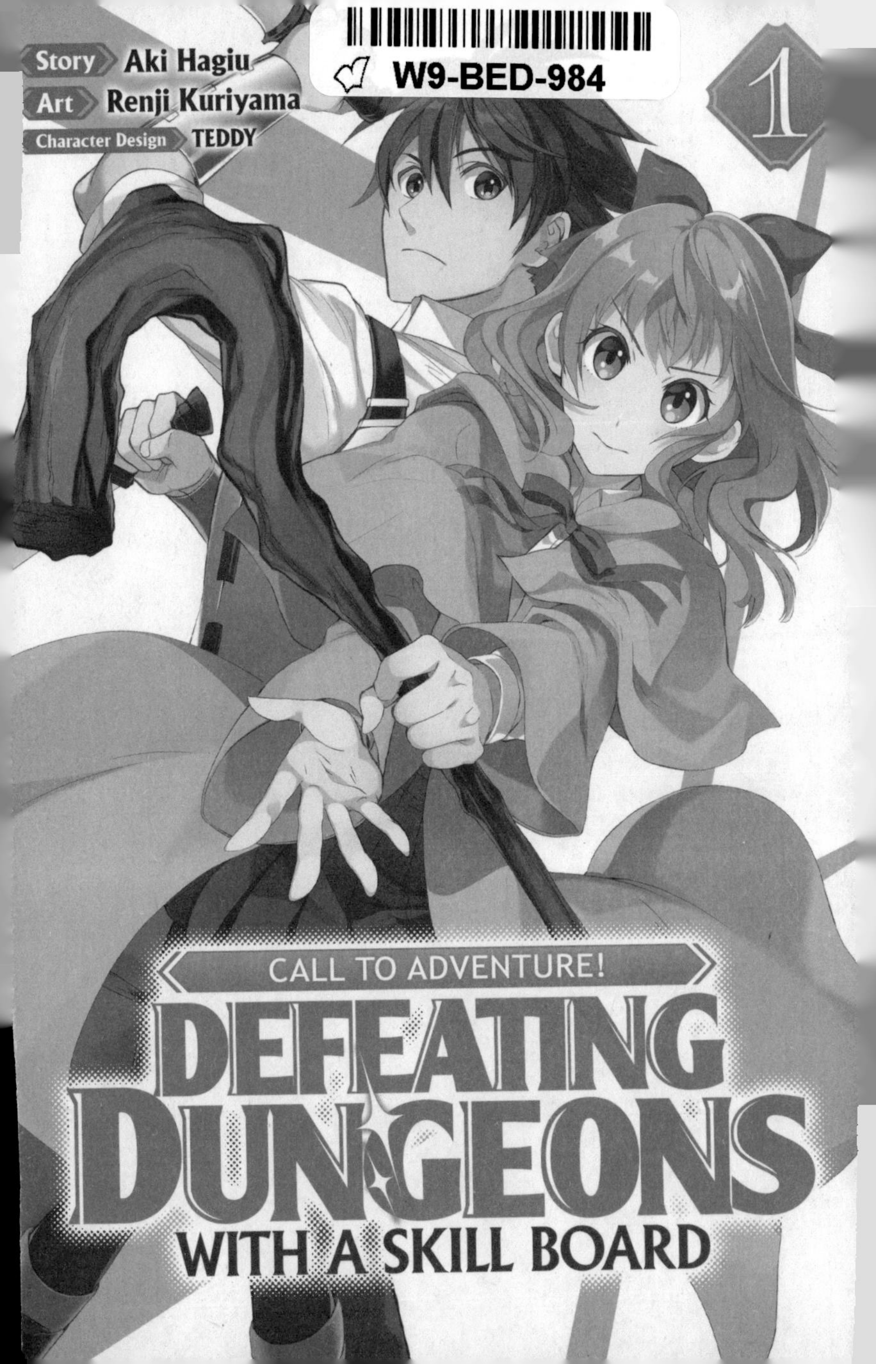
Story Aki Hagiu
Art Renji Kuriyama
Character Design TEDDY
1
CALL TO ADVENTURE!
DEFEATING DUNGEONS
WITH A SKILL BOARD

1

CONTENTS

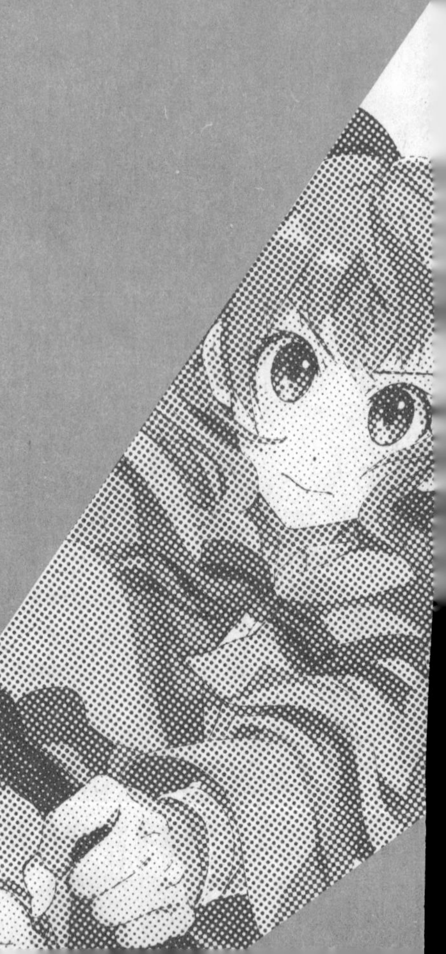

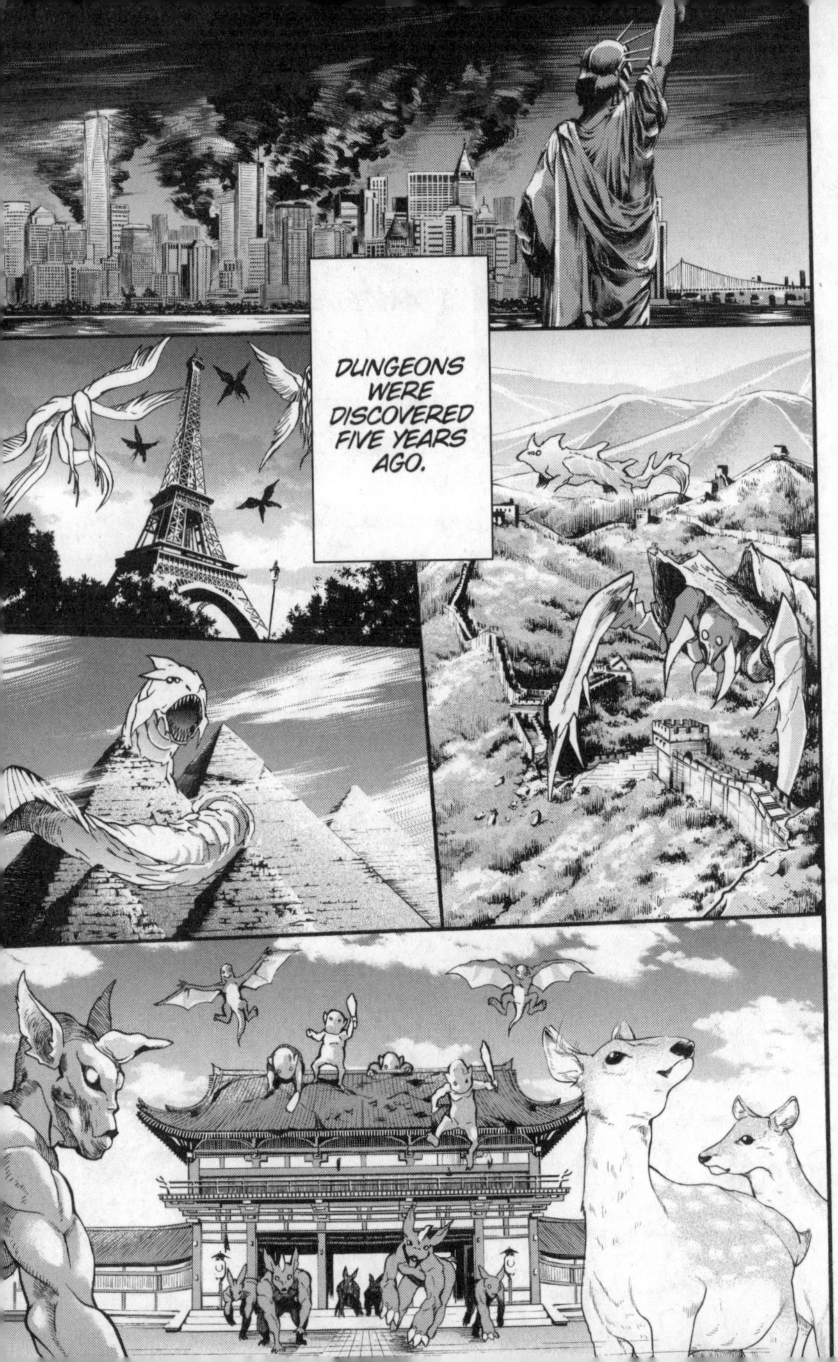
DUNGEONS WERE DISCOVERED FIVE YEARS AGO.

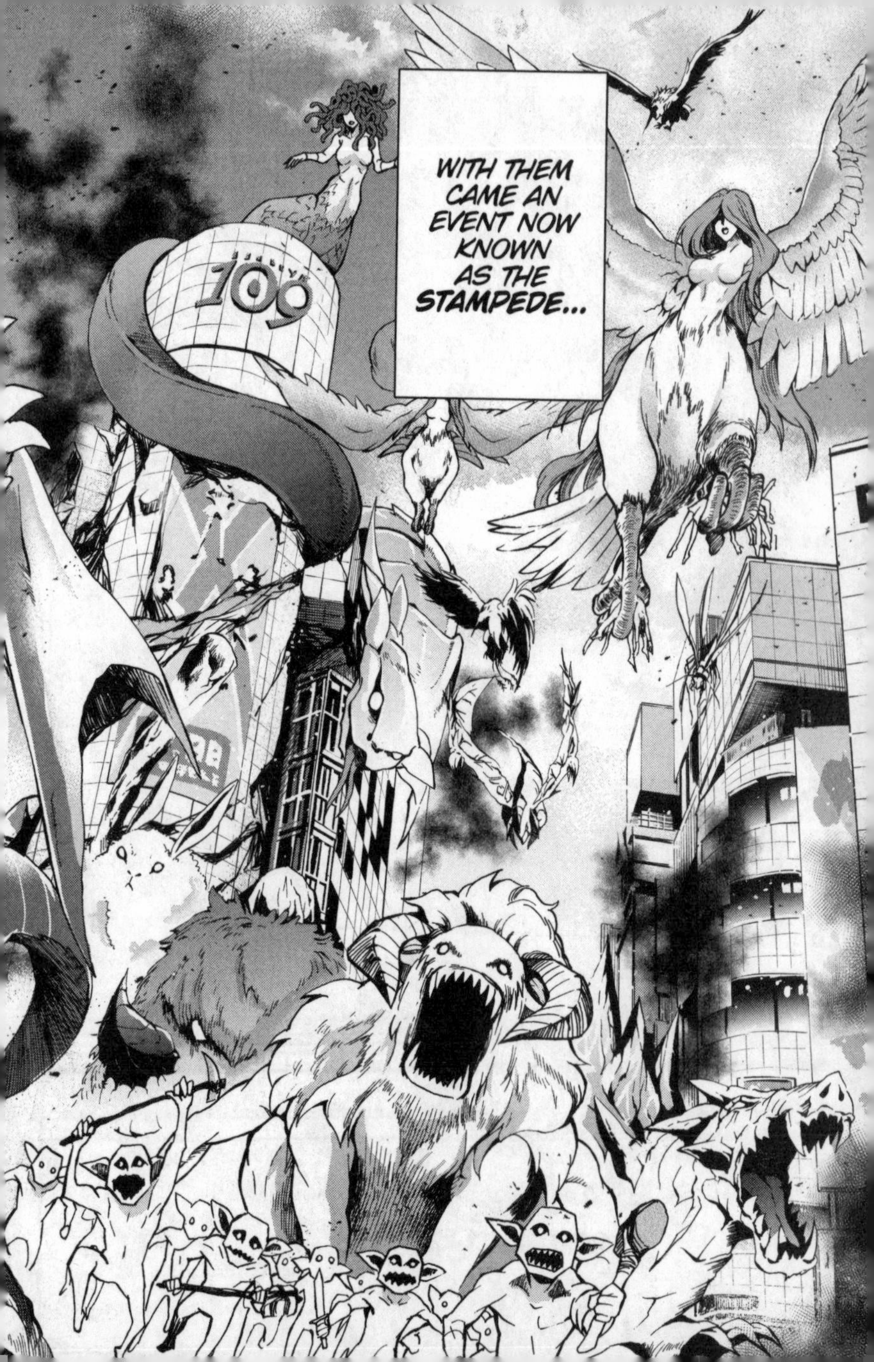
WITH THEM CAME AN EVENT NOW KNOWN AS THE STAMPEDE...
109

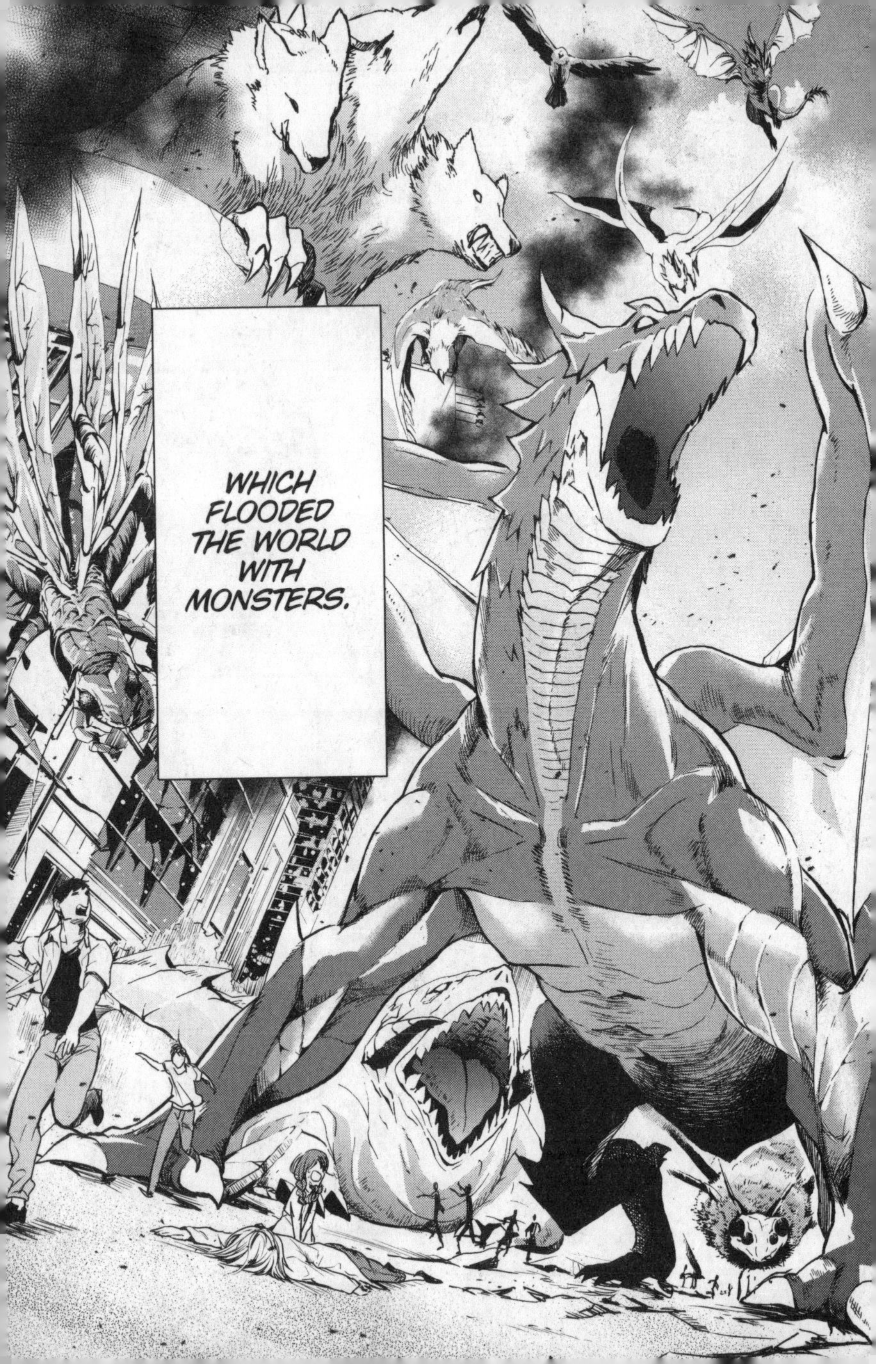
WHICH FLOODED THE WORLD WITH MONSTERS.

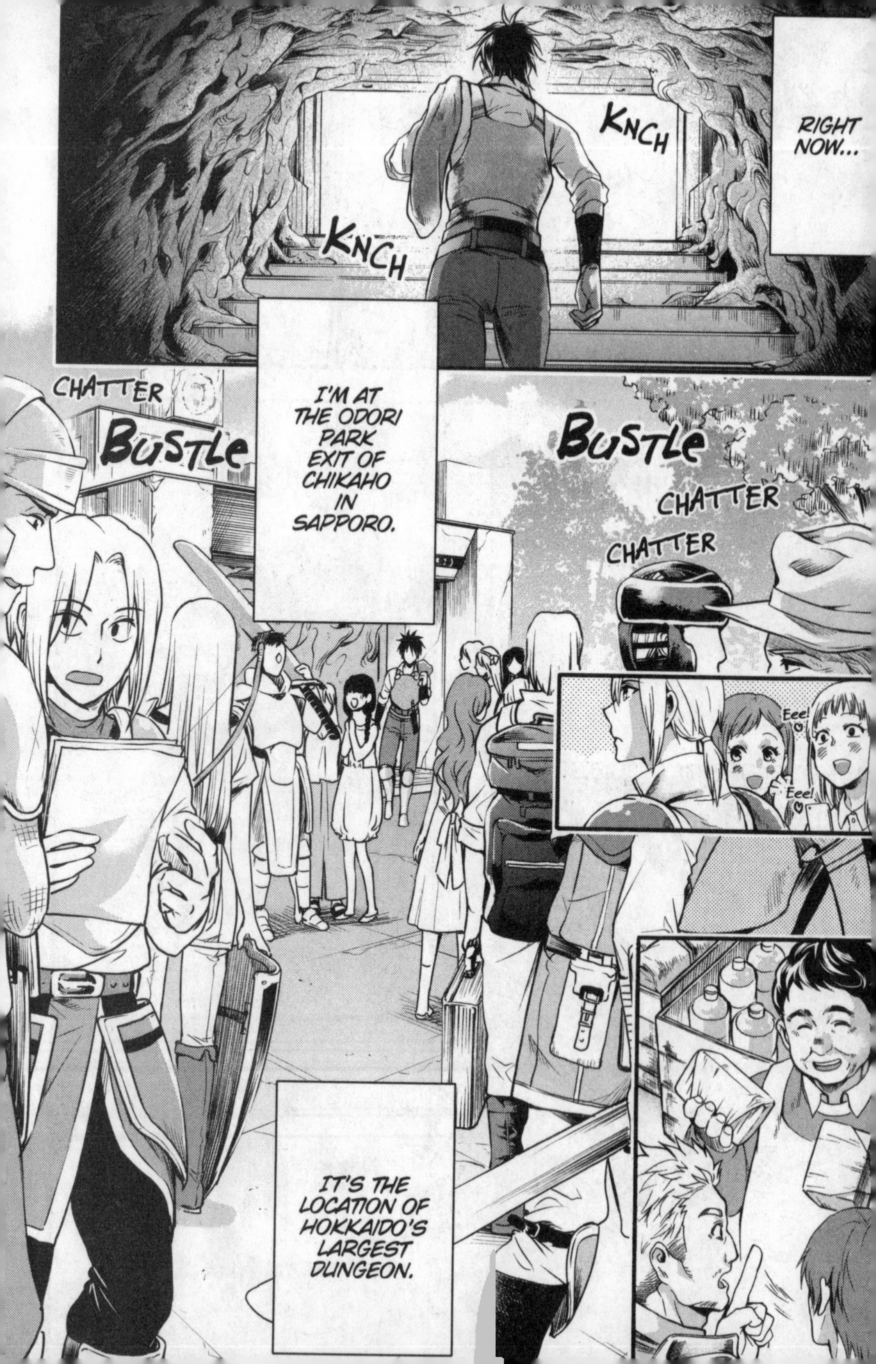
RIGHT NOW...
KNCH
KNCH
I'M AT THE ODORI PARK EXIT OF CHIKAHO IN SAPPORO.
BUSTLE
CHATTER
CHATTER
CHATTER
BUSTLE
Eee!
Eee!
IT'S THE LOCATION OF HOKKAIDO'S LARGEST DUNGEON.

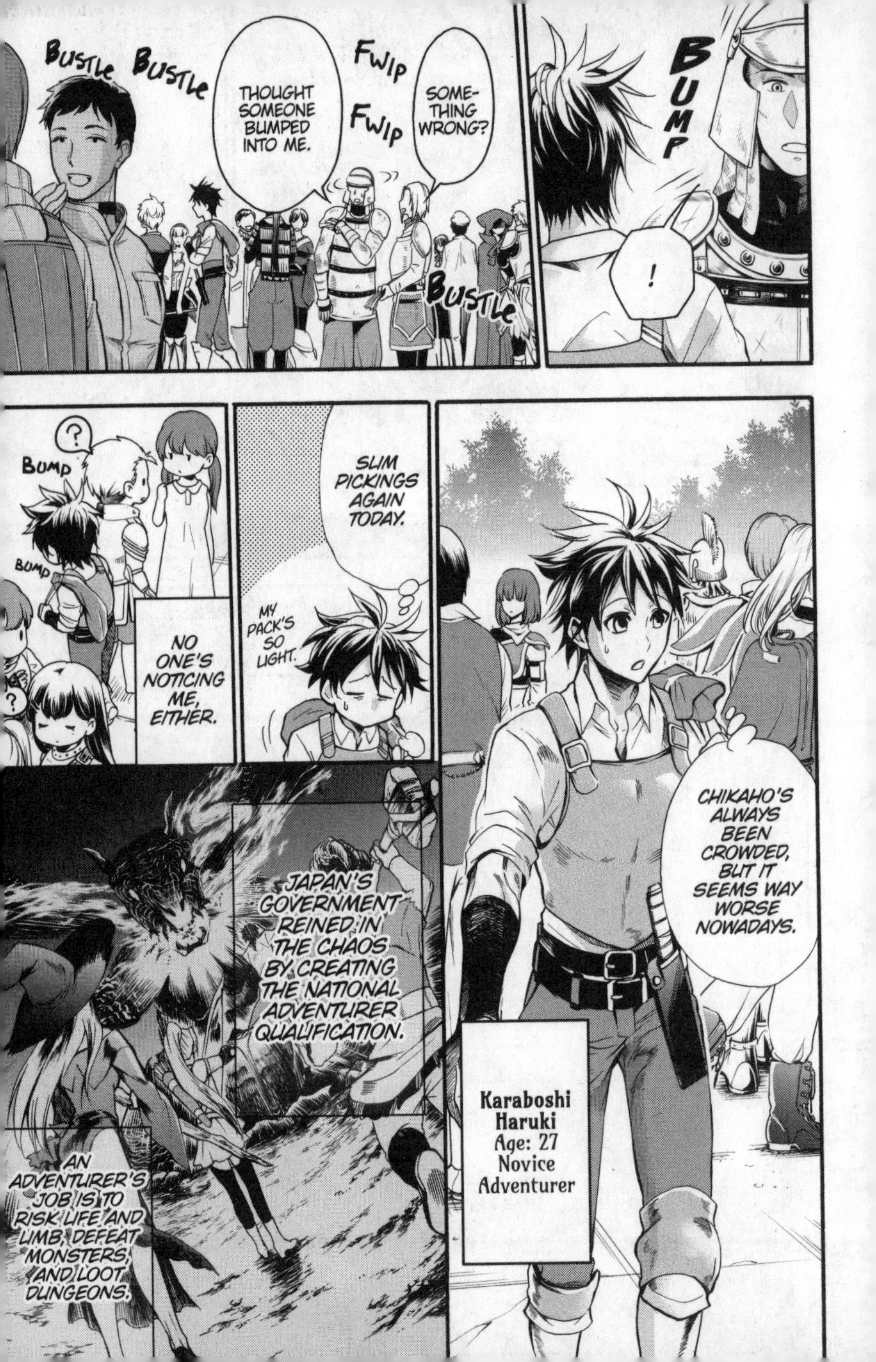
BUMP
!
BUSTLE BUSTLE
THOUGHT SOMEONE BUMPED INTO ME.
FWIP FWIP
SOME-THING WRONG?
BUSTLE
CHIKAHO'S ALWAYS BEEN CROWDED, BUT IT SEEMS WAY WORSE NOWADAYS.
Karaboshi Haruki Age: 27 Novice Adventurer
SLIM PICKINGS AGAIN TODAY.
MY PACK'S SO LIGHT.
?
BUMP
BUMP
NO ONE'S NOTICING ME, EITHER.
?
JAPAN'S GOVERNMENT REINED IN THE CHAOS BY CREATING THE NATIONAL ADVENTURER QUALIFICATION.
AN ADVENTURER'S JOB IS TO RISK LIFE AND LIMB, DEFEAT MONSTERS, AND LOOT DUNGEONS.

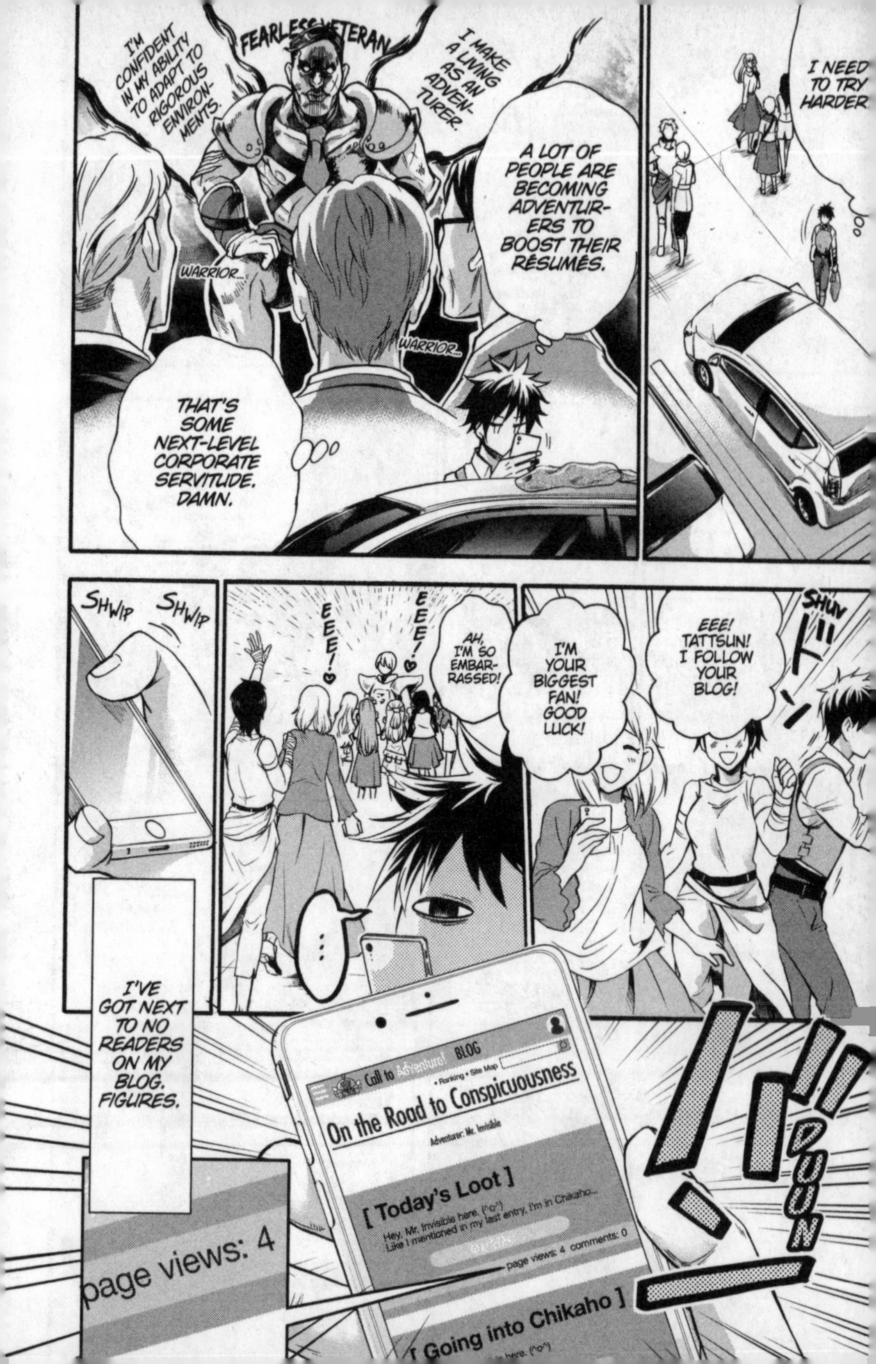
I NEED TO TRY HARDER.
I'M CONFIDENT IN MY ABILITY TO ADAPT TO RIGOROUS ENVIRONMENTS.
FEARLESS VETERAN
I MAKE A LIVING AS AN ADVENTURER.
A LOT OF PEOPLE ARE BECOMING ADVENTURERS TO BOOST THEIR RÉSUMÉS.
WARRIOR...
WARRIOR...
THAT'S SOME NEXT-LEVEL CORPORATE SERVITUDE. DAMN.
SHUV
EEE! TATTSUN! I FOLLOW YOUR BLOG!
I'M YOUR BIGGEST FAN! GOOD LUCK!
AH, I'M SO EMBARRASSED!
EEE!
EEE!
...
SHWIP
SHWIP
DUUN
Call to Adventure! BLOG
• Ranking • Site Map
On the Road to Conspicuousness
Adventurer: Mr. Invisible
[Today's Loot]
Hey, Mr. Invisible here. (^o^)
Like I mentioned in my last entry, I'm in Chikaho...
page views: 4 comments: 0
[Going into Chikaho]
page views: 4
I'VE GOT NEXT TO NO READERS ON MY BLOG. FIGURES.

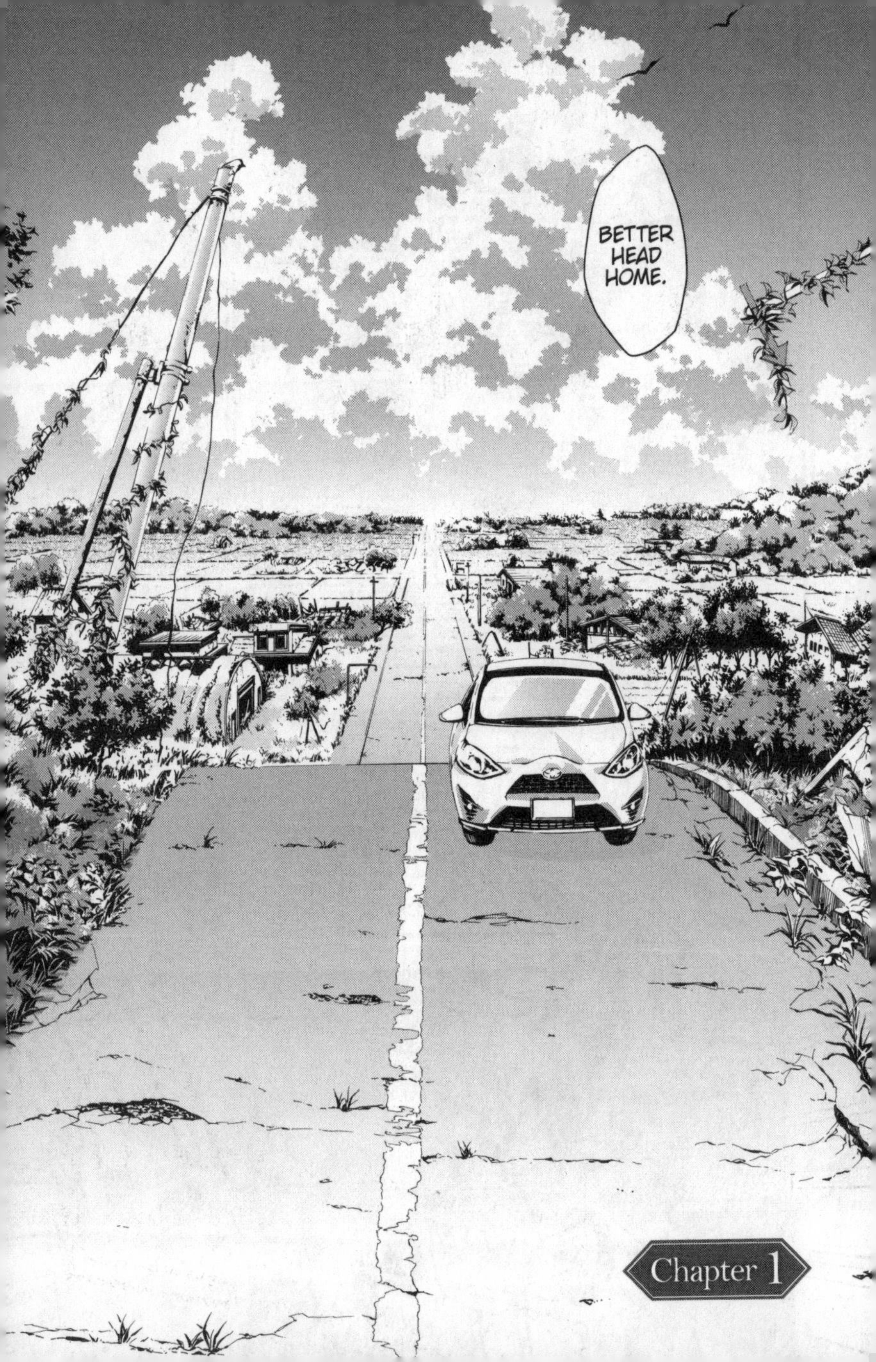
BETTER HEAD HOME.
Chapter 1

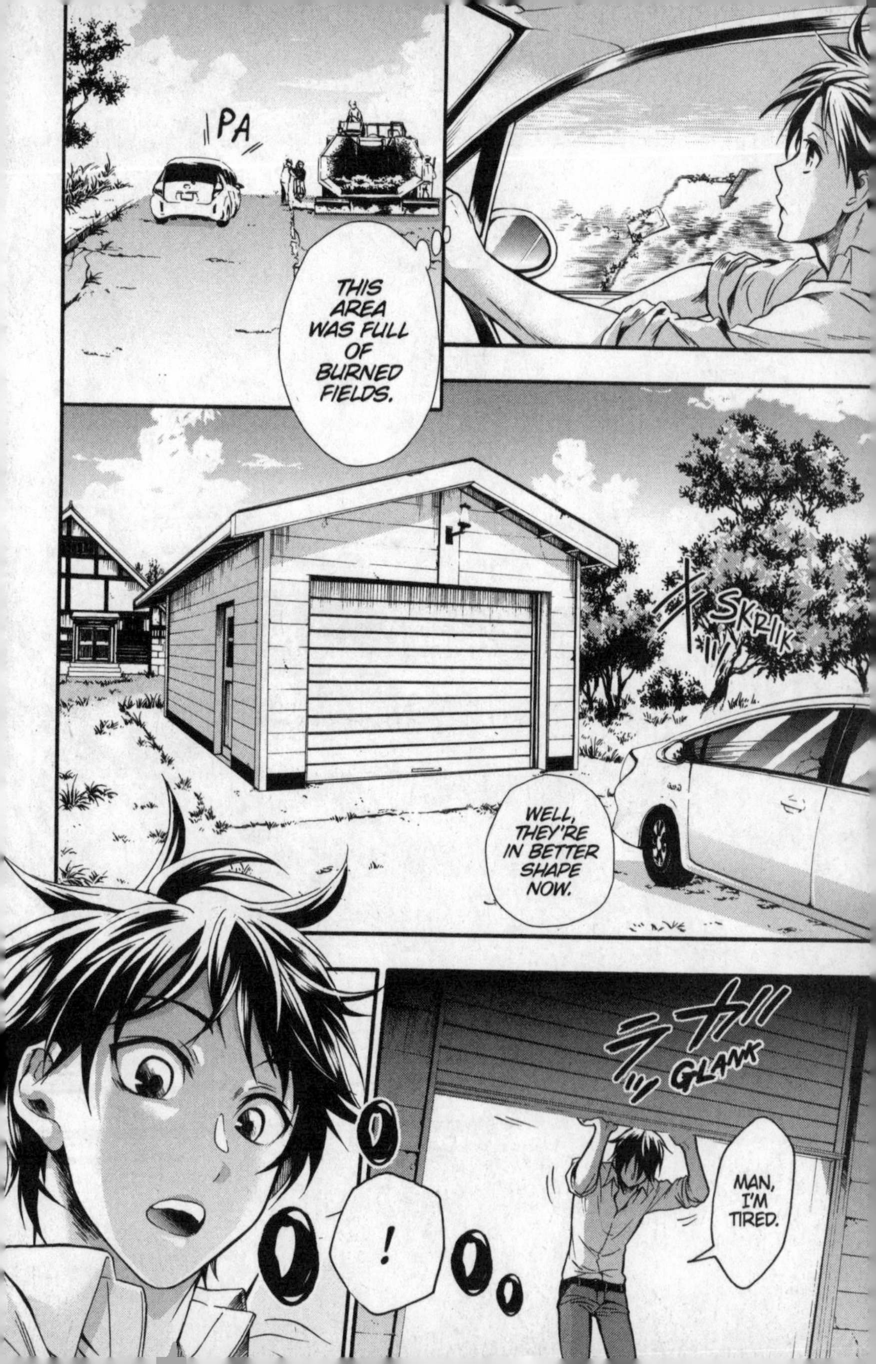
PA
THIS AREA WAS FULL OF BURNED FIELDS.
SKRIIK
WELL, THEY'RE IN BETTER SHAPE NOW.
GLANK
MAN, I'M TIRED.
!

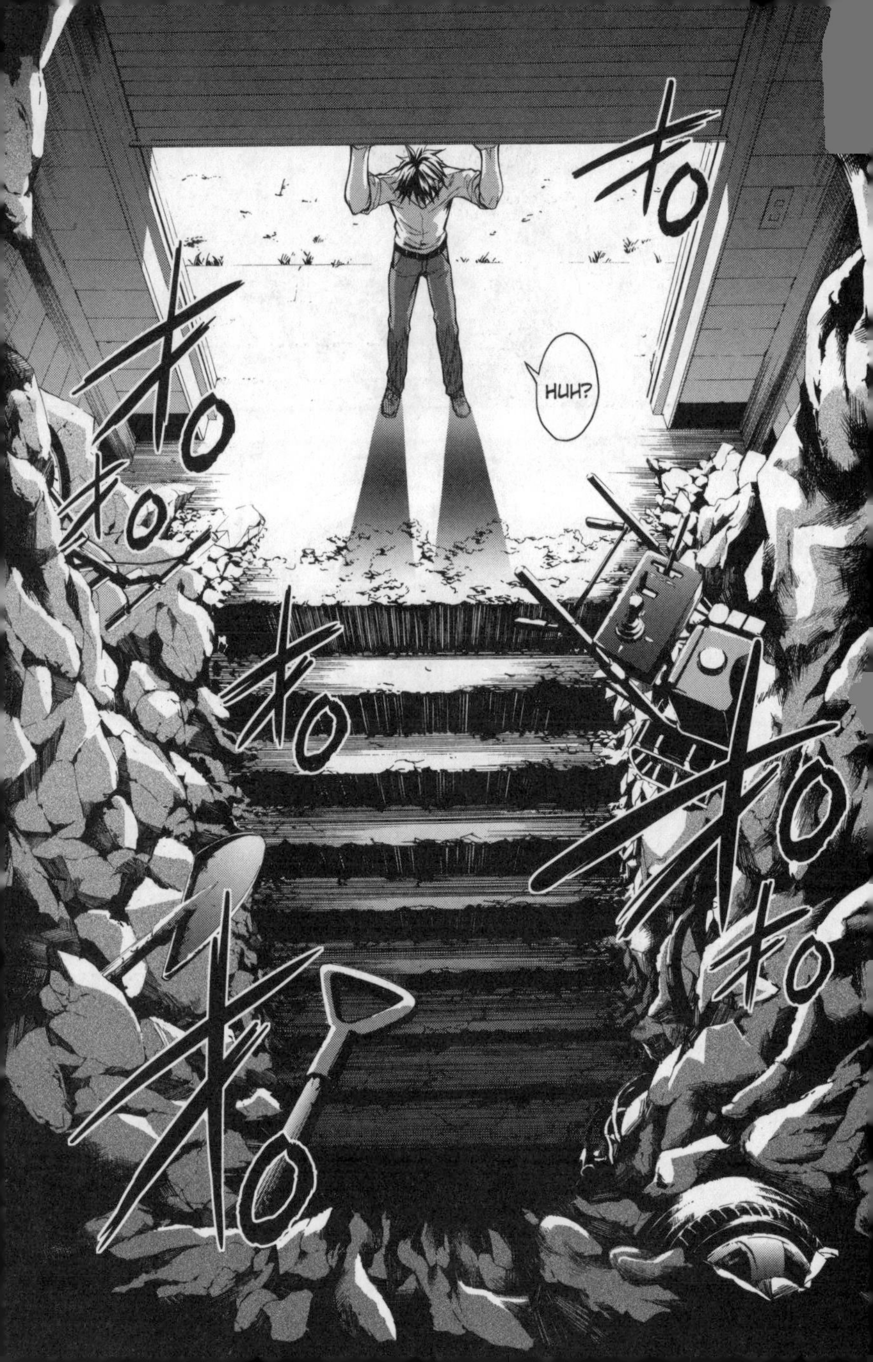
HUH?

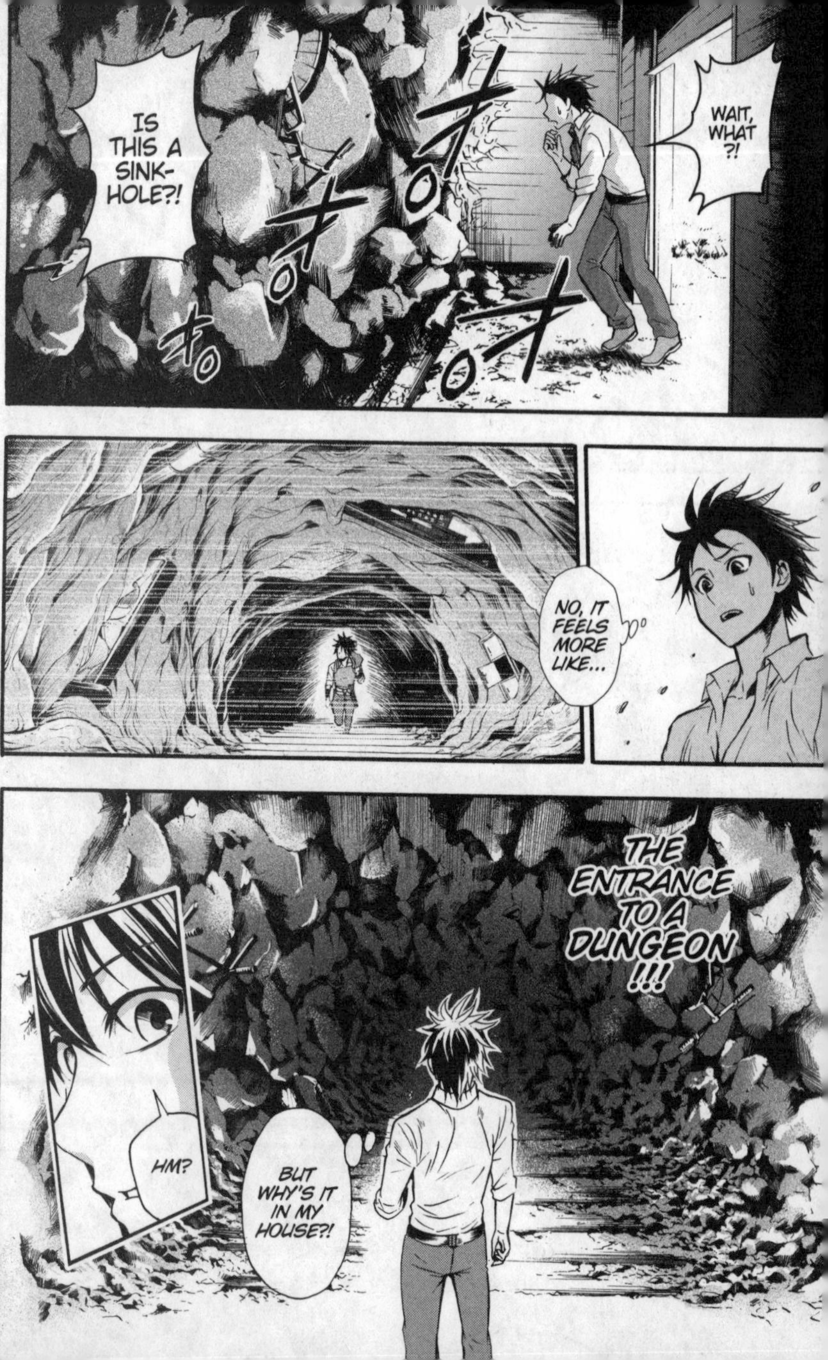
WAIT, WHAT ?!
IS THIS A SINK-HOLE?!
NO, IT FEELS MORE LIKE...
THE ENTRANCE TO A DUNGEON !!!
BUT WHY'S IT IN MY HOUSE?!
HM?

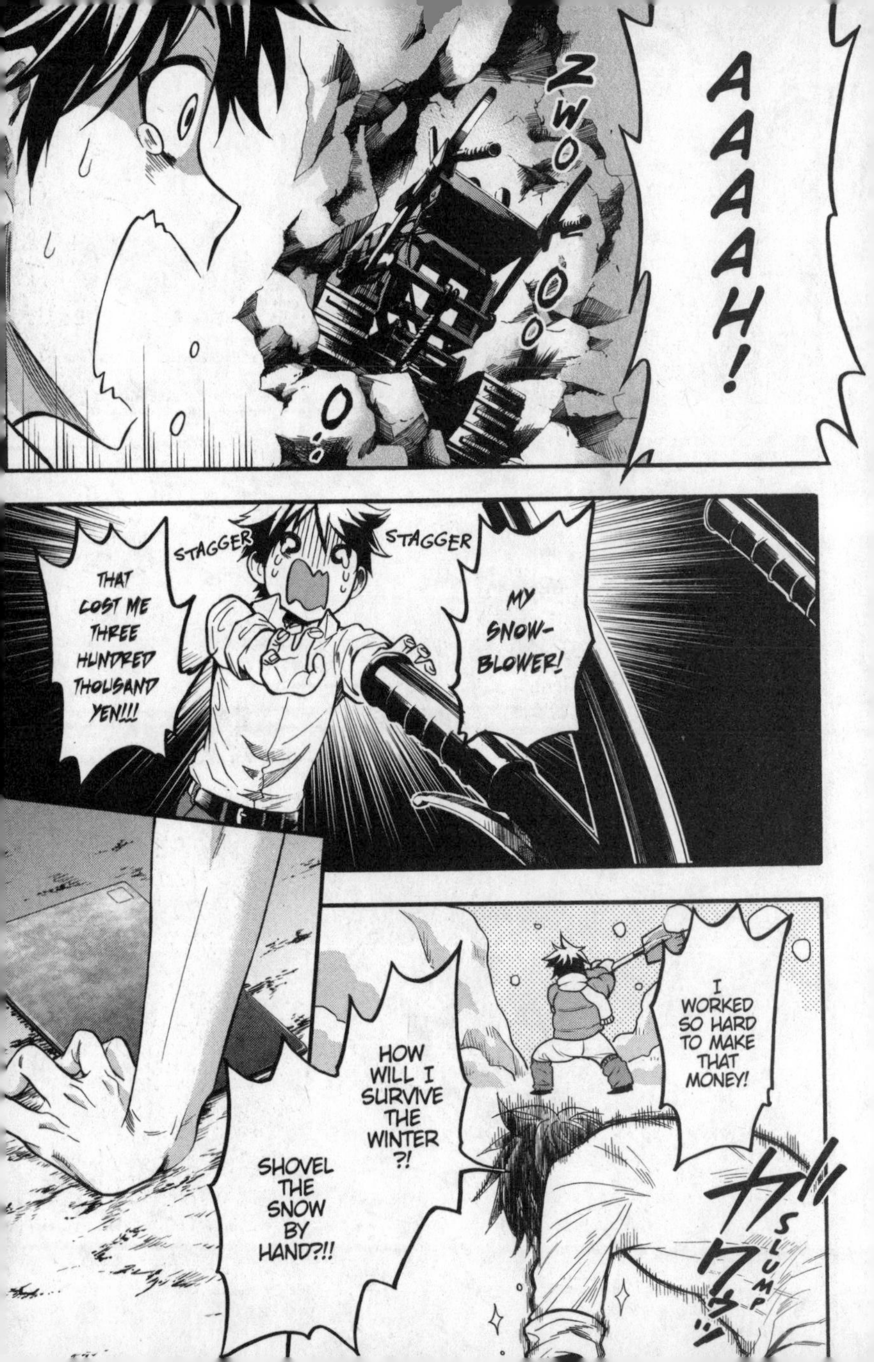
AAAAAH!
ZWOOOO
STAGGER
STAGGER
MY SNOW-BLOWER!
THAT COST ME THREE HUNDRED THOUSAND YEN!!!
I WORKED SO HARD TO MAKE THAT MONEY!
HOW WILL I SURVIVE THE WINTER ?!
SHOVEL THE SNOW BY HAND?!!
SLUMP

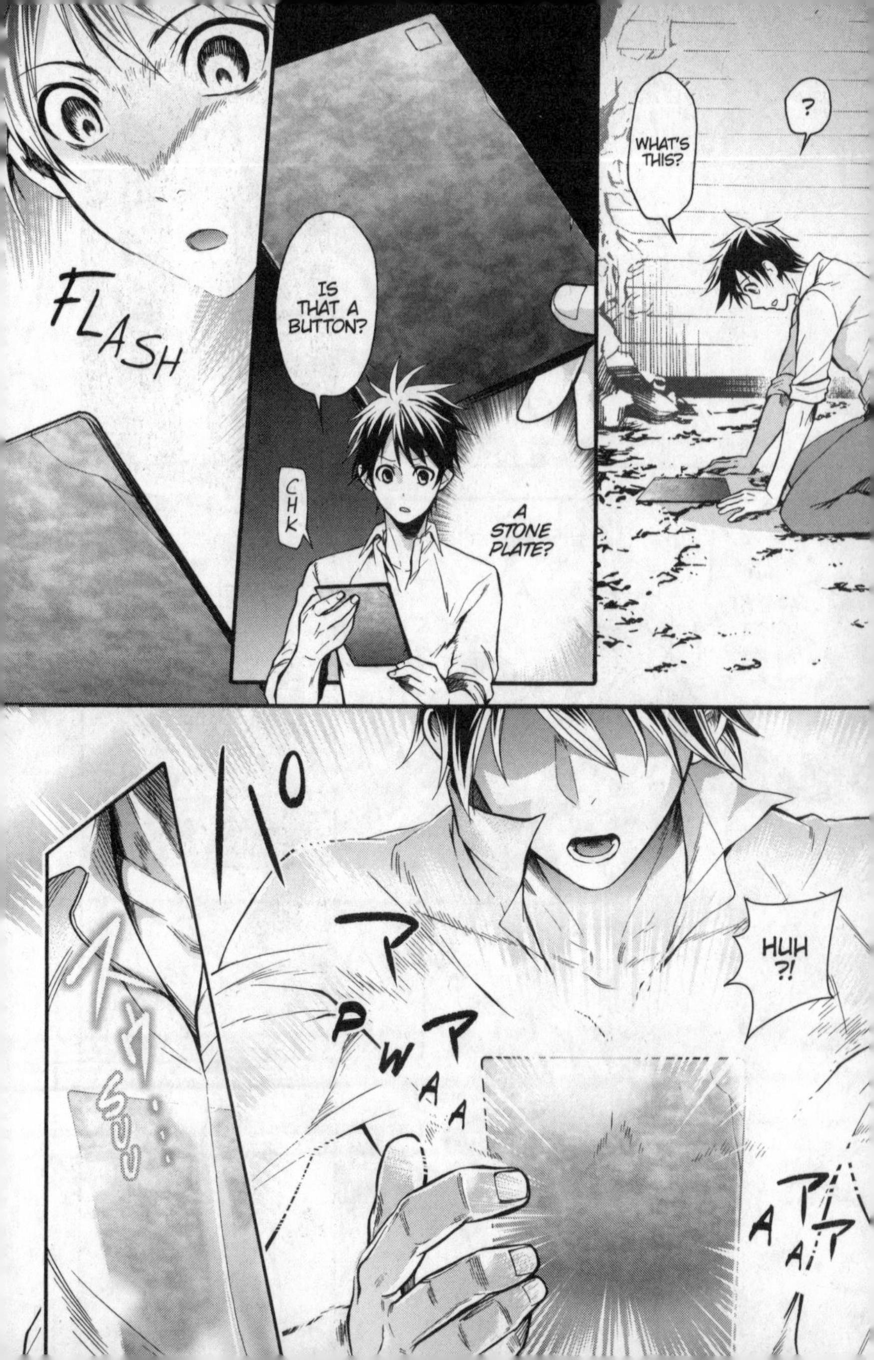
?
WHAT'S THIS?
IS THAT A BUTTON?
A STONE PLATE?
CHK
FLASH
HUH?!
PWAA
SUU

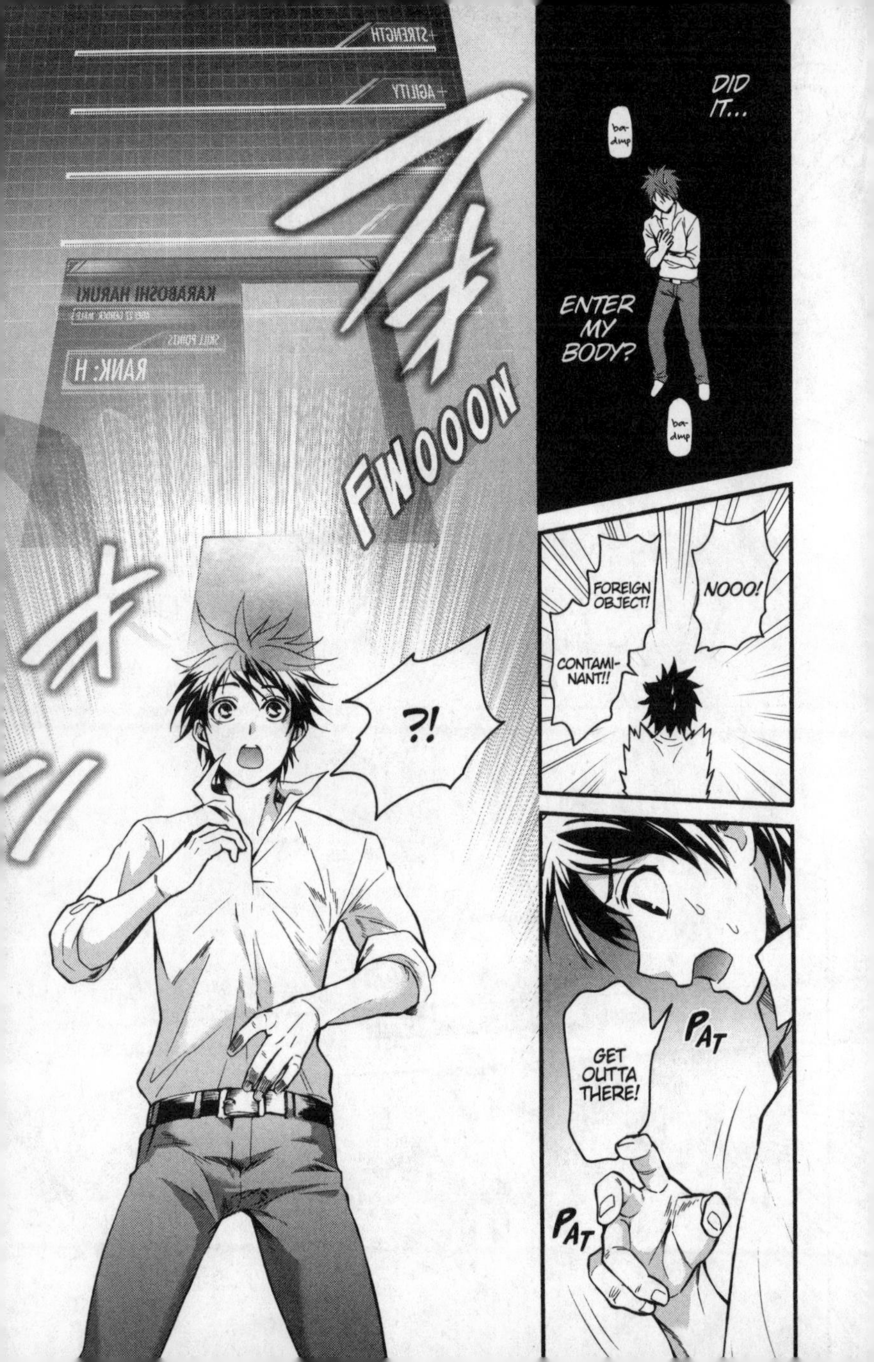
DID IT...
ba-dmp
ENTER MY BODY?
ba-dmp
NOOO!
FOREIGN OBJECT!
CONTAMI-NANT!!
PAT
GET OUTTA THERE!
PAT
STRENGTH
AGILITY
KARABOSHI HARUKI
RANK: H
FWOOON
?!

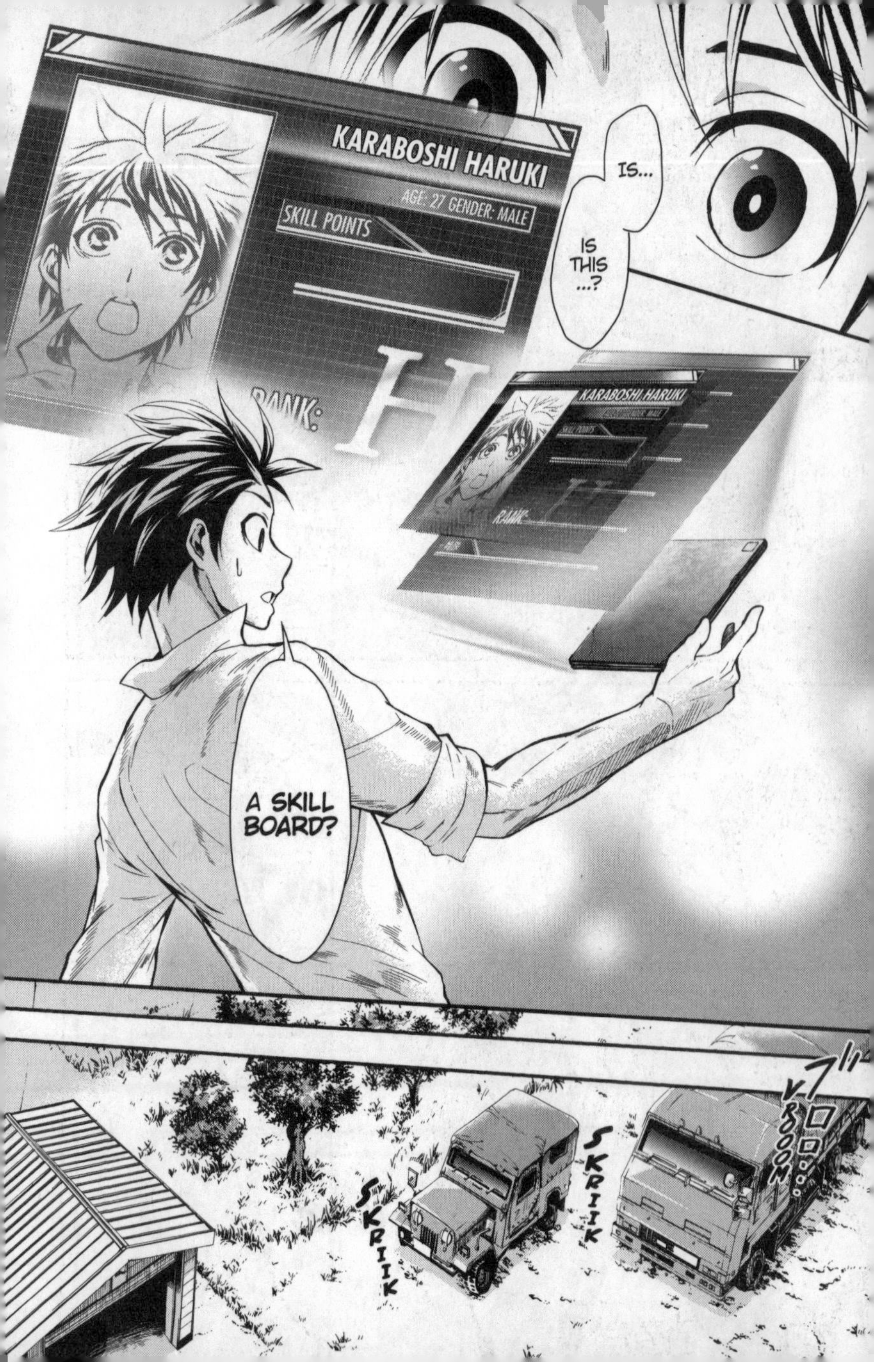
IS...
IS THIS ...?
KARABOSHI HARUKI
AGE: 27 GENDER: MALE
SKILL POINTS
RANK: H
A SKILL BOARD?
VROOOM...
SKRIIK
SKRIIK

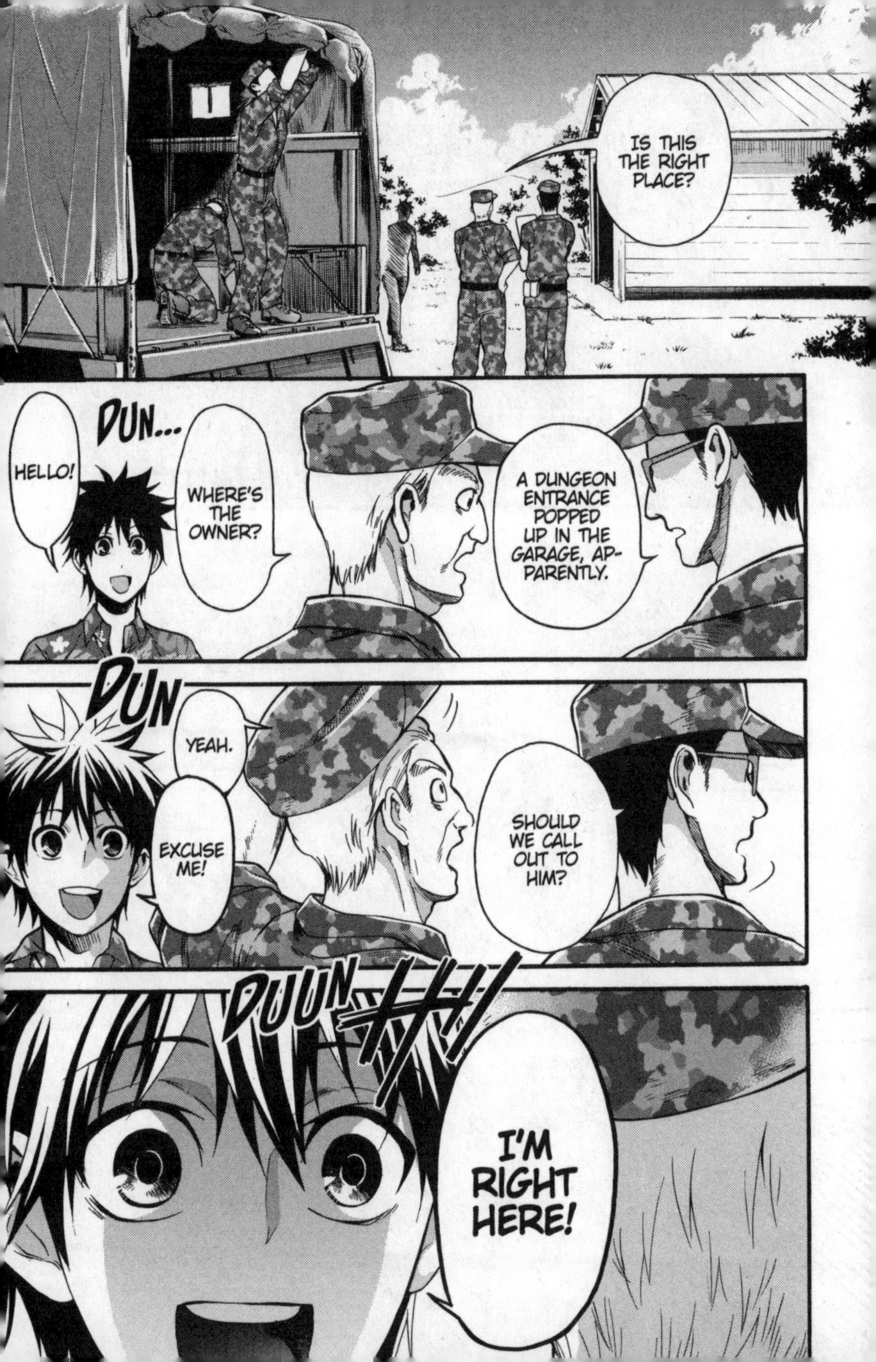
IS THIS THE RIGHT PLACE?
A DUNGEON ENTRANCE POPPED UP IN THE GARAGE, AP-PARENTLY.
DUN...
WHERE'S THE OWNER?
HELLO!
SHOULD WE CALL OUT TO HIM?
YEAH.
DUN
EXCUSE ME!
DUUN-!!
I'M RIGHT HERE!

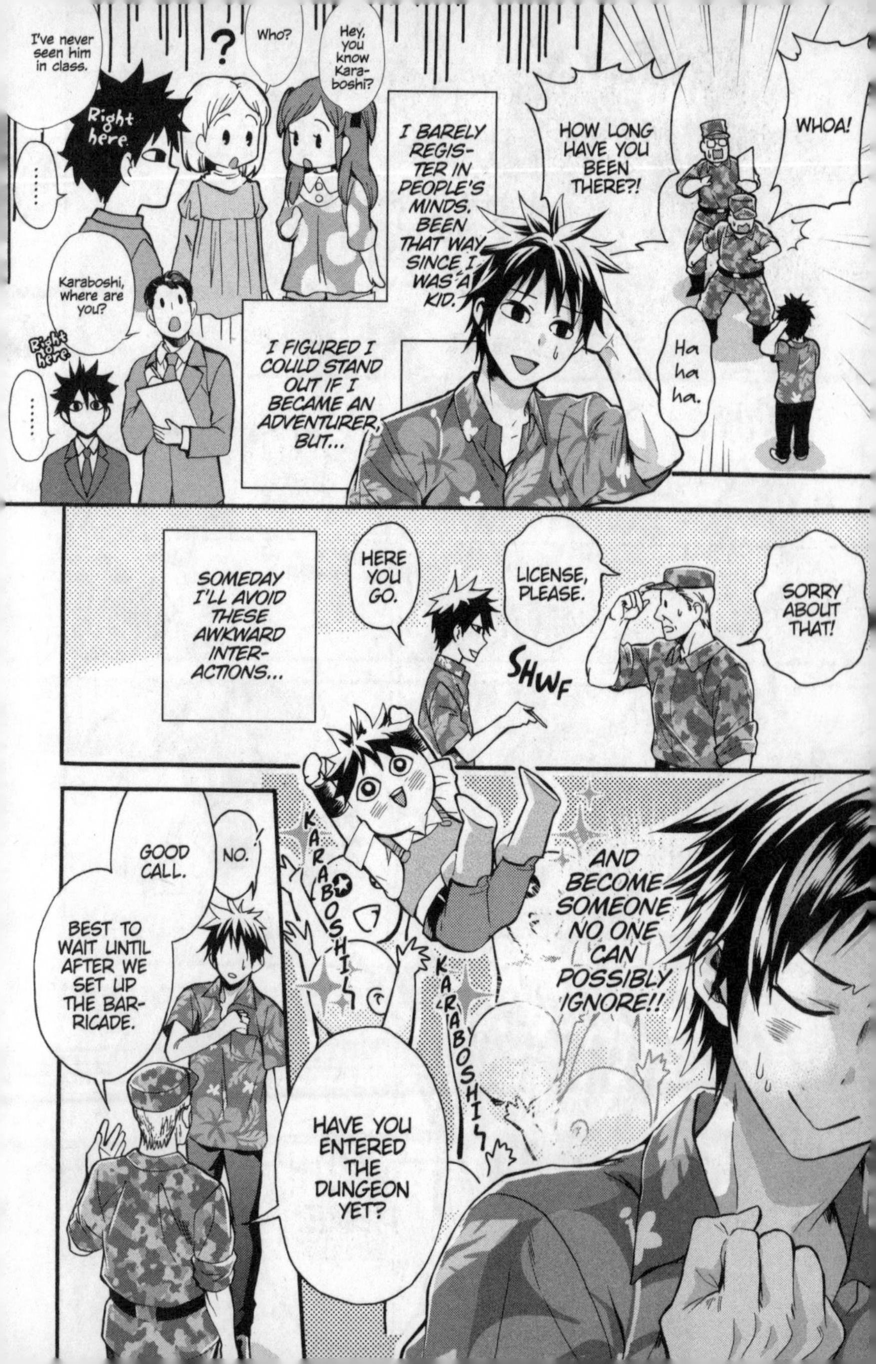
WHOA!
HOW LONG HAVE YOU BEEN THERE?!
Ha ha ha.
I BARELY REGISTER IN PEOPLE'S MINDS. BEEN THAT WAY SINCE I WAS A KID.
I FIGURED I COULD STAND OUT IF I BECAME AN ADVENTURER, BUT...
Hey, you know Karaboshi?
Who?
?
I've never seen him in class.
Right here.
......
Karaboshi, where are you?
Right here.
......
SORRY ABOUT THAT!
LICENSE, PLEASE.
SHWF
HERE YOU GO.
SOMEDAY I'LL AVOID THESE AWKWARD INTERACTIONS...
AND BECOME SOMEONE NO ONE CAN POSSIBLY IGNORE!!
KARABOSHI
KARABOSHI
HAVE YOU ENTERED THE DUNGEON YET?
NO.
GOOD CALL.
BEST TO WAIT UNTIL AFTER WE SET UP THE BARRICADE.

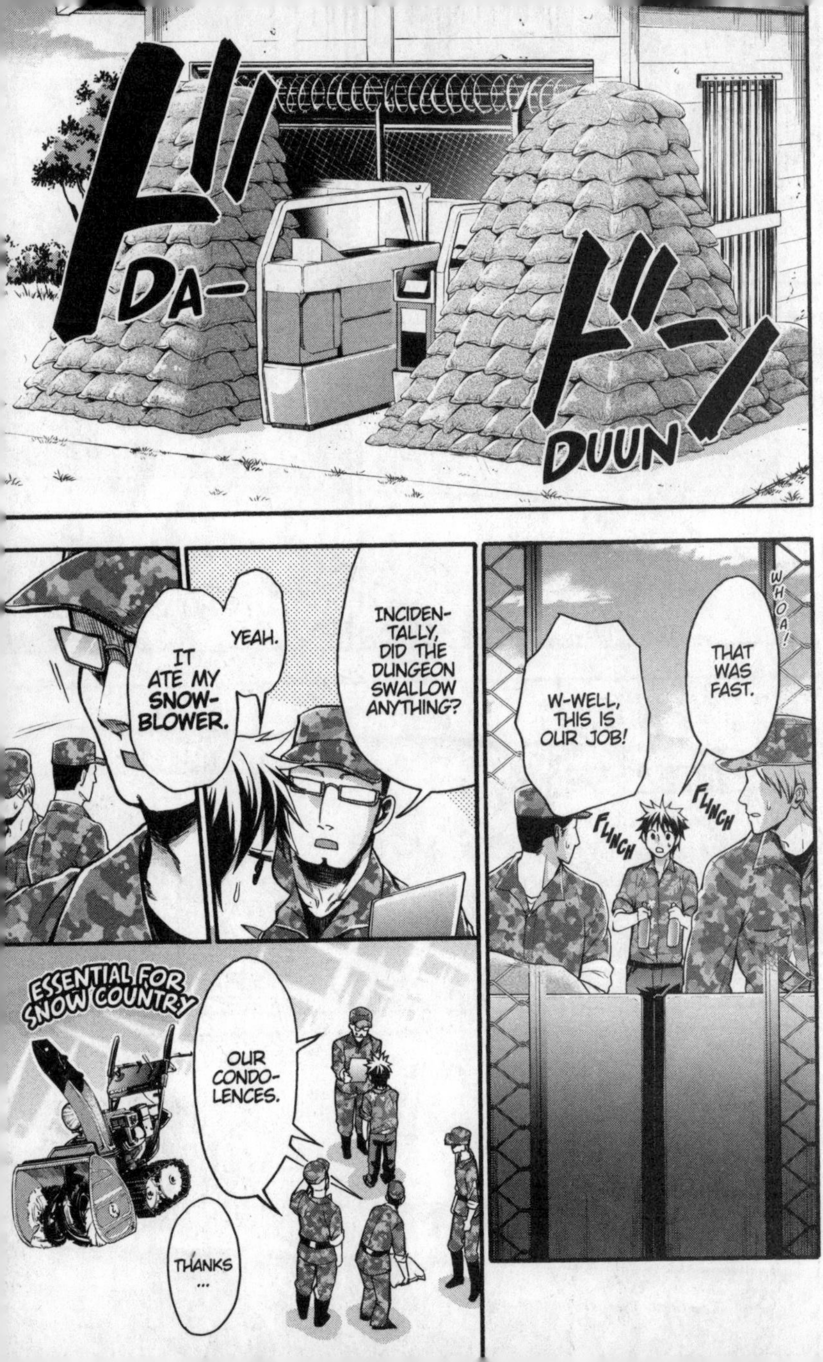
DA-
DUUN
WHOA!
THAT WAS FAST.
W-WELL, THIS IS OUR JOB!
FLINCH
FLINCH
INCIDENTALLY, DID THE DUNGEON SWALLOW ANYTHING?
YEAH.
IT ATE MY SNOWBLOWER.
OUR CONDOLENCES.
THANKS...
ESSENTIAL FOR SNOW COUNTRY

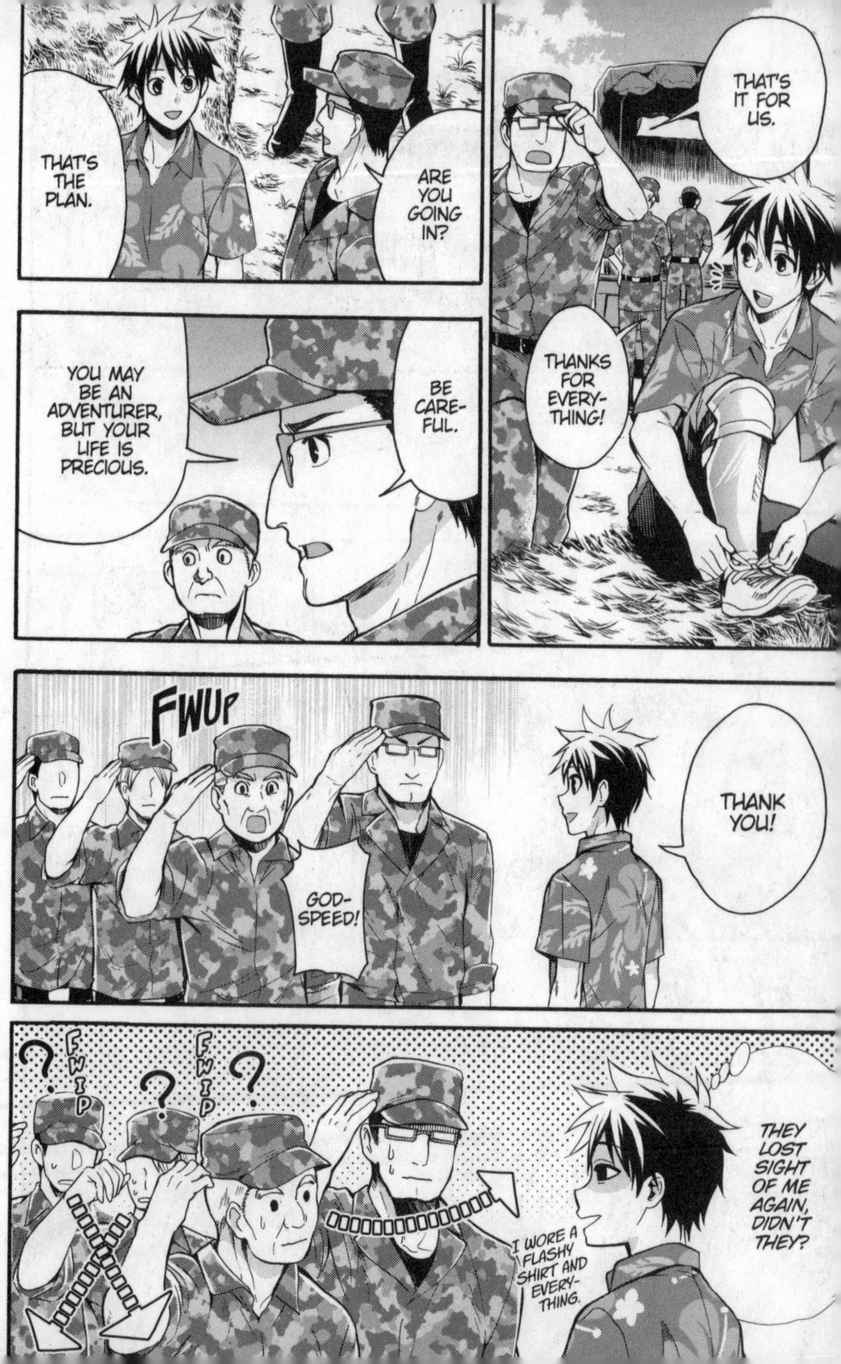
THAT'S IT FOR US.
THANKS FOR EVERY-THING!
ARE YOU GOING IN?
THAT'S THE PLAN.
BE CARE-FUL.
YOU MAY BE AN ADVENTURER, BUT YOUR LIFE IS PRECIOUS.
THANK YOU!
FWUP
GOD-SPEED!
THEY LOST SIGHT OF ME AGAIN, DIDN'T THEY?
I WORE A FLASHY SHIRT AND EVERY-THING.
FWIP
FWIP

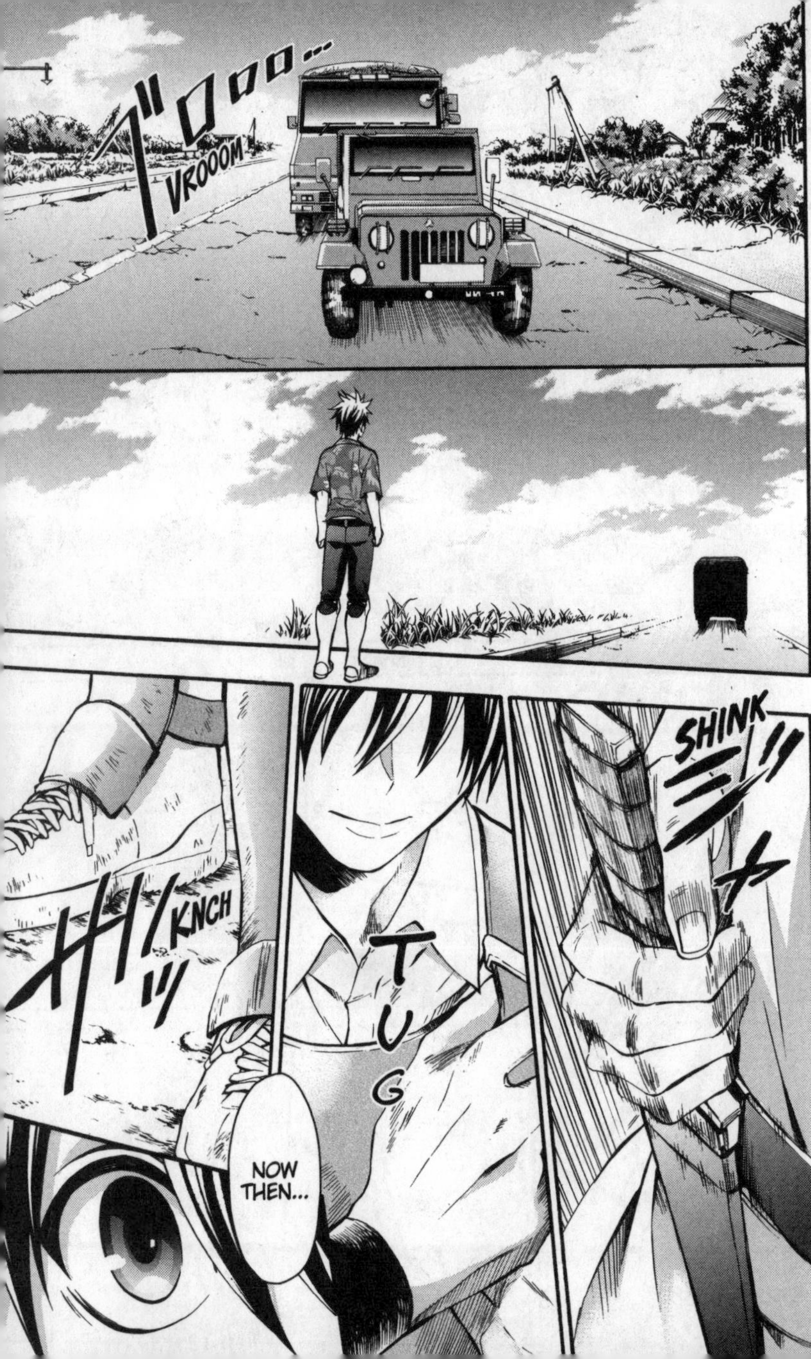
VROOOM
SHINK
TUG
NOW THEN...
KNCH

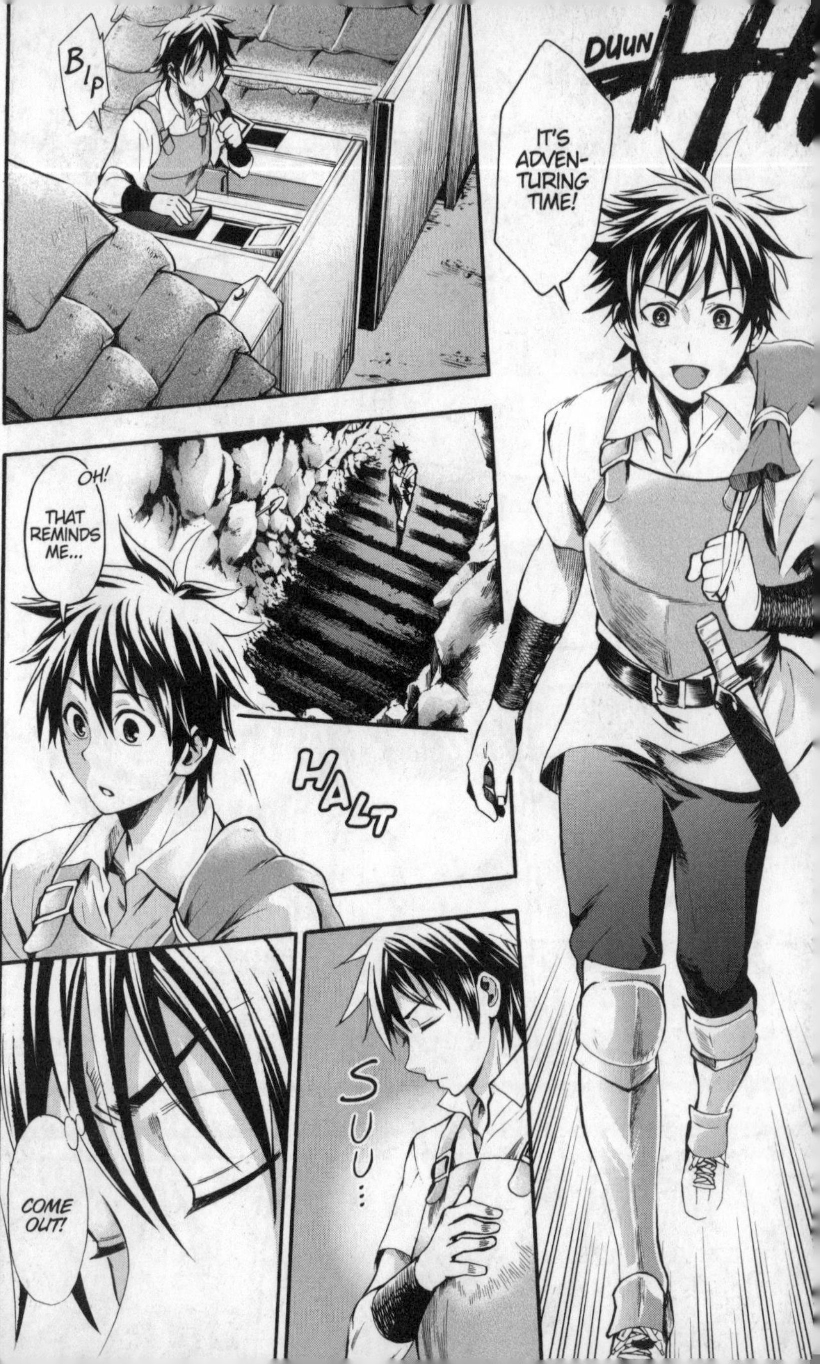
DUUN
IT'S ADVEN-TURING TIME!
BIP
OH!
THAT REMINDS ME...
HALT
SUU...
COME OUT!

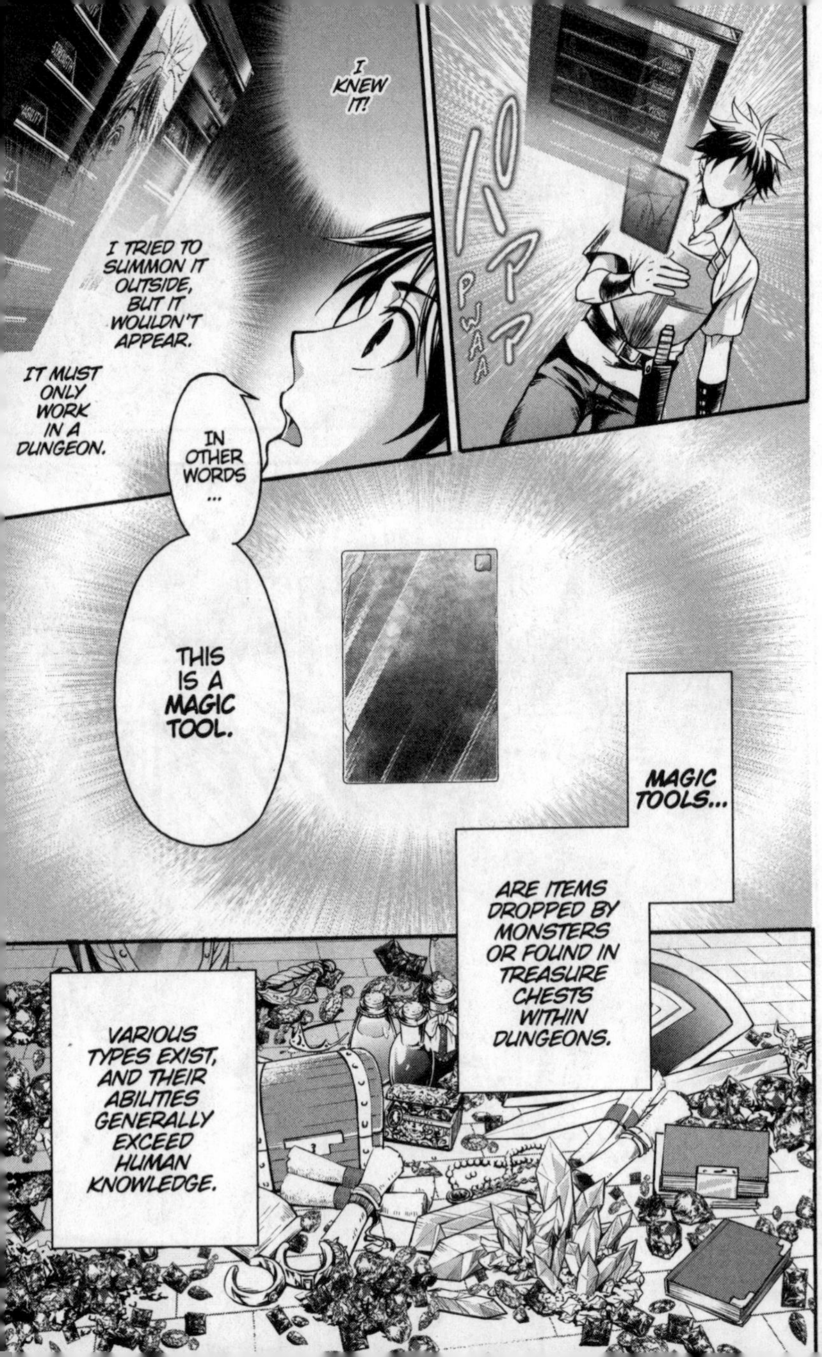
PWAA
I KNEW IT!
I TRIED TO SUMMON IT OUTSIDE, BUT IT WOULDN'T APPEAR.
IT MUST ONLY WORK IN A DUNGEON.
IN OTHER WORDS ...
THIS IS A MAGIC TOOL.
MAGIC TOOLS...
ARE ITEMS DROPPED BY MONSTERS OR FOUND IN TREASURE CHESTS WITHIN DUNGEONS.
VARIOUS TYPES EXIST, AND THEIR ABILITIES GENERALLY EXCEED HUMAN KNOWLEDGE.

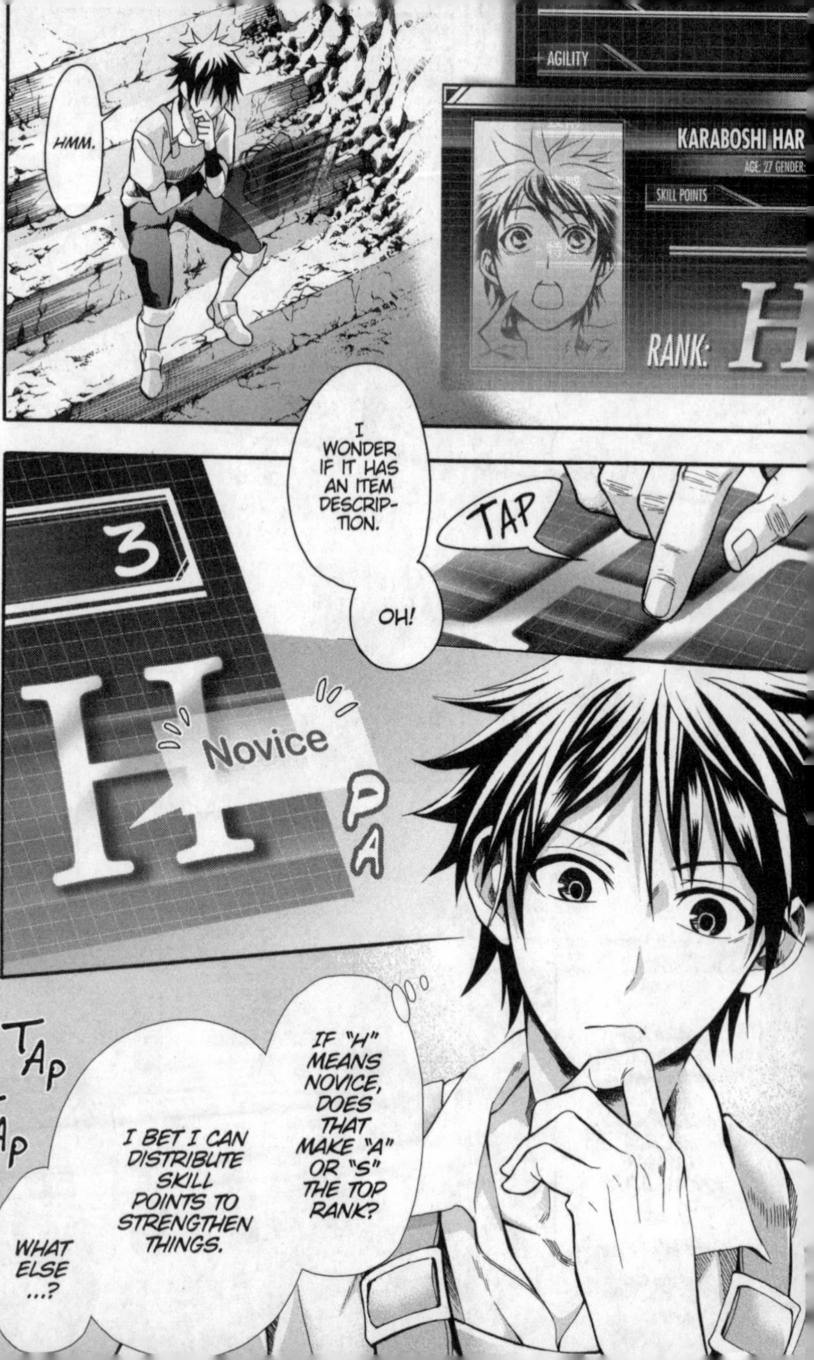
AGILITY
KARABOSHI HAR
AGE: 27 GENDER:
SKILL POINTS
RANK: H
HMM.
I WONDER IF IT HAS AN ITEM DESCRIP-TION.
TAP
OH!
3
H
Novice
PA
IF "H" MEANS NOVICE, DOES THAT MAKE "A" OR "S" THE TOP RANK?
I BET I CAN DISTRIBUTE SKILL POINTS TO STRENGTHEN THINGS.
WHAT ELSE ...?
TAP TAP

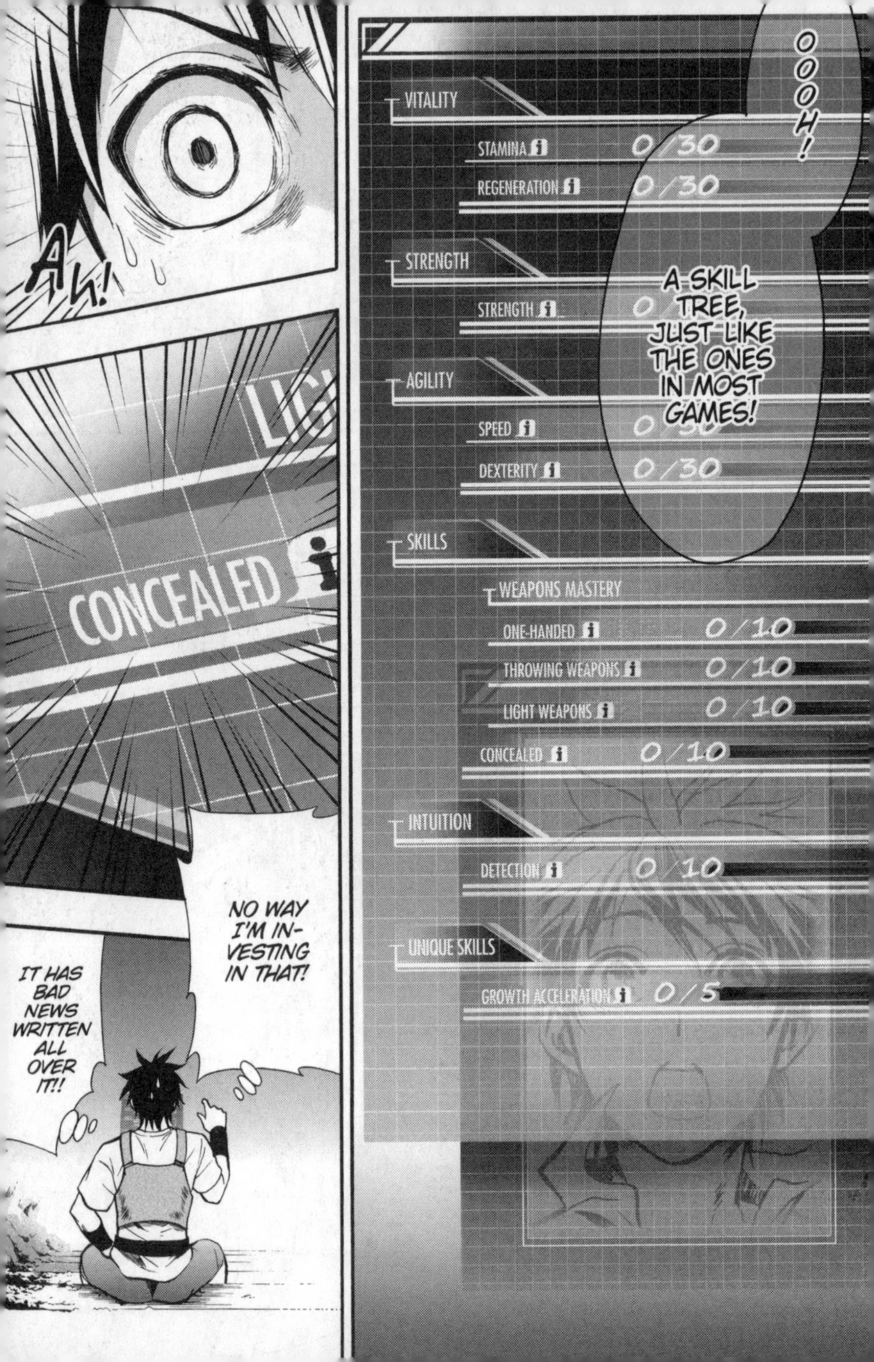
OOOOH!
A SKILL TREE, JUST LIKE THE ONES IN MOST GAMES!
VITALITY
STAMINA 0/30
REGENERATION 0/30
STRENGTH
STRENGTH 0
AGILITY
SPEED 0
DEXTERITY 0/30
SKILLS
WEAPONS MASTERY
ONE-HANDED 0/10
THROWING WEAPONS 0/10
LIGHT WEAPONS 0/10
CONCEALED 0/10
INTUITION
DETECTION 0/10
UNIQUE SKILLS
GROWTH ACCELERATION 0/5
AH!
CONCEALED
NO WAY I'M IN-VESTING IN THAT!
IT HAS BAD NEWS WRITTEN ALL OVER IT!!

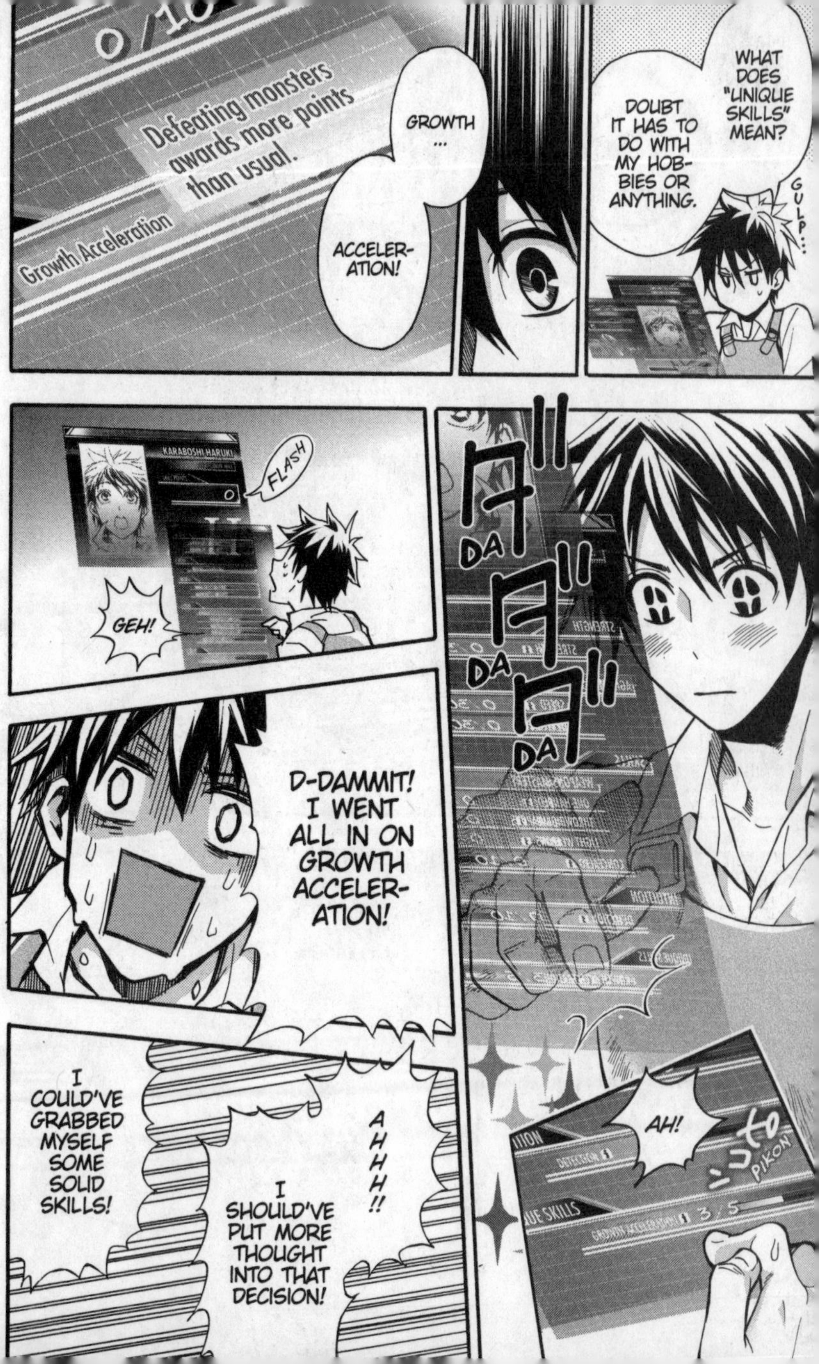
WHAT DOES "UNIQUE SKILLS" MEAN?
GULP...
DOUBT IT HAS TO DO WITH MY HOBBIES OR ANYTHING.
GROWTH...
ACCELERATION!
0 / 10
Growth Acceleration
Defeating monsters awards more points than usual.
DA DA DA
KARABOSHI HARUKI
FLASH
GEH!
D-DAMMIT! I WENT ALL IN ON GROWTH ACCELERATION!
AH!
PIKON
3 / 5
AHHH!!
I SHOULD'VE PUT MORE THOUGHT INTO THAT DECISION!
I COULD'VE GRABBED MYSELF SOME SOLID SKILLS!

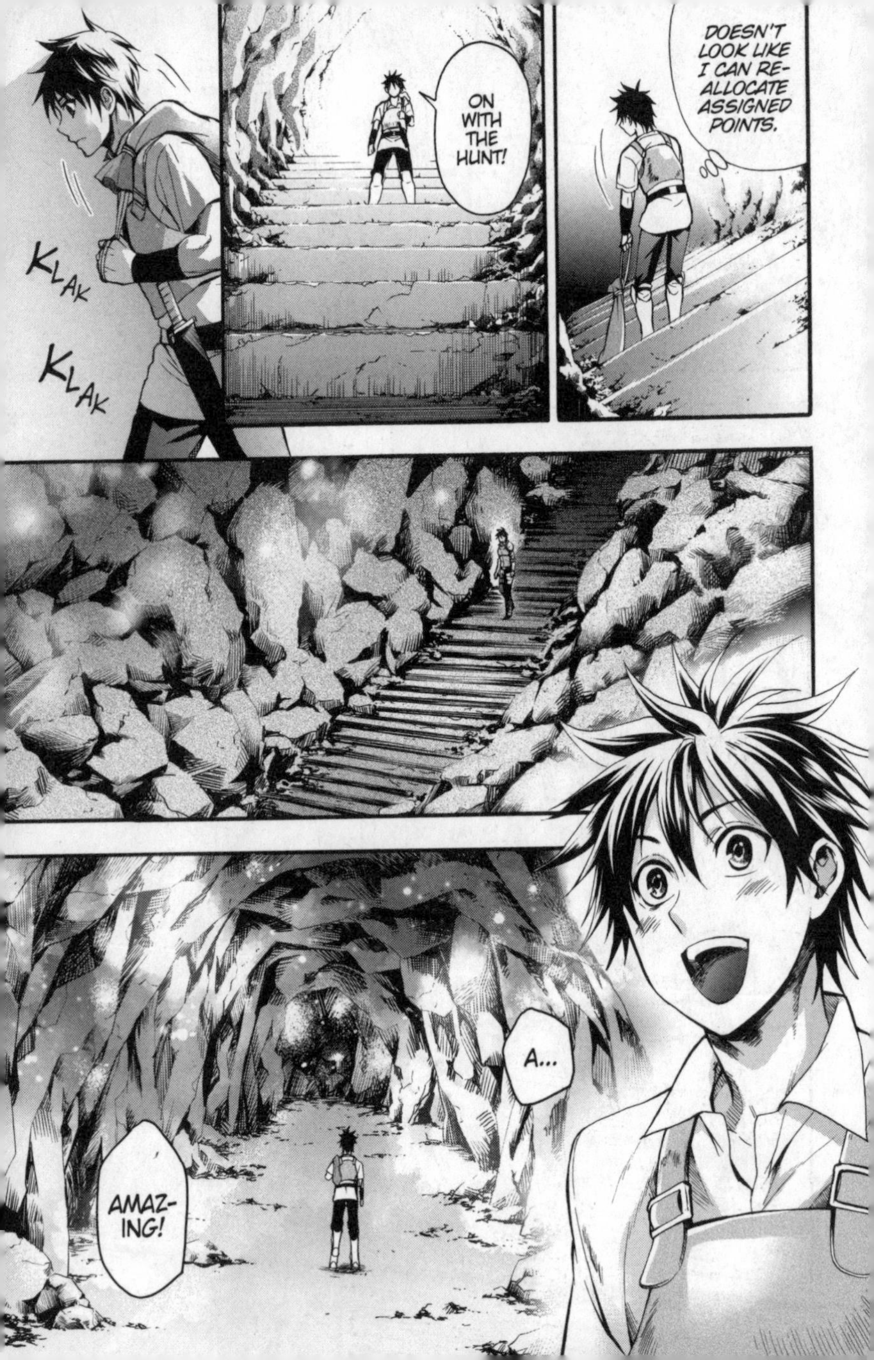
DOESN'T LOOK LIKE I CAN RE-ALLOCATE ASSIGNED POINTS.
ON WITH THE HUNT!
KLAK
KLAK
A...
AMAZ-ING!

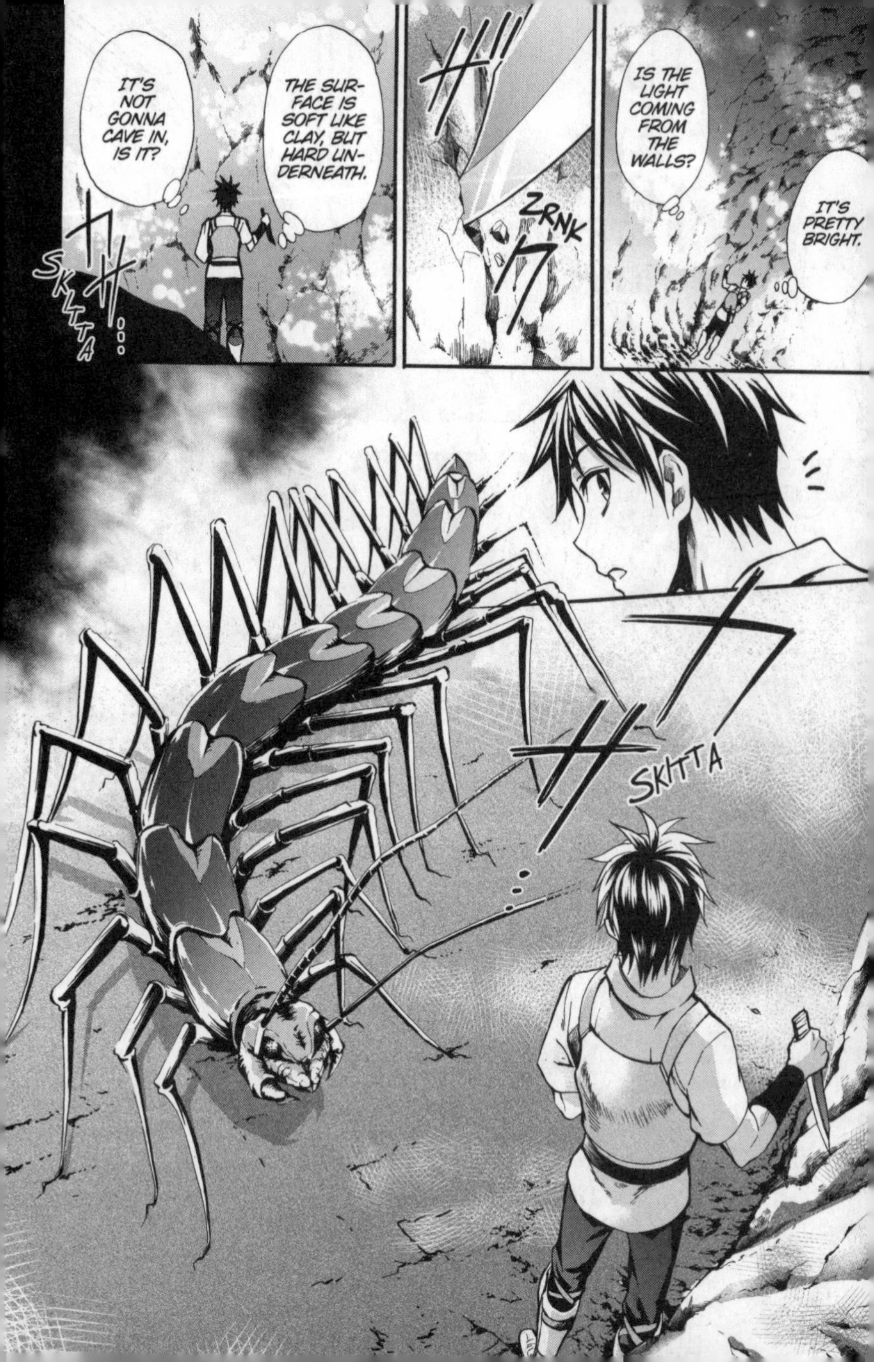
IT'S PRETTY BRIGHT.
IS THE LIGHT COMING FROM THE WALLS?
ZRNK
THE SURFACE IS SOFT LIKE CLAY, BUT HARD UNDERNEATH.
IT'S NOT GONNA CAVE IN, IS IT?
SKITTA...
SKITTA

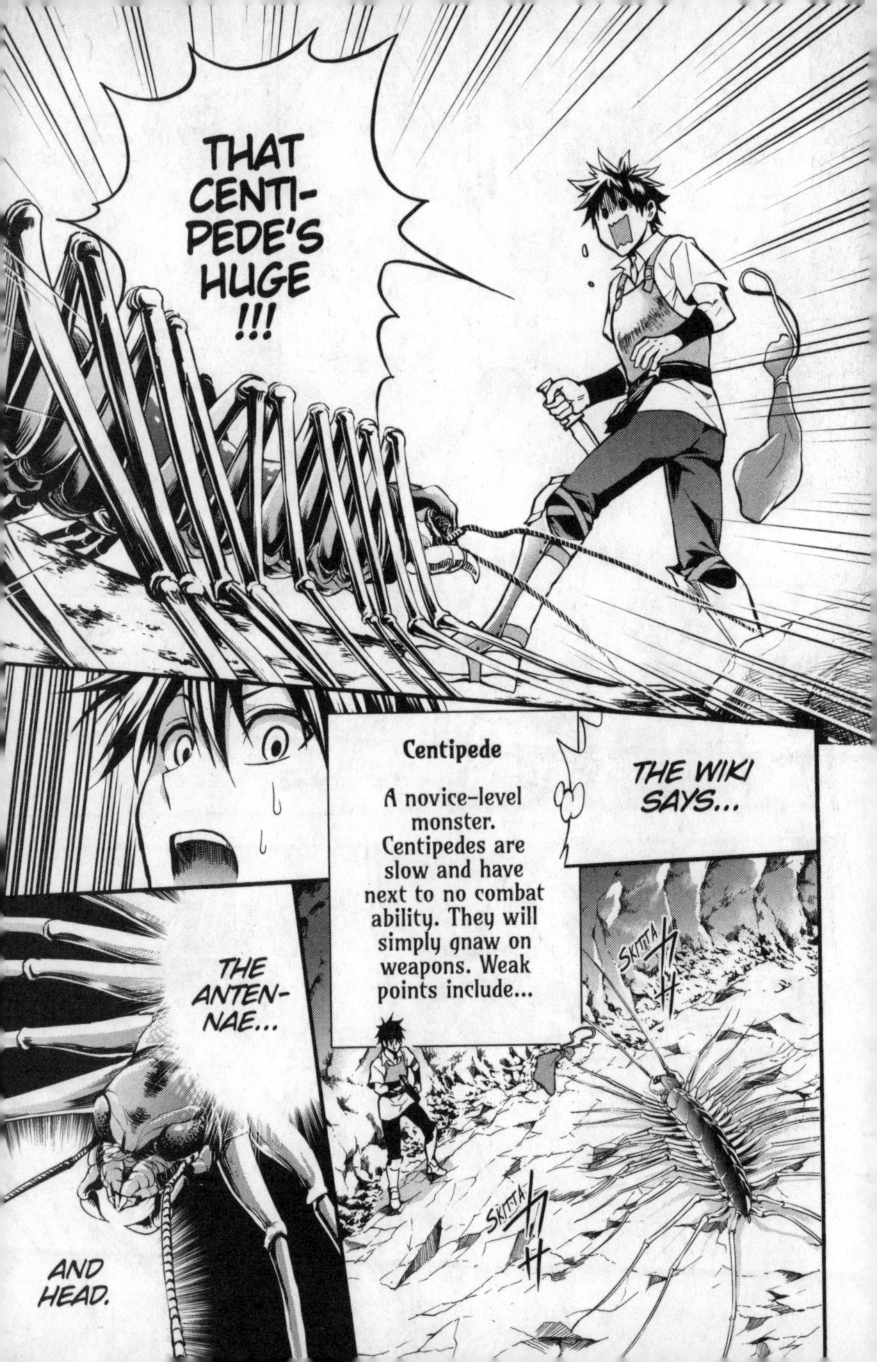
THAT CENTI-PEDE'S HUGE!!!
THE WIKI SAYS...
Centipede
A novice-level monster. Centipedes are slow and have next to no combat ability. They will simply gnaw on weapons. Weak points include...
SKITTA
SKITTA
THE ANTEN-NAE...
AND HEAD.

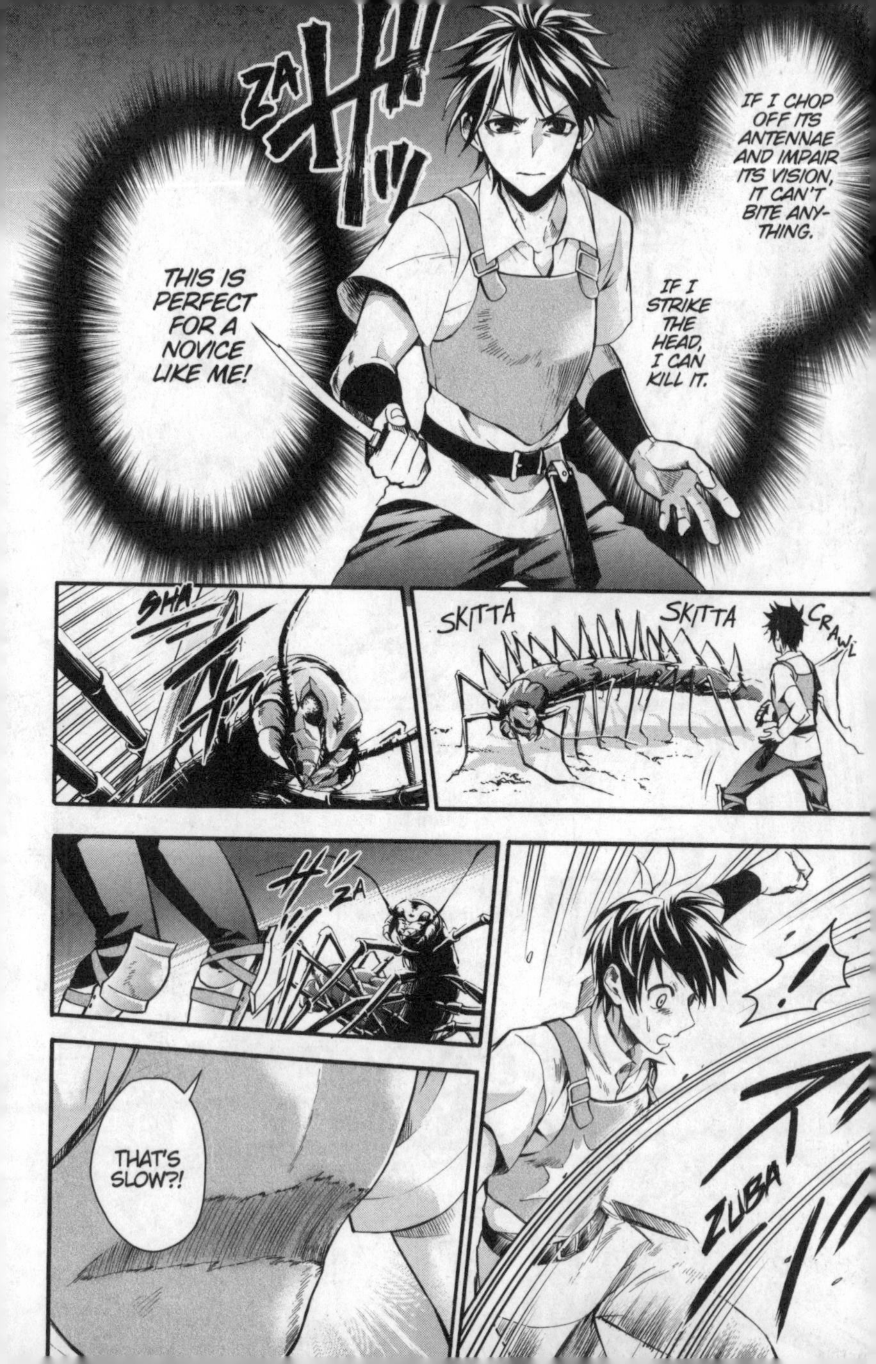
IF I CHOP OFF ITS ANTENNAE AND IMPAIR ITS VISION, IT CAN'T BITE ANY-THING.
IF I STRIKE THE HEAD, I CAN KILL IT.
THIS IS PERFECT FOR A NOVICE LIKE ME!
ZAH!!
SKITTA
SKITTA
CRAWL
SHA
!
ZUBA!!
ZA
THAT'S SLOW?!

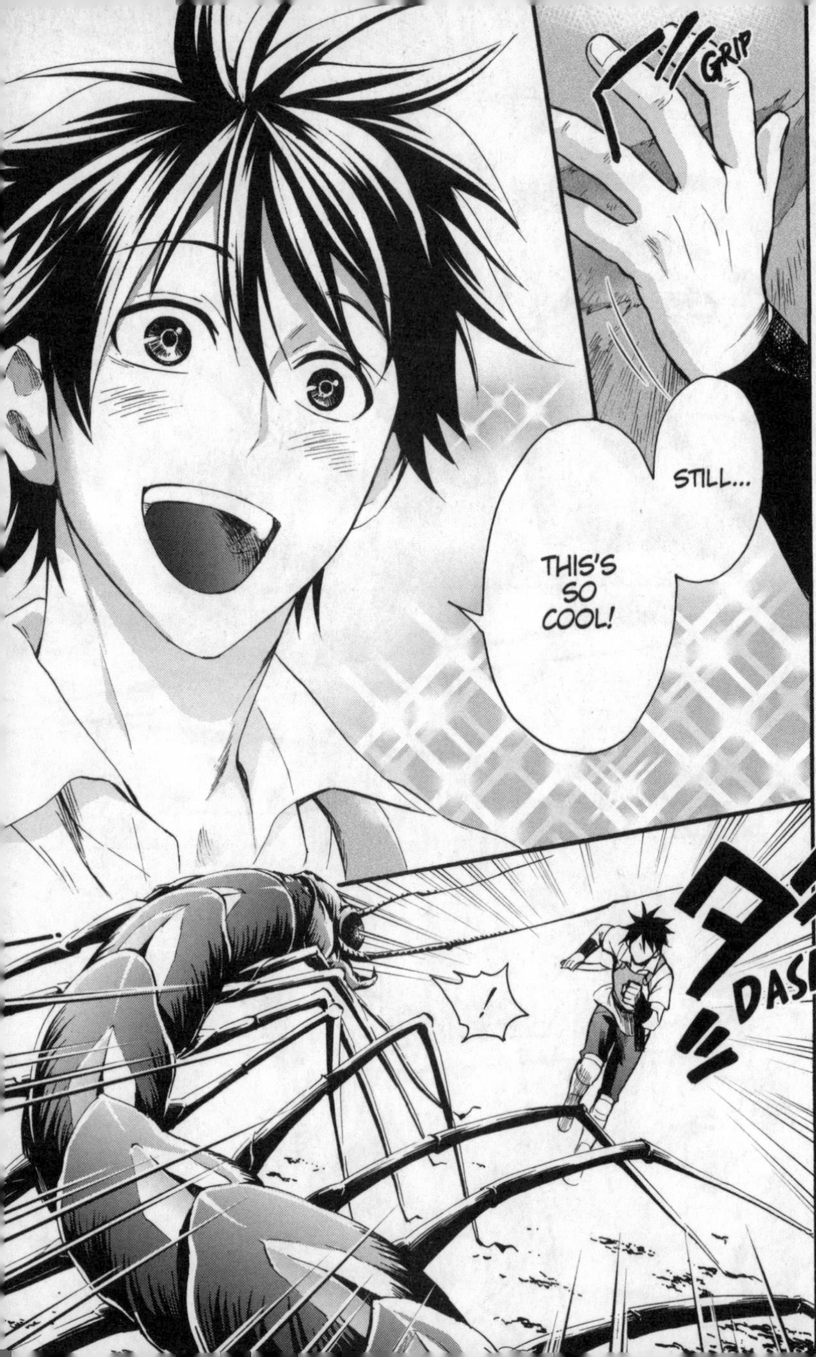
GRIP
STILL...
THIS'S SO COOL!
DASH
!

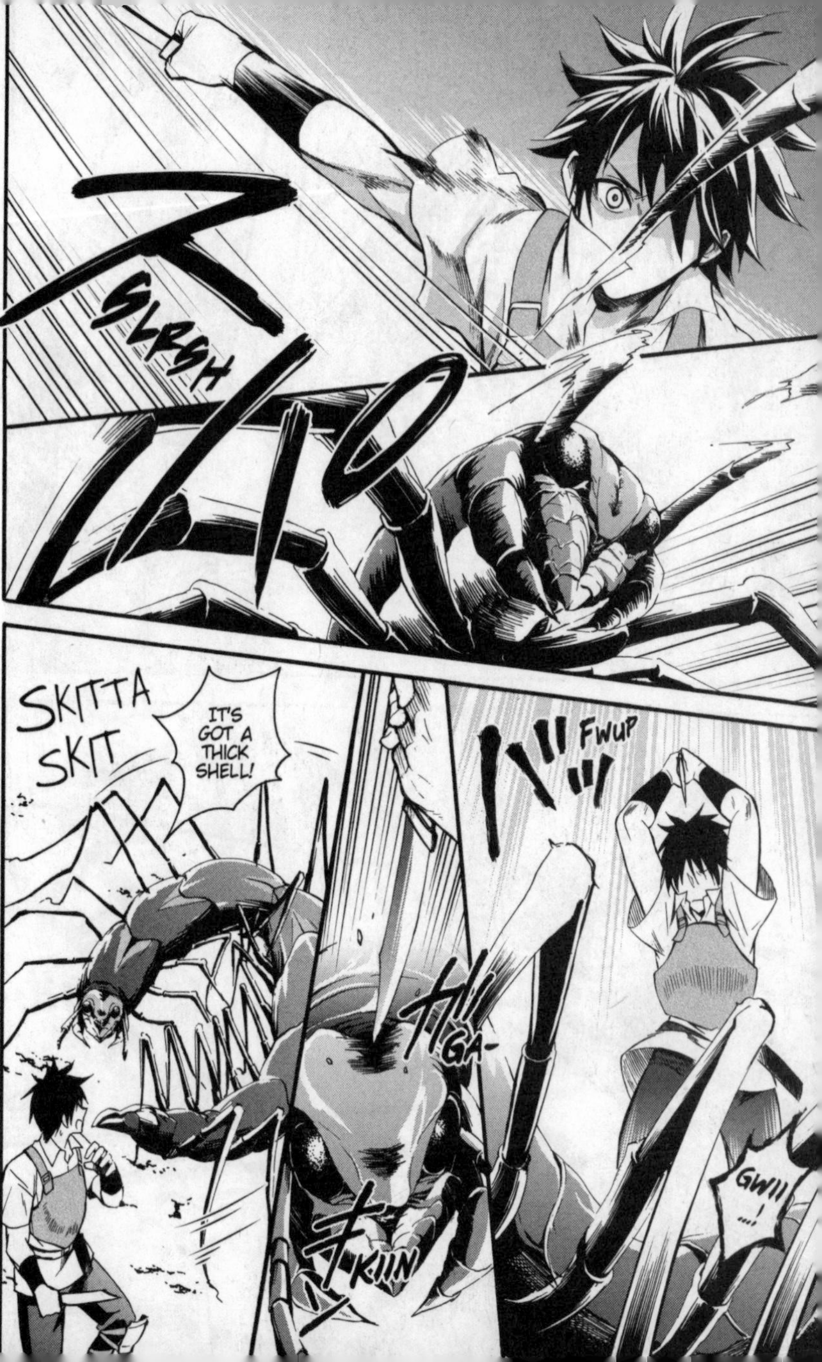
SLRSH
FWUP
HIGA-
GWII!...
KIIN
SKITTA SKIT
IT'S GOT A THICK SHELL!

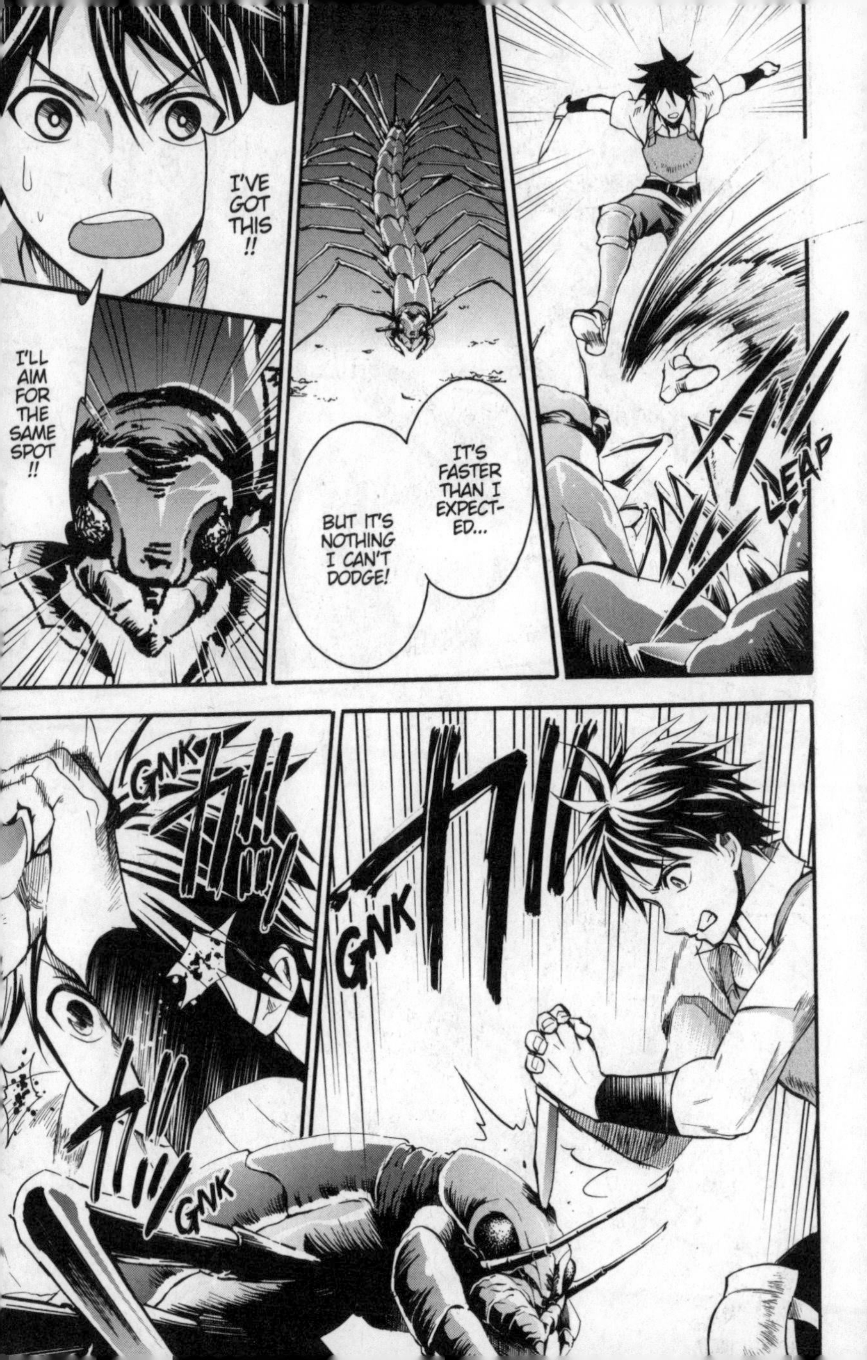
LEAP
IT'S FASTER THAN I EXPECTED...
BUT IT'S NOTHING I CAN'T DODGE!
I'VE GOT THIS!!
I'LL AIM FOR THE SAME SPOT!!
GNK
GNK
GNK

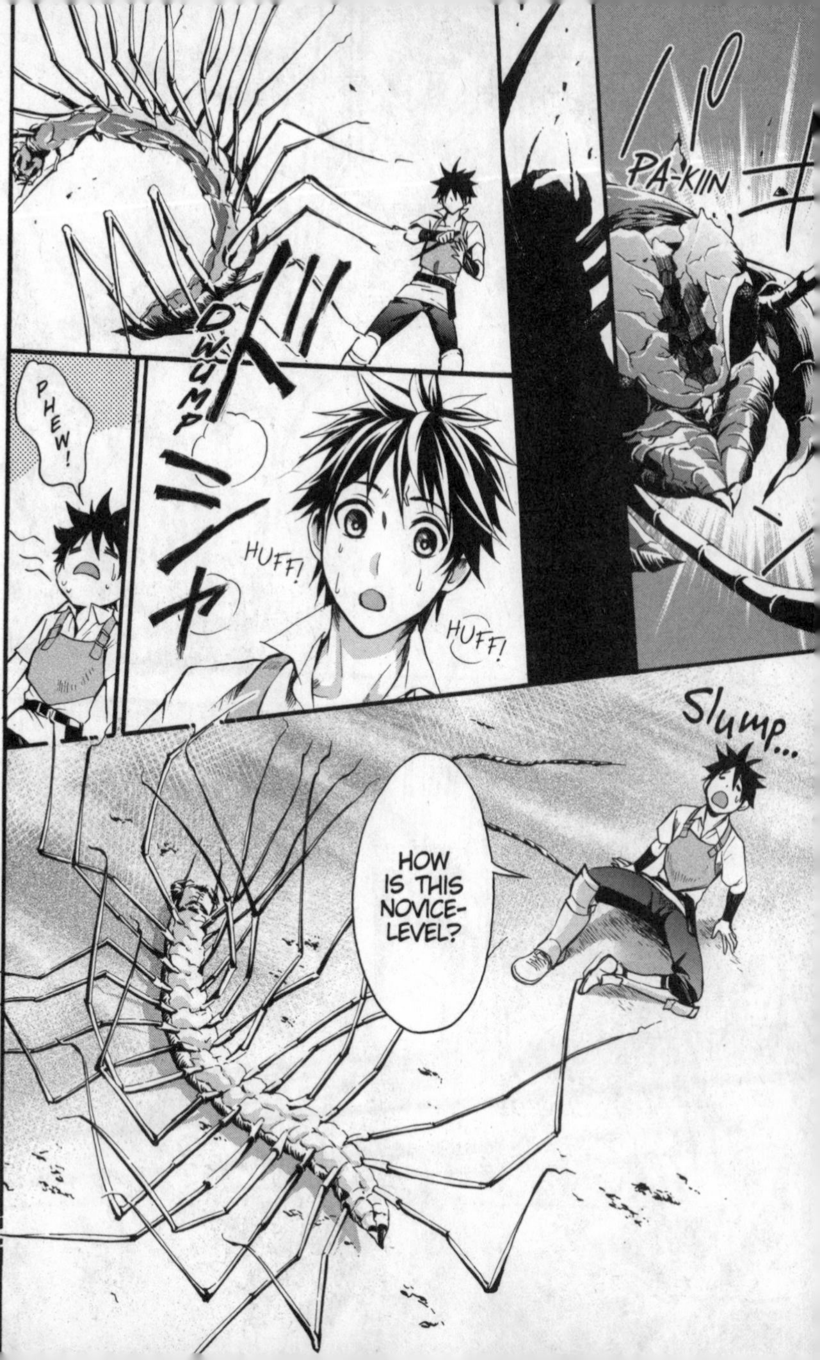
PA-KIIN
DWUMP
HUFF!
HUFF!
PHEW!
Slump...
HOW IS THIS NOVICE-LEVEL?

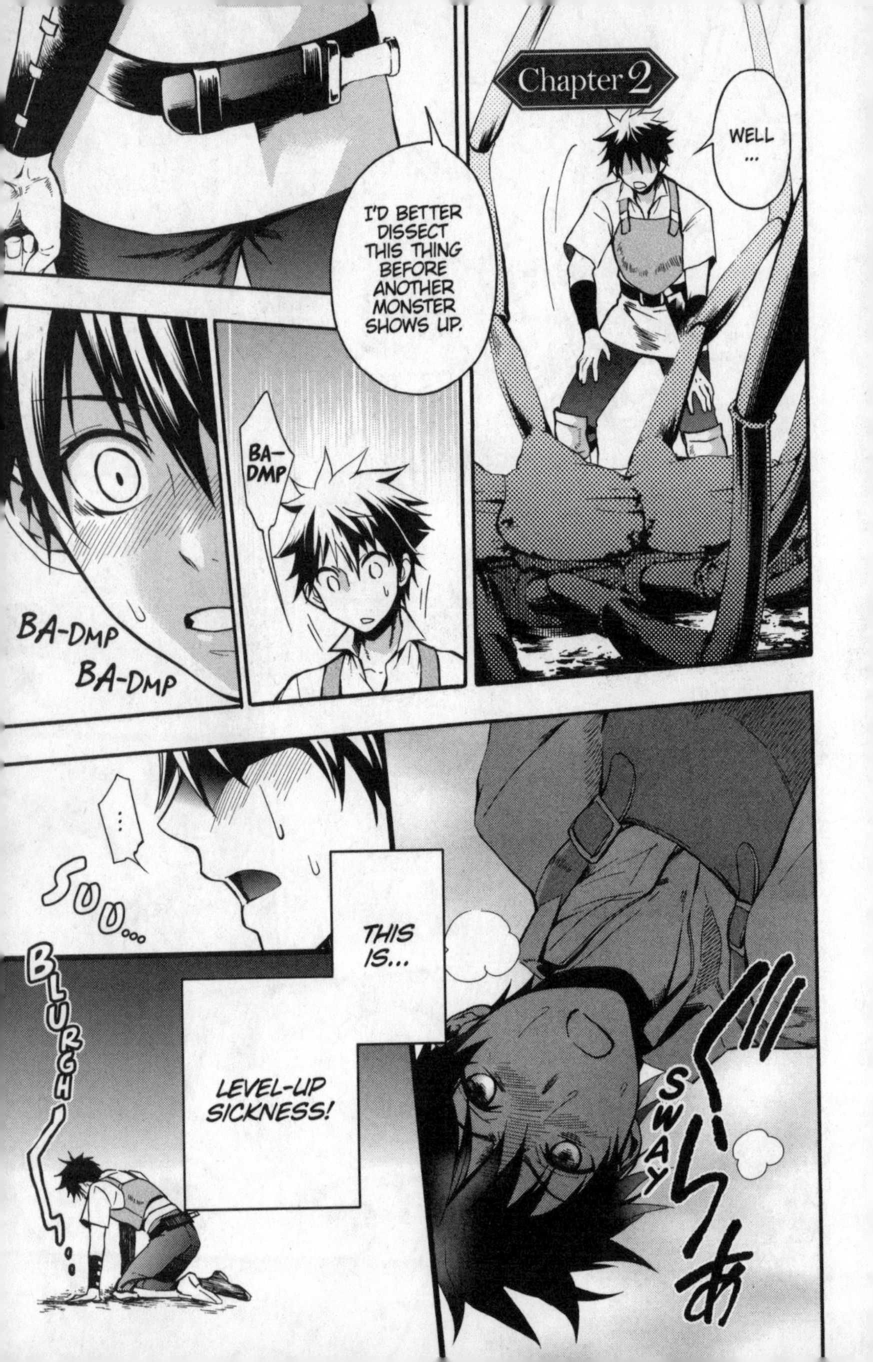
Chapter 2
WELL ...
I'D BETTER DISSECT THIS THING BEFORE ANOTHER MONSTER SHOWS UP.
BA-DMP
BA-DMP BA-DMP
SWAY
THIS IS...
...
SUU...
LEVEL-UP SICKNESS!
BLURGH...

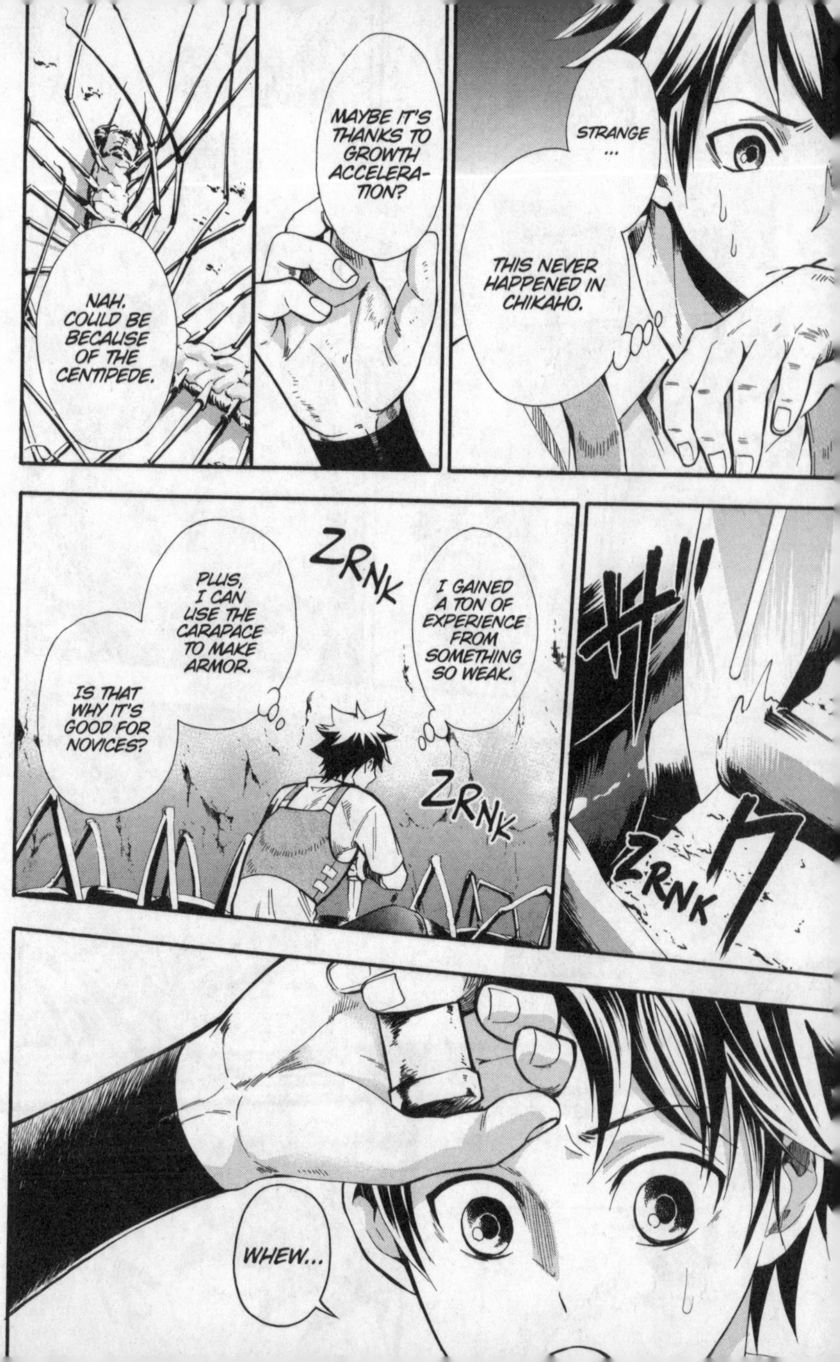
STRANGE ...
THIS NEVER HAPPENED IN CHIKAHO.
MAYBE IT'S THANKS TO GROWTH ACCELERATION?
NAH. COULD BE BECAUSE OF THE CENTIPEDE.
ZRNK
ZRNK
I GAINED A TON OF EXPERIENCE FROM SOMETHING SO WEAK.
PLUS, I CAN USE THE CARAPACE TO MAKE ARMOR.
IS THAT WHY IT'S GOOD FOR NOVICES?
ZRNK
WHEW...

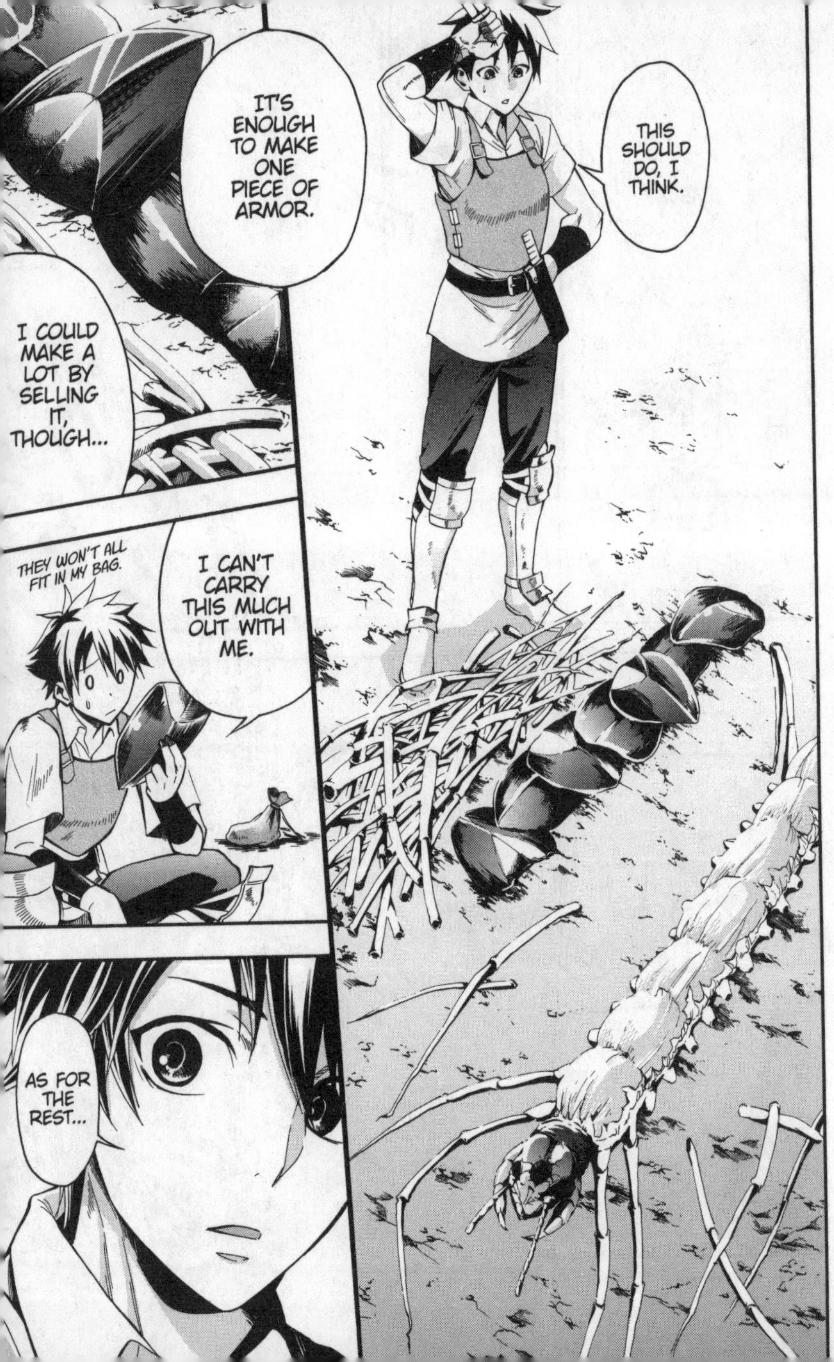
THIS SHOULD DO, I THINK.
IT'S ENOUGH TO MAKE ONE PIECE OF ARMOR.
I COULD MAKE A LOT BY SELLING IT, THOUGH...
I CAN'T CARRY THIS MUCH OUT WITH ME.
THEY WON'T ALL FIT IN MY BAG.
AS FOR THE REST...

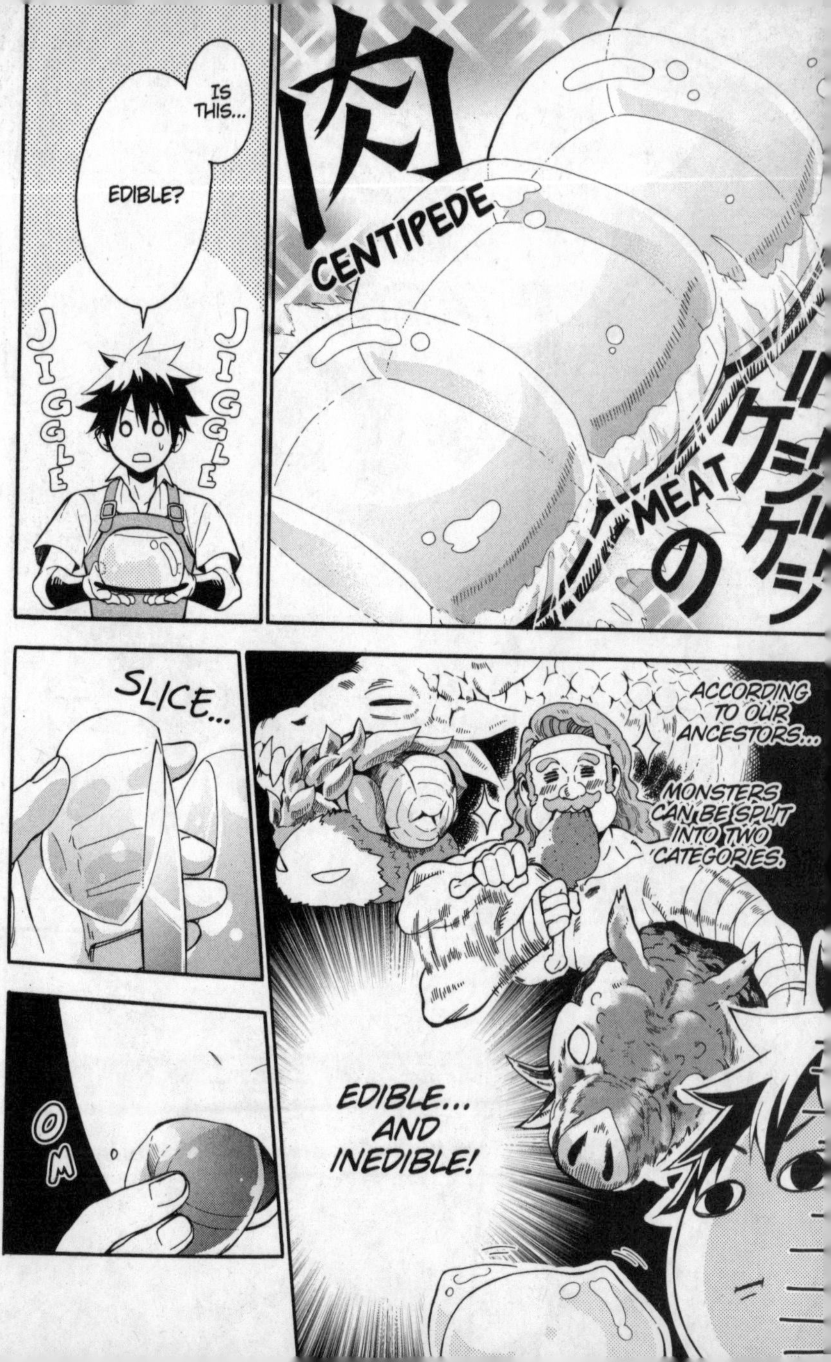
ゲジゲジの肉
CENTIPEDE MEAT
IS THIS...
EDIBLE?
JIGGLE
JIGGLE
ACCORDING TO OUR ANCESTORS...
MONSTERS CAN BE SPLIT INTO TWO CATEGORIES.
EDIBLE... AND INEDIBLE!
SLICE...
OM

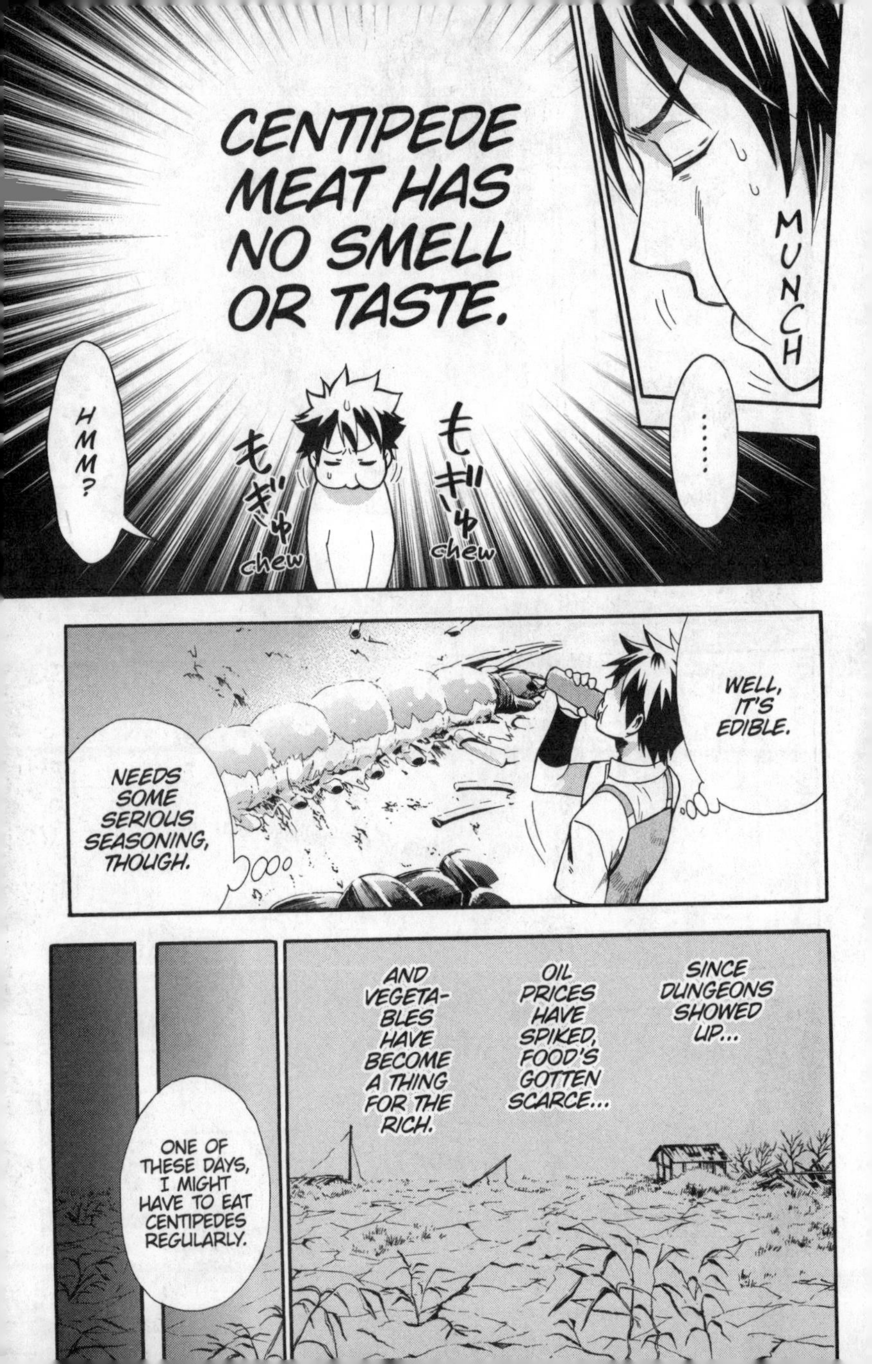
MUNCH
......
CENTIPEDE MEAT HAS NO SMELL OR TASTE.
もぎゅ chew
もぎゅ chew
HMM?
WELL, IT'S EDIBLE.
NEEDS SOME SERIOUS SEASONING, THOUGH.
SINCE DUNGEONS SHOWED UP...
OIL PRICES HAVE SPIKED, FOOD'S GOTTEN SCARCE...
AND VEGETA-BLES HAVE BECOME A THING FOR THE RICH.
ONE OF THESE DAYS, I MIGHT HAVE TO EAT CENTIPEDES REGULARLY.

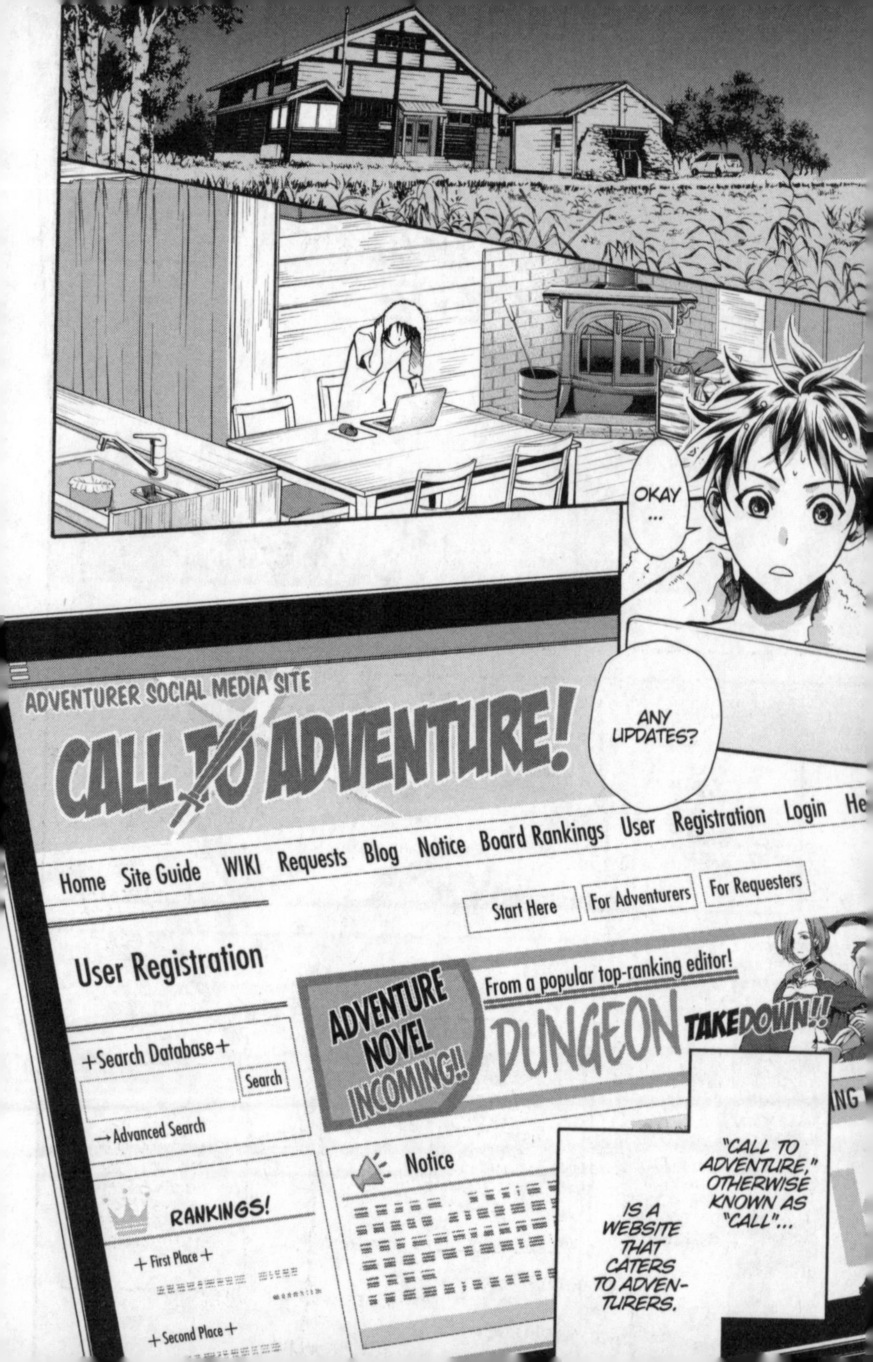
OKAY ...
ANY UPDATES?
ADVENTURER SOCIAL MEDIA SITE
CALL TO ADVENTURE!
Home Site Guide WIKI Requests Blog Notice Board Rankings User Registration Login He
Start Here
For Adventurers
For Requesters
User Registration
+Search Database+
Search
→Advanced Search
ADVENTURE NOVEL INCOMING!!
From a popular top-ranking editor!
DUNGEON TAKEDOWN!!
Notice
RANKINGS!
+First Place+
+Second Place+
"CALL TO ADVENTURE," OTHERWISE KNOWN AS "CALL"...
IS A WEBSITE THAT CATERS TO ADVEN-TURERS.

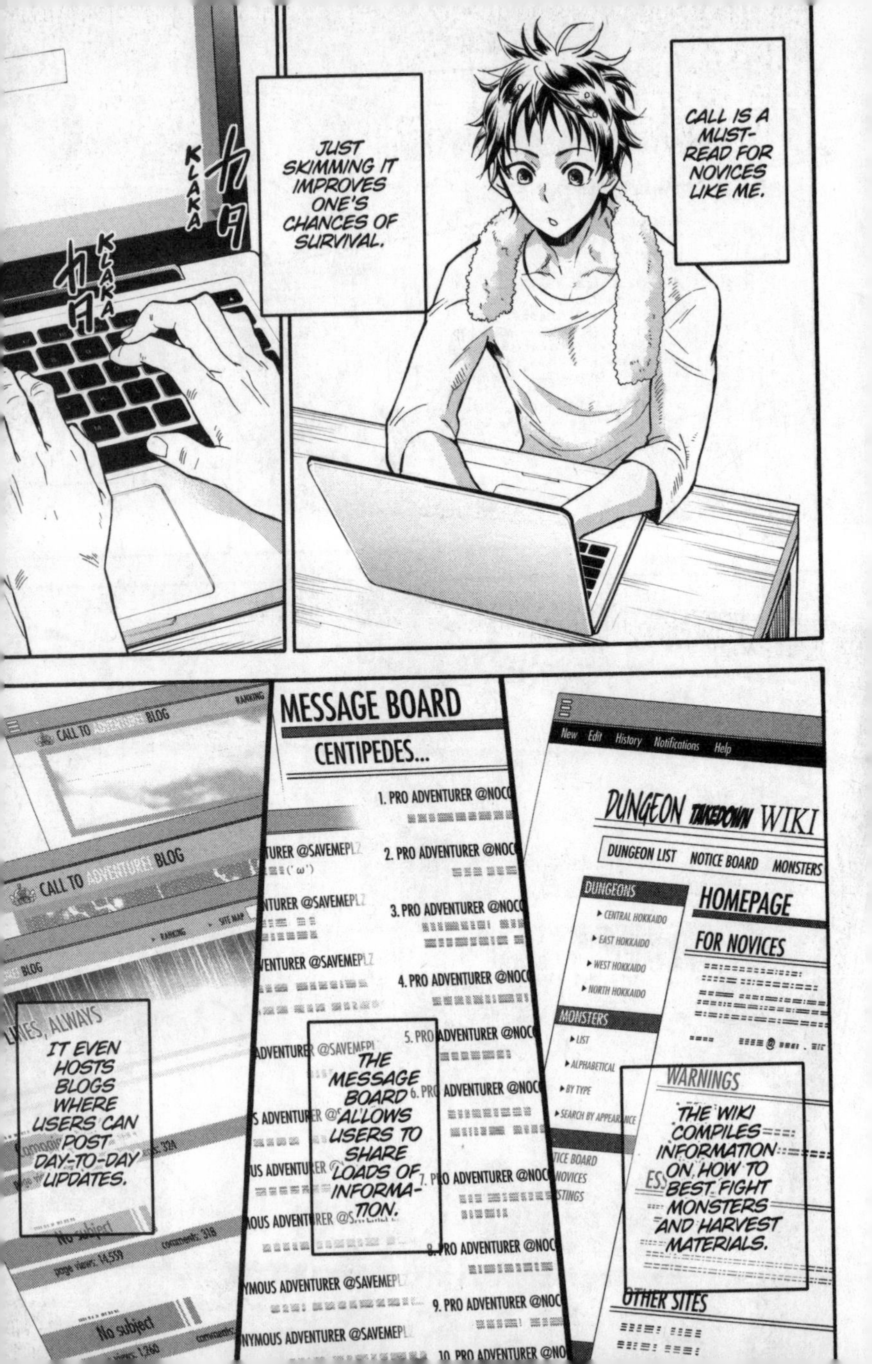
CALL IS A MUST-READ FOR NOVICES LIKE ME.
JUST SKIMMING IT IMPROVES ONE'S CHANCES OF SURVIVAL.
KLAKA
KLAKA
New Edit History Notifications Help
DUNGEON TAKEDOWN WIKI
DUNGEON LIST NOTICE BOARD MONSTERS
DUNGEONS
CENTRAL HOKKAIDO
EAST HOKKAIDO
WEST HOKKAIDO
NORTH HOKKAIDO
MONSTERS
LIST
ALPHABETICAL
BY TYPE
SEARCH BY APPEARANCE
HOMEPAGE
FOR NOVICES
WARNINGS
OTHER SITES
THE WIKI COMPILES INFORMATION ON HOW TO BEST FIGHT MONSTERS AND HARVEST MATERIALS.
MESSAGE BOARD
CENTIPEDES...
1. PRO ADVENTURER @NOC
2. PRO ADVENTURER @NOC
3. PRO ADVENTURER @NOC
4. PRO ADVENTURER @NOC
5. PRO ADVENTURER @NOC
6. PRO ADVENTURER @NOC
7. PRO ADVENTURER @NOC
8. PRO ADVENTURER @NOC
9. PRO ADVENTURER @NOC
10. PRO ADVENTURER @NO
THE MESSAGE BOARD ALLOWS USERS TO SHARE LOADS OF INFORMATION.
CALL TO ADVENTURE! BLOG
RANKING
SITE MAP
No subject
page views: 14,559
comments: 318
IT EVEN HOSTS BLOGS WHERE USERS CAN POST DAY-TO-DAY UPDATES.

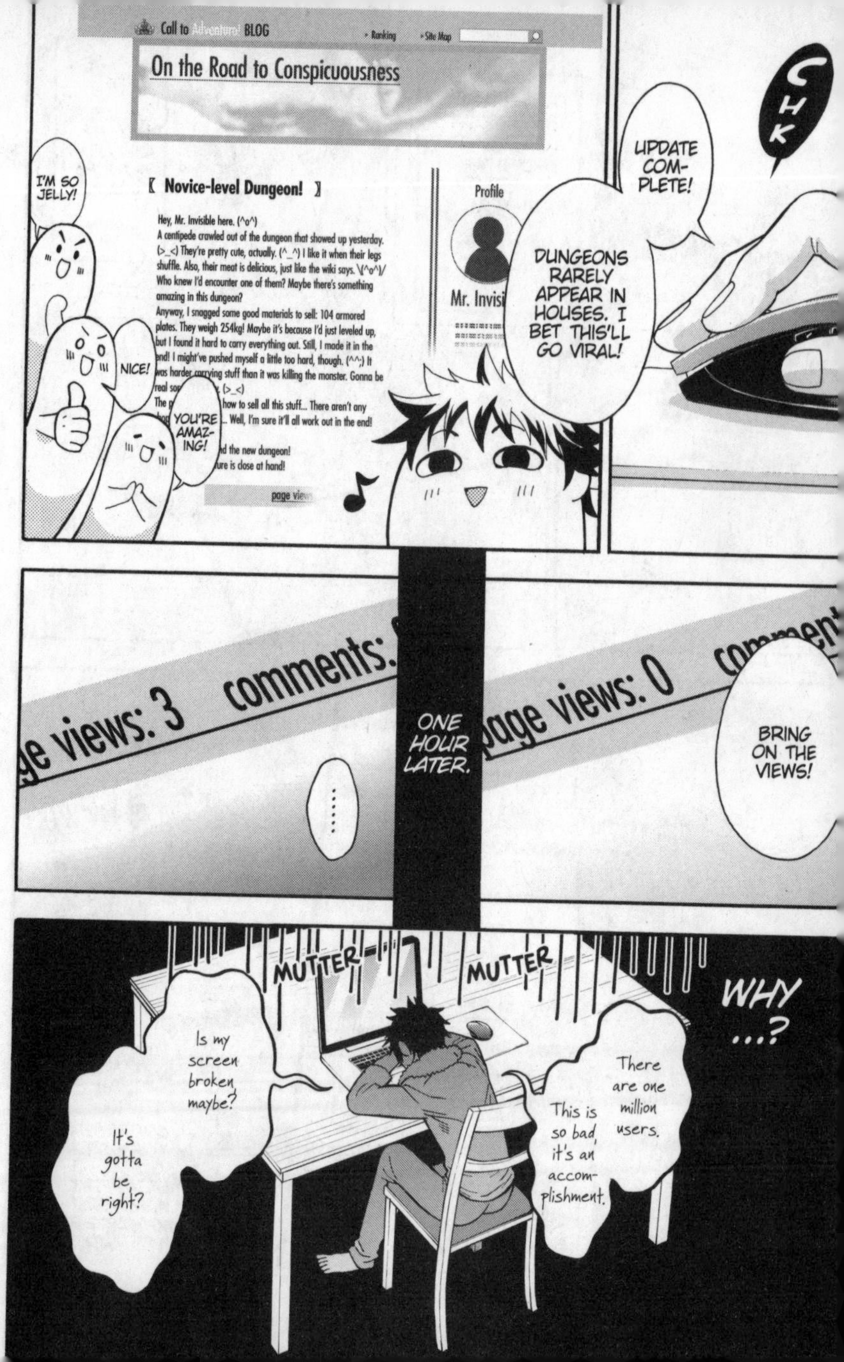
CHK
UPDATE COM-PLETE!
DUNGEONS RARELY APPEAR IN HOUSES. I BET THIS'LL GO VIRAL!
Call to Adventure! BLOG
Ranking
Site Map
On the Road to Conspicuousness
Profile
Mr. Invisi
【 Novice-level Dungeon! 】
Hey, Mr. Invisible here. (^o^)
A centipede crawled out of the dungeon that showed up yesterday. (>_<) They're pretty cute, actually. (^_^) I like it when their legs shuffle. Also, their meat is delicious, just like the wiki says. \(^o^)/ Who knew I'd encounter one of them? Maybe there's something amazing in this dungeon?
Anyway, I snagged some good materials to sell: 104 armored plates. They weigh 254kg! Maybe it's because I'd just leveled up, but I found it hard to carry everything out. Still, I made it in the end! I might've pushed myself a little too hard, though. (^^;) It was harder carrying stuff than it was killing the monster. Gonna be real so (>_<)
The p how to sell all this stuff... There aren't any ... Well, I'm sure it'll all work out in the end!
d the new dungeon!
ure is close at hand!
page view
I'M SO JELLY!
NICE!
YOU'RE AMAZ-ING!
page views: 0
comment
BRING ON THE VIEWS!
ONE HOUR LATER.
page views: 3
comments:
......
WHY ...?
MUTTER
MUTTER
There are one million users.
This is so bad, it's an accom-plishment.
Is my screen broken, maybe?
It's gotta be right?

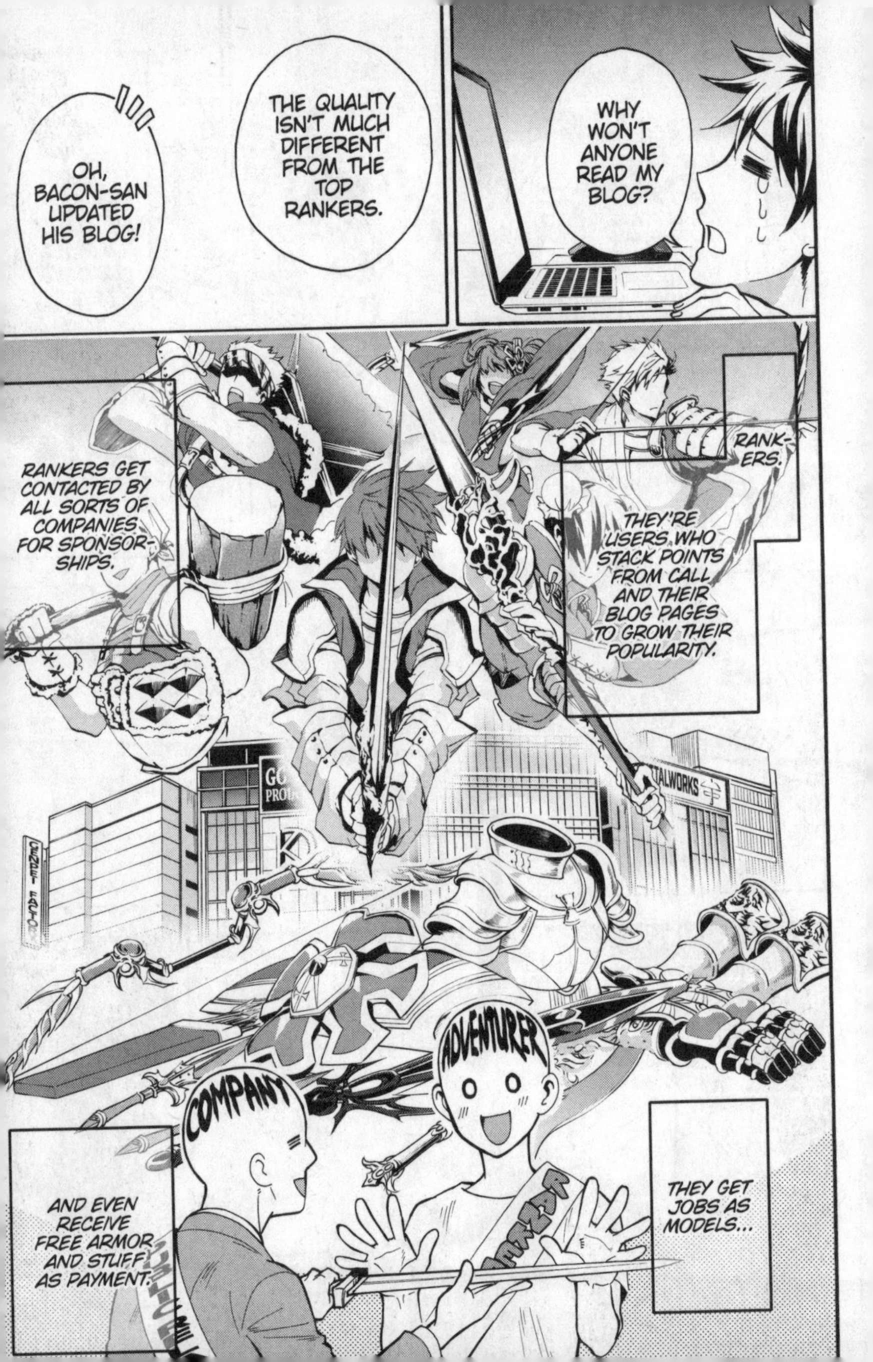
WHY WON'T ANYONE READ MY BLOG?
OH, BACON-SAN UPDATED HIS BLOG!
THE QUALITY ISN'T MUCH DIFFERENT FROM THE TOP RANKERS.
RANK-ERS.
THEY'RE USERS WHO STACK POINTS FROM CALL AND THEIR BLOG PAGES TO GROW THEIR POPULARITY.
RANKERS GET CONTACTED BY ALL SORTS OF COMPANIES FOR SPONSOR-SHIPS.
GENPEI FACTORY
TALWORKS
ADVENTURER
COMPANY
THEY GET JOBS AS MODELS...
AND EVEN RECEIVE FREE ARMOR AND STUFF AS PAYMENT.

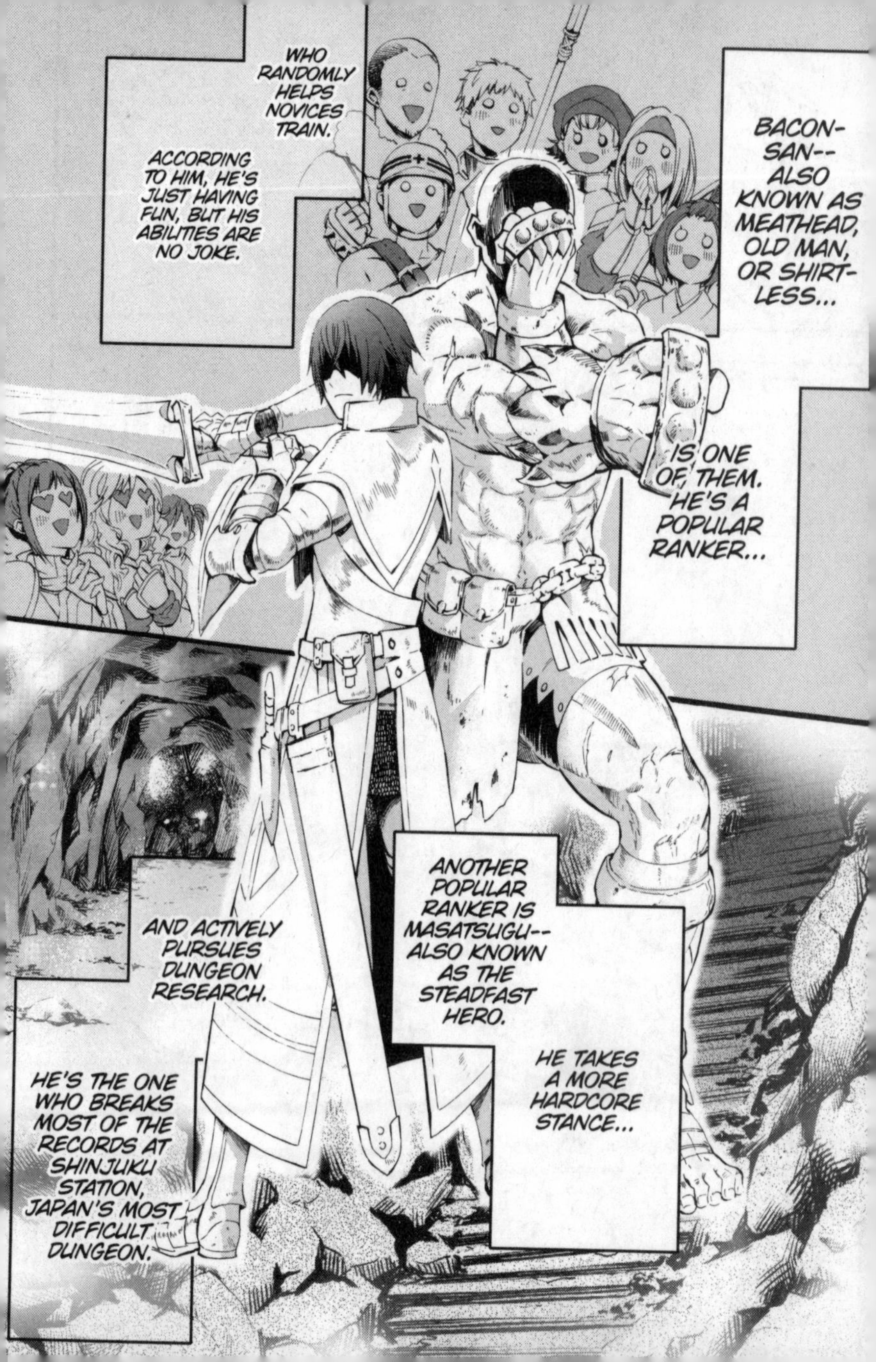
BACON-SAN--ALSO KNOWN AS MEATHEAD, OLD MAN, OR SHIRTLESS...
IS ONE OF THEM. HE'S A POPULAR RANKER...
WHO RANDOMLY HELPS NOVICES TRAIN.
ACCORDING TO HIM, HE'S JUST HAVING FUN, BUT HIS ABILITIES ARE NO JOKE.
ANOTHER POPULAR RANKER IS MASATSUGU--ALSO KNOWN AS THE STEADFAST HERO.
HE TAKES A MORE HARDCORE STANCE...
AND ACTIVELY PURSUES DUNGEON RESEARCH.
HE'S THE ONE WHO BREAKS MOST OF THE RECORDS AT SHINJUKU STATION, JAPAN'S MOST DIFFICULT DUNGEON.

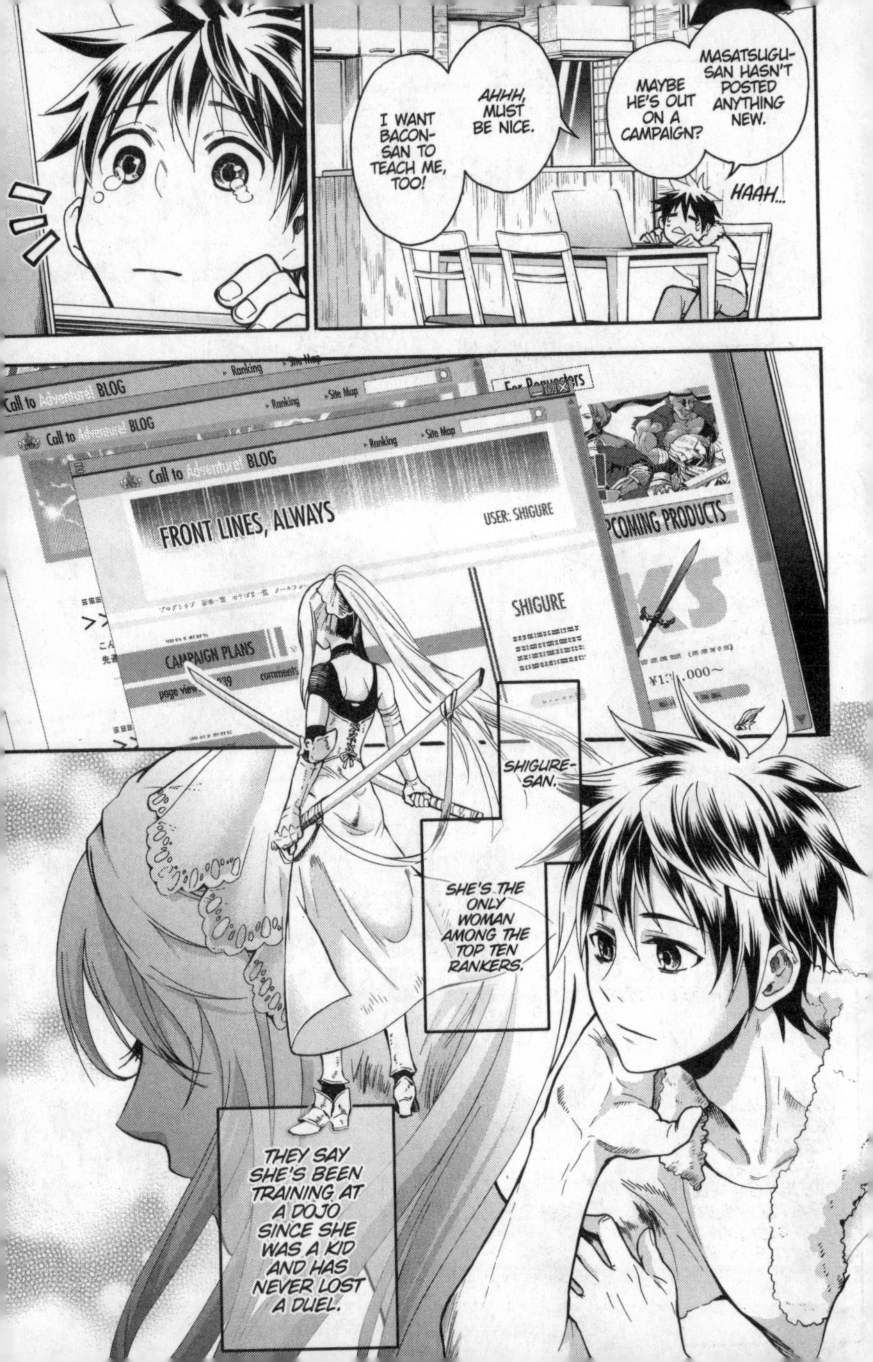
MASATSUGU-SAN HASN'T POSTED ANYTHING NEW.
MAYBE HE'S OUT ON A CAMPAIGN?
HAAH...
AHHH, MUST BE NICE.
I WANT BACON-SAN TO TEACH ME, TOO!
Call to Adventure! BLOG
Ranking
Site Map
For Requesters
UPCOMING PRODUCTS
FRONT LINES, ALWAYS
USER: SHIGURE
SHIGURE
CAMPAIGN PLANS
comments
page views
SHIGURE-SAN.
SHE'S THE ONLY WOMAN AMONG THE TOP TEN RANKERS.
THEY SAY SHE'S BEEN TRAINING AT A DOJO SINCE SHE WAS A KID AND HAS NEVER LOST A DUEL.

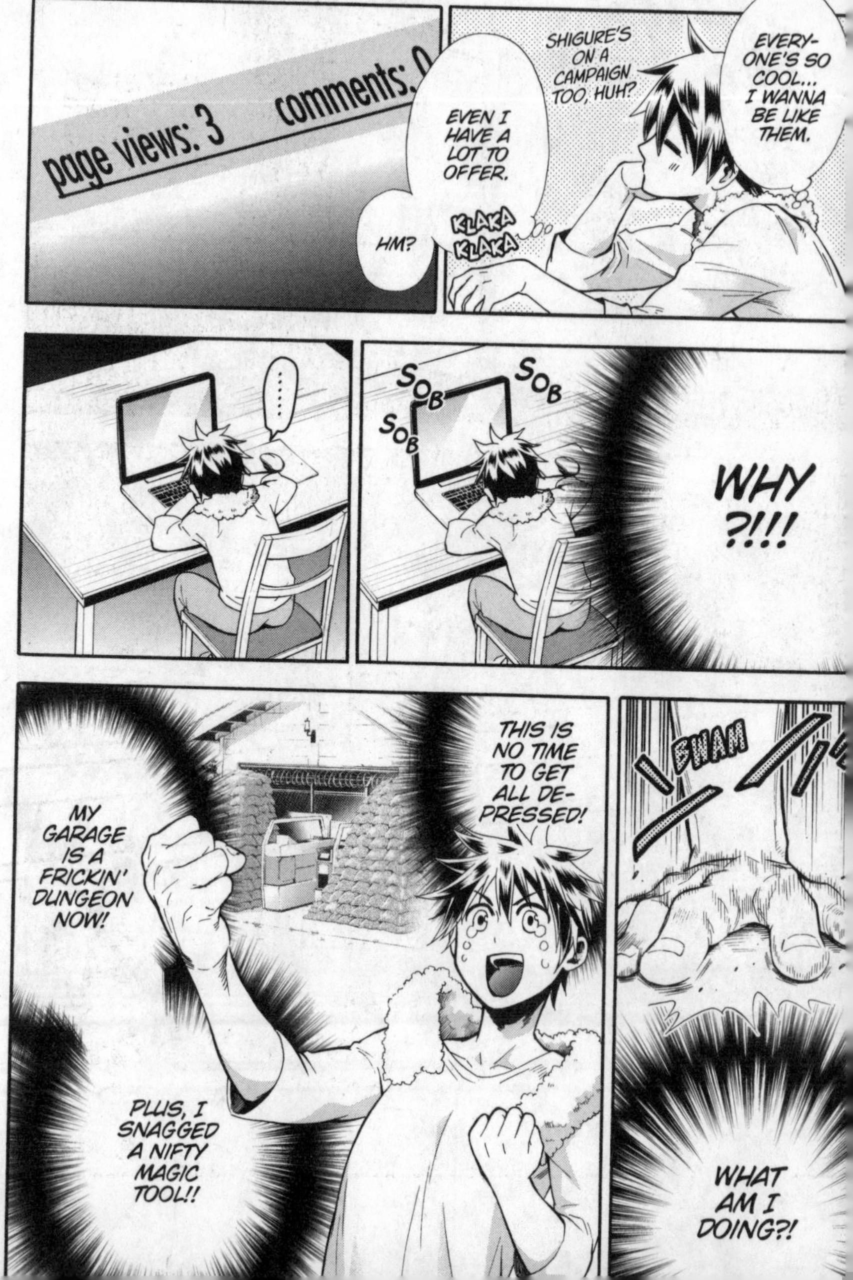
EVERY-ONE'S SO COOL... I WANNA BE LIKE THEM.
SHIGURE'S ON A CAMPAIGN TOO, HUH?
EVEN I HAVE A LOT TO OFFER.
KLAKA KLAKA
HM?
page views: 3 comments: 0
WHY ?!!!
SOB SOB SOB
......
BWAM
WHAT AM I DOING?!
THIS IS NO TIME TO GET ALL DE-PRESSED!
MY GARAGE IS A FRICKIN' DUNGEON NOW!
PLUS, I SNAGGED A NIFTY MAGIC TOOL!!

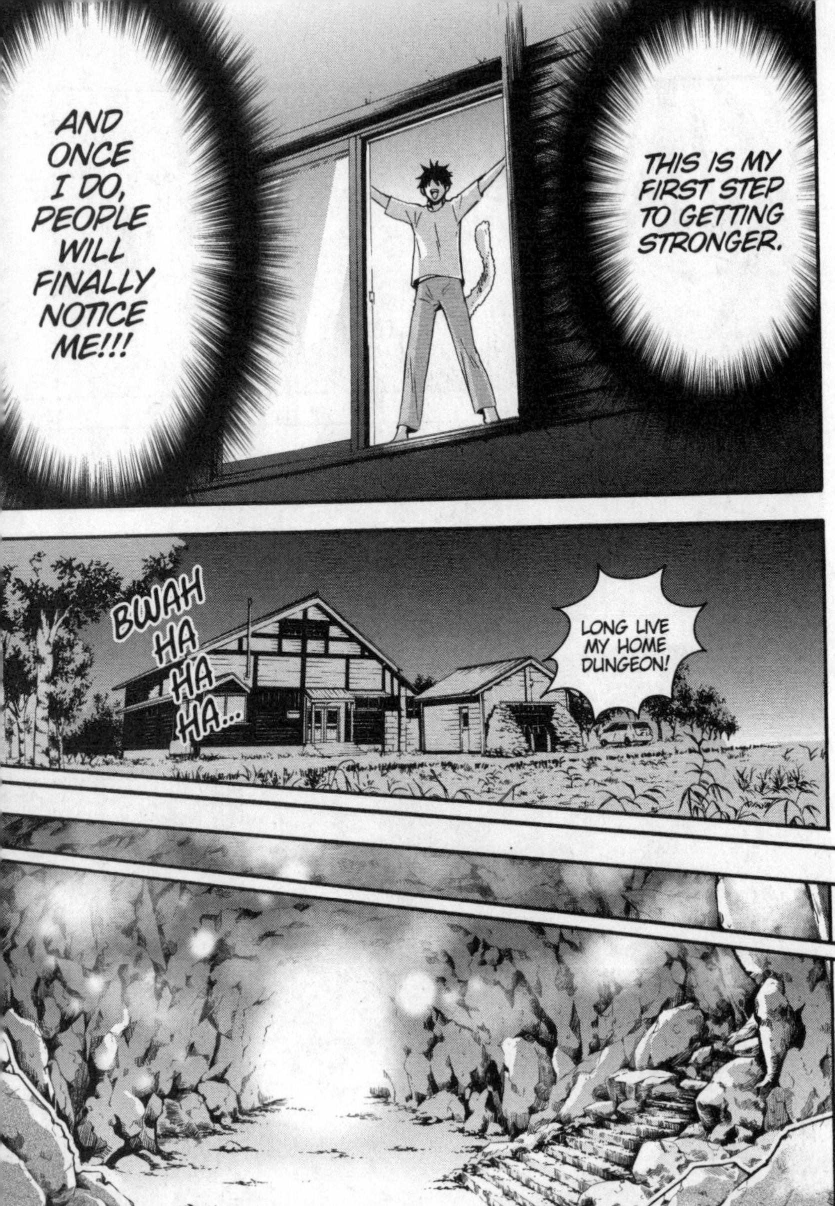
THIS IS MY FIRST STEP TO GETTING STRONGER.
AND ONCE I DO, PEOPLE WILL FINALLY NOTICE ME!!!
LONG LIVE MY HOME DUNGEON!
BWAH HA HA HA...

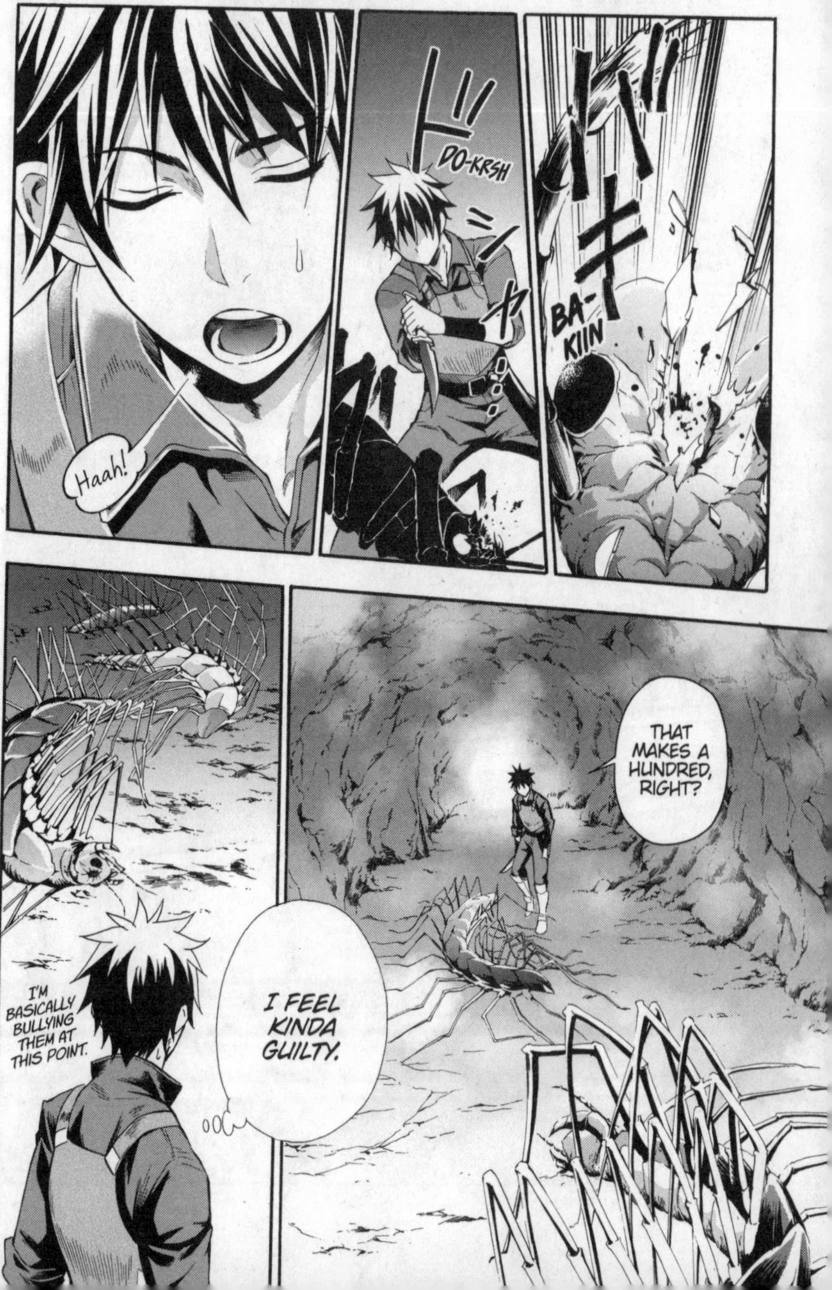
BA-KIIN
DO-KRSH
Haah!
THAT MAKES A HUNDRED, RIGHT?
I FEEL KINDA GUILTY.
I'M BASICALLY BULLYING THEM AT THIS POINT.

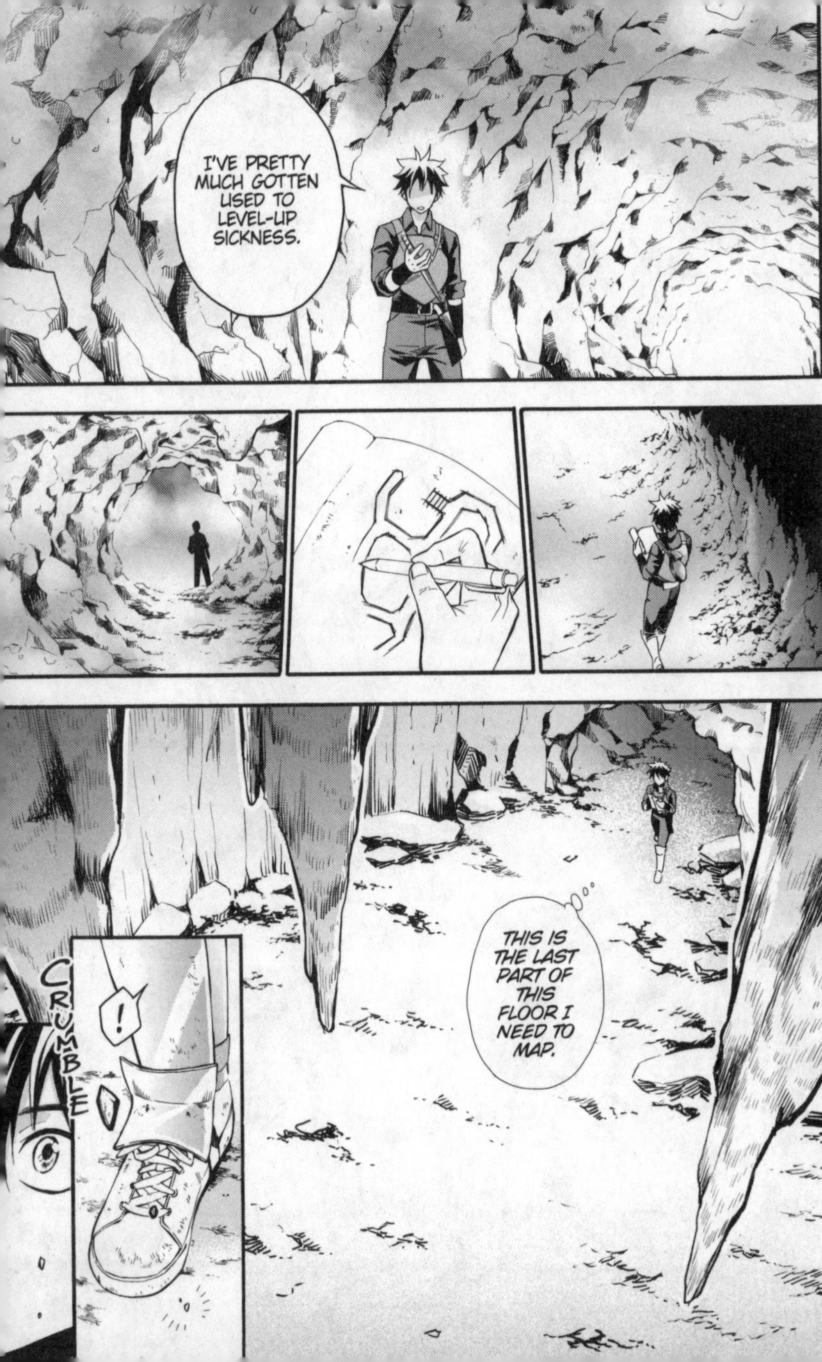
I'VE PRETTY MUCH GOTTEN USED TO LEVEL-UP SICKNESS.
THIS IS THE LAST PART OF THIS FLOOR I NEED TO MAP.
!
CRUMBLE

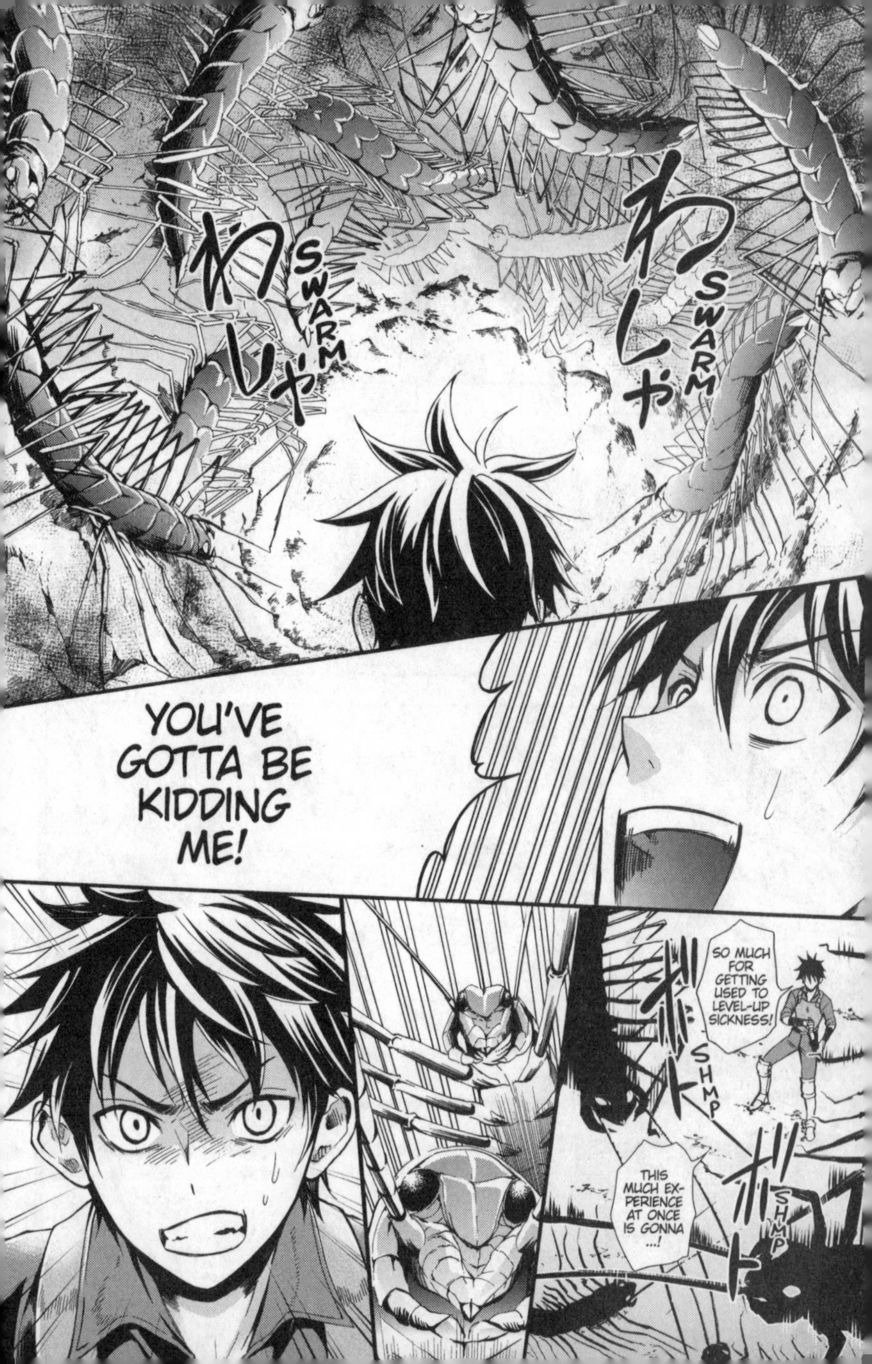
SWARM
SWARM
YOU'VE GOTTA BE KIDDING ME!
SO MUCH FOR GETTING USED TO LEVEL-UP SICKNESS!
SHMP
THIS MUCH EX-PERIENCE AT ONCE IS GONNA ...!
SHMP

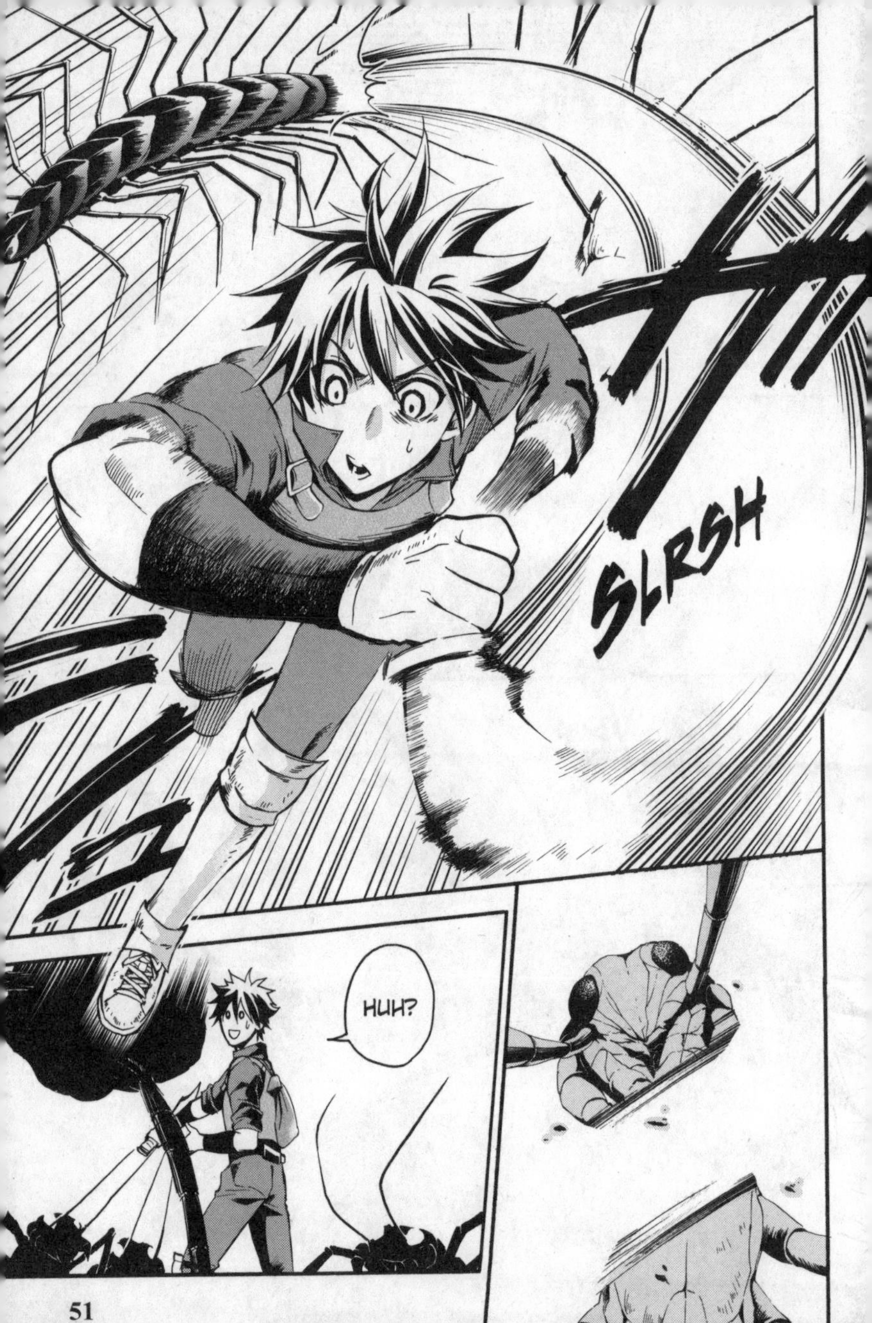
SLRSH
HUH?

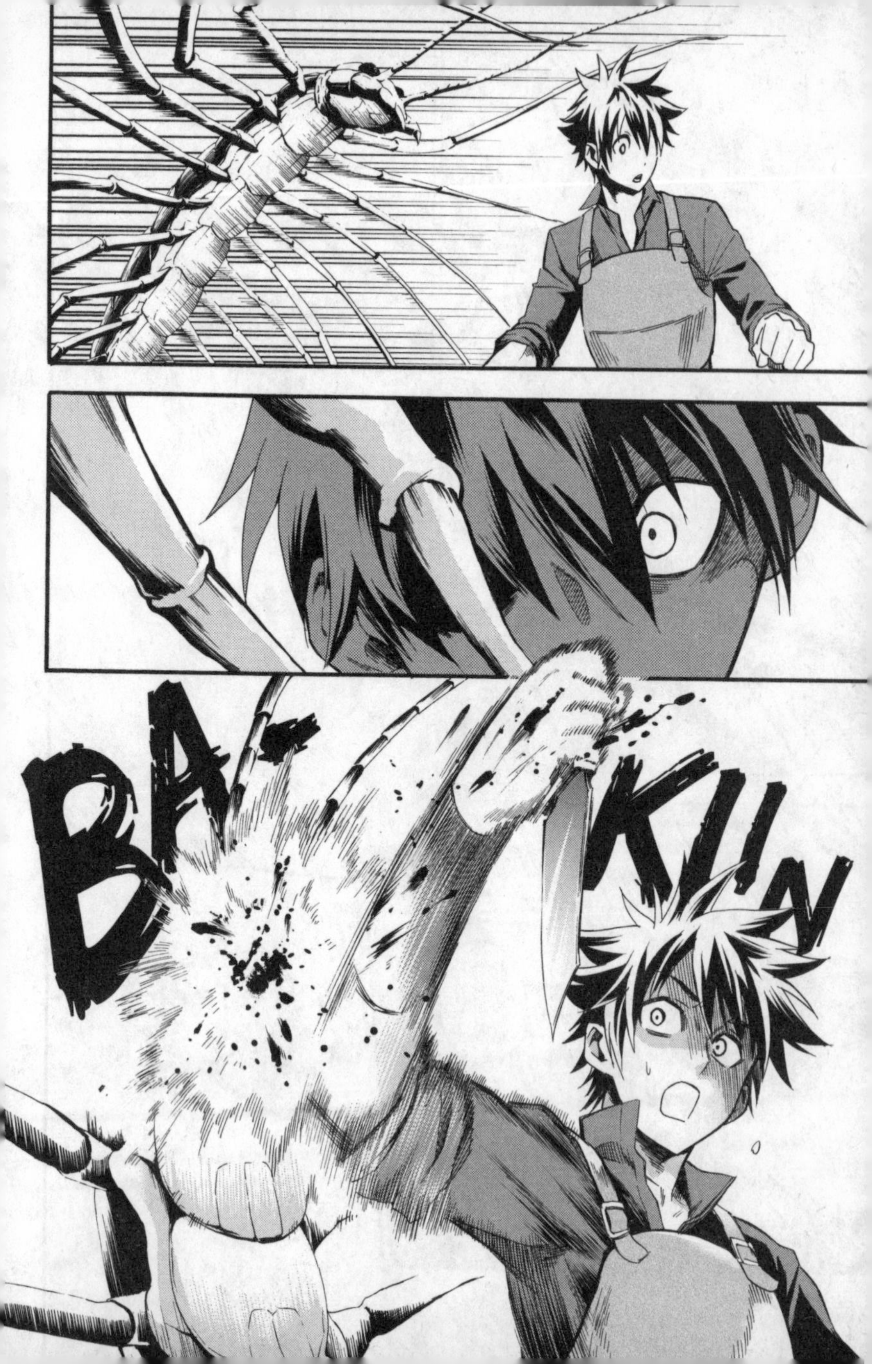
BAKIN

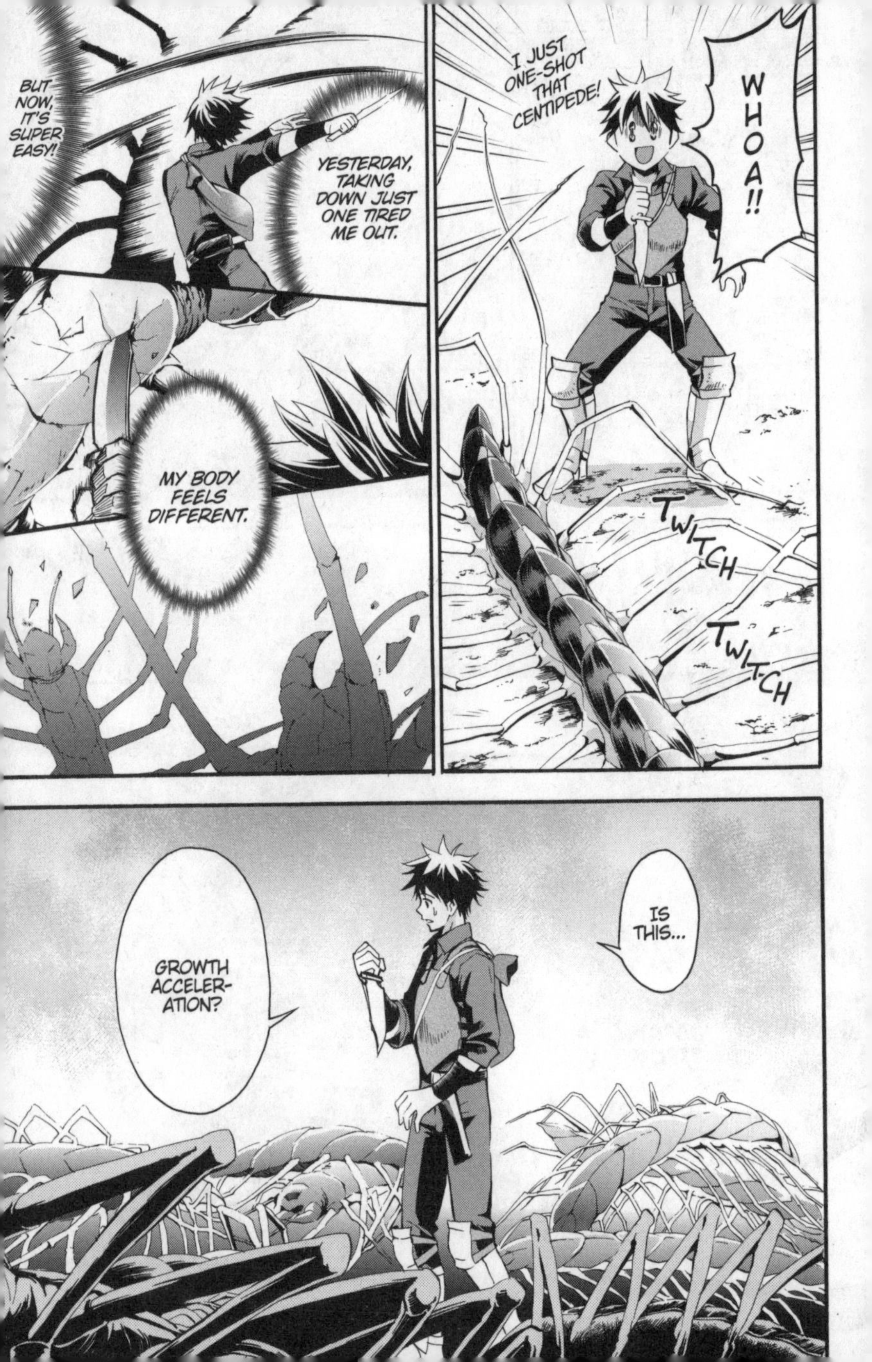
WHOA!!
I JUST ONE-SHOT THAT CENTIPEDE!
TWITCH
TWITCH
YESTERDAY, TAKING DOWN JUST ONE TIRED ME OUT.
BUT NOW, IT'S SUPER EASY!
MY BODY FEELS DIFFERENT.
IS THIS...
GROWTH ACCELER-ATION?

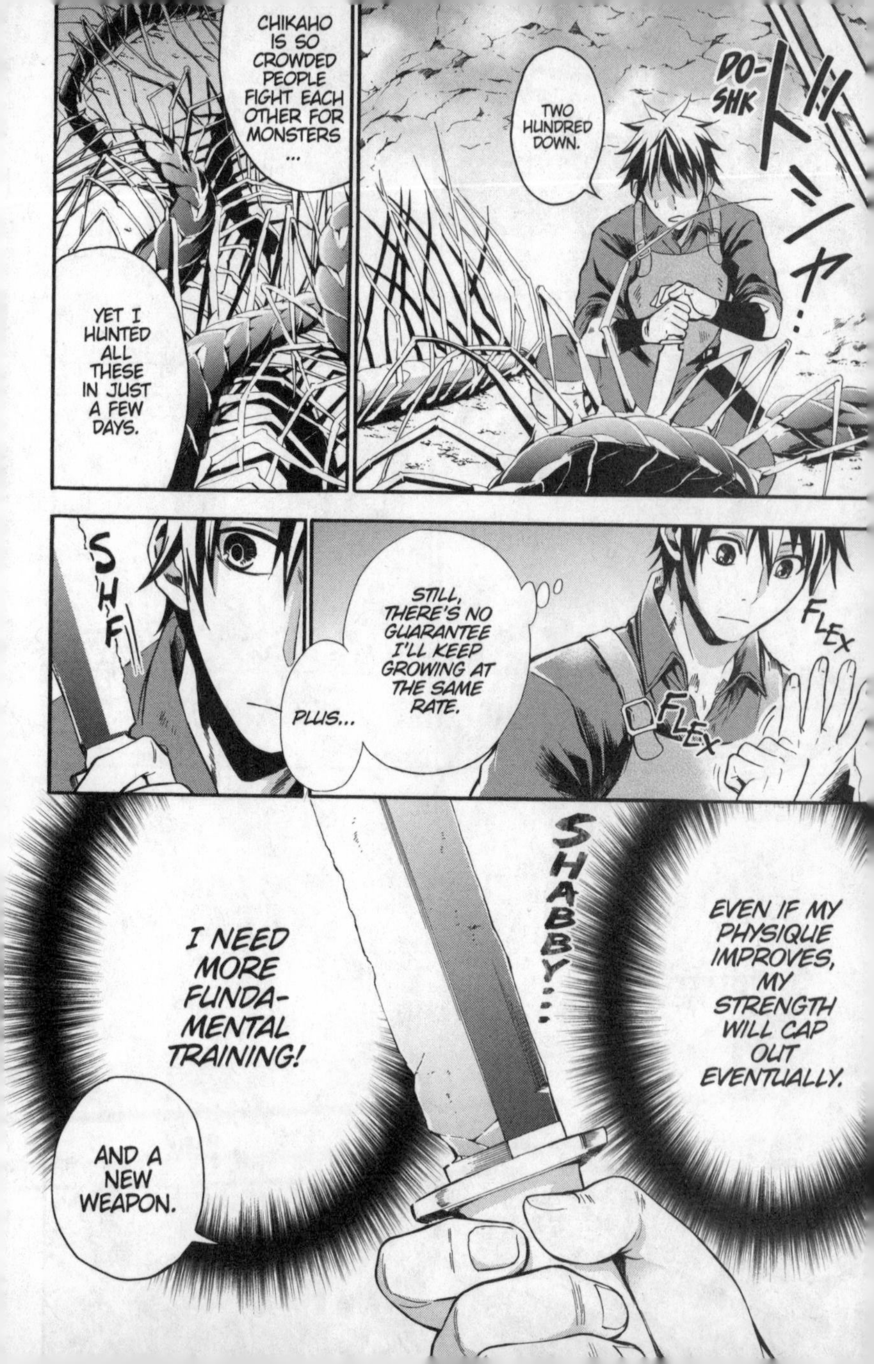
DO-SHK
TWO HUNDRED DOWN.
CHIKAHO IS SO CROWDED PEOPLE FIGHT EACH OTHER FOR MONSTERS...
YET I HUNTED ALL THESE IN JUST A FEW DAYS.
FLEX
FLEX
STILL, THERE'S NO GUARANTEE I'LL KEEP GROWING AT THE SAME RATE.
PLUS...
SHF
EVEN IF MY PHYSIQUE IMPROVES, MY STRENGTH WILL CAP OUT EVENTUALLY.
SHABBY...
I NEED MORE FUNDA-MENTAL TRAINING!
AND A NEW WEAPON.

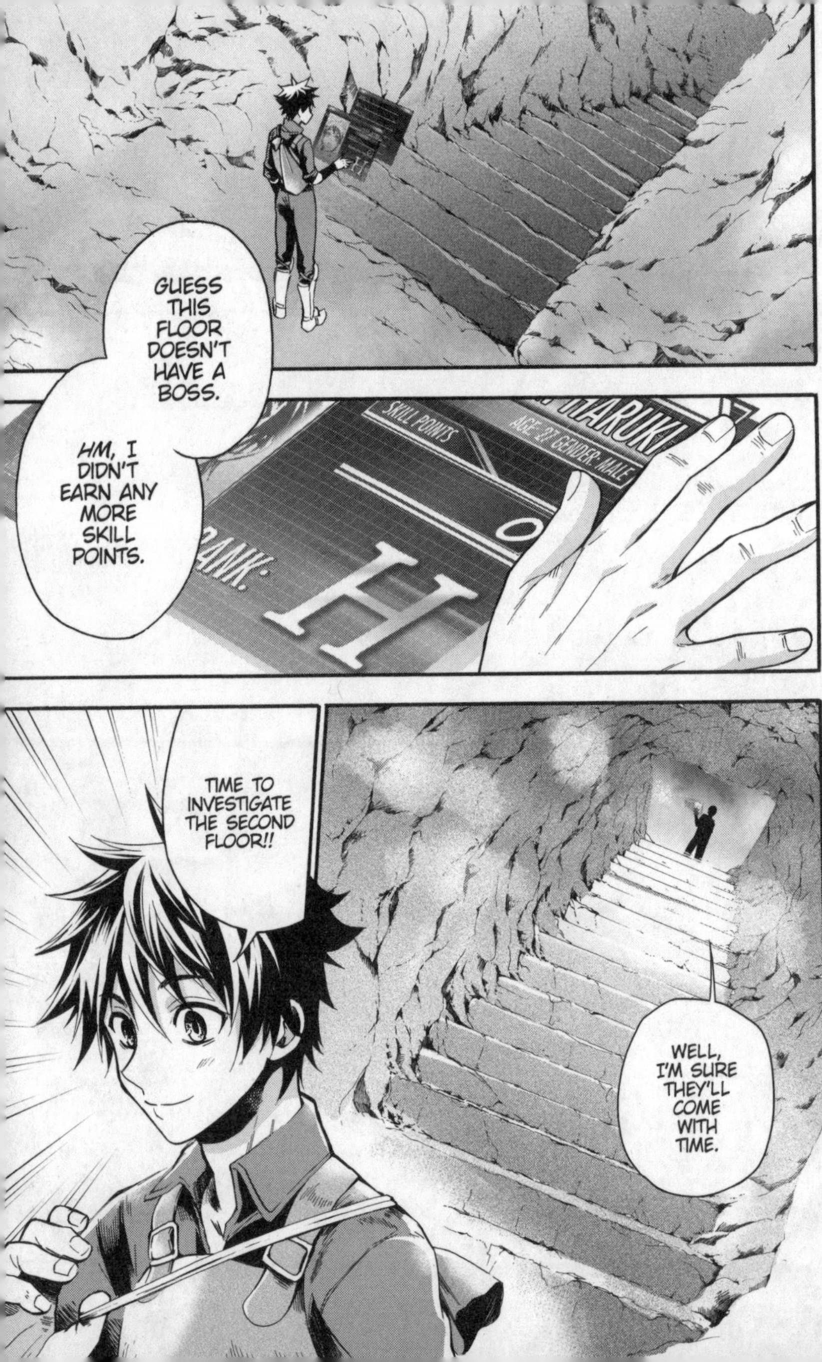
GUESS THIS FLOOR DOESN'T HAVE A BOSS.
HM, I DIDN'T EARN ANY MORE SKILL POINTS.
SKILL POINTS
AGE: 27 GENDER: MALE
0
H
WELL, I'M SURE THEY'LL COME WITH TIME.
TIME TO INVESTIGATE THE SECOND FLOOR!!

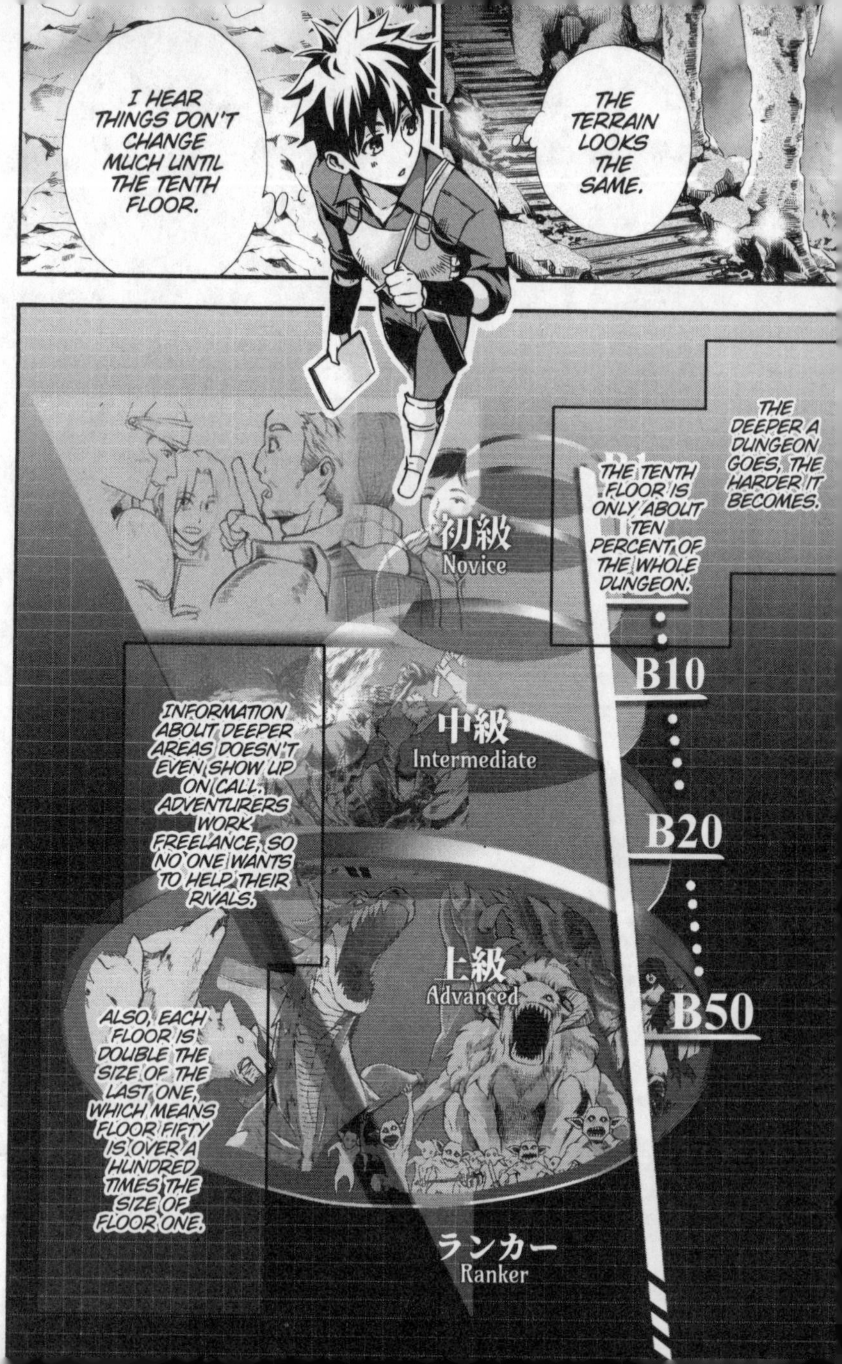
THE TERRAIN LOOKS THE SAME.
I HEAR THINGS DON'T CHANGE MUCH UNTIL THE TENTH FLOOR.
THE DEEPER A DUNGEON GOES, THE HARDER IT BECOMES.
THE TENTH FLOOR IS ONLY ABOUT TEN PERCENT OF THE WHOLE DUNGEON.
B10
B20
B50
初級
Novice
中級
Intermediate
上級
Advanced
ランカー
Ranker
INFORMATION ABOUT DEEPER AREAS DOESN'T EVEN SHOW UP ON CALL. ADVENTURERS WORK FREELANCE, SO NO ONE WANTS TO HELP THEIR RIVALS.
ALSO, EACH FLOOR IS DOUBLE THE SIZE OF THE LAST ONE, WHICH MEANS FLOOR FIFTY IS OVER A HUNDRED TIMES THE SIZE OF FLOOR ONE.

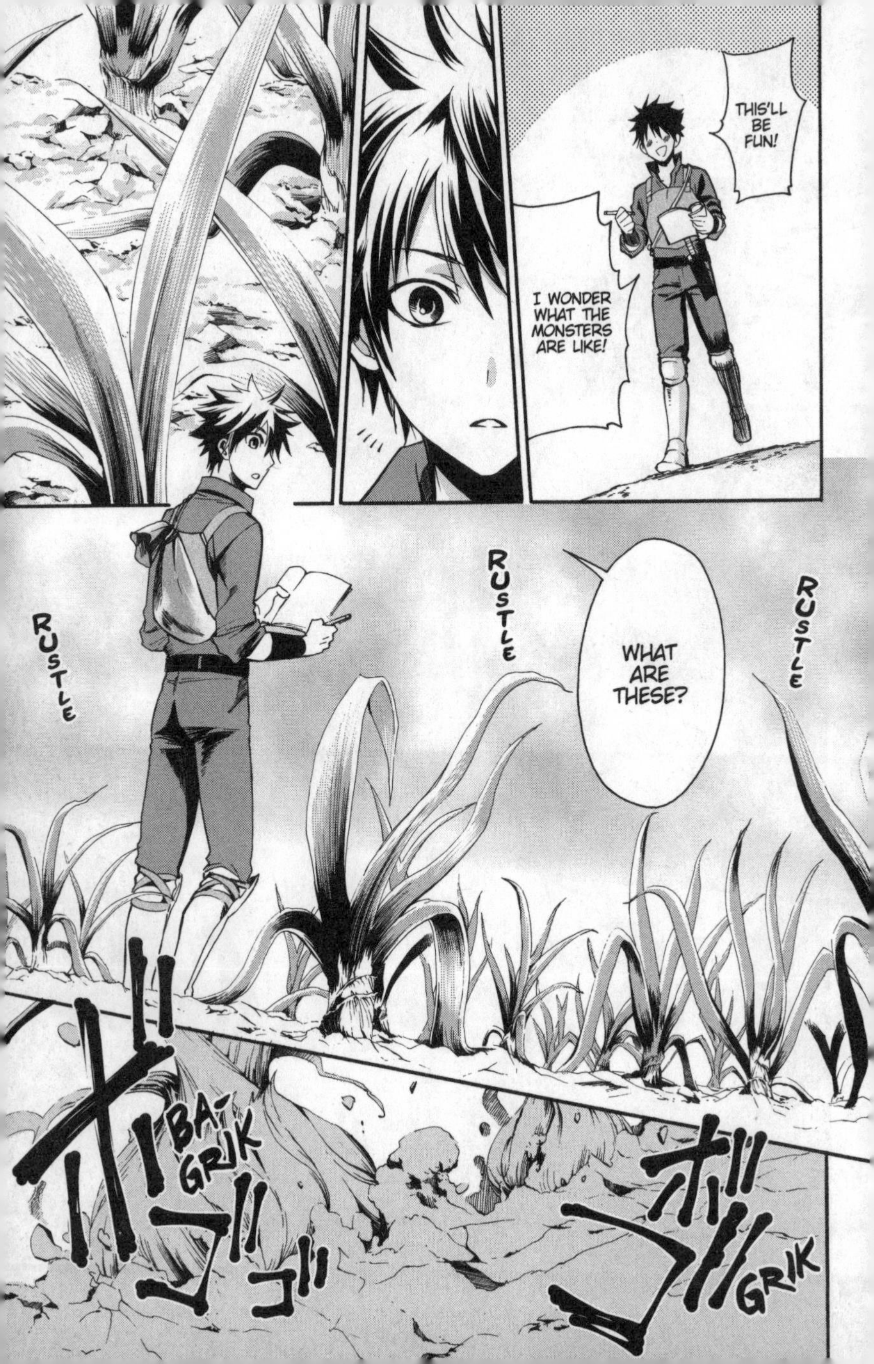
THIS'LL BE FUN!
I WONDER WHAT THE MONSTERS ARE LIKE!
RUSTLE
WHAT ARE THESE?
RUSTLE
RUSTLE
GRIK
BA-GRIK

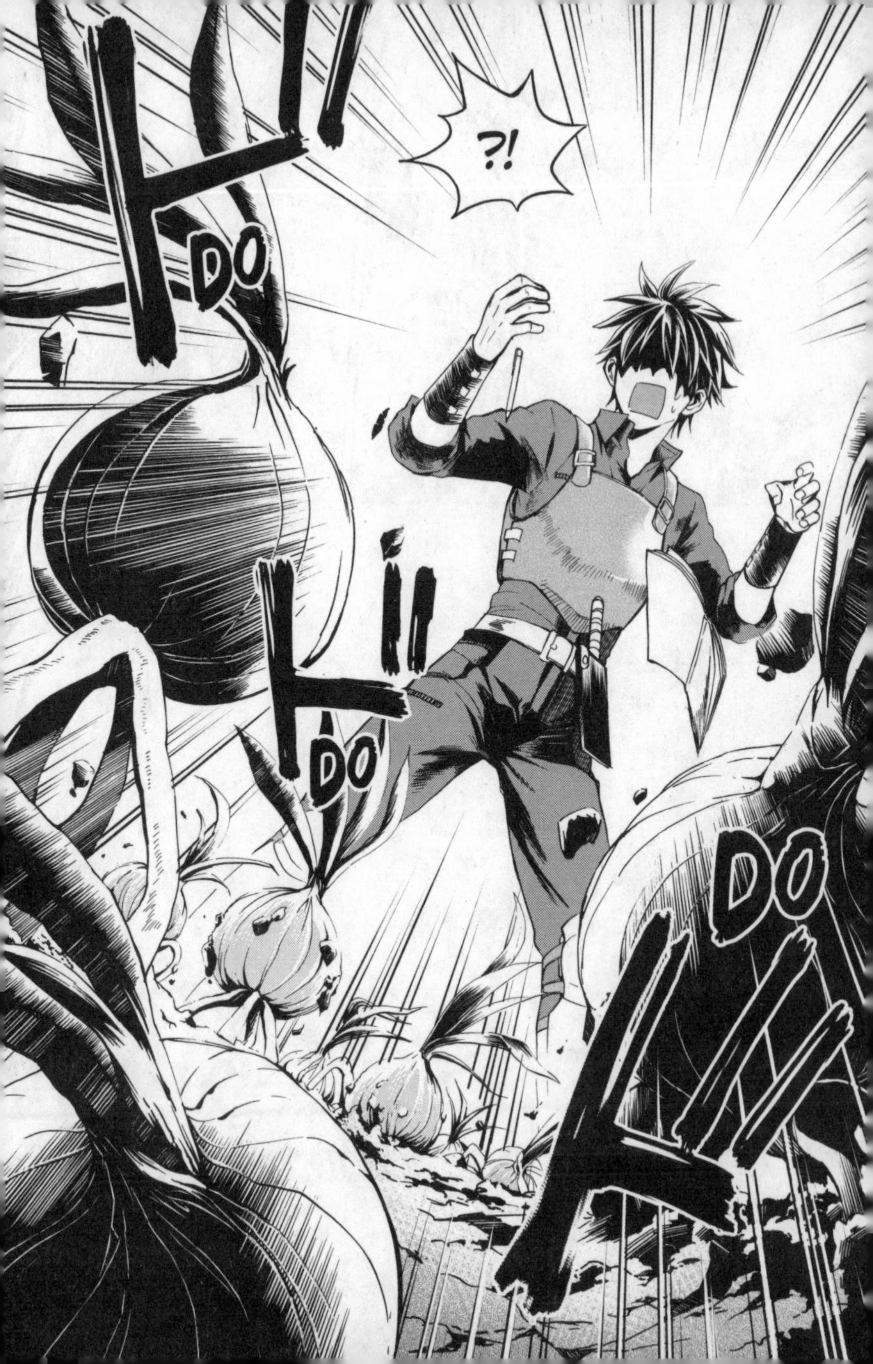

?!
DO
DO
DO

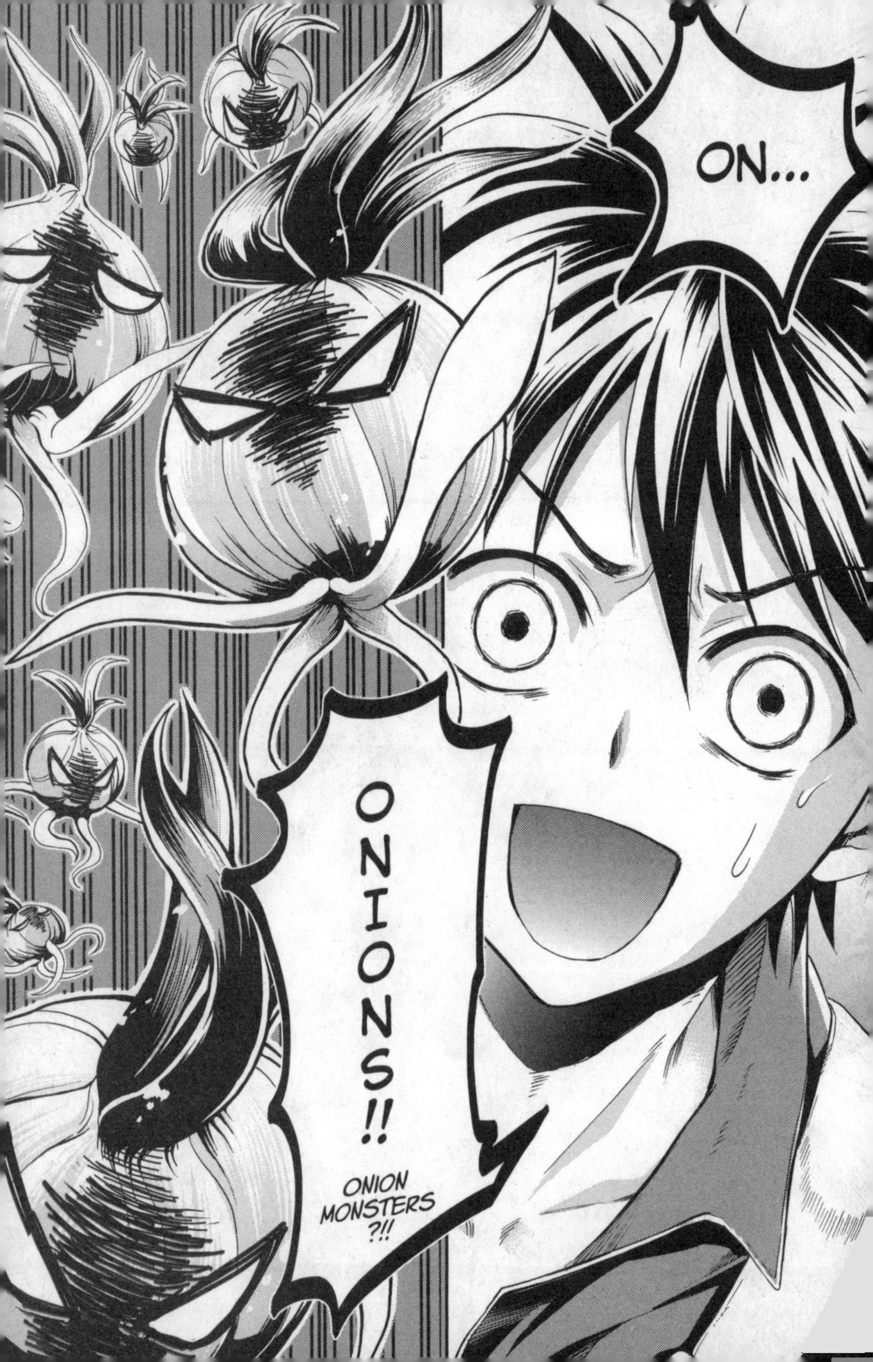
ON...
ONIONS!!
ONION MONSTERS ?!!

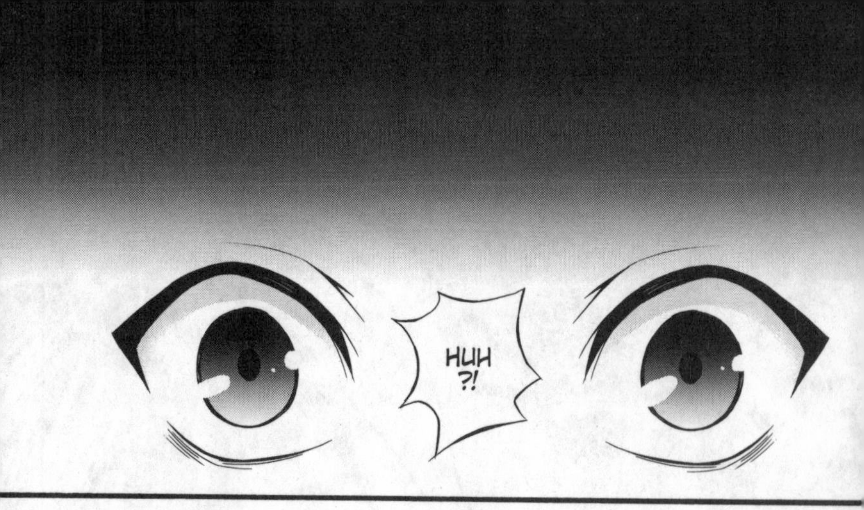
HUH ?!
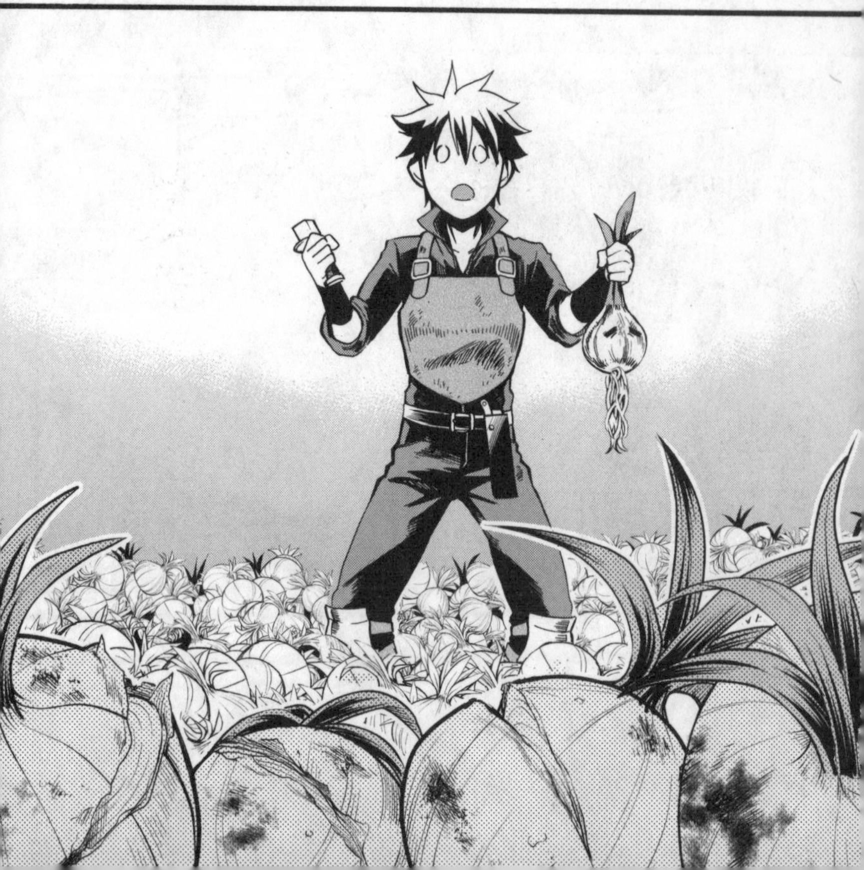

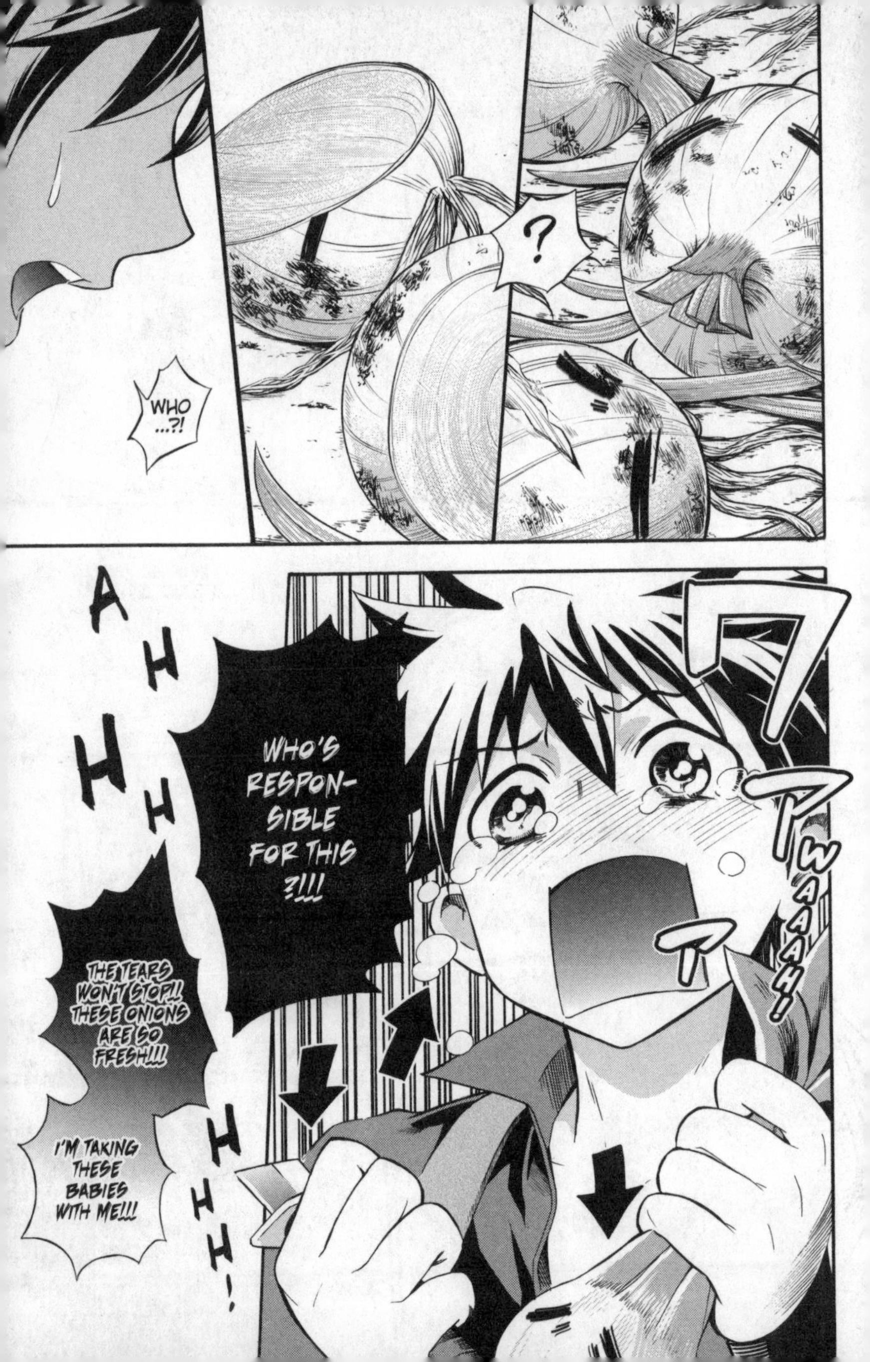
?
WHO ...?!
WAAAAH!
WHO'S RESPON-SIBLE FOR THIS ?!!!
AHHHHHHHH!
THE TEARS WON'T STOP!! THESE ONIONS ARE SO FRESH!!!
I'M TAKING THESE BABIES WITH ME!!!

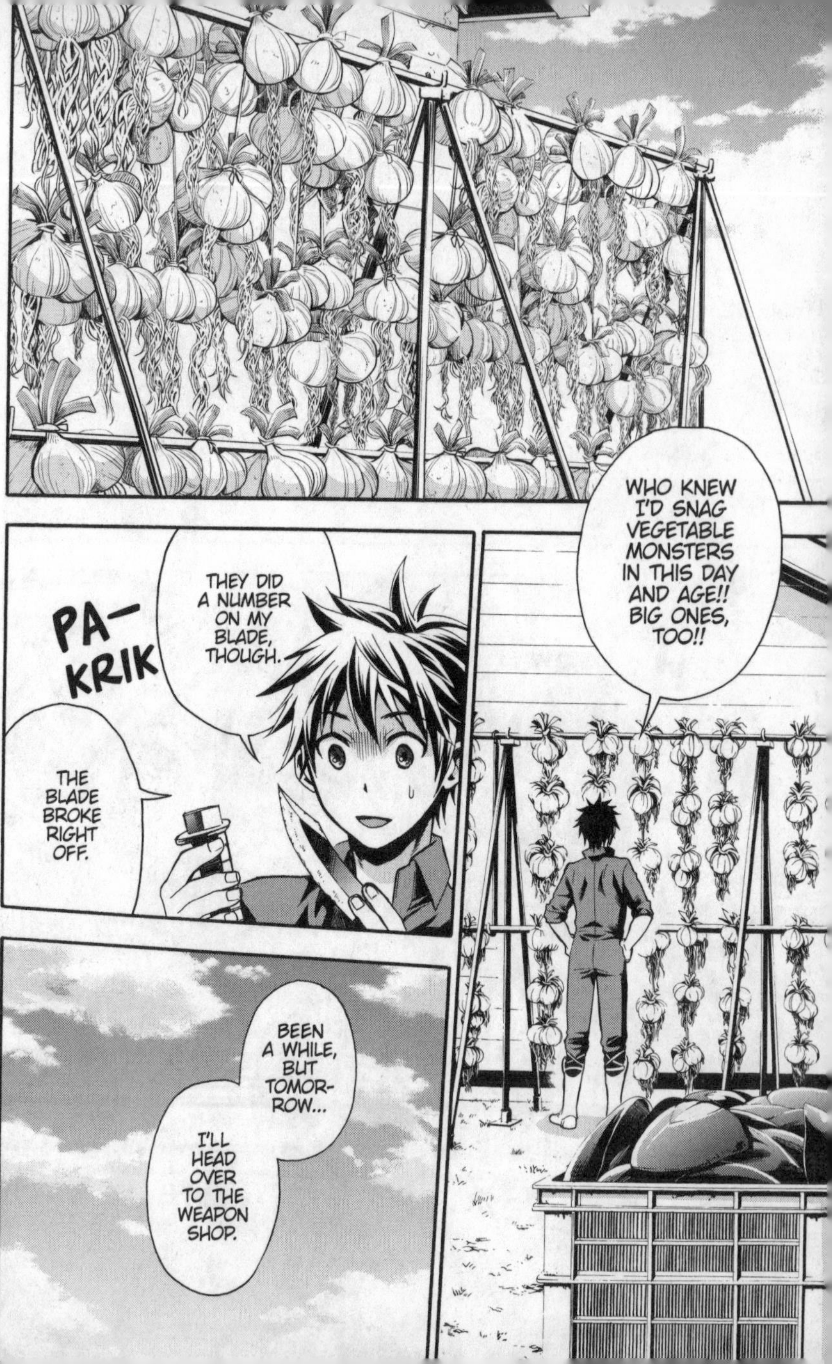
WHO KNEW I'D SNAG VEGETABLE MONSTERS IN THIS DAY AND AGE!! BIG ONES, TOO!!
THEY DID A NUMBER ON MY BLADE, THOUGH.
PA-KRIK
THE BLADE BROKE RIGHT OFF.
BEEN A WHILE, BUT TOMORROW...
I'LL HEAD OVER TO THE WEAPON SHOP.

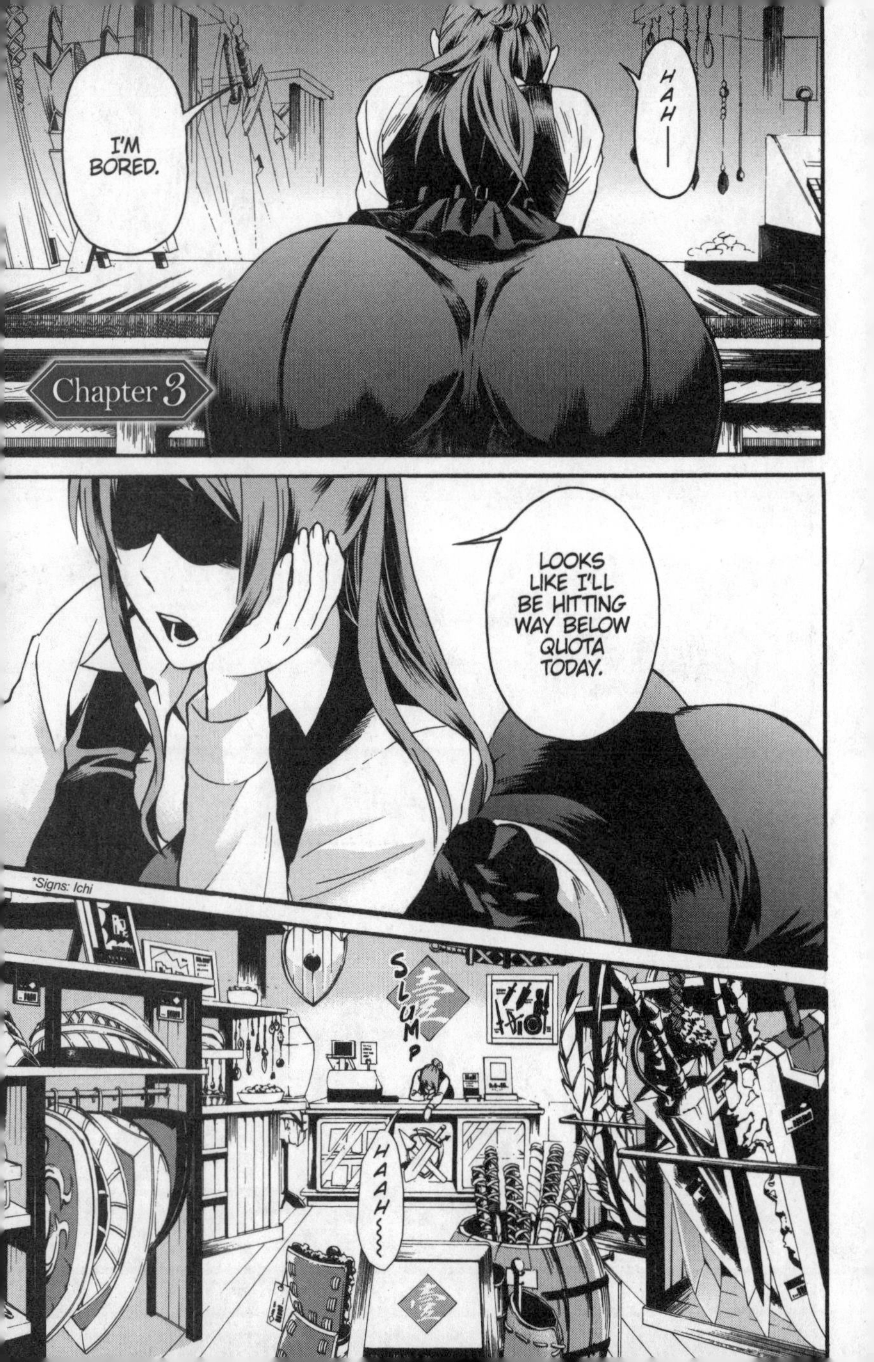
HAH—
I'M BORED.
Chapter 3
LOOKS LIKE I'LL BE HITTING WAY BELOW QUOTA TODAY.
*Signs: Ichi
SLUMP
HAAAH~~

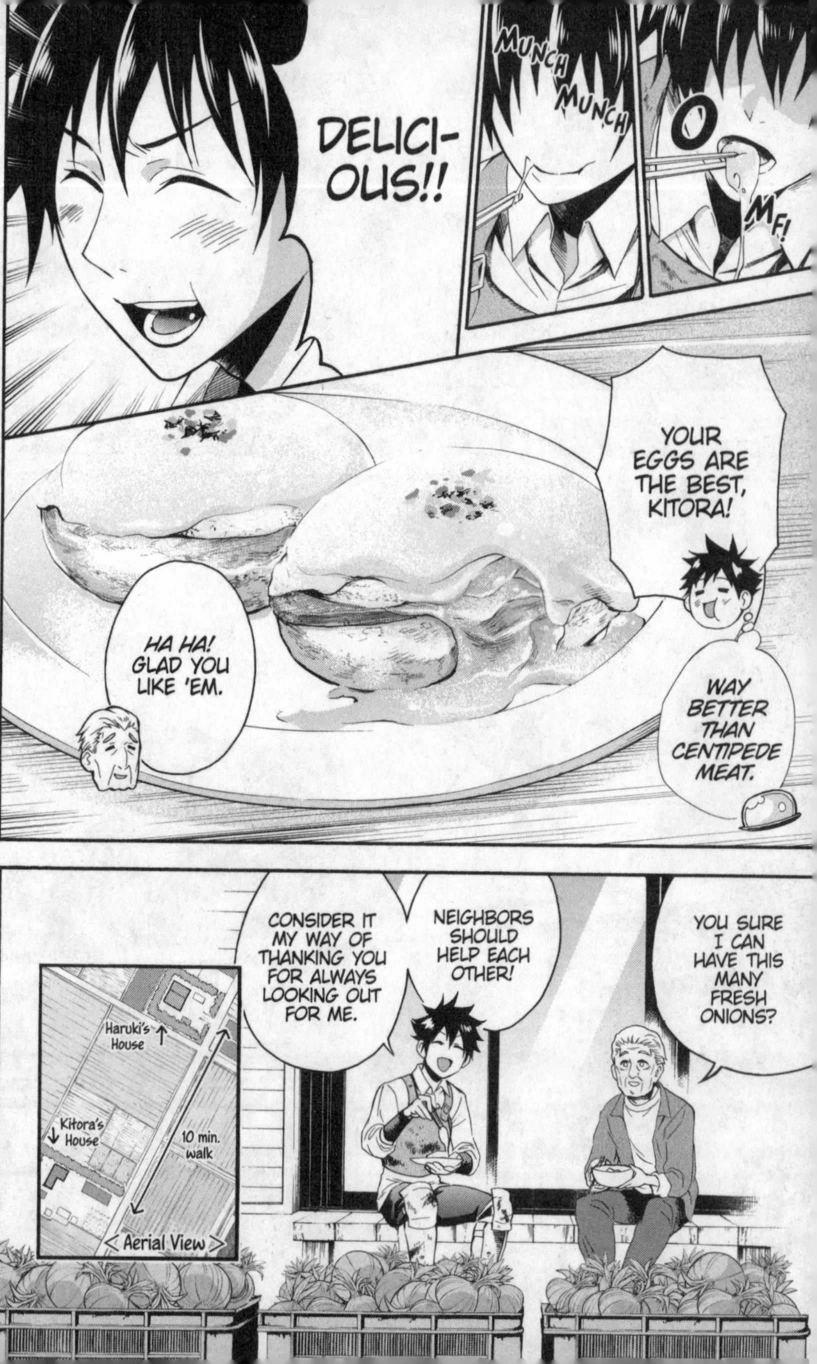
MUNCH MUNCH
O
MF!
DELICI-OUS!!
YOUR EGGS ARE THE BEST, KITORA!
WAY BETTER THAN CENTIPEDE MEAT.
HA HA! GLAD YOU LIKE 'EM.
YOU SURE I CAN HAVE THIS MANY FRESH ONIONS?
NEIGHBORS SHOULD HELP EACH OTHER!
CONSIDER IT MY WAY OF THANKING YOU FOR ALWAYS LOOKING OUT FOR ME.
Haruki's House
Kitora's House
10 min. walk
< Aerial View >

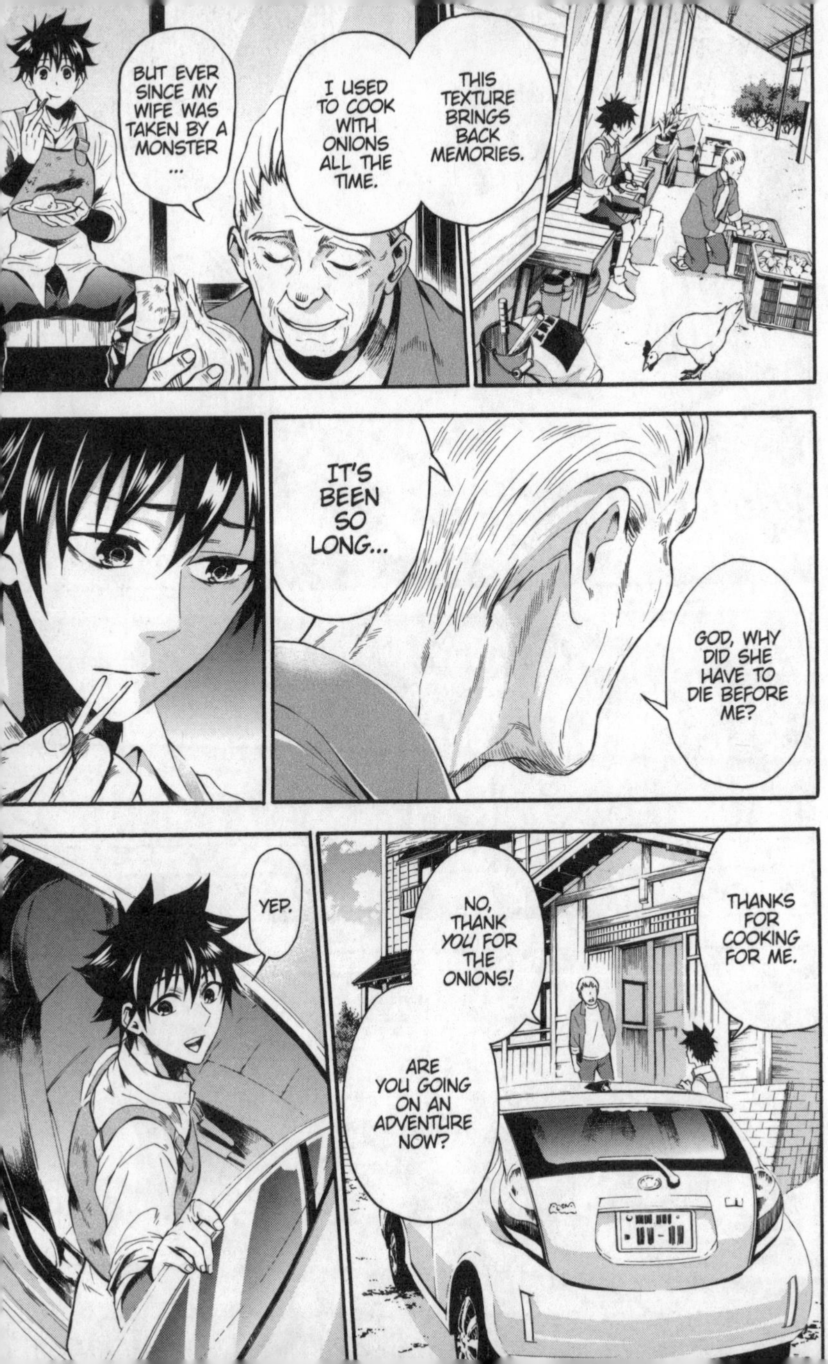
THIS TEXTURE BRINGS BACK MEMORIES.
I USED TO COOK WITH ONIONS ALL THE TIME.
BUT EVER SINCE MY WIFE WAS TAKEN BY A MONSTER ...
IT'S BEEN SO LONG...
GOD, WHY DID SHE HAVE TO DIE BEFORE ME?
THANKS FOR COOKING FOR ME.
NO, THANK *YOU* FOR THE ONIONS!
ARE YOU GOING ON AN ADVENTURE NOW?
YEP.

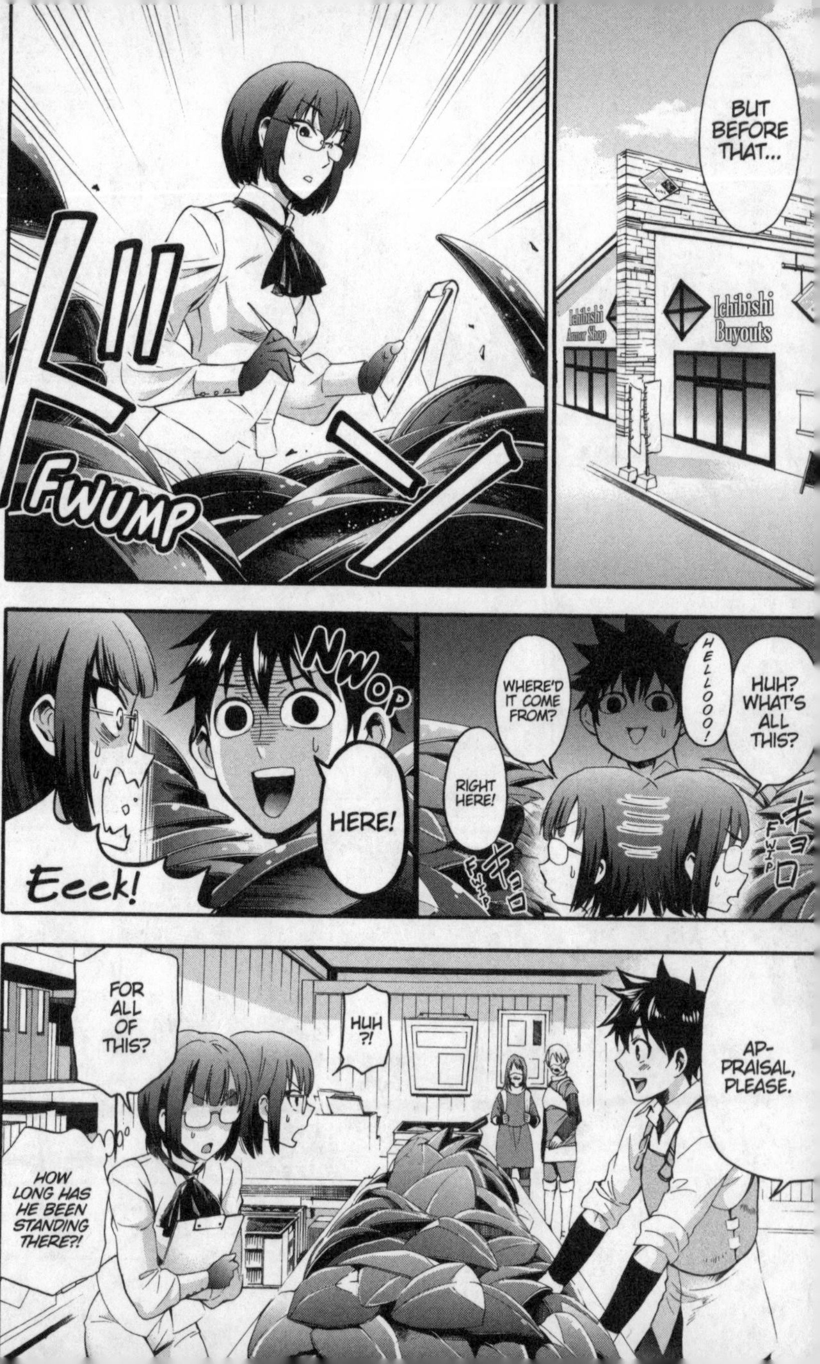
BUT BEFORE THAT...
Ichibishi Buyouts
Ichibishi Armor Shop
FWUMP
HUH? WHAT'S ALL THIS?
FWIP
HELLOOO!
WHERE'D IT COME FROM?
RIGHT HERE!
FWIP
NWOP
HERE!
Eeek!
AP-PRAISAL, PLEASE.
HUH?!
FOR ALL OF THIS?
HOW LONG HAS HE BEEN STANDING THERE?!

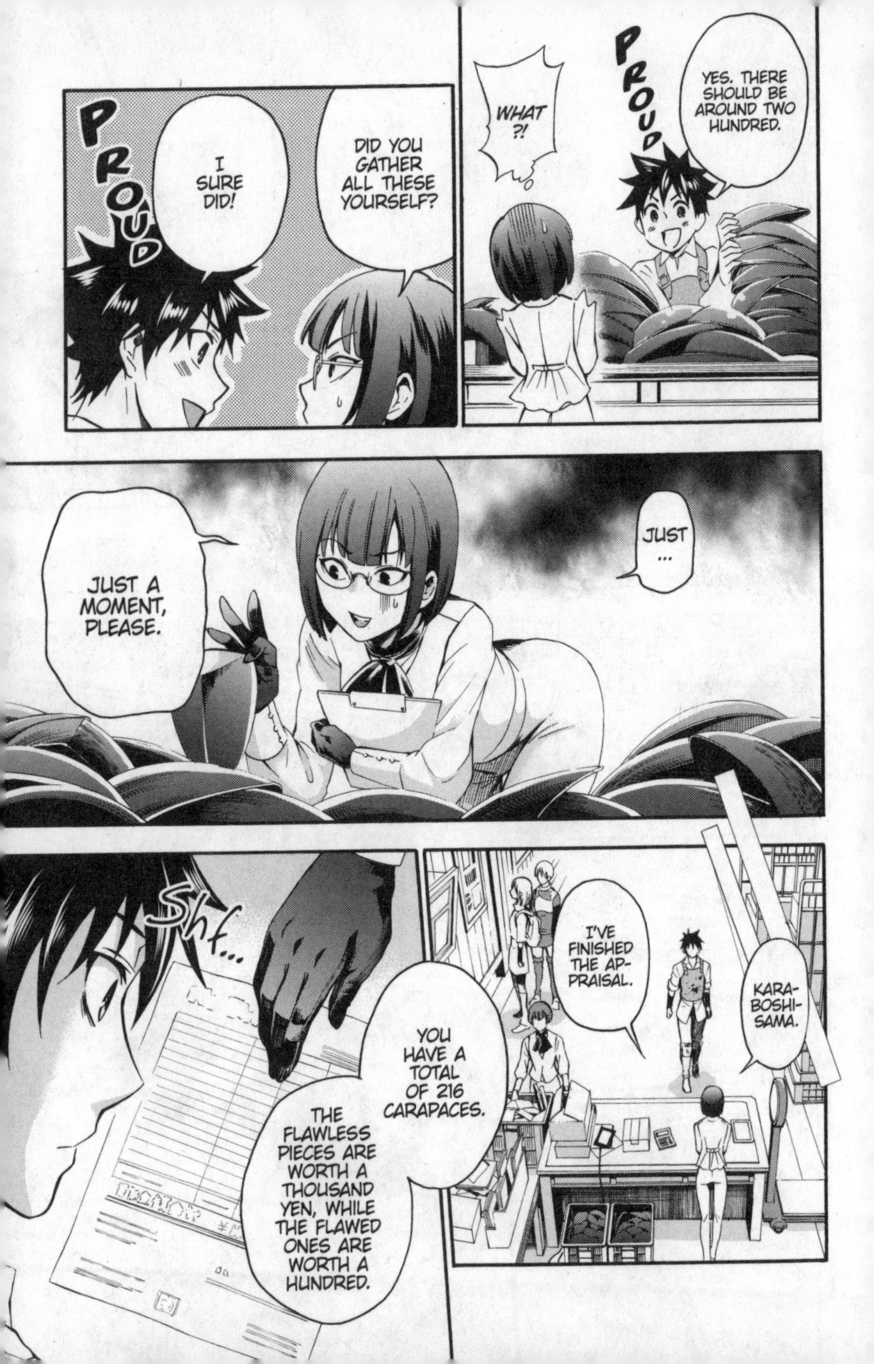
YES. THERE SHOULD BE AROUND TWO HUNDRED.
PROUD
WHAT ?!
DID YOU GATHER ALL THESE YOURSELF?
I SURE DID!
PROUD
JUST ...
JUST A MOMENT, PLEASE.
KARA-BOSHI-SAMA.
I'VE FINISHED THE AP-PRAISAL.
SHF...
YOU HAVE A TOTAL OF 216 CARAPACES.
THE FLAWLESS PIECES ARE WORTH A THOUSAND YEN, WHILE THE FLAWED ONES ARE WORTH A HUNDRED.

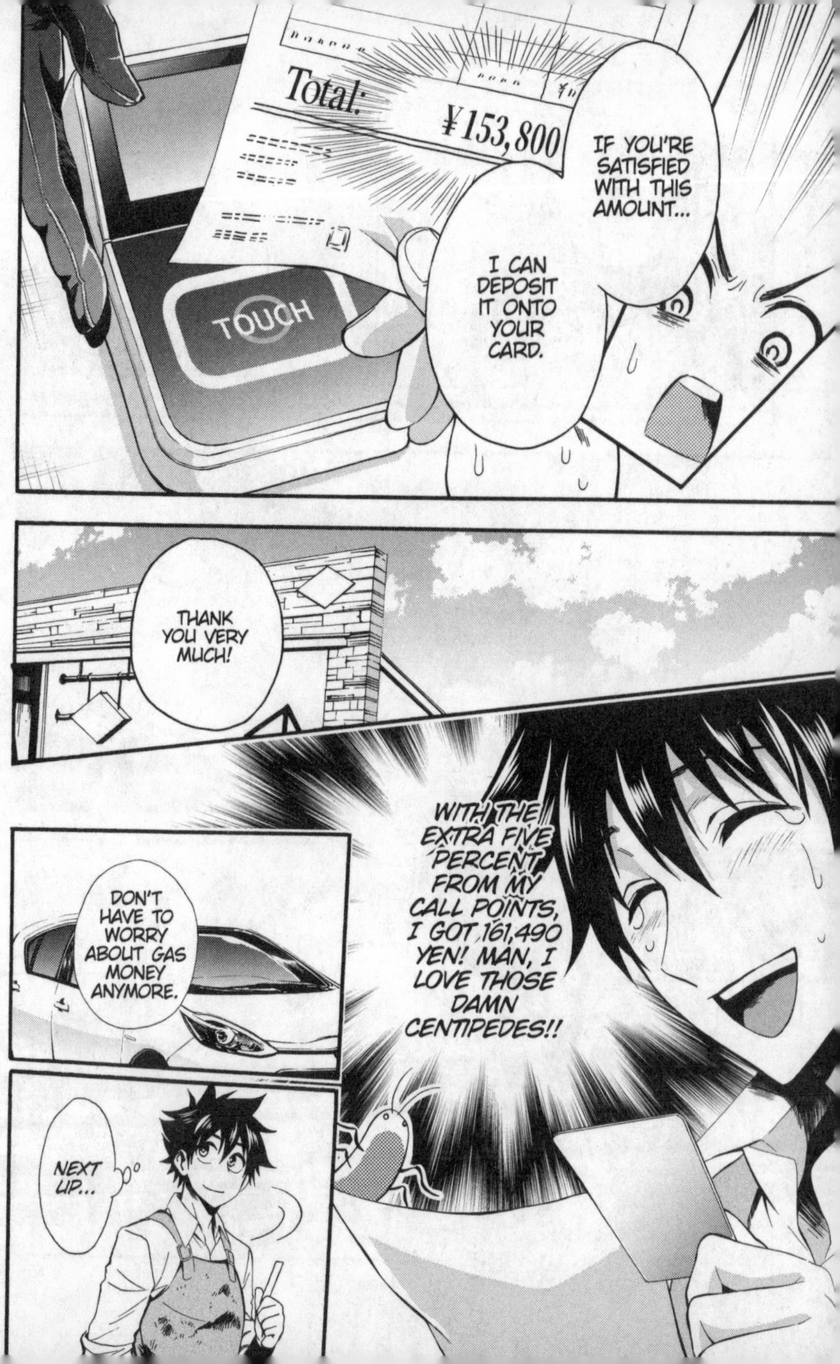
Total:
¥153,800
IF YOU'RE SATISFIED WITH THIS AMOUNT...
I CAN DEPOSIT IT ONTO YOUR CARD.
TOUCH
THANK YOU VERY MUCH!
WITH THE EXTRA FIVE PERCENT FROM MY CALL POINTS, I GOT 161,490 YEN! MAN, I LOVE THOSE DAMN CENTIPEDES!!
DON'T HAVE TO WORRY ABOUT GAS MONEY ANYMORE.
NEXT UP...

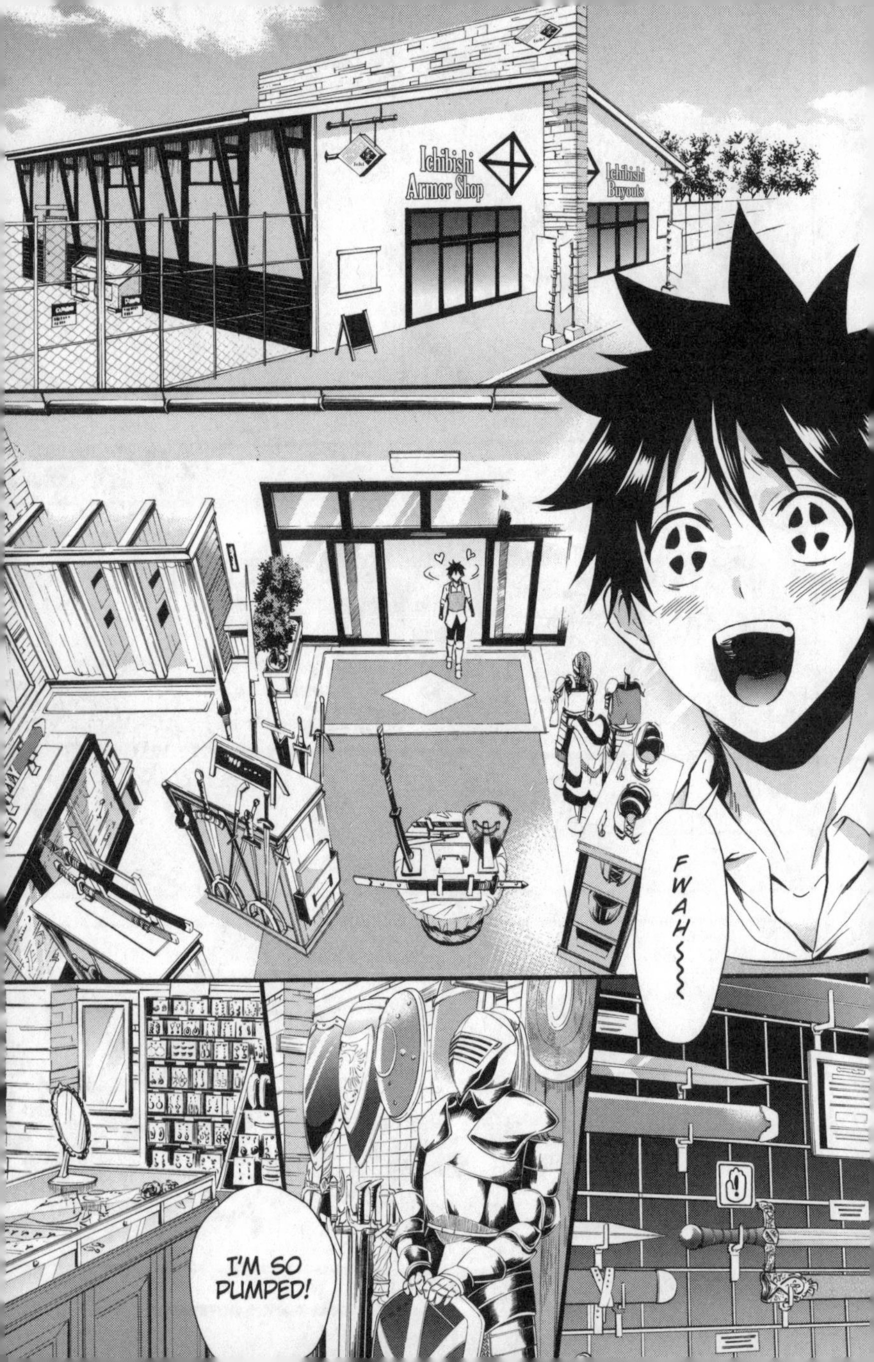
Ichibishi Armor Shop
Ichibishi Buyouts
FWAH~~
I'M SO PUMPED!

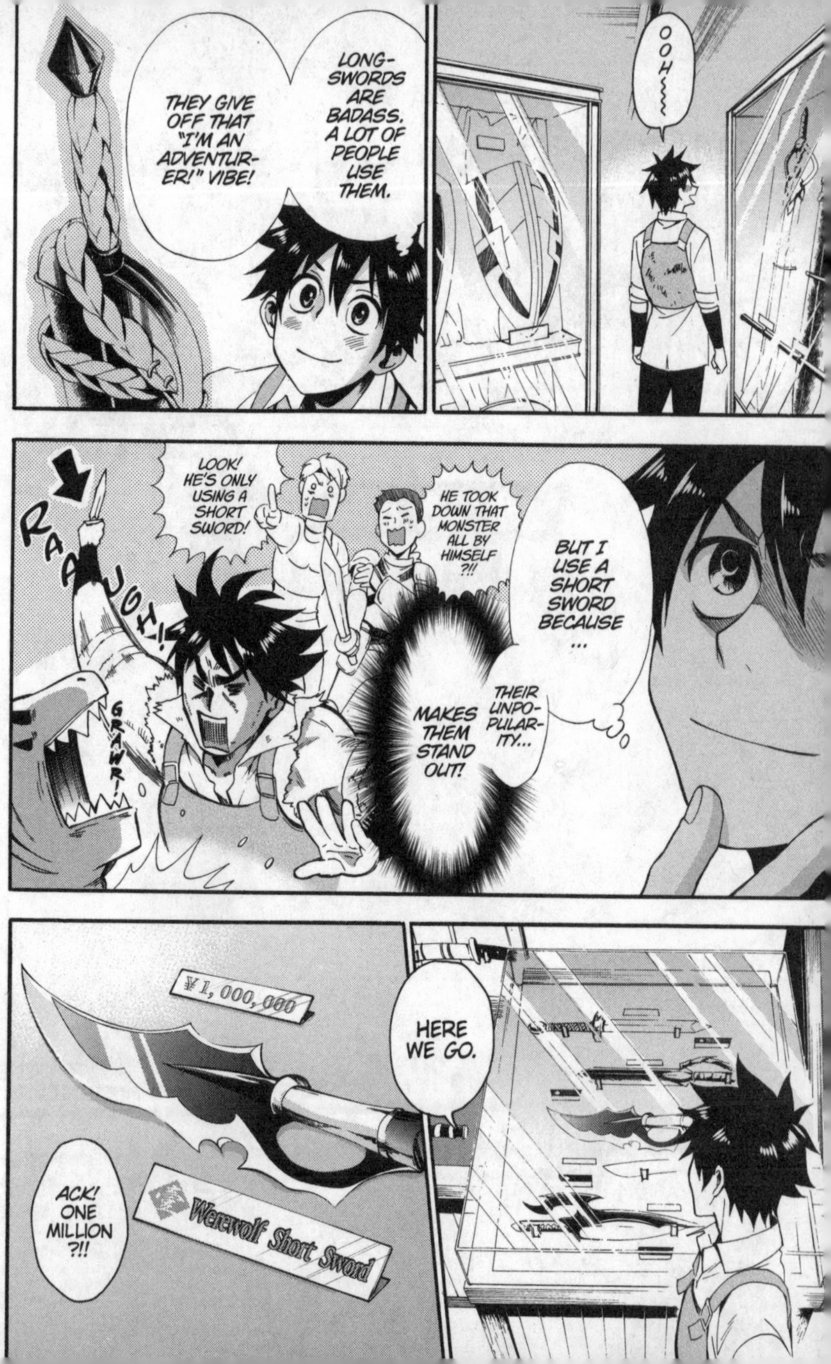
OOH~~~
LONG-SWORDS ARE BADASS. A LOT OF PEOPLE USE THEM.
THEY GIVE OFF THAT "I'M AN ADVENTURER!" VIBE!
BUT I USE A SHORT SWORD BECAUSE ...
THEIR UNPOPULARITY...
MAKES THEM STAND OUT!
HE TOOK DOWN THAT MONSTER ALL BY HIMSELF ?!!
LOOK! HE'S ONLY USING A SHORT SWORD!
RAAUGH!!
GRAWR!
HERE WE GO.
¥1,000,000
Werewolf Short Sword
ACK! ONE MILLION ?!!

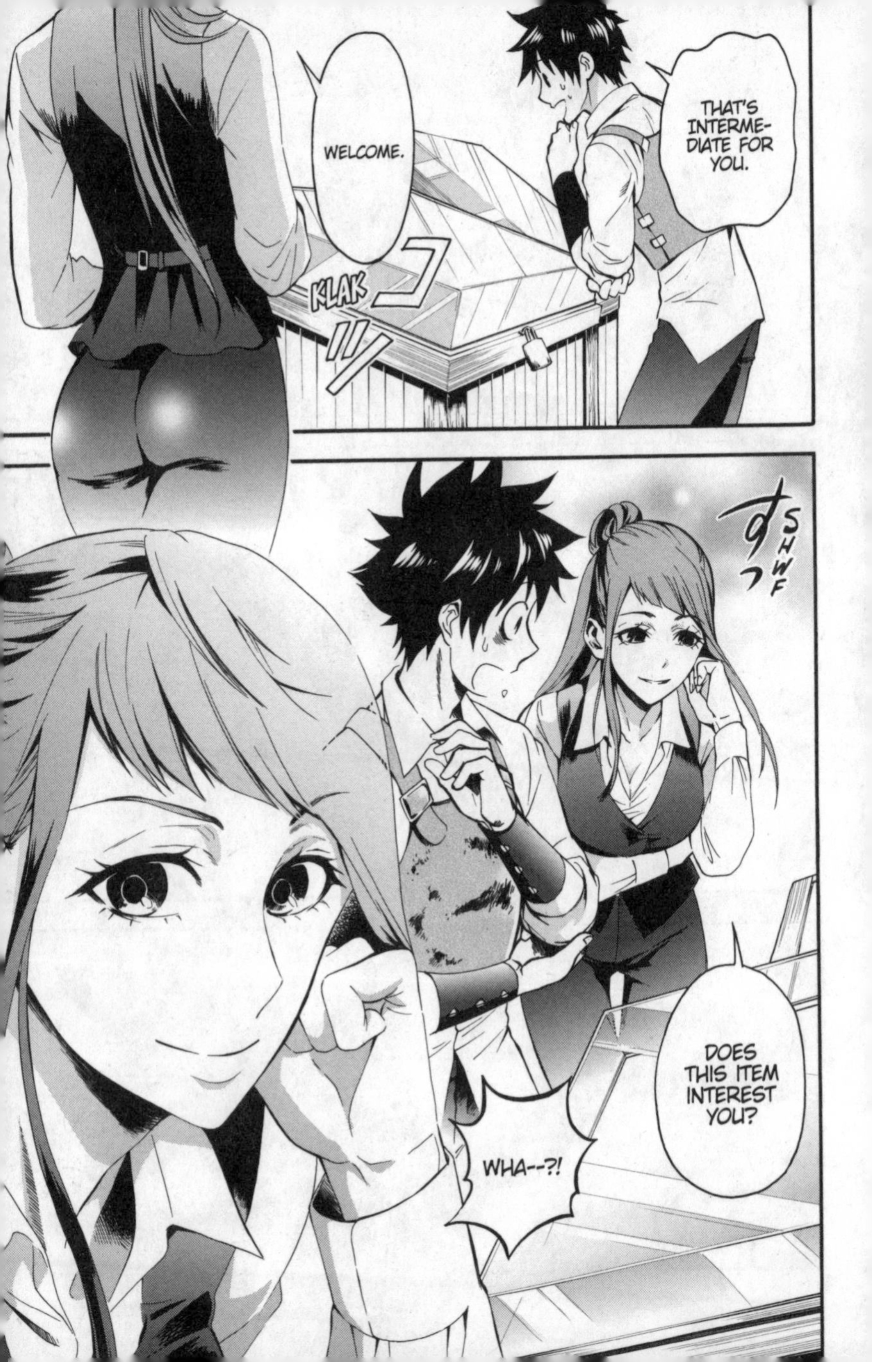
THAT'S INTERMEDIATE FOR YOU.
WELCOME.
KLAK
SHWF
DOES THIS ITEM INTEREST YOU?
WHA--?!

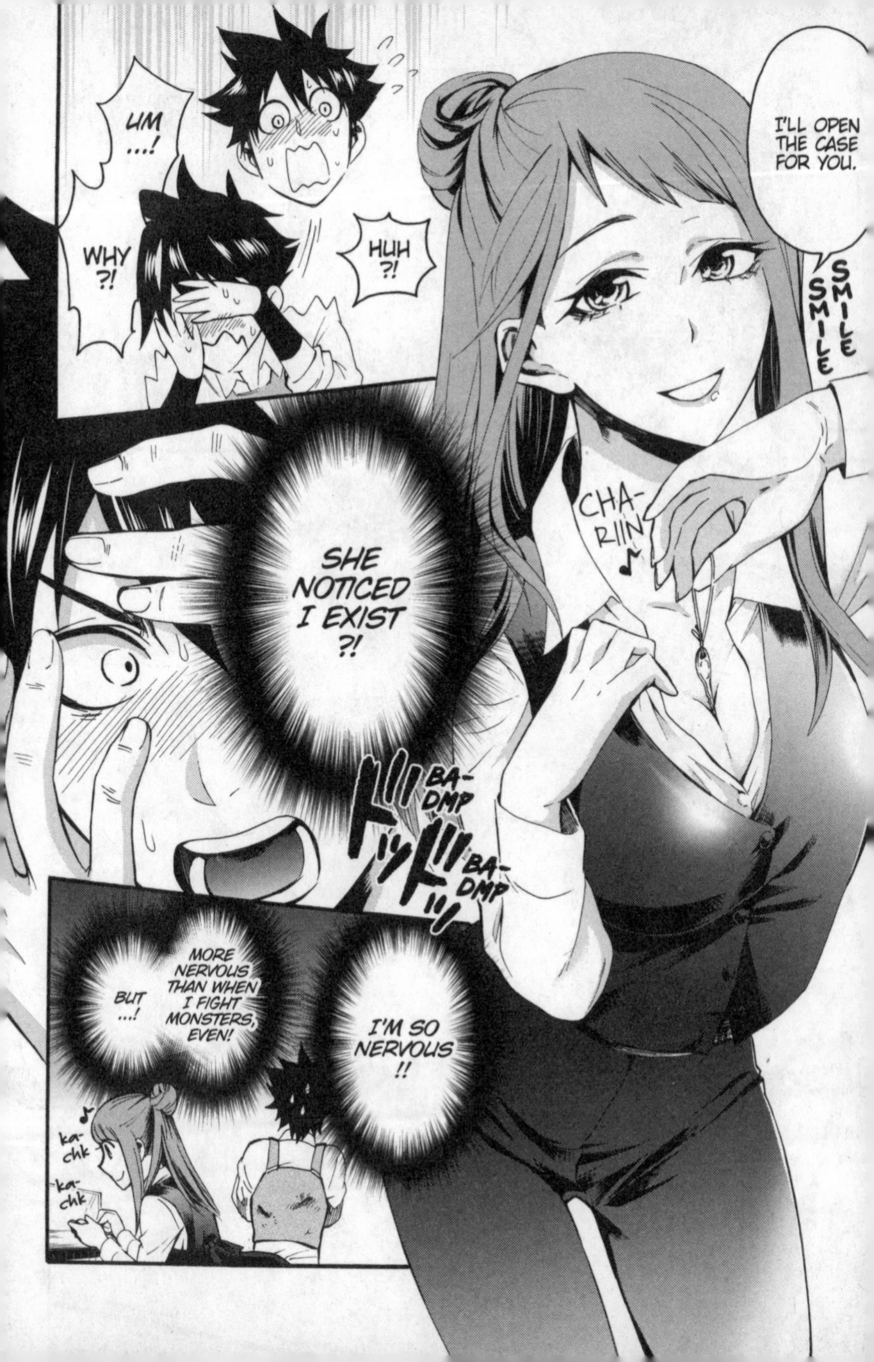
I'LL OPEN THE CASE FOR YOU.
SMILE SMILE
CHA-RIIN♪
UM ...!
HUH ?!
WHY ?!
SHE NOTICED I EXIST ?!
BA-DMP
BA-DMP
I'M SO NERVOUS !!
MORE NERVOUS THAN WHEN I FIGHT MONSTERS, EVEN!
BUT ...!
ka-chk
ka-chk

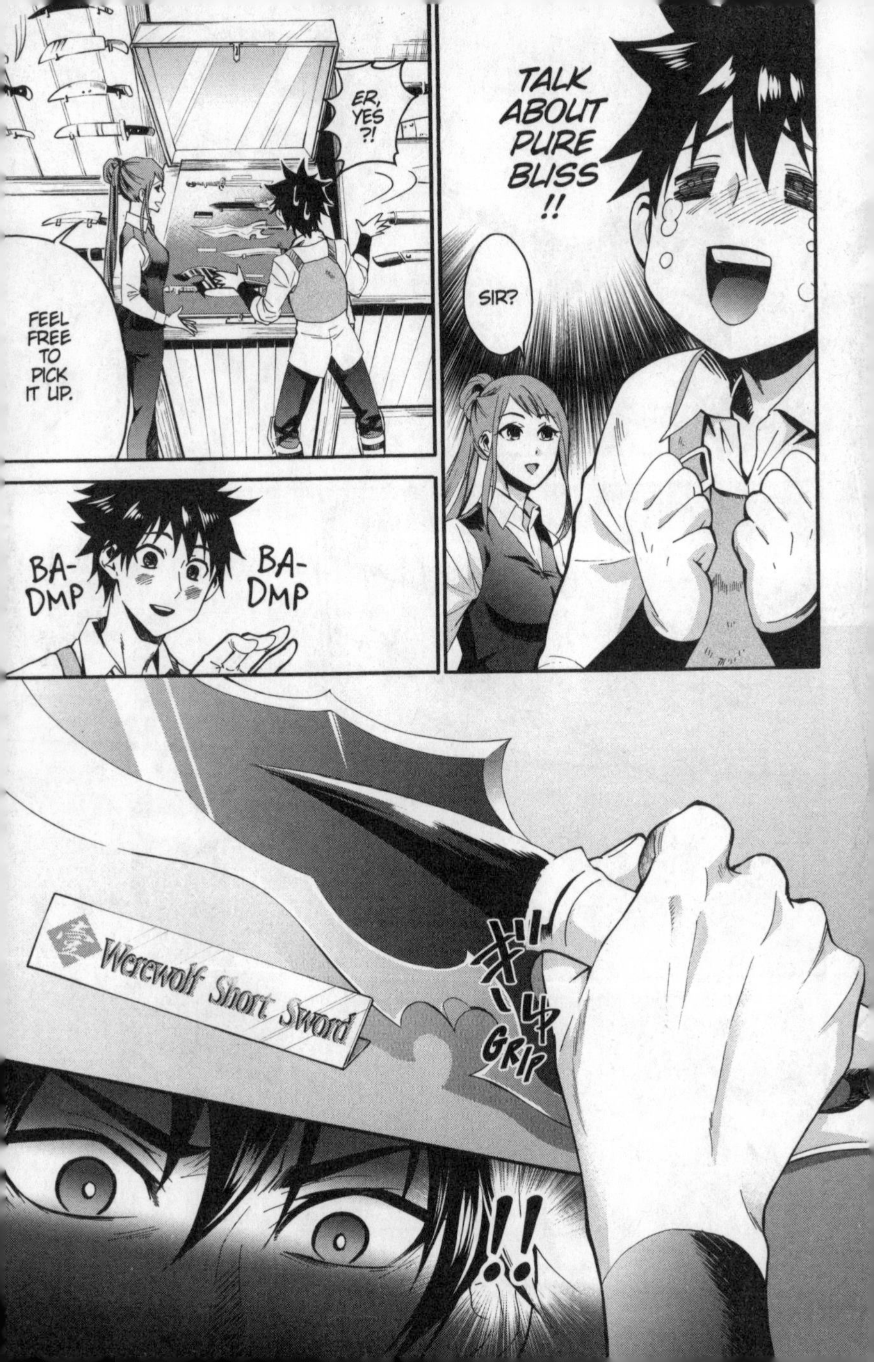
TALK ABOUT PURE BLISS !!
SIR?
ER, YES?!
FEEL FREE TO PICK IT UP.
BA-DMP
BA-DMP
GRIP
Werewolf Short Sword
!!

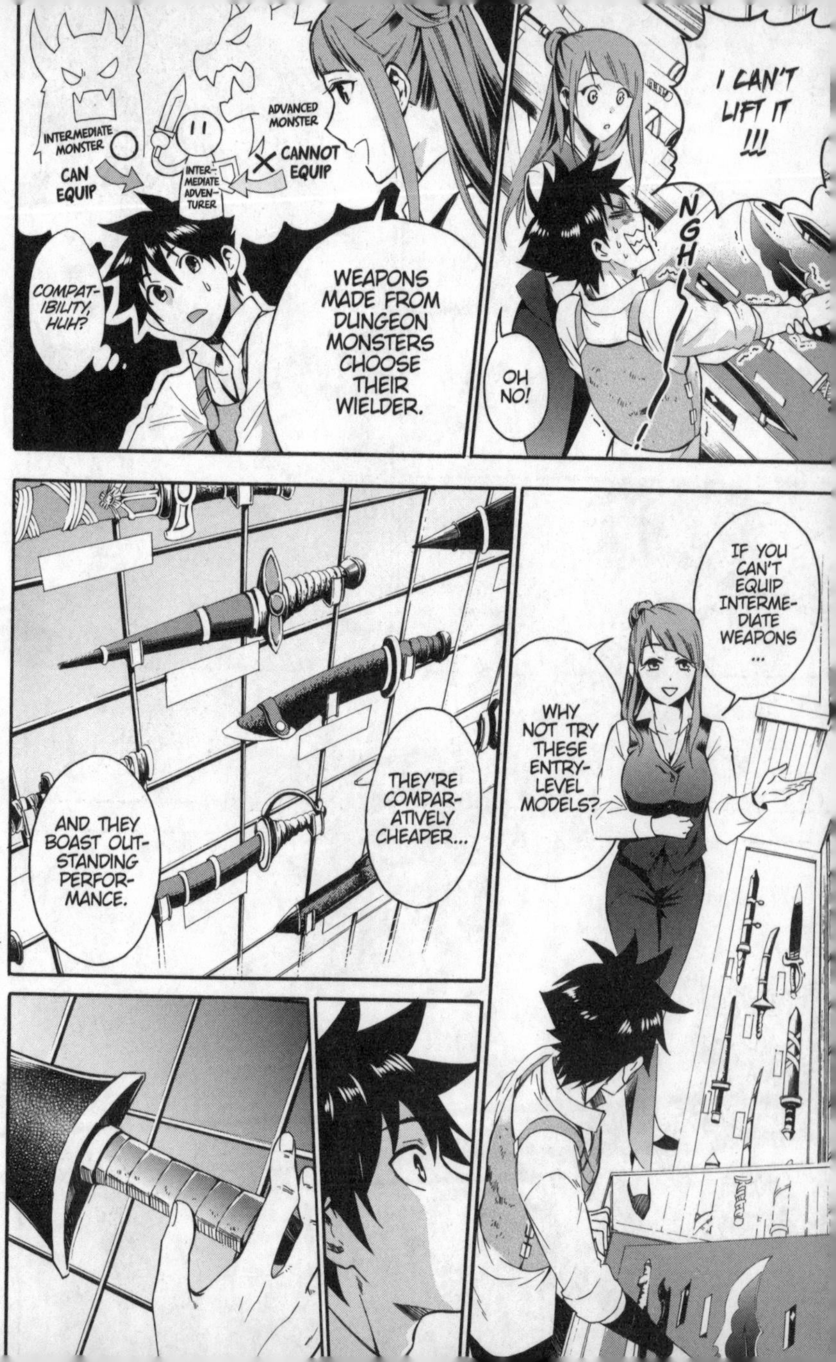
I CAN'T LIFT IT !!!
NGH!
OH NO!
WEAPONS MADE FROM DUNGEON MONSTERS CHOOSE THEIR WIELDER.
ADVANCED MONSTER
CANNOT EQUIP
INTERMEDIATE MONSTER
CAN EQUIP
INTER-MEDIATE ADVEN-TURER
COMPAT-IBILITY, HUH?
IF YOU CAN'T EQUIP INTERME-DIATE WEAPONS ...
WHY NOT TRY THESE ENTRY-LEVEL MODELS?
THEY'RE COMPAR-ATIVELY CHEAPER...
AND THEY BOAST OUT-STANDING PERFOR-MANCE.

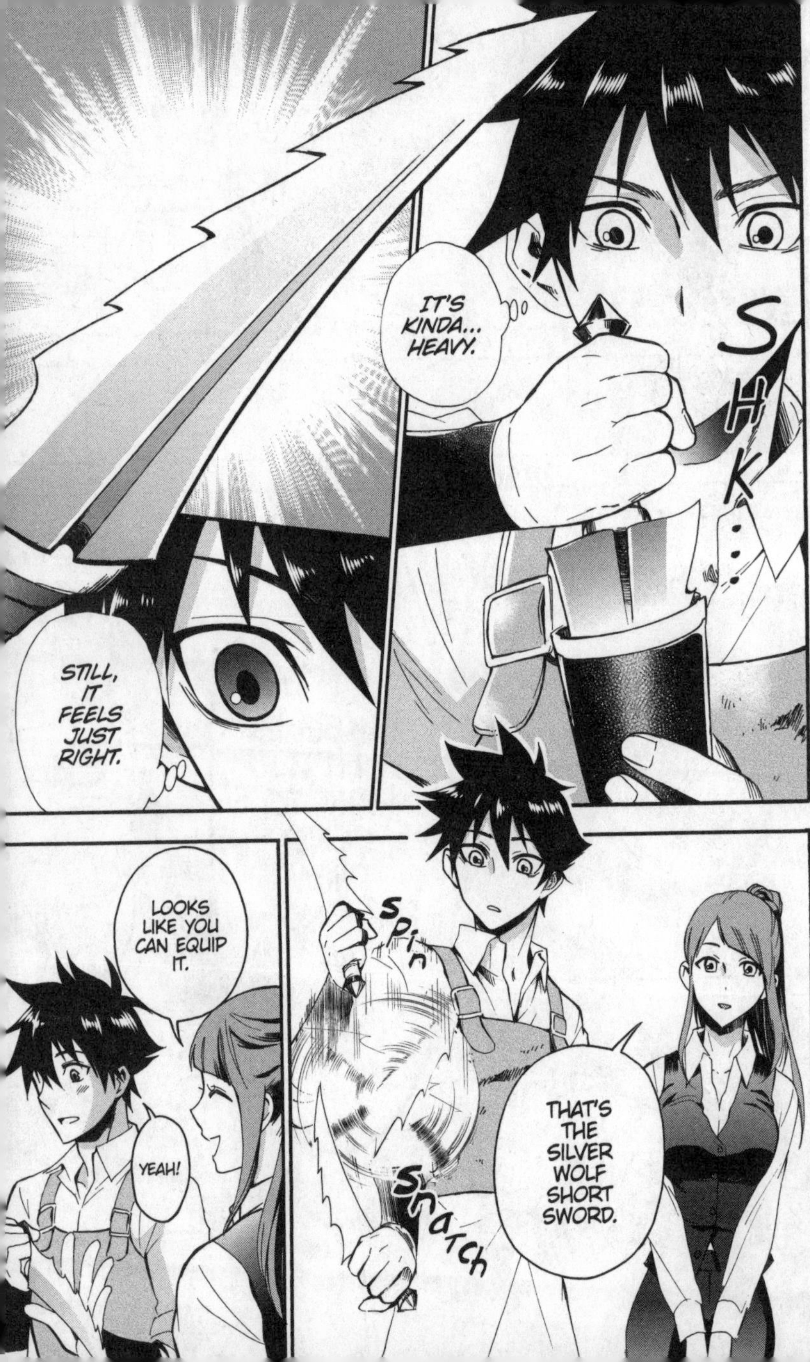
S H K . . .
IT'S KINDA... HEAVY.
STILL, IT FEELS JUST RIGHT.
spin
THAT'S THE SILVER WOLF SHORT SWORD.
snatch
LOOKS LIKE YOU CAN EQUIP IT.
YEAH!

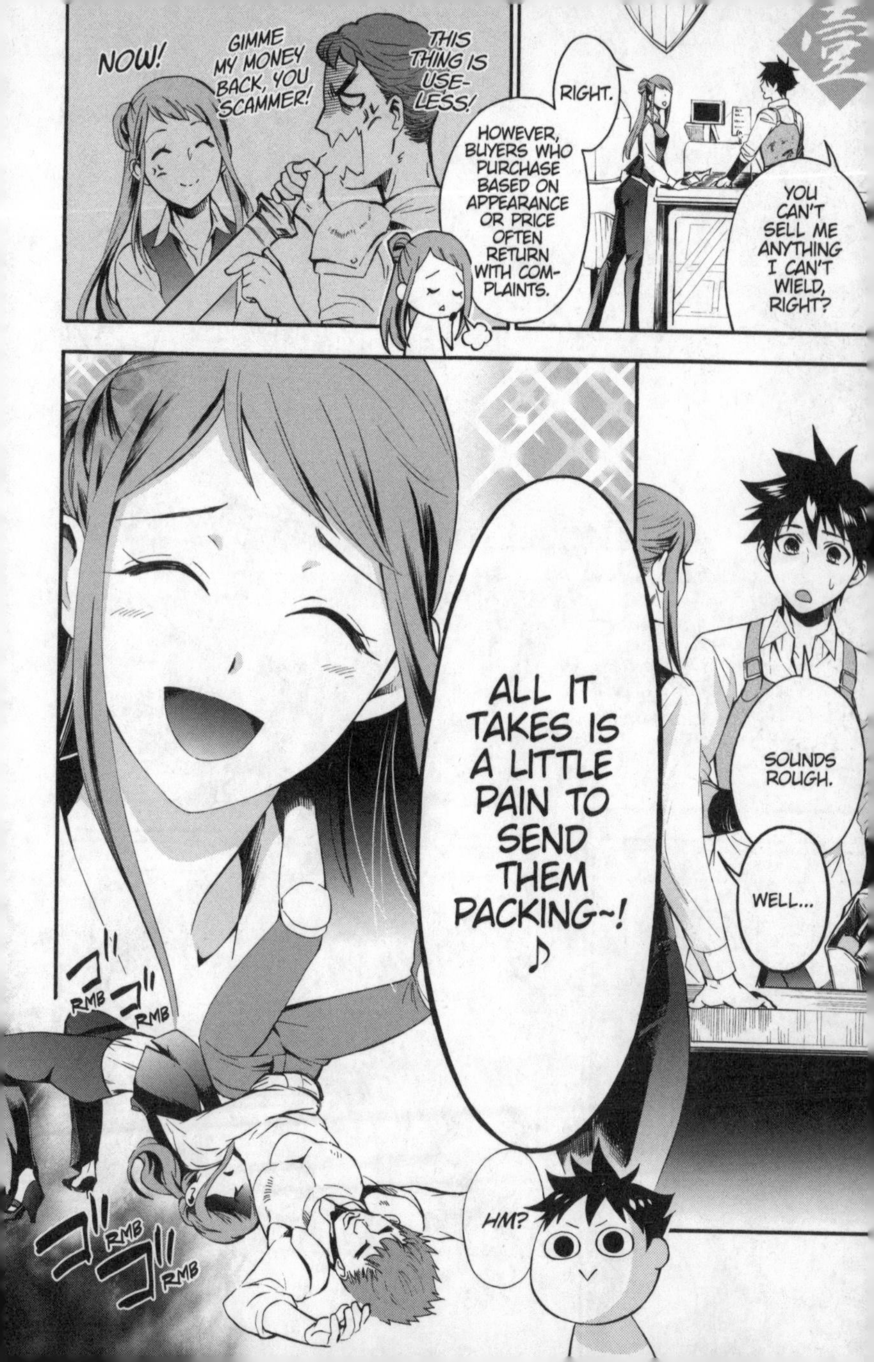
YOU CAN'T SELL ME ANYTHING I CAN'T WIELD, RIGHT?
RIGHT.
HOWEVER, BUYERS WHO PURCHASE BASED ON APPEARANCE OR PRICE OFTEN RETURN WITH COM-PLAINTS.
THIS THING IS USE-LESS!
GIMME MY MONEY BACK, YOU SCAMMER!
NOW!
SOUNDS ROUGH.
WELL...
ALL IT TAKES IS A LITTLE PAIN TO SEND THEM PACKING~! ♪
ゴ RMB ゴ RMB
HM?
ゴ RMB ゴ RMB

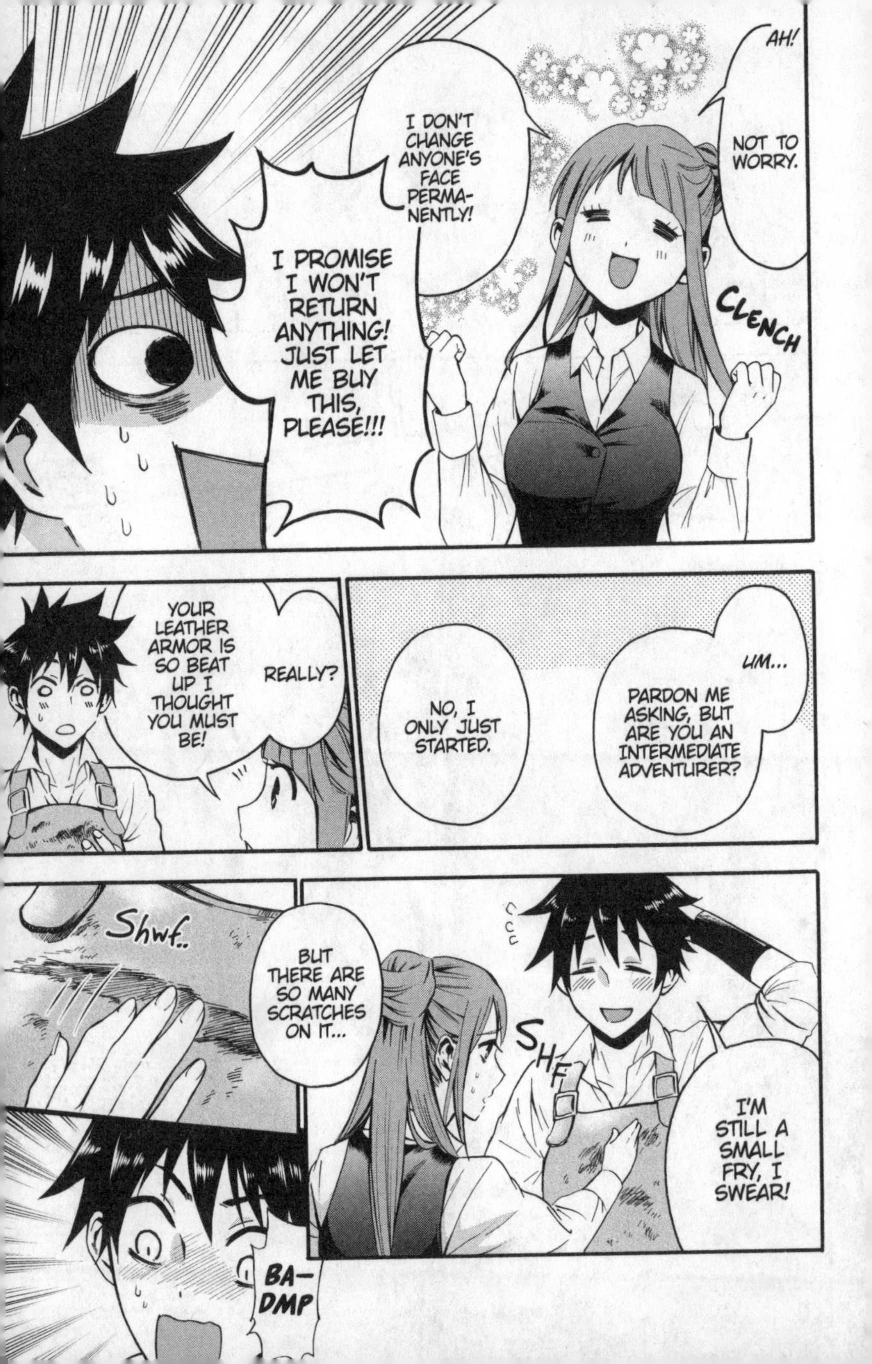
AH!
NOT TO WORRY.
CLENCH
I DON'T CHANGE ANYONE'S FACE PERMA-NENTLY!
I PROMISE I WON'T RETURN ANYTHING! JUST LET ME BUY THIS, PLEASE!!!
UM...
PARDON ME ASKING, BUT ARE YOU AN INTERMEDIATE ADVENTURER?
NO, I ONLY JUST STARTED.
REALLY?
YOUR LEATHER ARMOR IS SO BEAT UP I THOUGHT YOU MUST BE!
I'M STILL A SMALL FRY, I SWEAR!
SHF
BUT THERE ARE SO MANY SCRATCHES ON IT...
Shwf..
BA-DMP

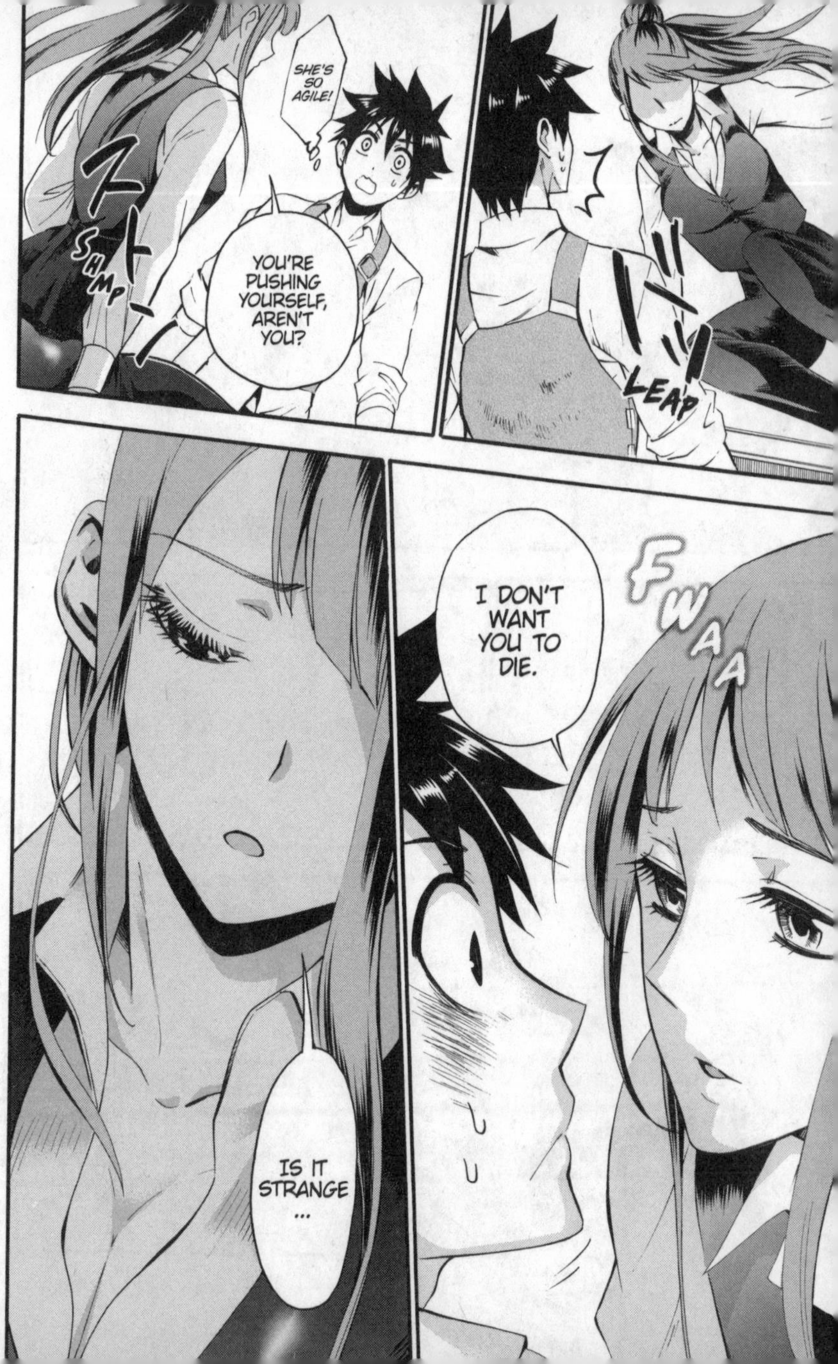
LEAP
SHMP
SHE'S SO AGILE!
YOU'RE PUSHING YOURSELF, AREN'T YOU?
FWAA
I DON'T WANT YOU TO DIE.
IS IT STRANGE ...

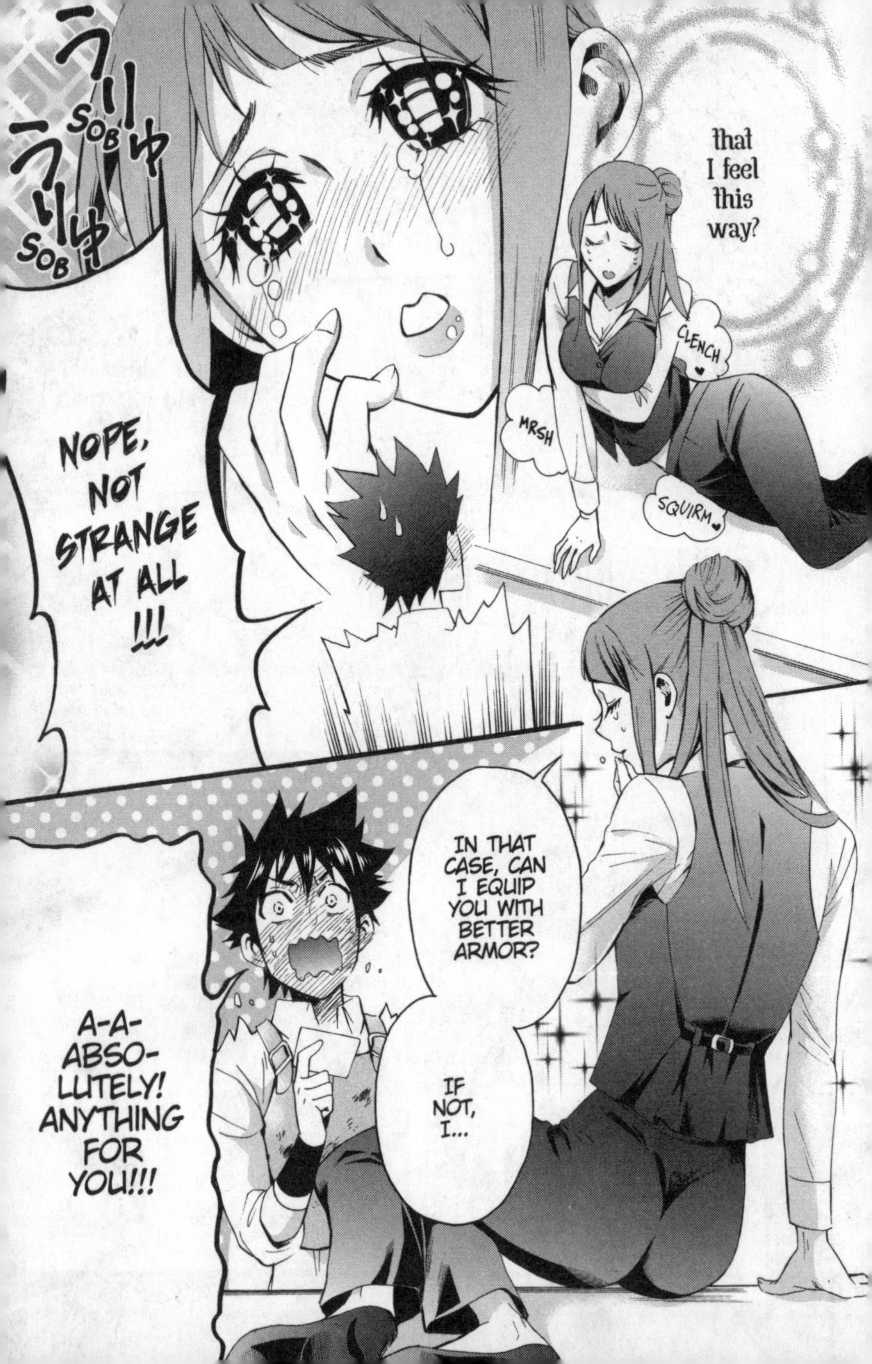
that I feel this way?
CLENCH
MRSH
SQUIRM
うりゅ SOB
うりゅ SOB
NOPE, NOT STRANGE AT ALL !!!
IN THAT CASE, CAN I EQUIP YOU WITH BETTER ARMOR?
IF NOT, I...
A-A-ABSO-LUTELY! ANYTHING FOR YOU!!!

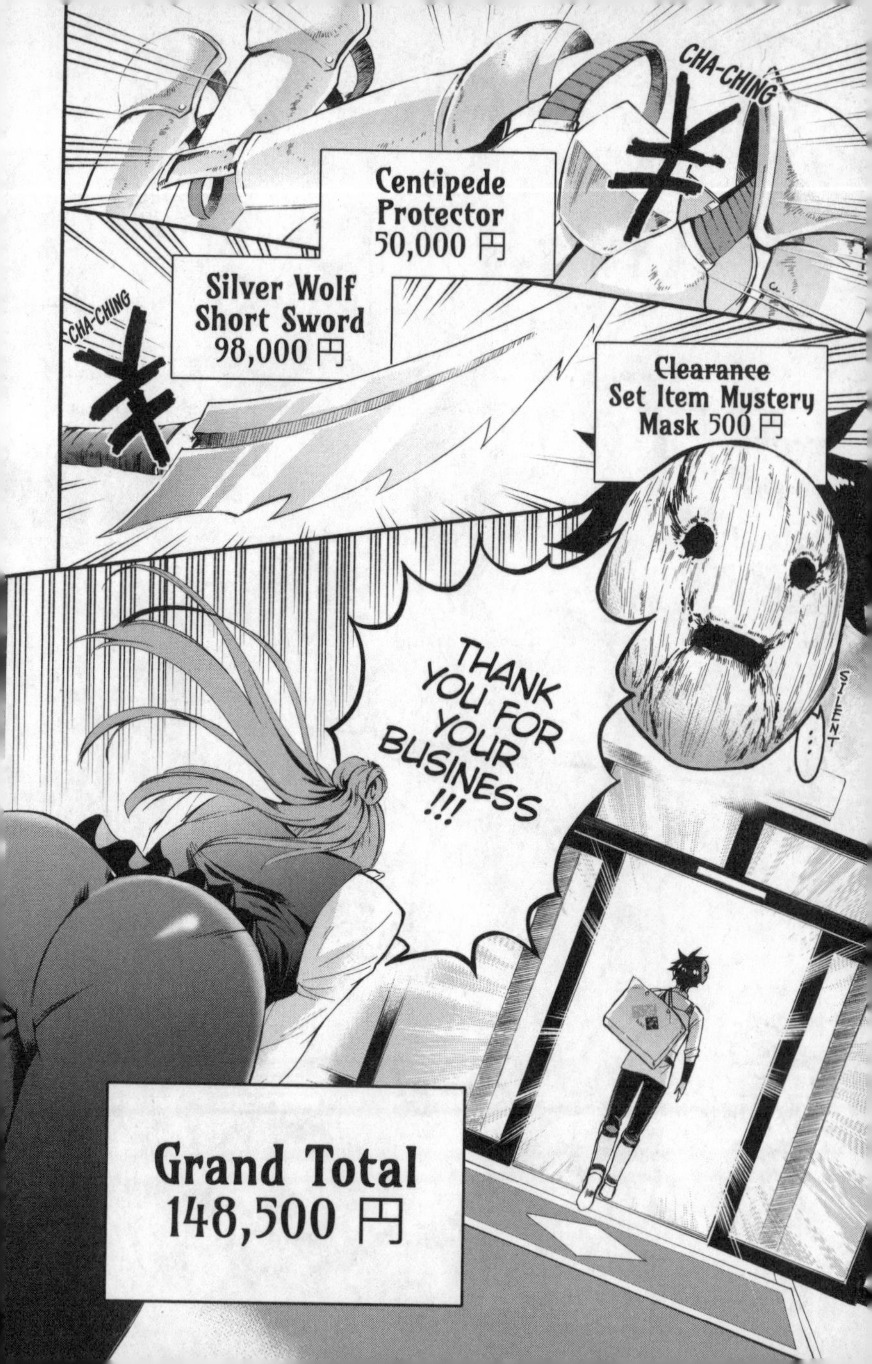
CHA-CHING
Centipede Protector 50,000 円
Silver Wolf Short Sword 98,000 円
CHA-CHING
Clearance Set Item Mystery Mask 500 円
SILENT
...
THANK YOU FOR YOUR BUSINESS!!!
Grand Total 148,500 円

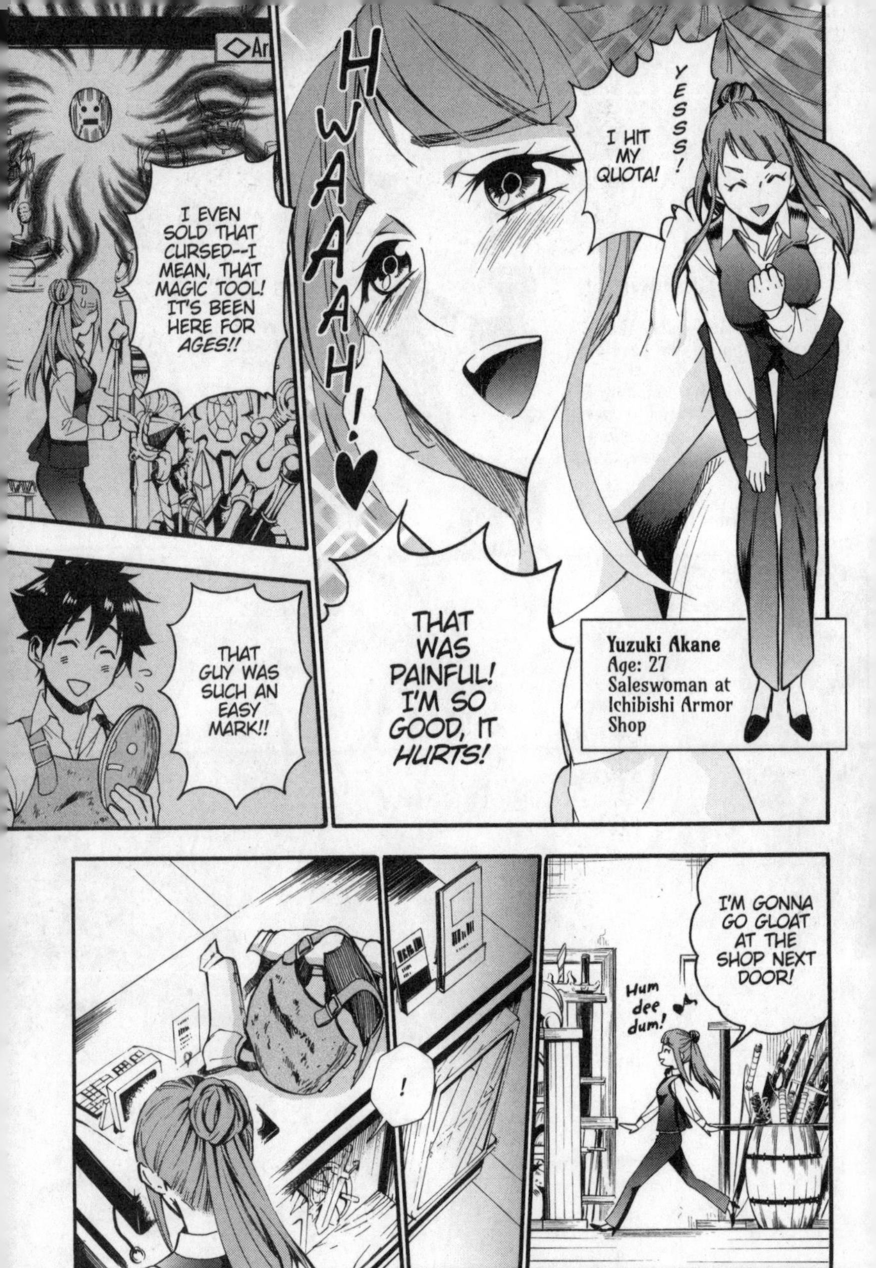
YESSS!
I HIT MY QUOTA!
Yuzuki Akane
Age: 27
Saleswoman at Ichibishi Armor Shop
HWAAAAH!♥
THAT WAS PAINFUL! I'M SO GOOD, IT HURTS!
I EVEN SOLD THAT CURSED--I MEAN, THAT MAGIC TOOL! IT'S BEEN HERE FOR AGES!!
THAT GUY WAS SUCH AN EASY MARK!!
I'M GONNA GO GLOAT AT THE SHOP NEXT DOOR!
Hum dee dum!
!

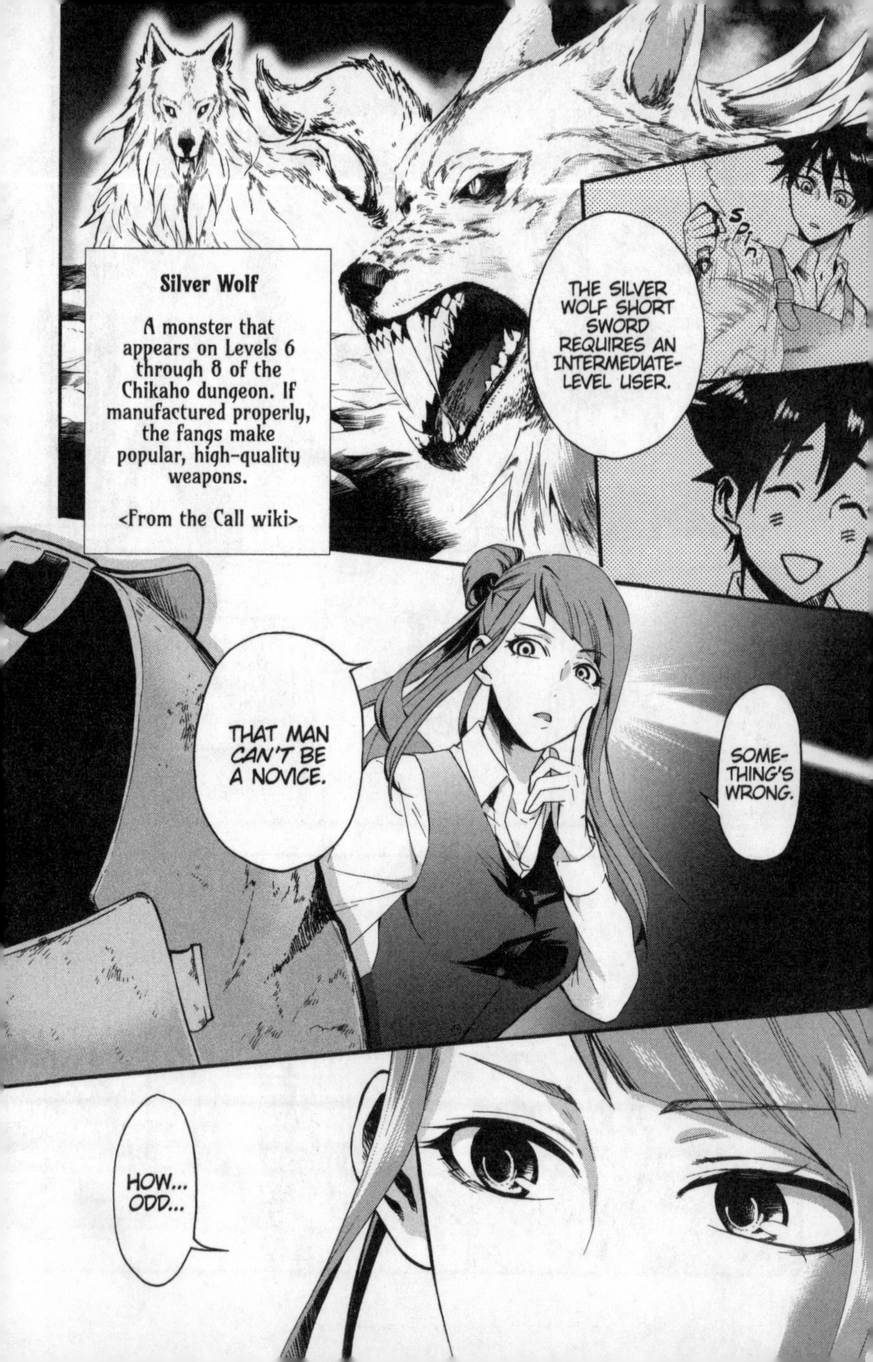
Spin
THE SILVER WOLF SHORT SWORD REQUIRES AN INTERMEDIATE-LEVEL USER.
Silver Wolf
A monster that appears on Levels 6 through 8 of the Chikaho dungeon. If manufactured properly, the fangs make popular, high-quality weapons.
<From the Call wiki>
SOME-THING'S WRONG.
THAT MAN CAN'T BE A NOVICE.
HOW... ODD...

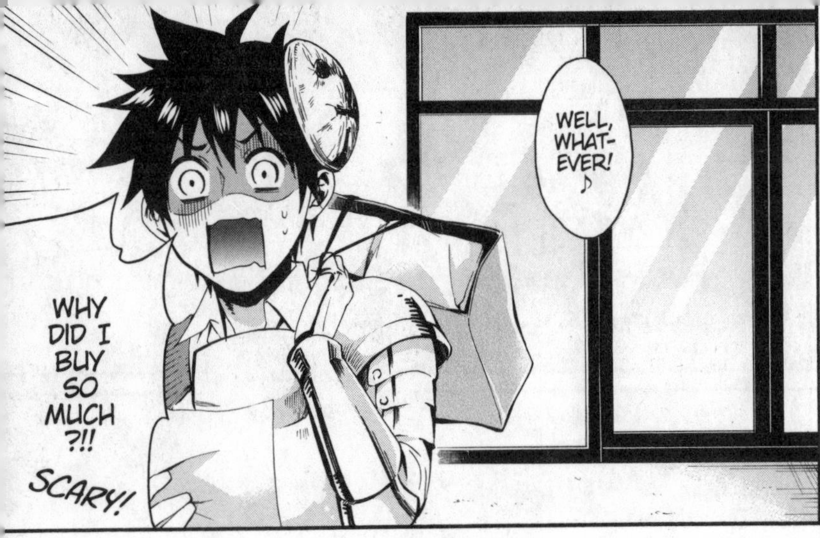
WELL, WHAT-EVER! ♪
WHY DID I BUY SO MUCH?!!
SCARY!

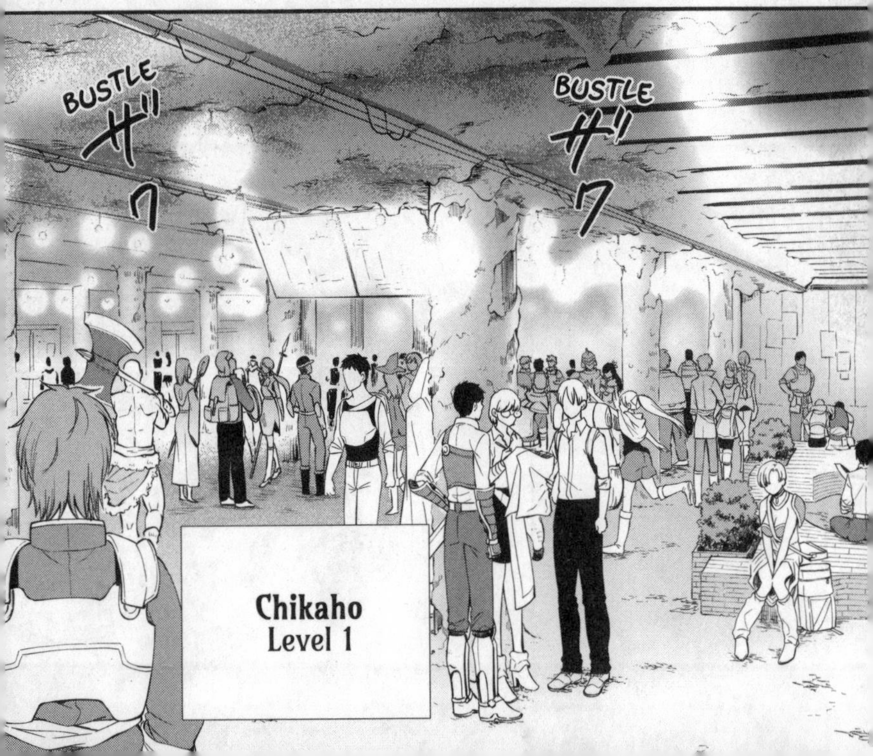
BUSTLE ザワ
BUSTLE ザワ
Chikaho Level 1

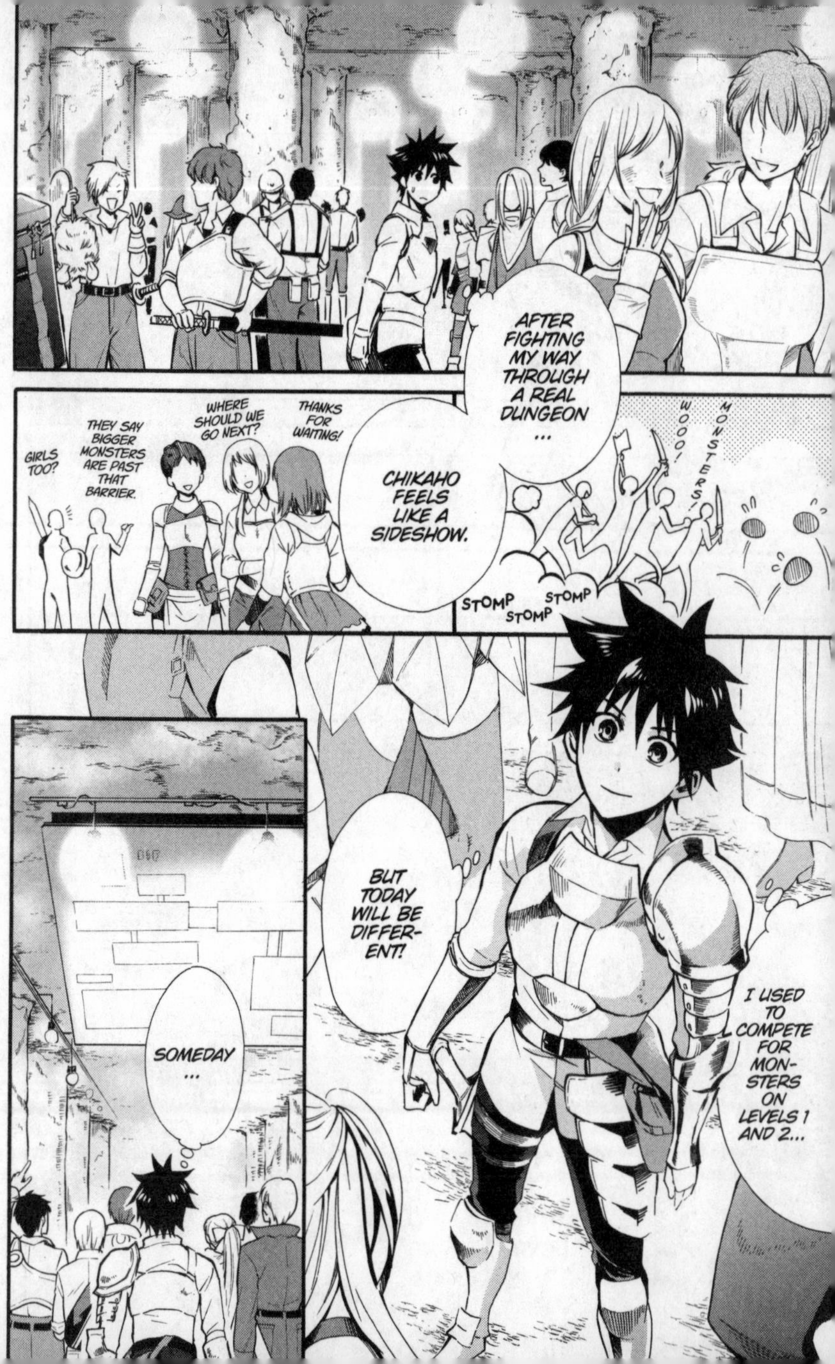
AFTER FIGHTING MY WAY THROUGH A REAL DUNGEON ...
MONSTERS!
WOOOO!
STOMP STOMP STOMP
CHIKAHO FEELS LIKE A SIDESHOW.
THANKS FOR WAITING!
WHERE SHOULD WE GO NEXT?
THEY SAY BIGGER MONSTERS ARE PAST THAT BARRIER.
GIRLS TOO?
I USED TO COMPETE FOR MON-STERS ON LEVELS 1 AND 2...
BUT TODAY WILL BE DIFFER-ENT!
SOMEDAY ...

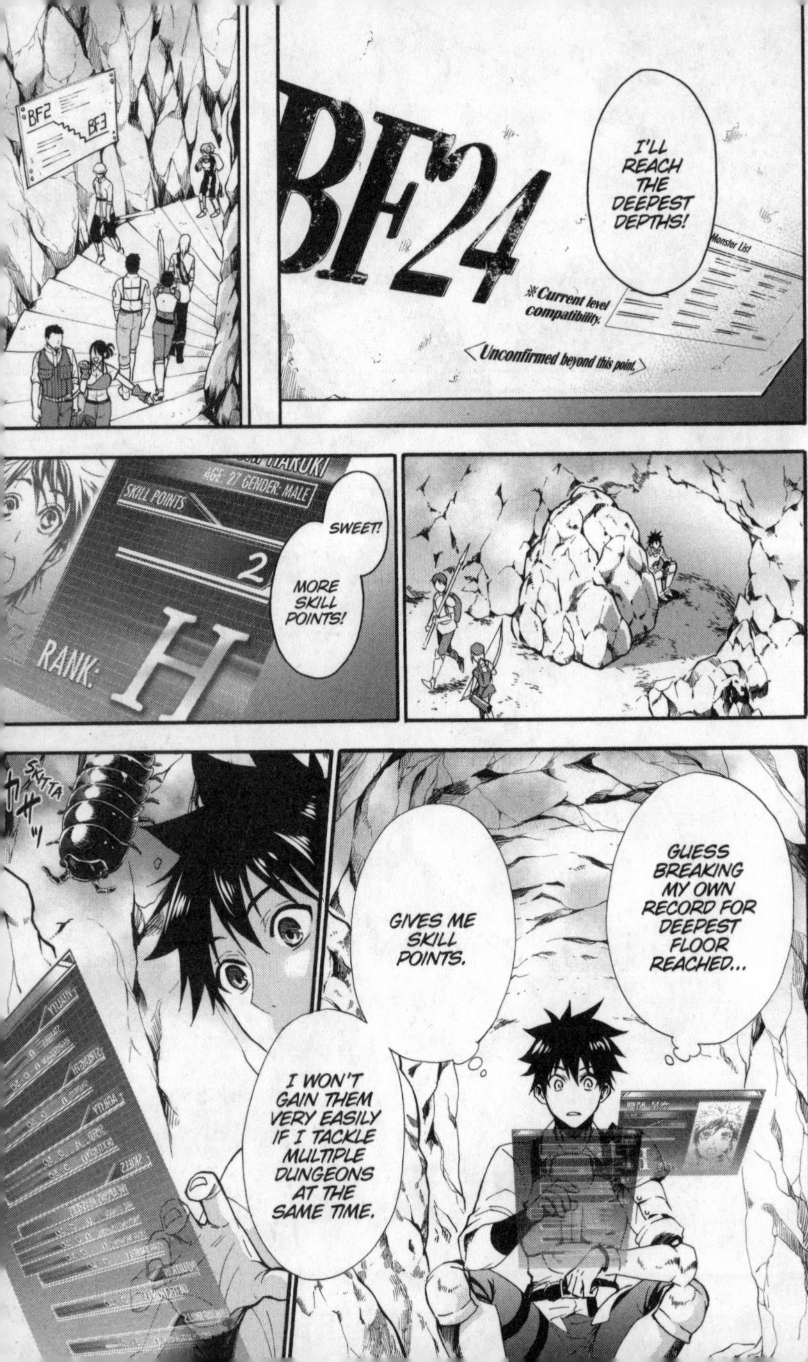
I'LL REACH THE DEEPEST DEPTHS!
BF24
Monster List
※Current level compatibility.
<Unconfirmed beyond this point.>
BF2
BF3
AGE: 27 GENDER: MALE
SKILL POINTS
2
RANK: H
SWEET!
MORE SKILL POINTS!
GUESS BREAKING MY OWN RECORD FOR DEEPEST FLOOR REACHED...
GIVES ME SKILL POINTS.
I WON'T GAIN THEM VERY EASILY IF I TACKLE MULTIPLE DUNGEONS AT THE SAME TIME.
SKITTA

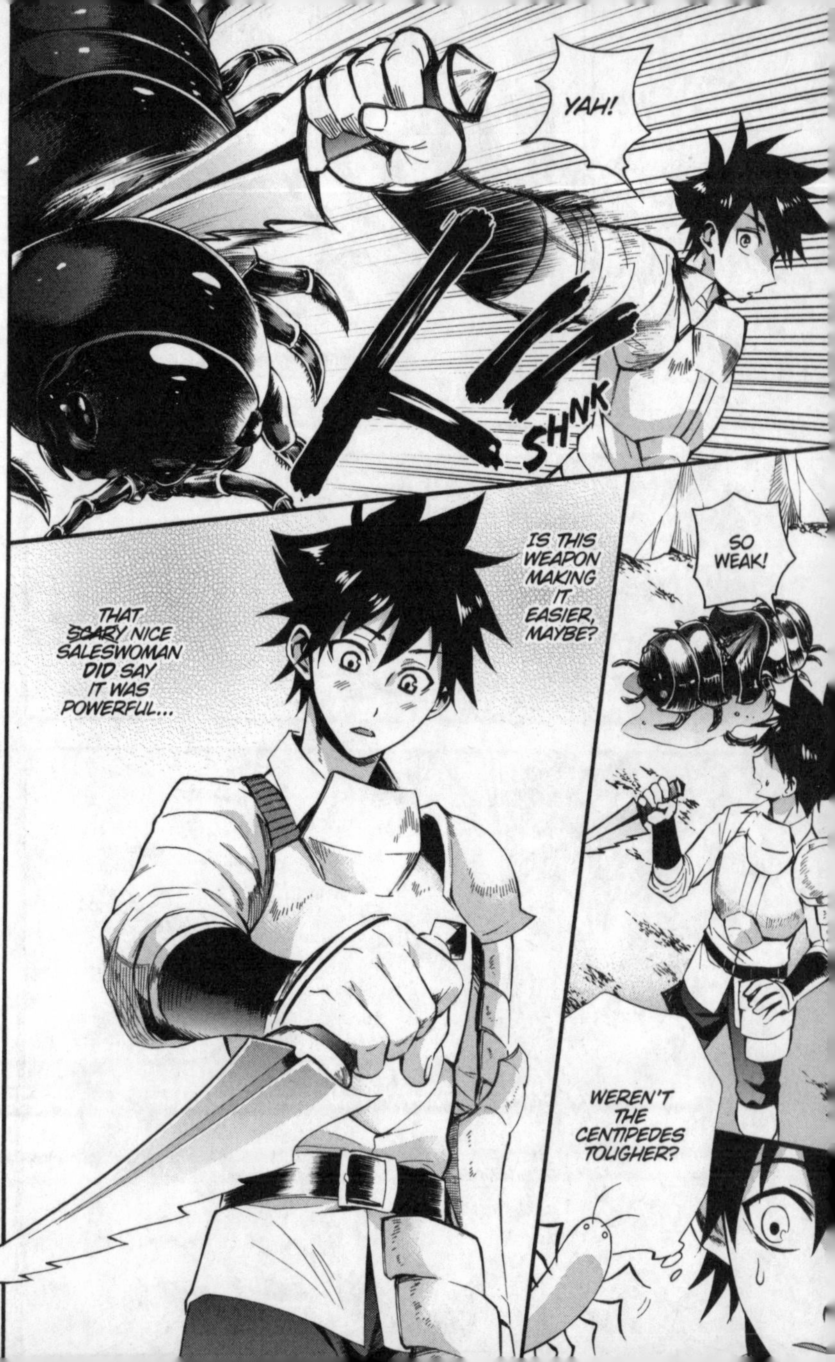
YAH!
SHNK
SO WEAK!
WEREN'T THE CENTIPEDES TOUGHER?
IS THIS WEAPON MAKING IT EASIER, MAYBE?
THAT ~~SCARY~~ NICE SALESWOMAN DID SAY IT WAS POWERFUL...

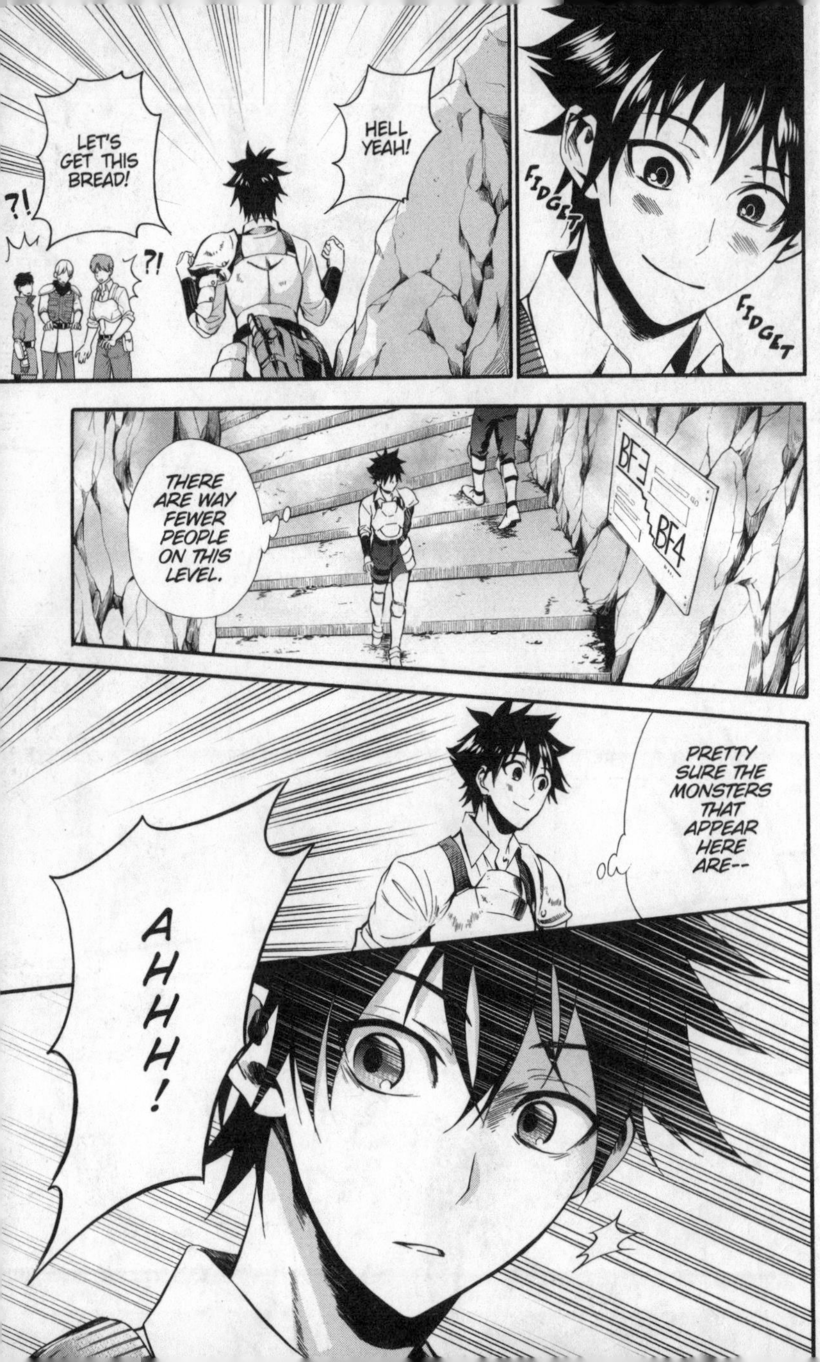
FIDGET
FIDGET
HELL YEAH!
LET'S GET THIS BREAD!
?!
?!
BF3
BF4
THERE ARE WAY FEWER PEOPLE ON THIS LEVEL.
PRETTY SURE THE MONSTERS THAT APPEAR HERE ARE--
AHHH!

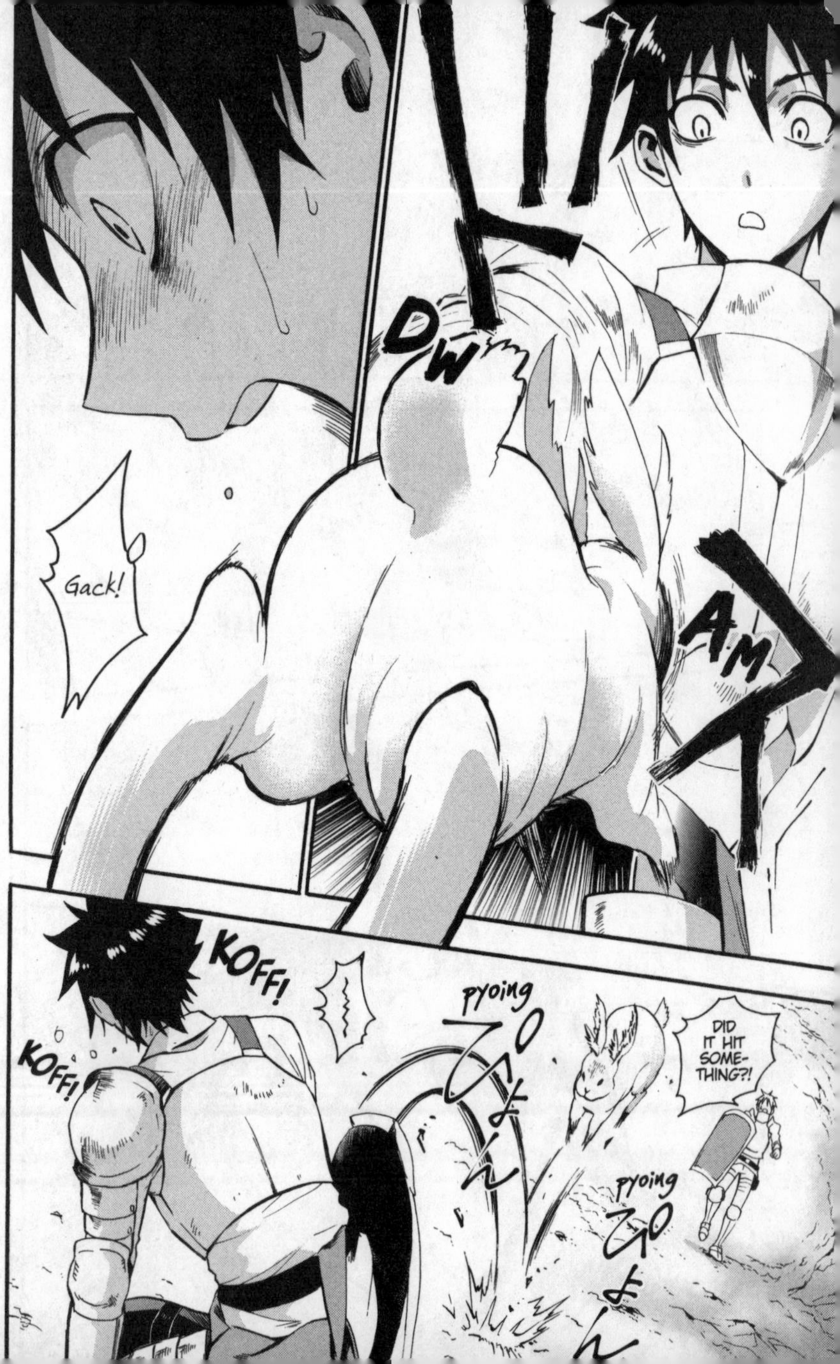
AM
DW
Gack!
DID IT HIT SOME-THING?!
pyoing
pyoing
...!
KOFF!
KOFF!

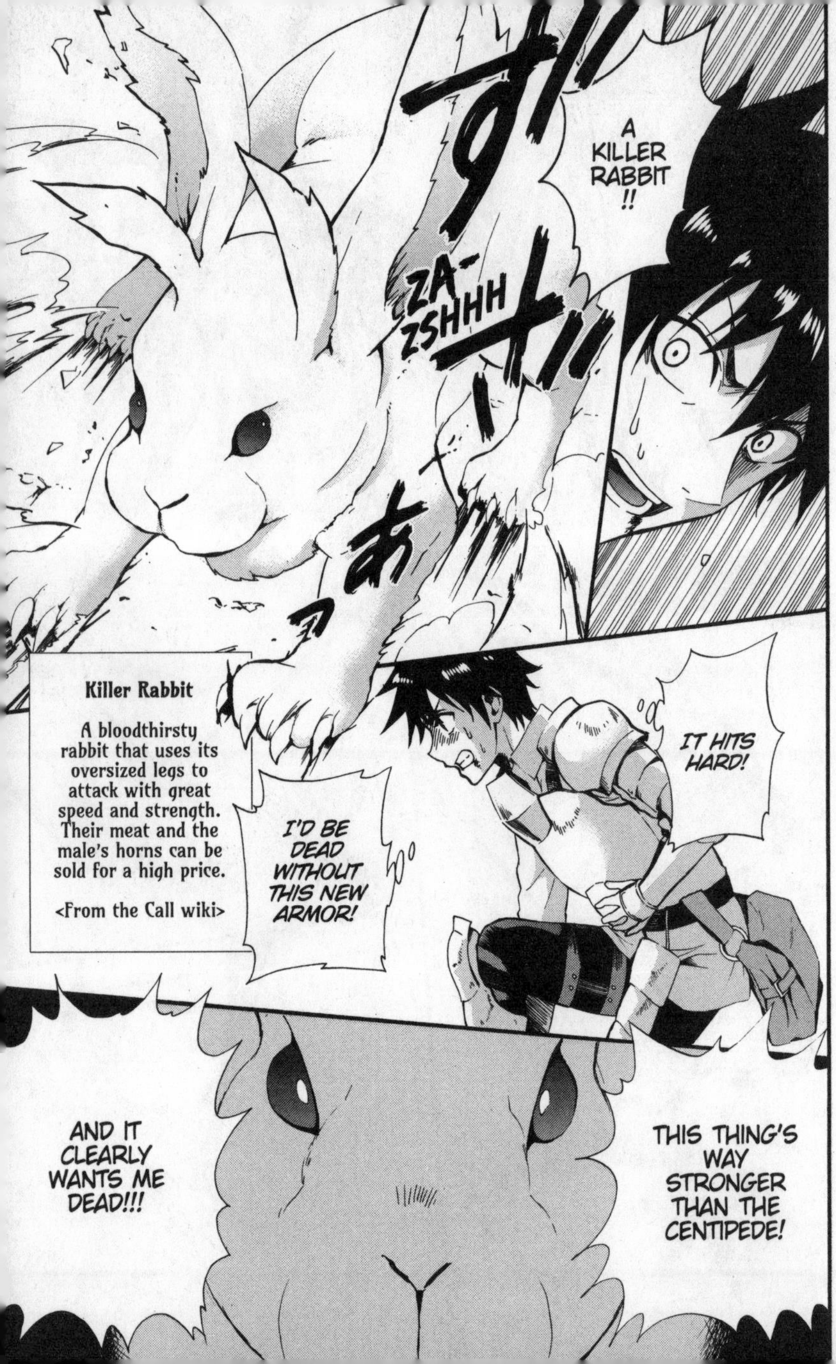
A KILLER RABBIT !!
ZA-ZSHHH
IT HITS HARD!
I'D BE DEAD WITHOUT THIS NEW ARMOR!
Killer Rabbit
A bloodthirsty rabbit that uses its oversized legs to attack with great speed and strength. Their meat and the male's horns can be sold for a high price.
<From the Call wiki>
THIS THING'S WAY STRONGER THAN THE CENTIPEDE!
AND IT CLEARLY WANTS ME DEAD!!!

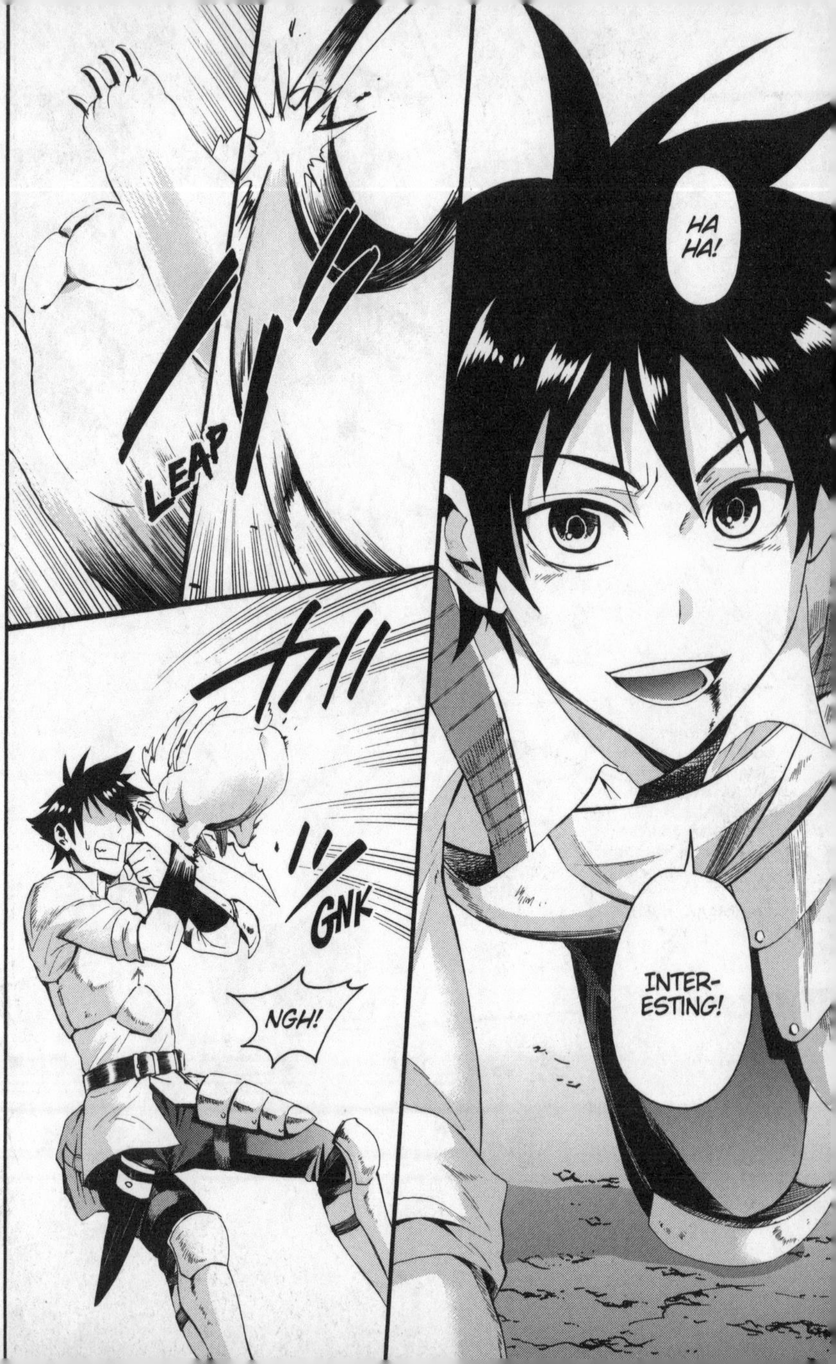
HA HA!
INTER-ESTING!
LEAP
GNK
NGH!

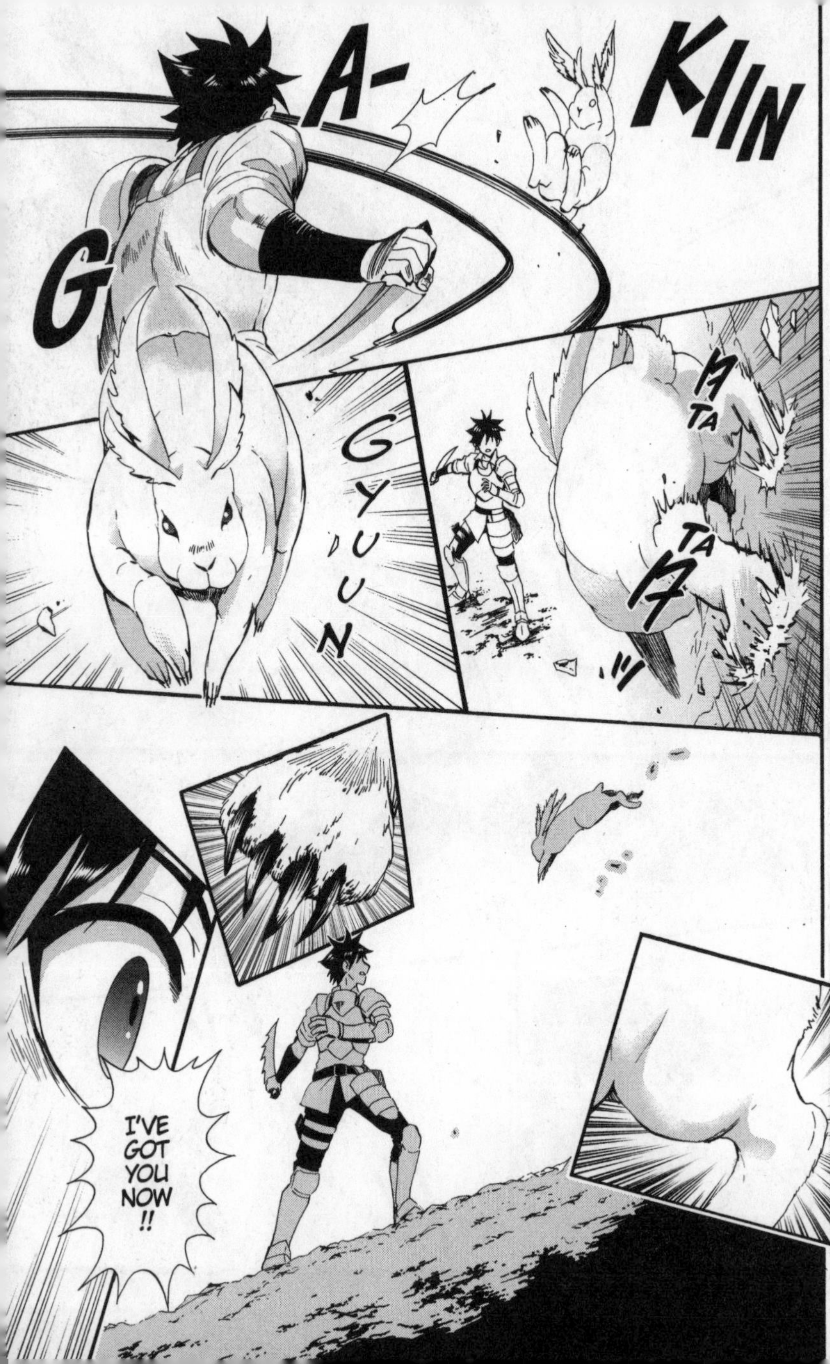
GA-KIIN
TATA TATA
GYUUN
I'VE GOT YOU NOW!!

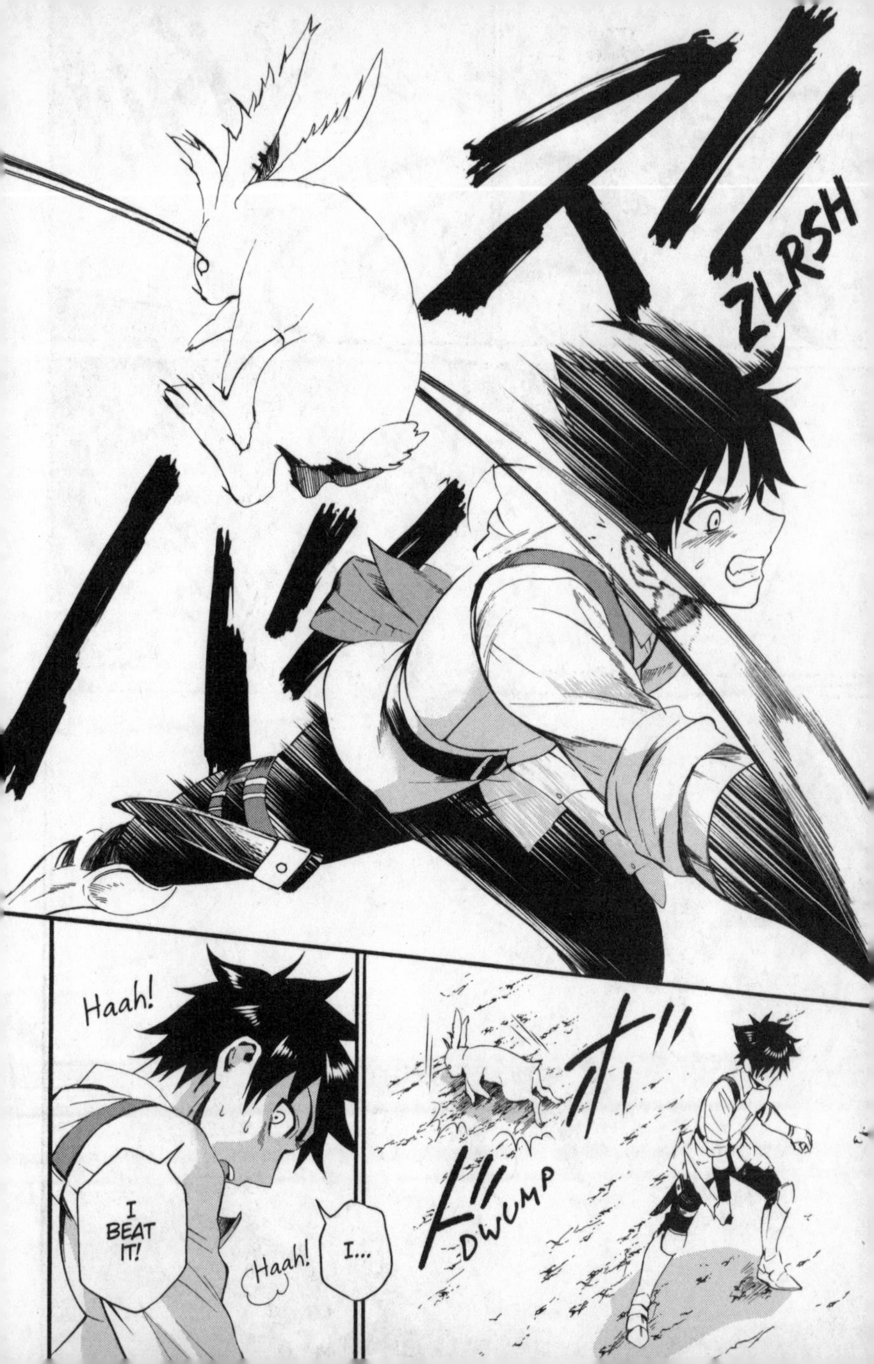
ZLRSH
DWUMP
Haah!
I...
Haah!
I BEAT IT!

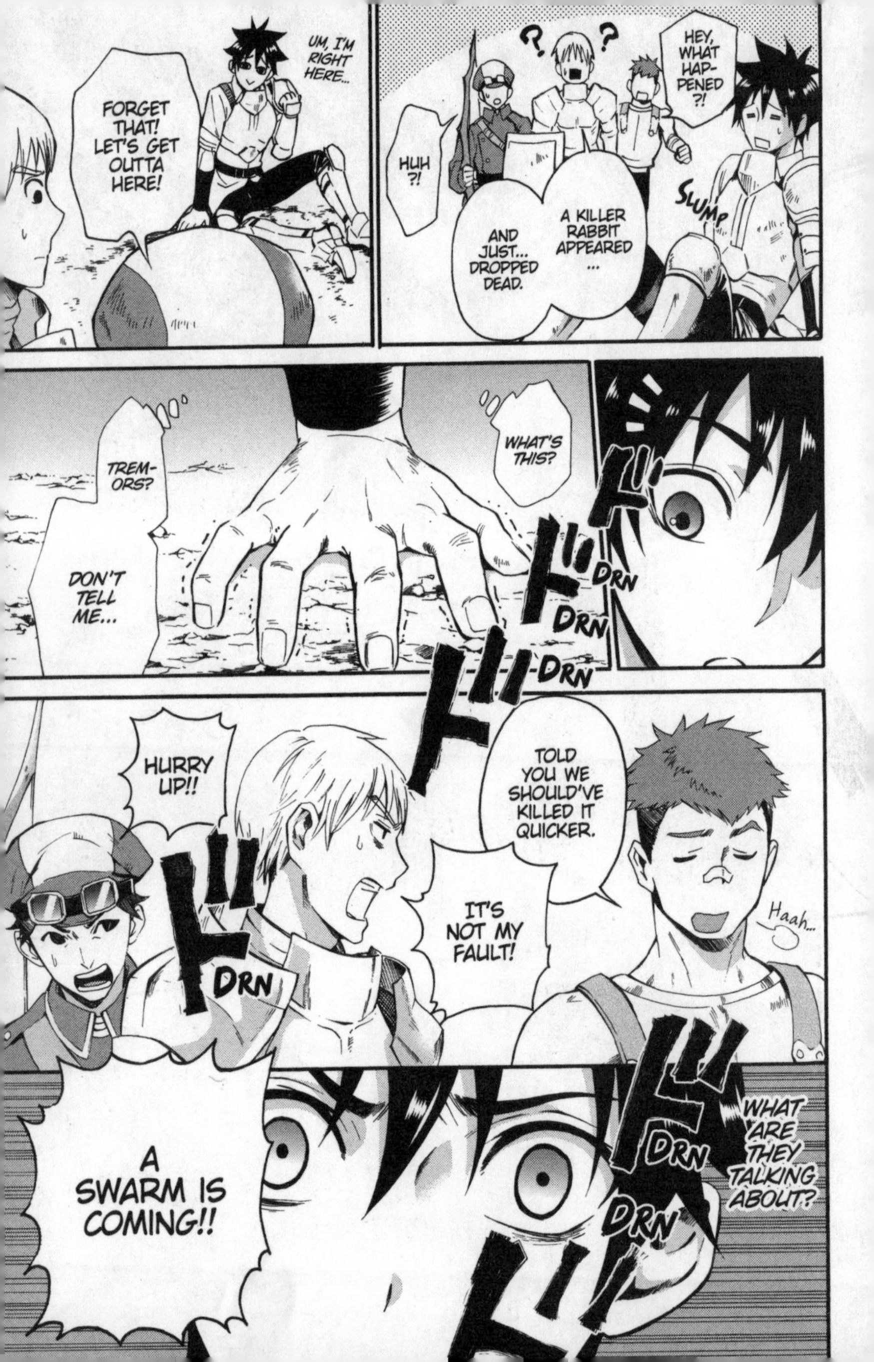
HEY, WHAT HAPPENED?!
SLUMP
?
?
HUH?!
A KILLER RABBIT APPEARED...
AND JUST... DROPPED DEAD.
UM, I'M RIGHT HERE...
FORGET THAT! LET'S GET OUTTA HERE!
DRN
DRN
WHAT'S THIS?
TREMORS?
DON'T TELL ME...
-DRN
TOLD YOU WE SHOULD'VE KILLED IT QUICKER.
Haah...
IT'S NOT MY FAULT!
HURRY UP!!
DRN
WHAT ARE THEY TALKING ABOUT?
DRN
DRN
A SWARM IS COMING!!

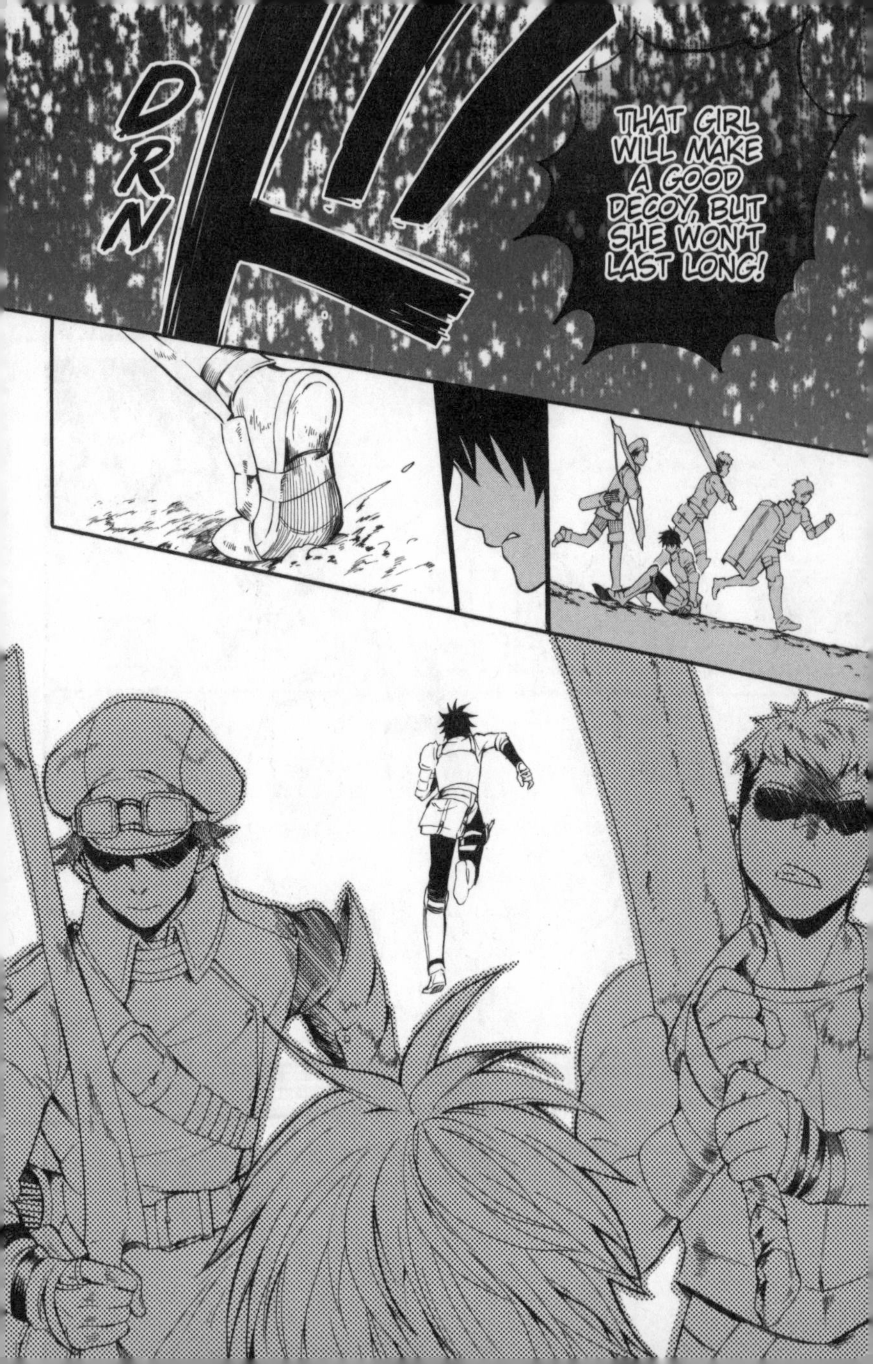
THAT GIRL WILL MAKE A GOOD DECOY, BUT SHE WON'T LAST LONG!
DRN

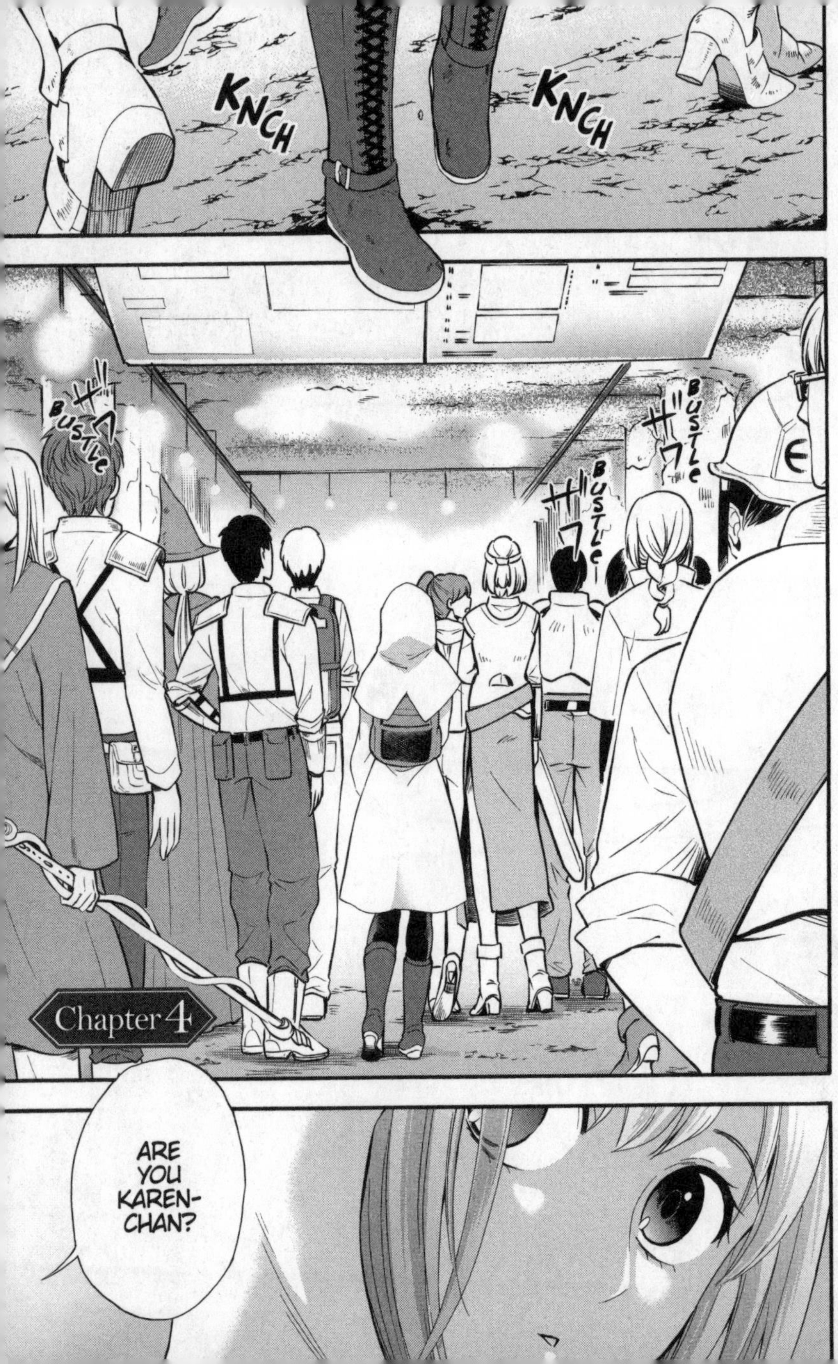
KNCH
KNCH
BUSTLE
BUSTLE
BUSTLE
Chapter 4
ARE YOU KAREN-CHAN?

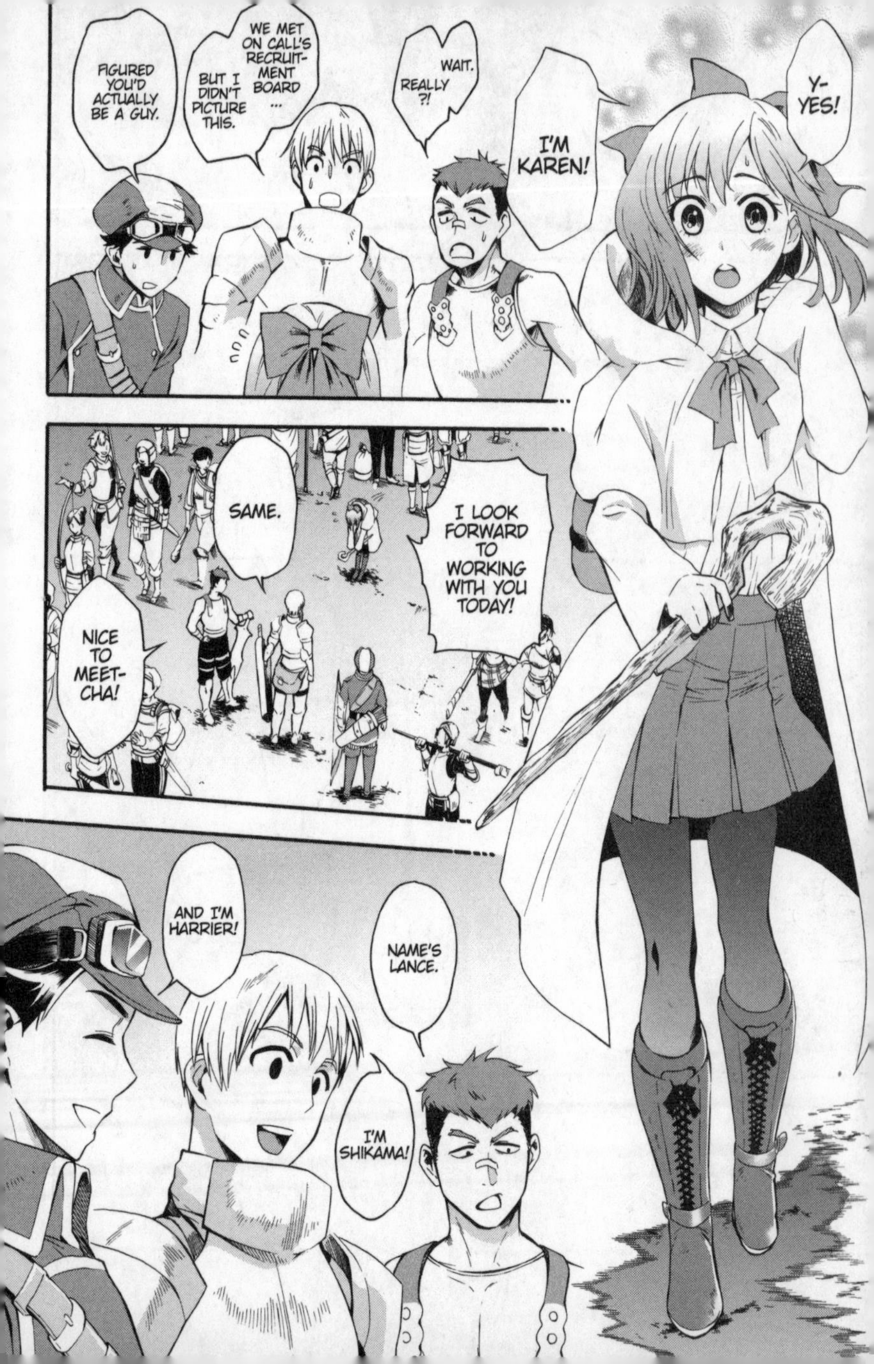
Y-YES!
I'M KAREN!
WAIT. REALLY?!
WE MET ON CALL'S RECRUIT-MENT BOARD ...
BUT I DIDN'T PICTURE THIS.
FIGURED YOU'D ACTUALLY BE A GUY.
I LOOK FORWARD TO WORKING WITH YOU TODAY!
SAME.
NICE TO MEET-CHA!
NAME'S LANCE.
I'M SHIKAMA!
AND I'M HARRIER!

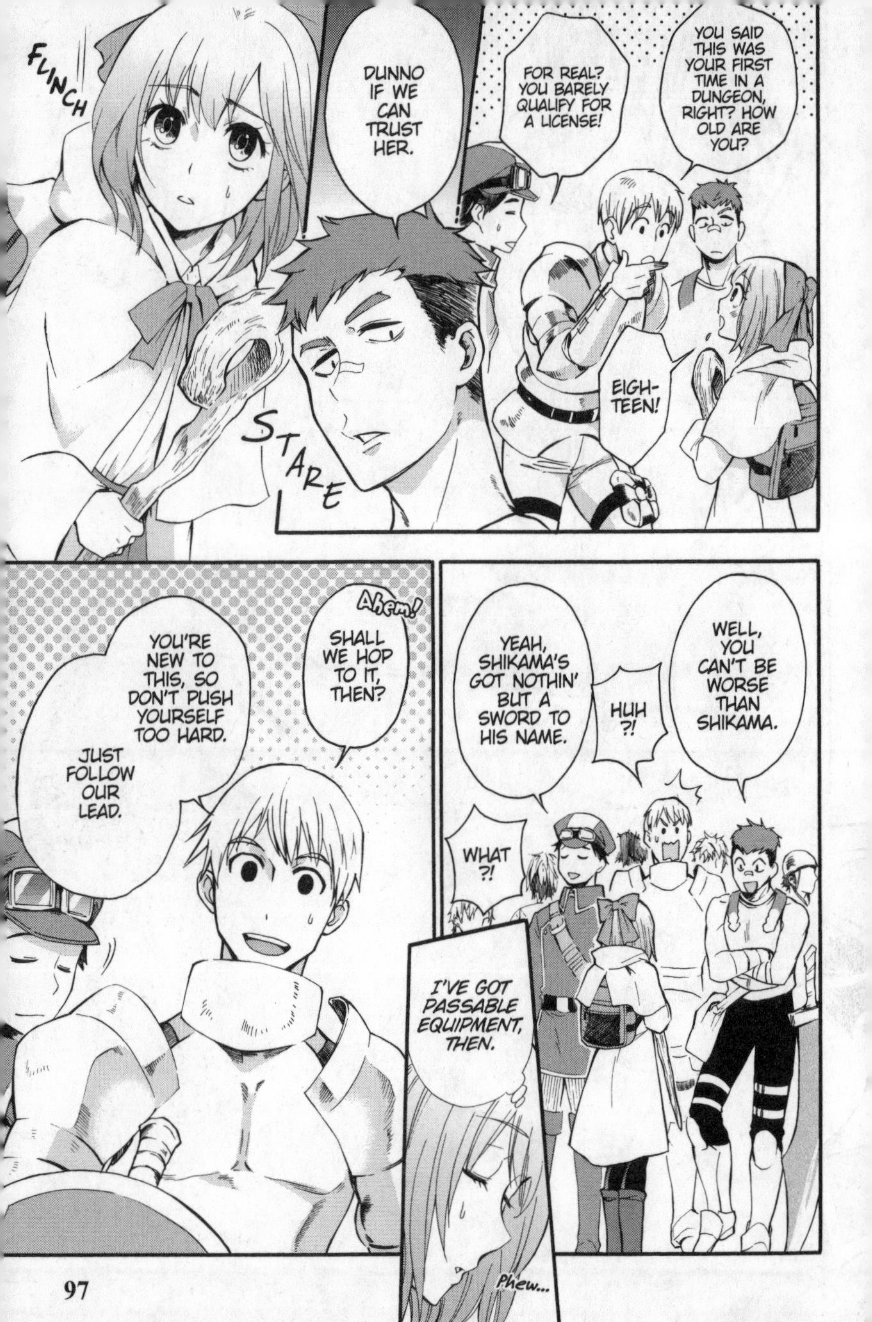
YOU SAID THIS WAS YOUR FIRST TIME IN A DUNGEON, RIGHT? HOW OLD ARE YOU?
EIGH-TEEN!
FOR REAL? YOU BARELY QUALIFY FOR A LICENSE!
DUNNO IF WE CAN TRUST HER.
FLINCH
STARE
WELL, YOU CAN'T BE WORSE THAN SHIKAMA.
HUH ?!
YEAH, SHIKAMA'S GOT NOTHIN' BUT A SWORD TO HIS NAME.
WHAT ?!
Ahem!
SHALL WE HOP TO IT, THEN?
YOU'RE NEW TO THIS, SO DON'T PUSH YOURSELF TOO HARD.
JUST FOLLOW OUR LEAD.
I'VE GOT PASSABLE EQUIPMENT, THEN.
Phew...

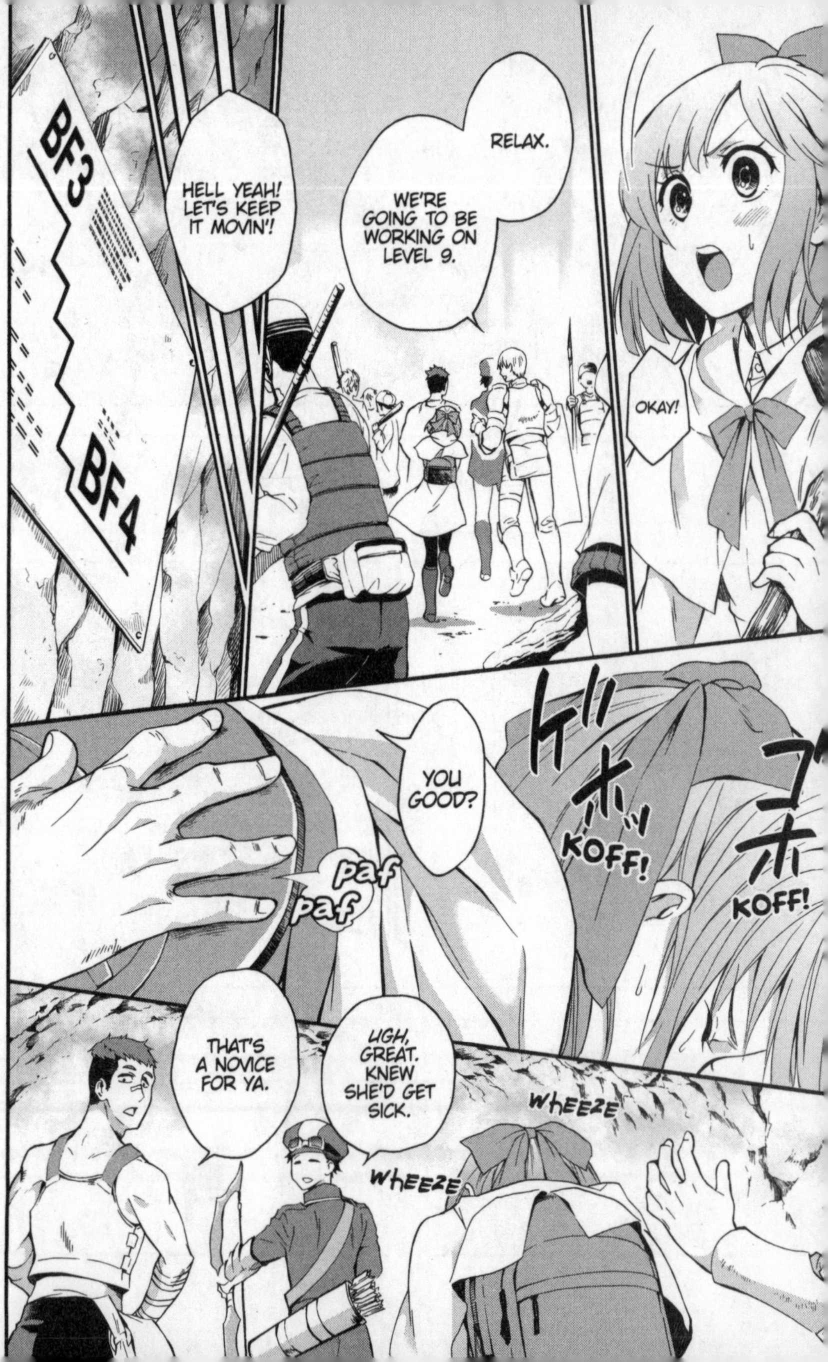
OKAY!
RELAX.
WE'RE GOING TO BE WORKING ON LEVEL 9.
HELL YEAH! LET'S KEEP IT MOVIN'!
BF3
BF4
ゴホ
KOFF!
ゲホッ
KOFF!
YOU GOOD?
paf paf
wheeze
wheeze
UGH, GREAT. KNEW SHE'D GET SICK.
THAT'S A NOVICE FOR YA.

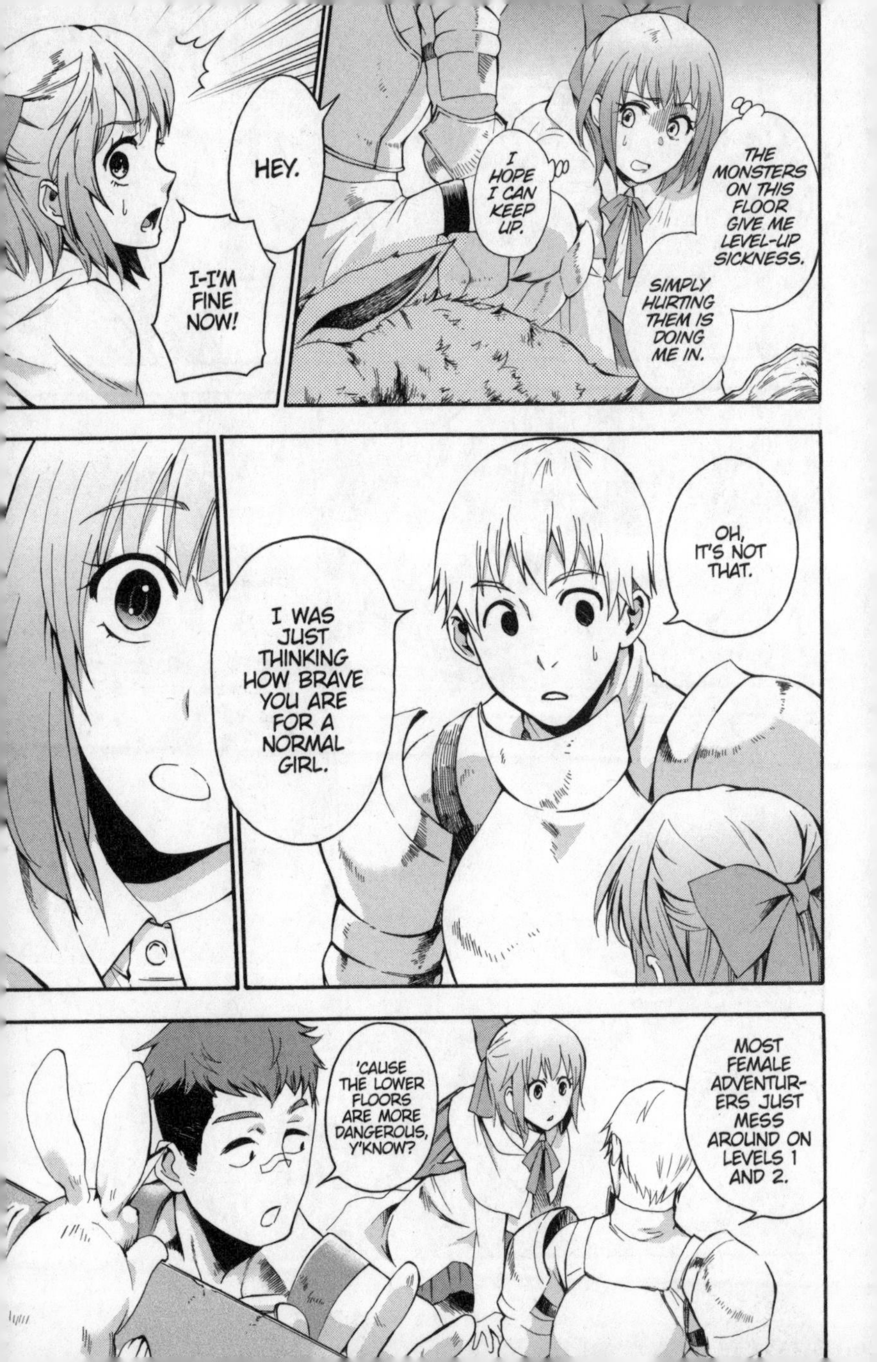
THE MONSTERS ON THIS FLOOR GIVE ME LEVEL-UP SICKNESS.
SIMPLY HURTING THEM IS DOING ME IN.
I HOPE I CAN KEEP UP.
HEY.
I-I'M FINE NOW!
OH, IT'S NOT THAT.
I WAS JUST THINKING HOW BRAVE YOU ARE FOR A NORMAL GIRL.
MOST FEMALE ADVENTUR-ERS JUST MESS AROUND ON LEVELS 1 AND 2.
'CAUSE THE LOWER FLOORS ARE MORE DANGEROUS, Y'KNOW?

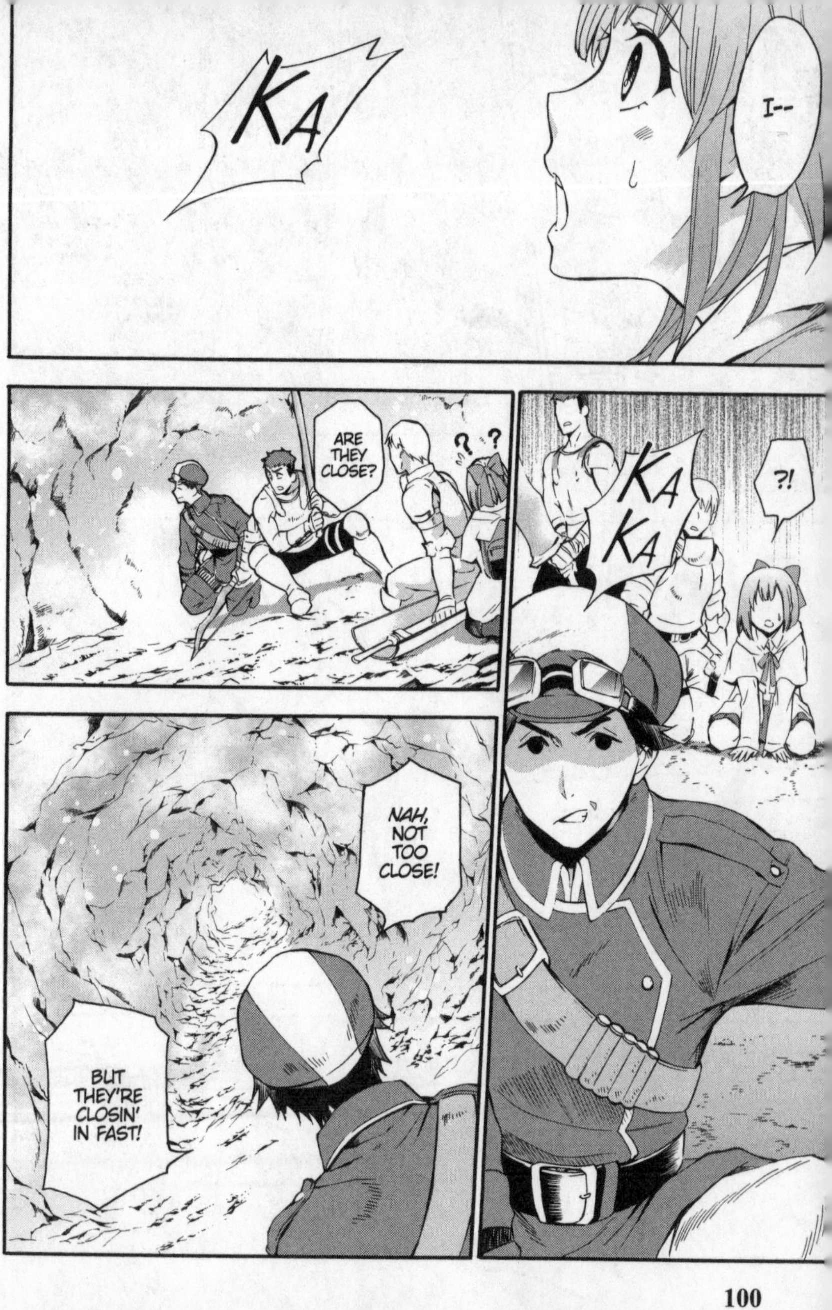
I--
KA
?!
KA KA
? ?
ARE THEY CLOSE?
NAH, NOT TOO CLOSE!
BUT THEY'RE CLOSIN' IN FAST!

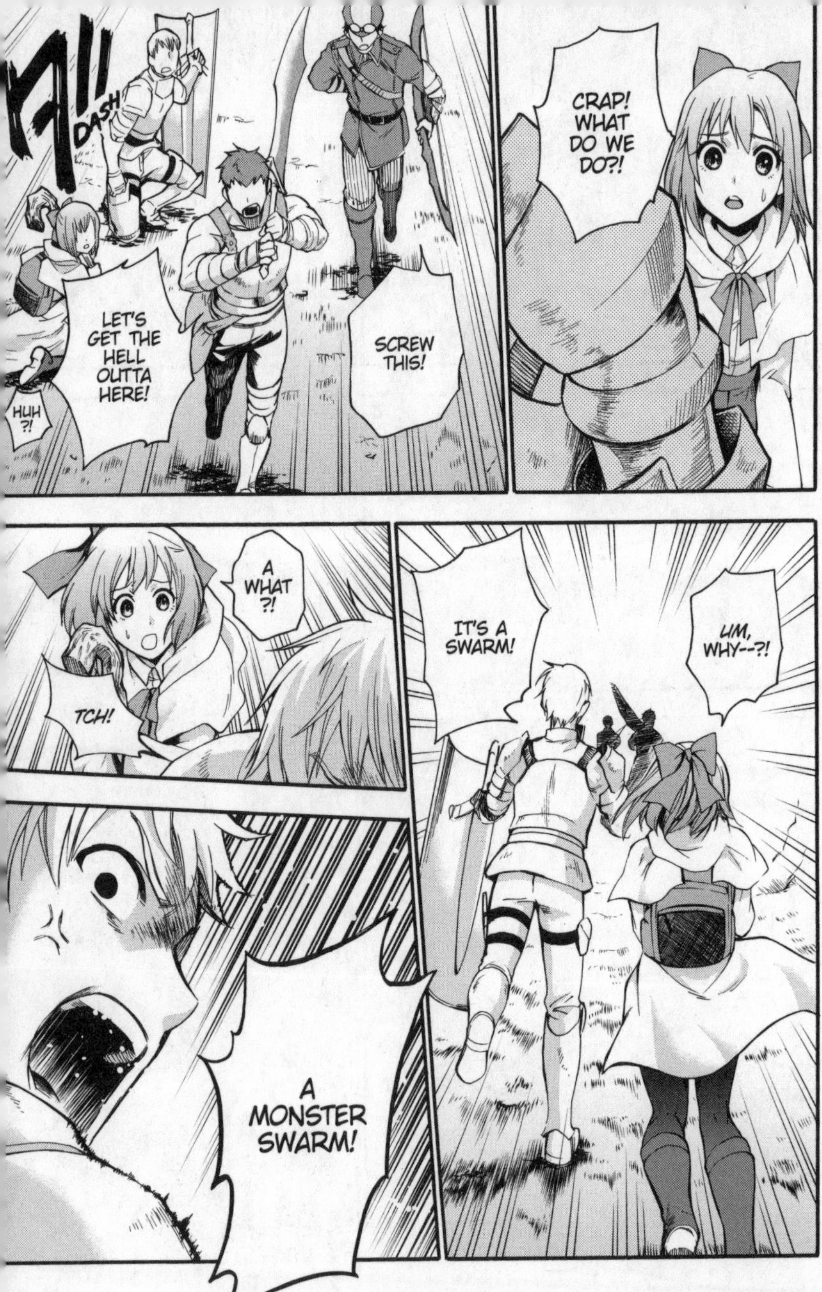
CRAP! WHAT DO WE DO?!
SCREW THIS!
DASH
LET'S GET THE HELL OUTTA HERE!
HUH ?!
UM, WHY--?!
IT'S A SWARM!
A WHAT ?!
TCH!
A MONSTER SWARM!

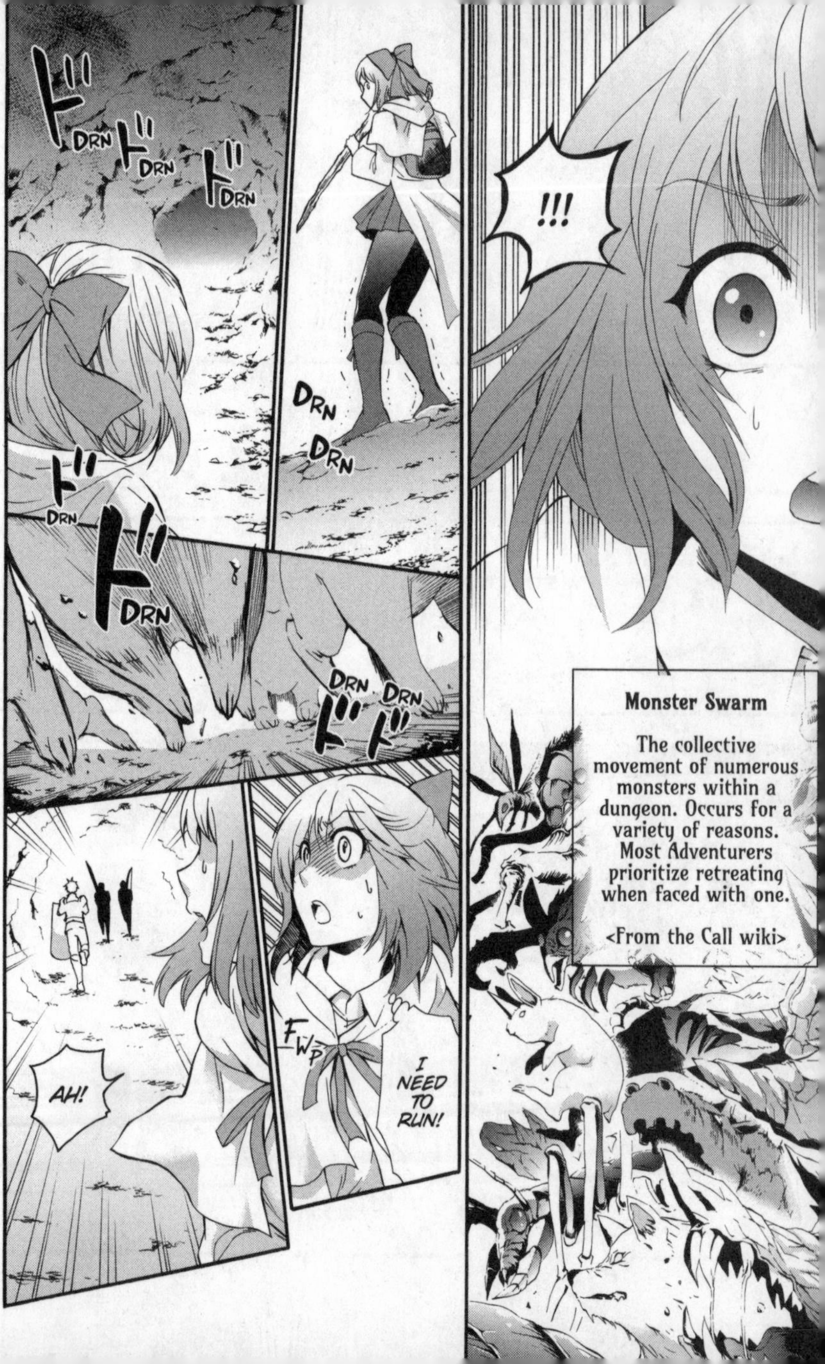
!!!
Monster Swarm
The collective movement of numerous monsters within a dungeon. Occurs for a variety of reasons. Most Adventurers prioritize retreating when faced with one.
<From the Call wiki>
DRN
DRN
DRN DRN DRN
DRN
DRN DRN
DRN
FWP
I NEED TO RUN!
AH!

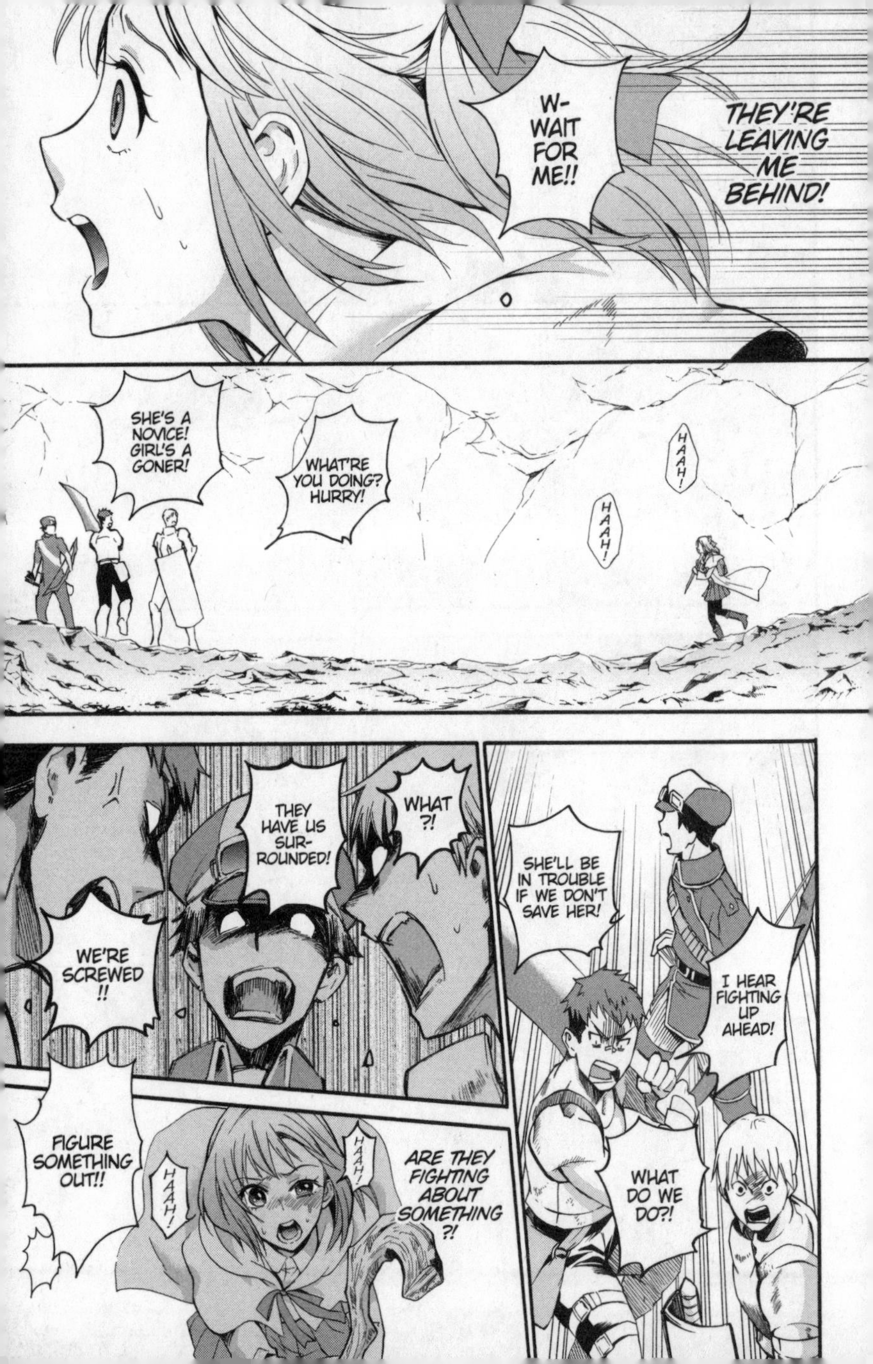
THEY'RE LEAVING ME BEHIND!
W-WAIT FOR ME!!
HAAH!
HAAH!
WHAT'RE YOU DOING? HURRY!
SHE'S A NOVICE! GIRL'S A GONER!
I HEAR FIGHTING UP AHEAD!
SHE'LL BE IN TROUBLE IF WE DON'T SAVE HER!
WHAT DO WE DO?!
WHAT ?!
THEY HAVE US SUR-ROUNDED!
WE'RE SCREWED !!
HAAH!
HAAH!
ARE THEY FIGHTING ABOUT SOMETHING ?!
FIGURE SOMETHING OUT!!

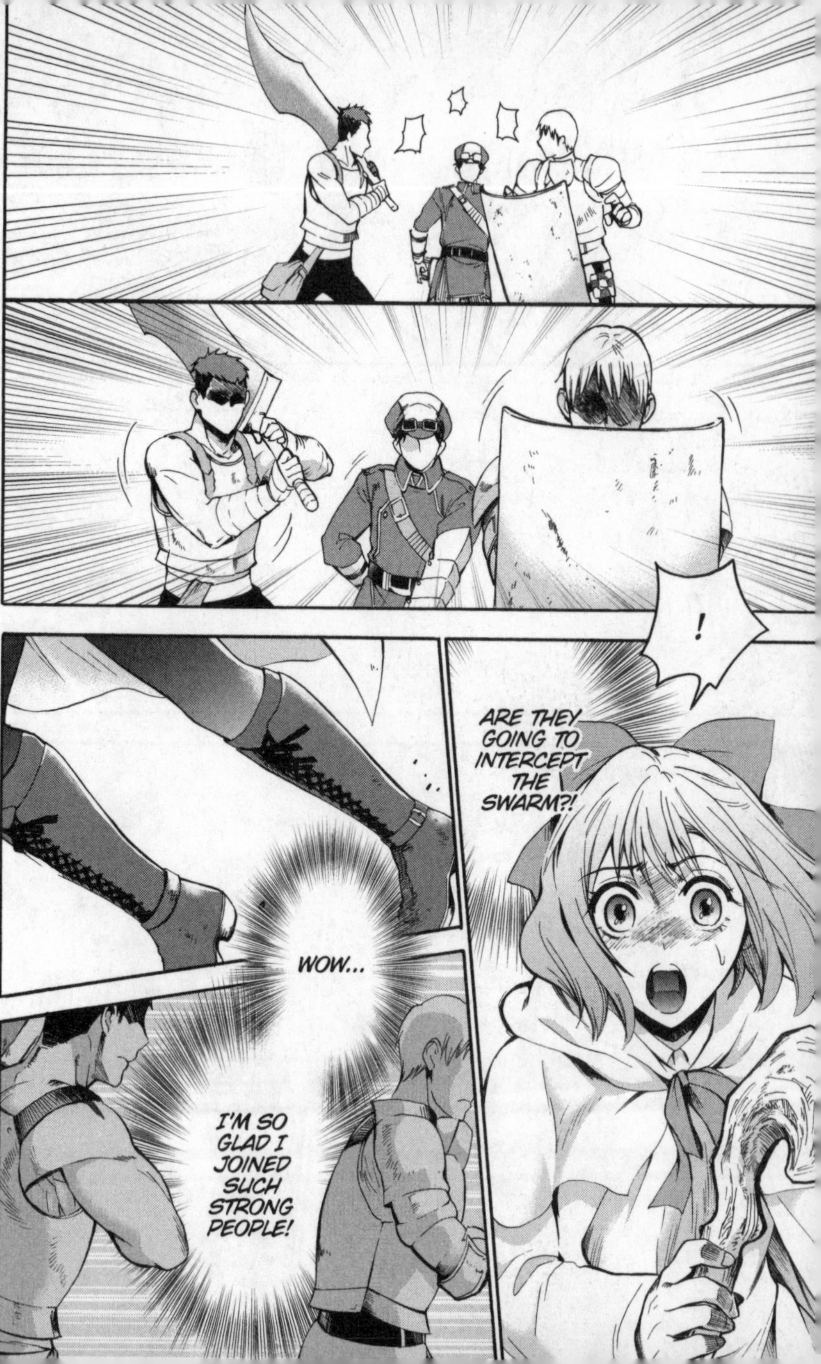
!
ARE THEY GOING TO INTERCEPT THE SWARM?!
WOW...
I'M SO GLAD I JOINED SUCH STRONG PEOPLE!

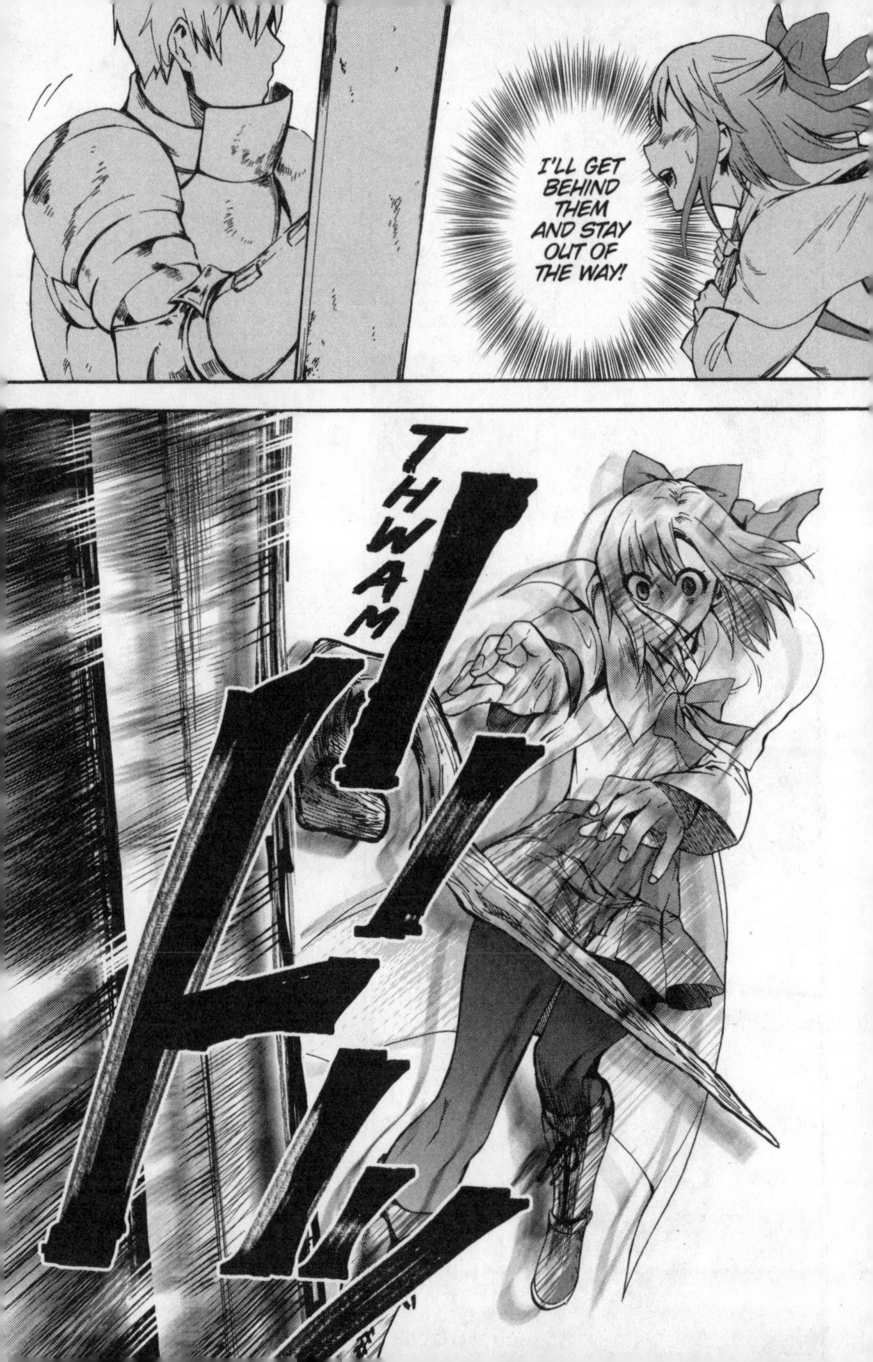
I'LL GET BEHIND THEM AND STAY OUT OF THE WAY!
THWAM

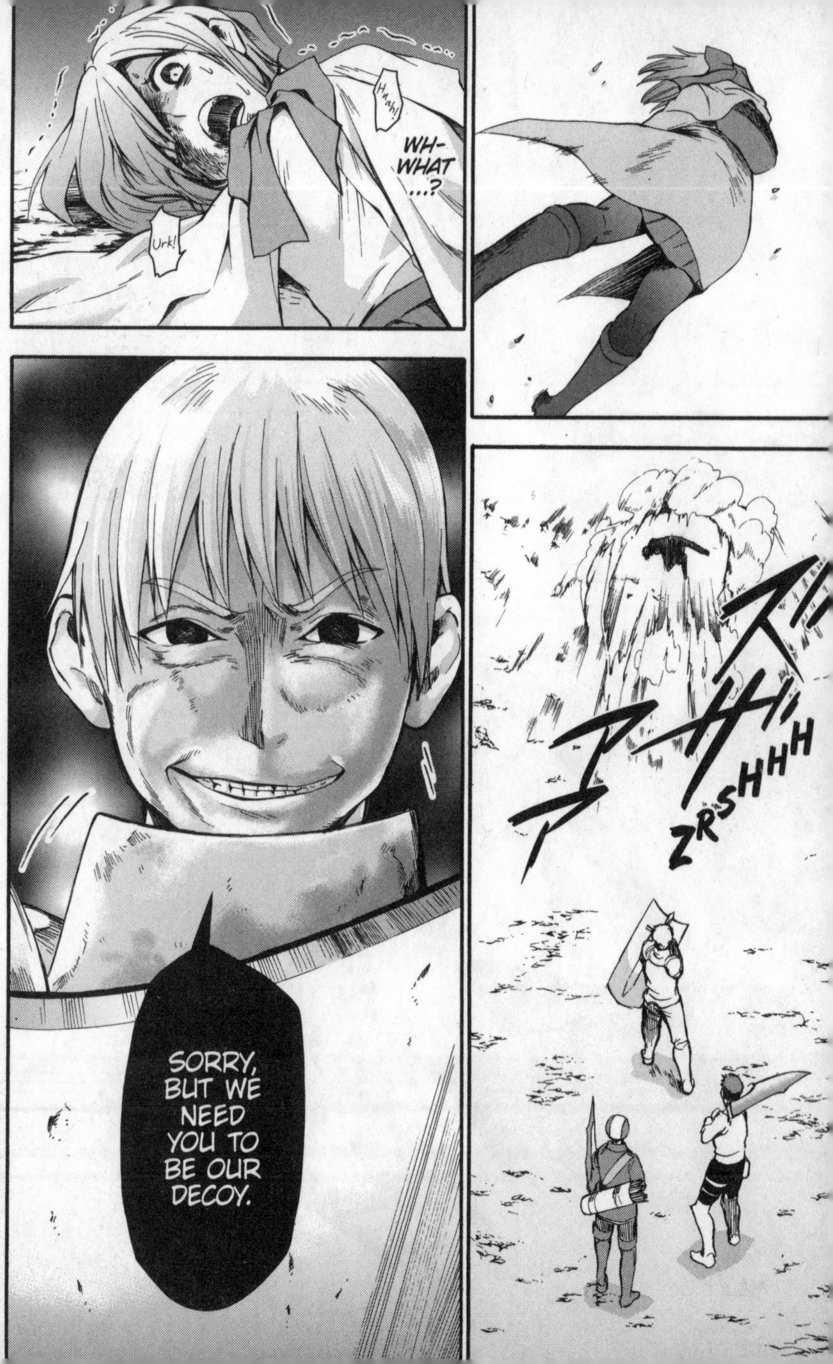
Hnah!
WH-WHAT ...?
Urk!
ZRSHHH
SORRY, BUT WE NEED YOU TO BE OUR DECOY.

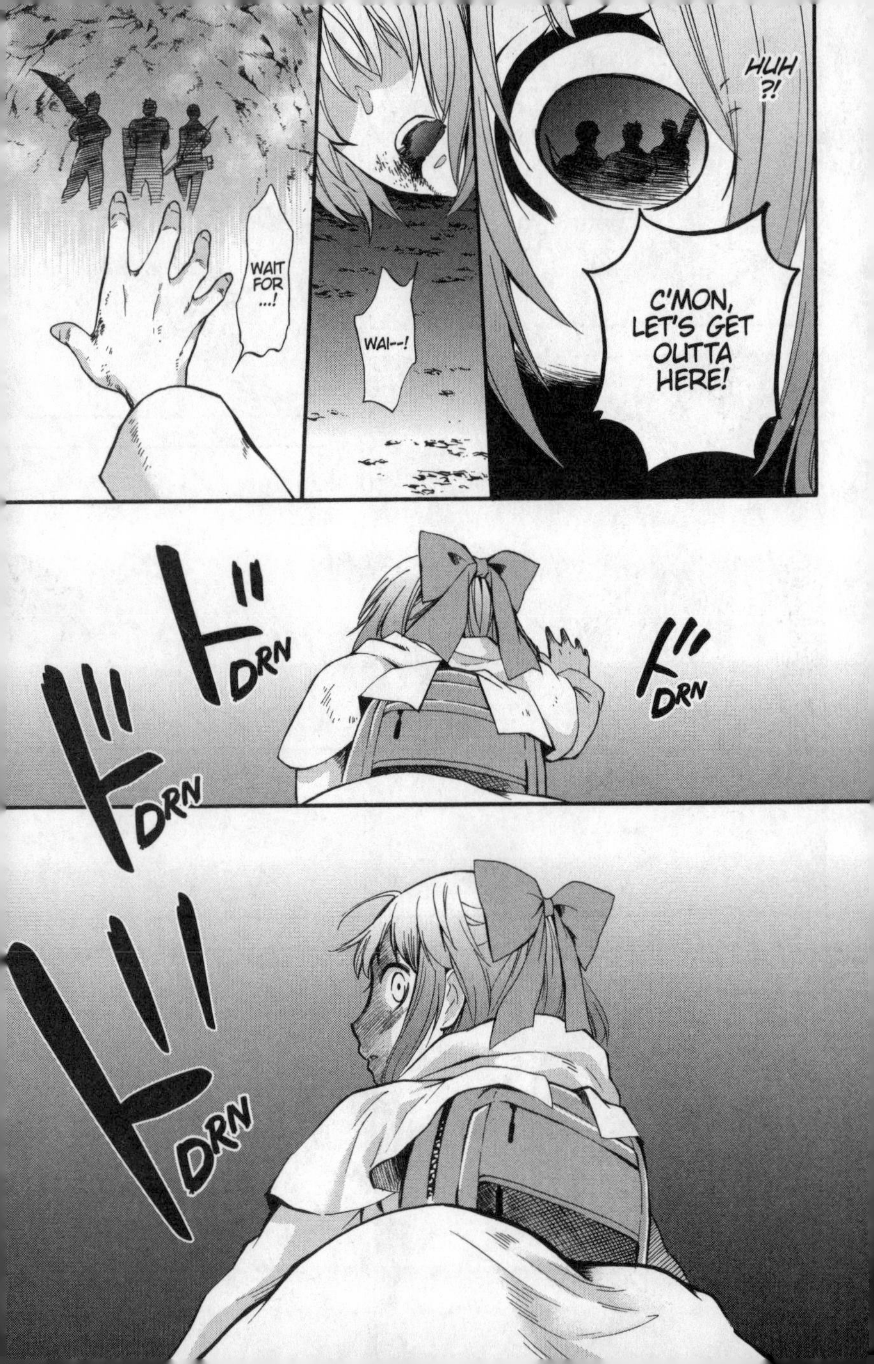
HUH ?!
C'MON, LET'S GET OUTTA HERE!
WAI--!
WAIT FOR ...!
ドド DRN
ドド DRN
ドド DRN
ドド DRN

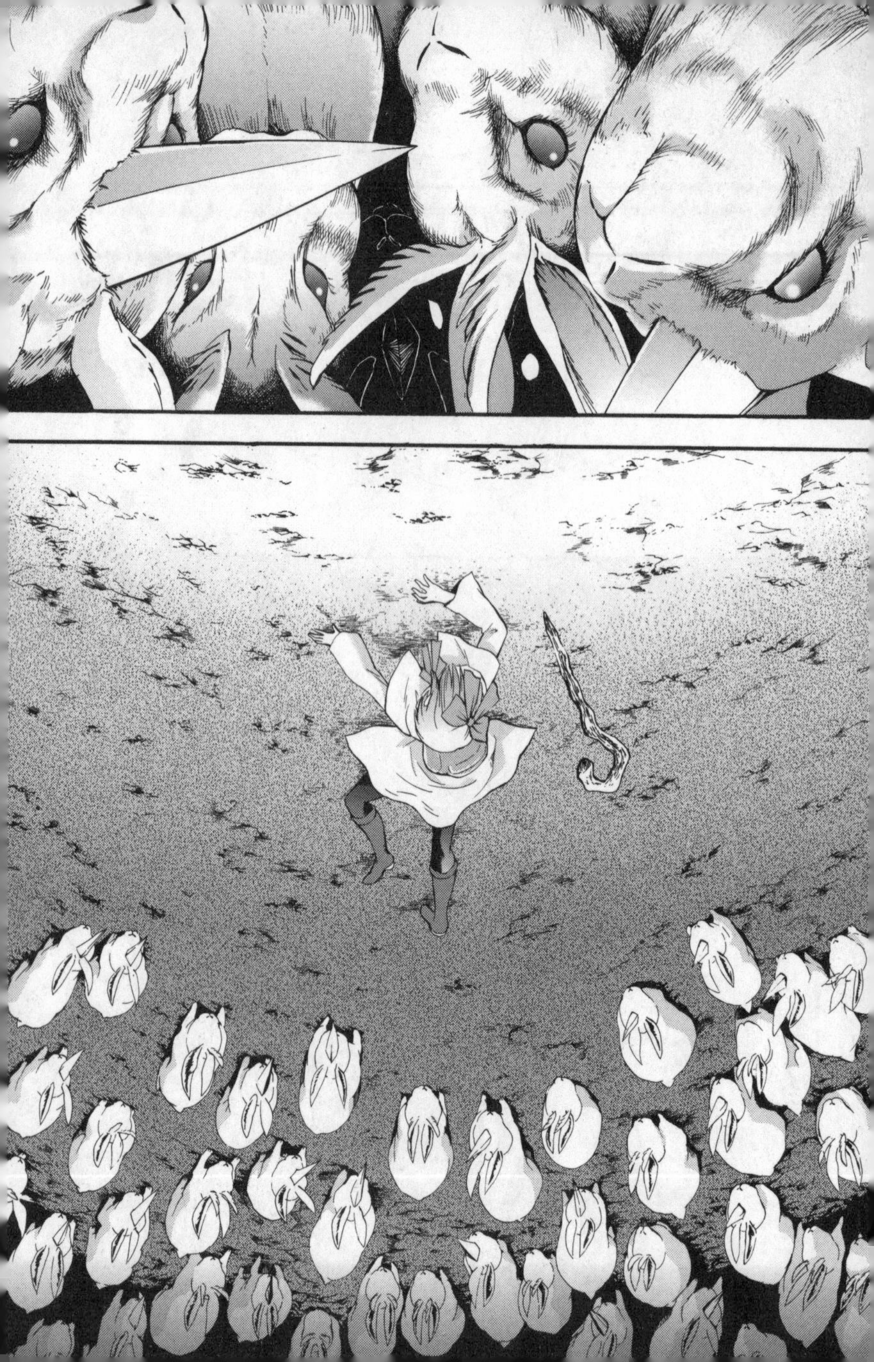

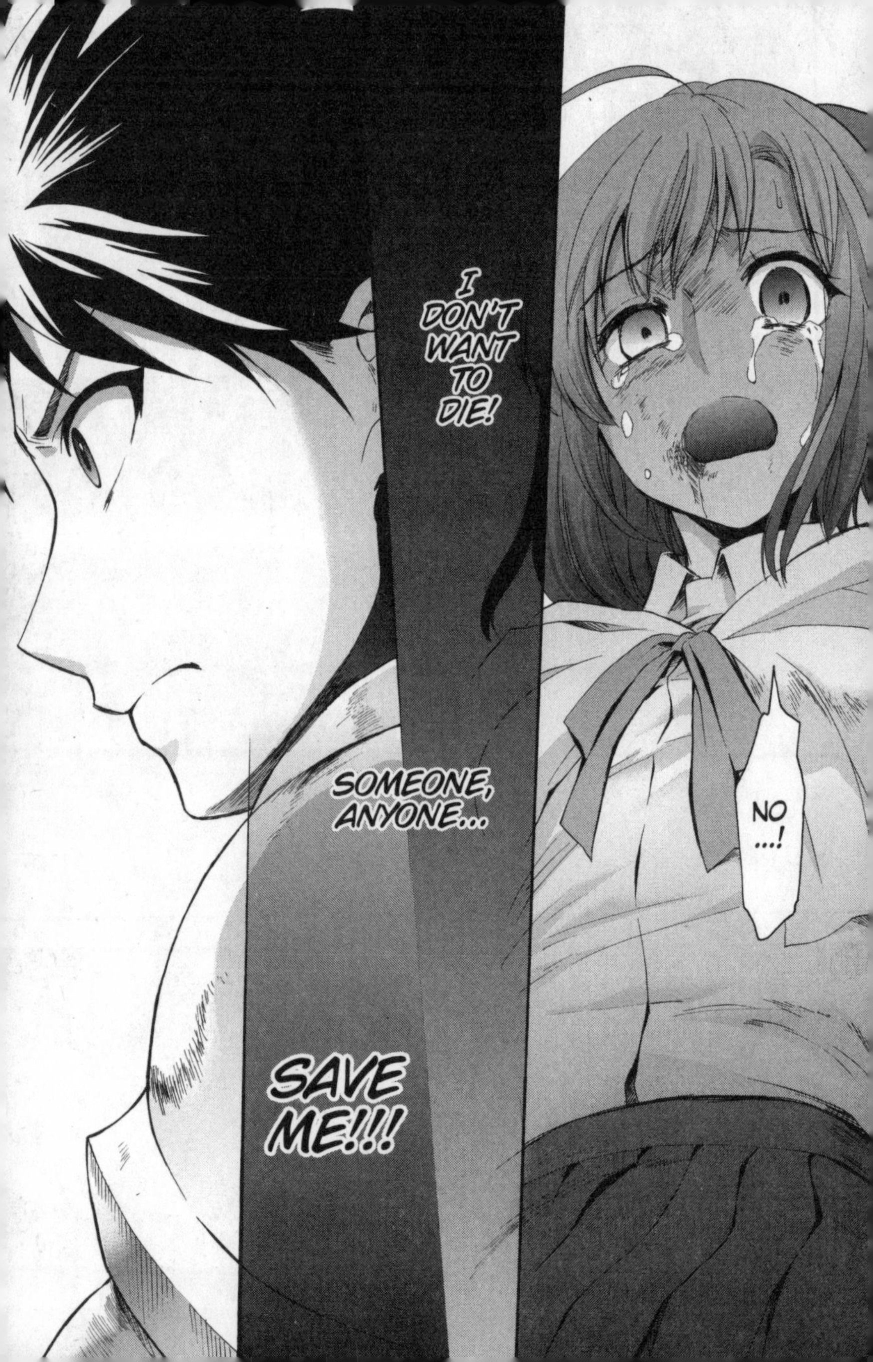
I DON'T WANT TO DIE!
NO ...!
SOMEONE, ANYONE...
SAVE ME!!!

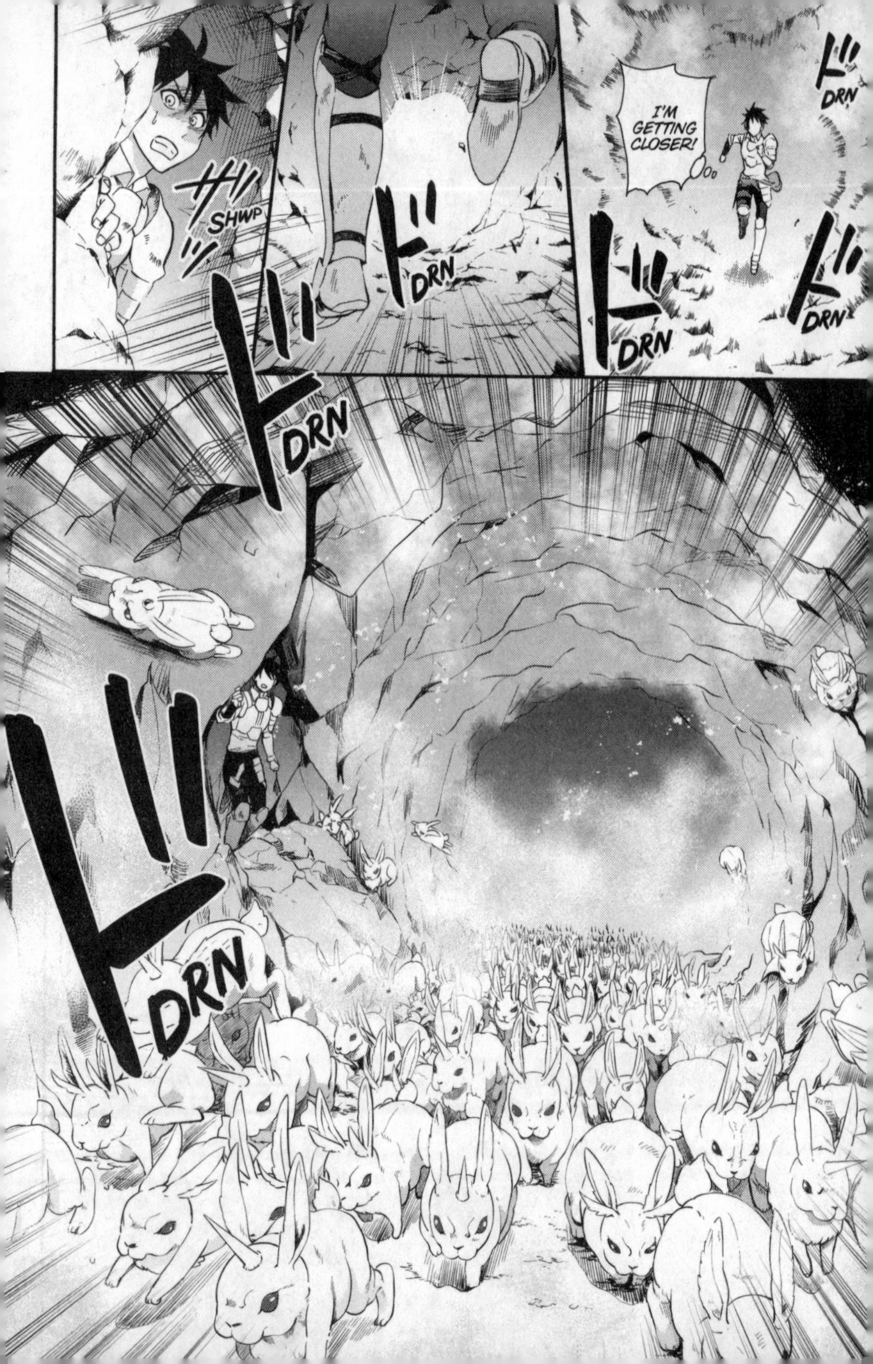
DRN
I'M GETTING CLOSER!
DRN
DRN
DRN
SHWP
DRN
DRN

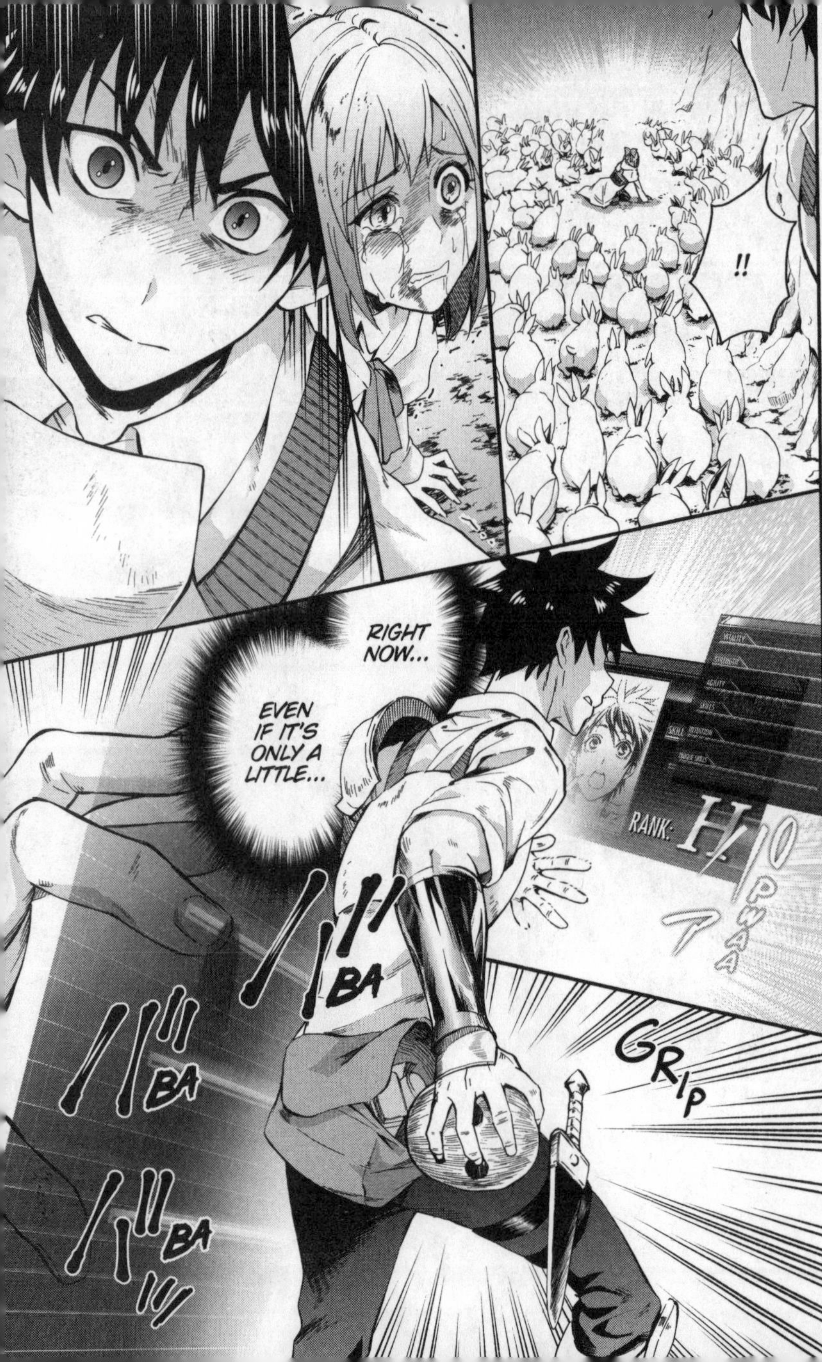
!!
RIGHT NOW...
EVEN IF IT'S ONLY A LITTLE...
RANK: H
PWAA
GRIP
BA
BA
BA

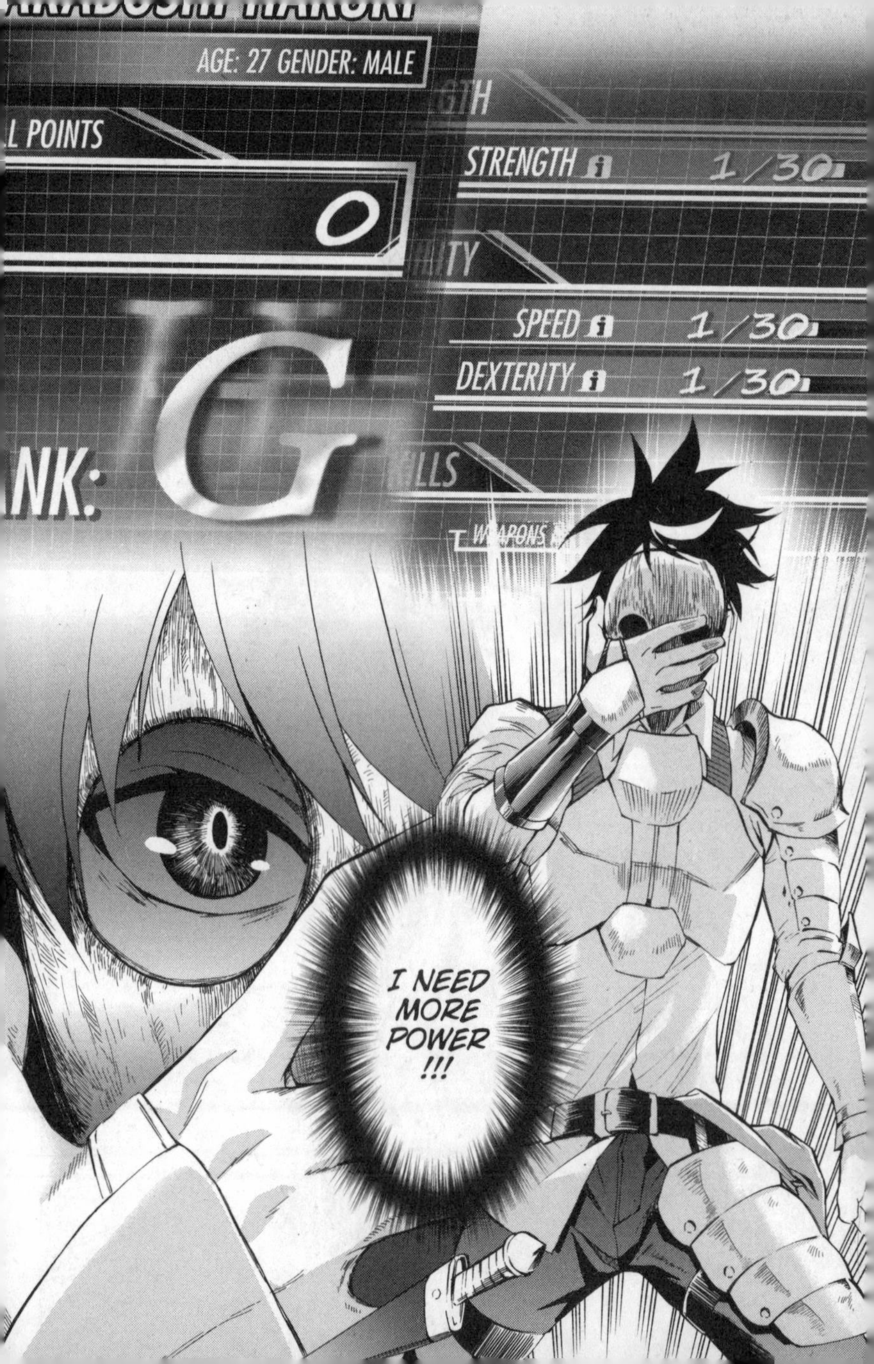
AGE: 27 GENDER: MALE
L POINTS
0
STRENGTH 1/30
SPEED 1/30
DEXTERITY 1/30
NK: G
I NEED MORE POWER !!!

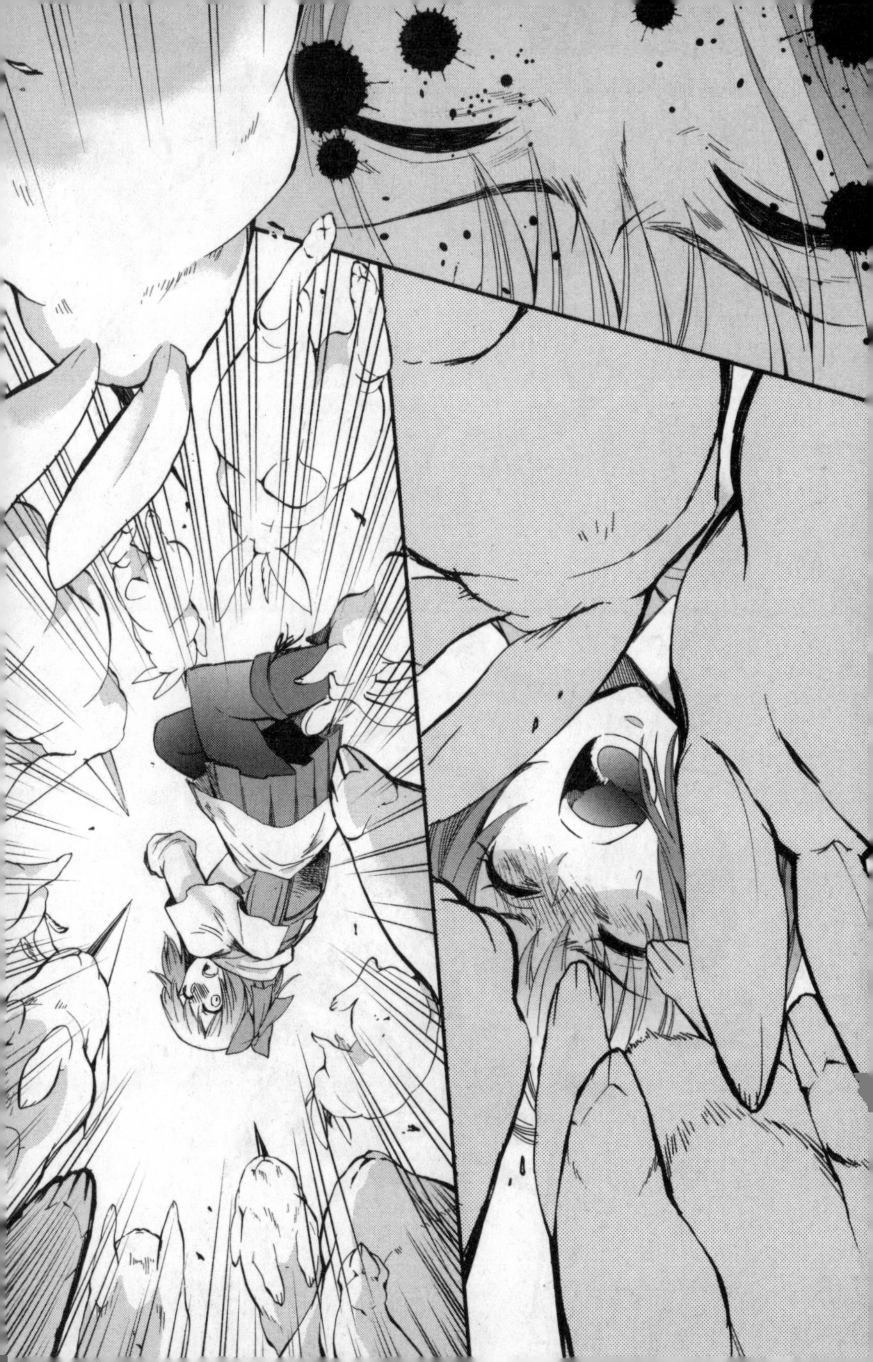

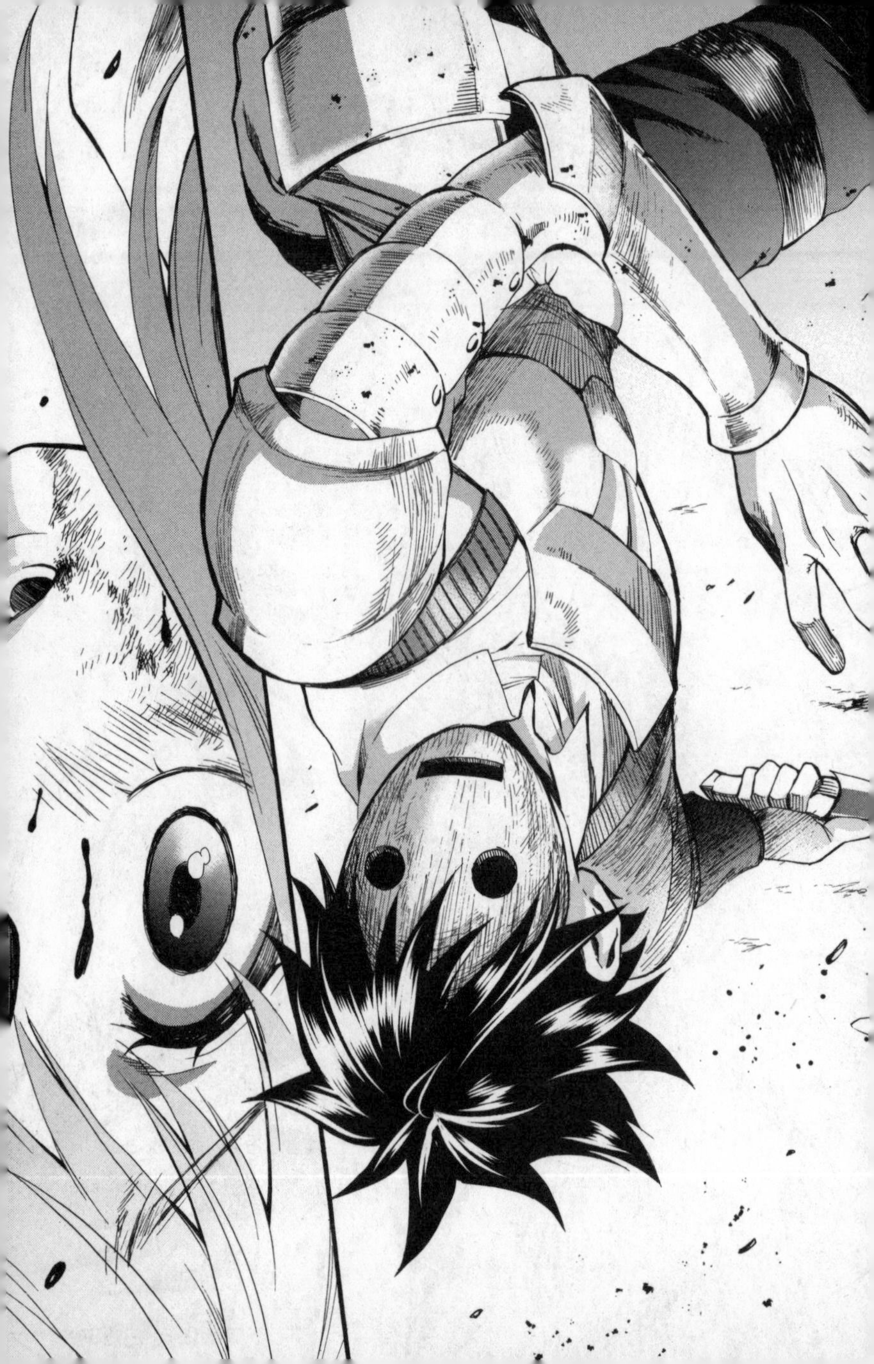

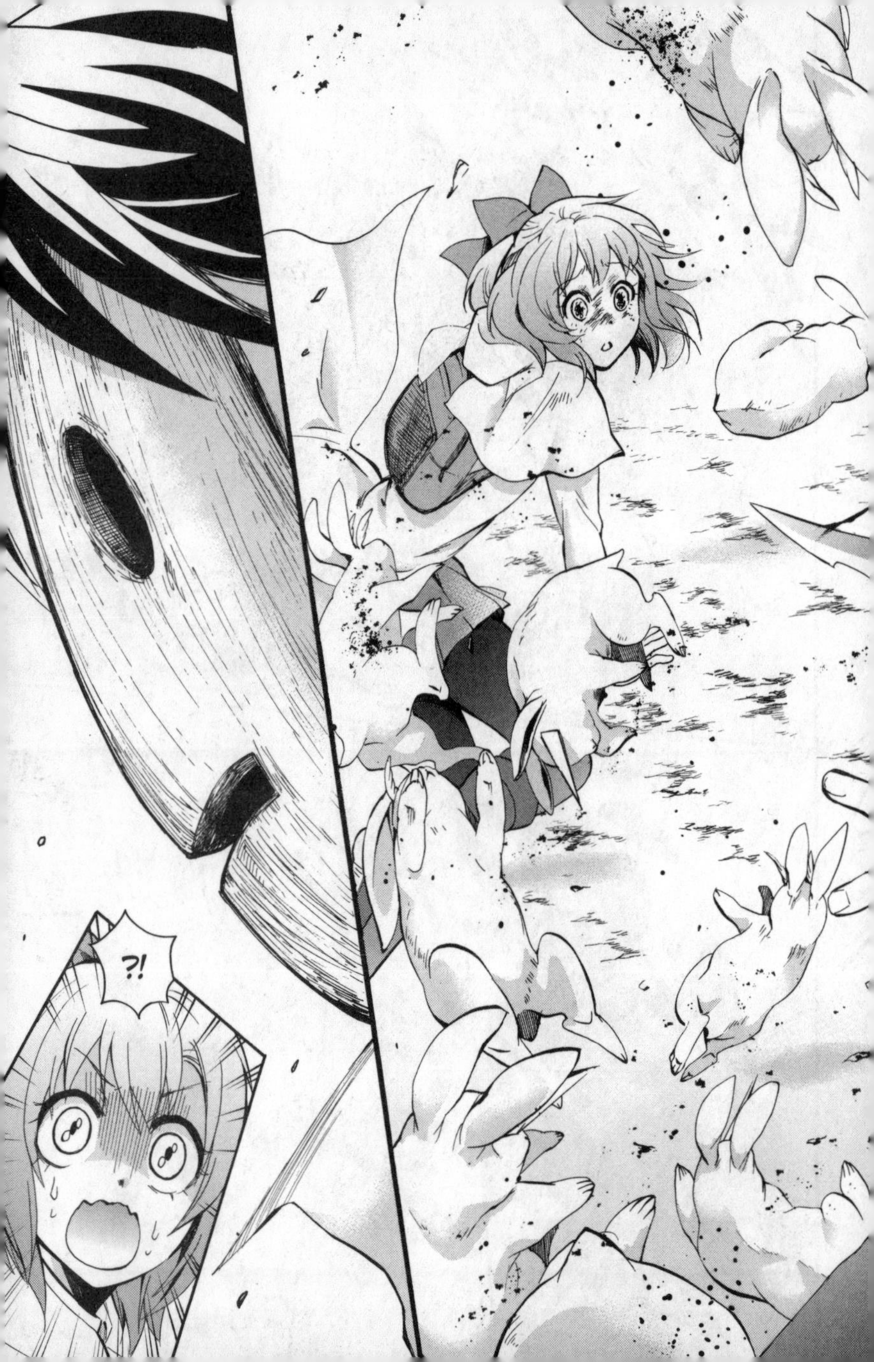
?!

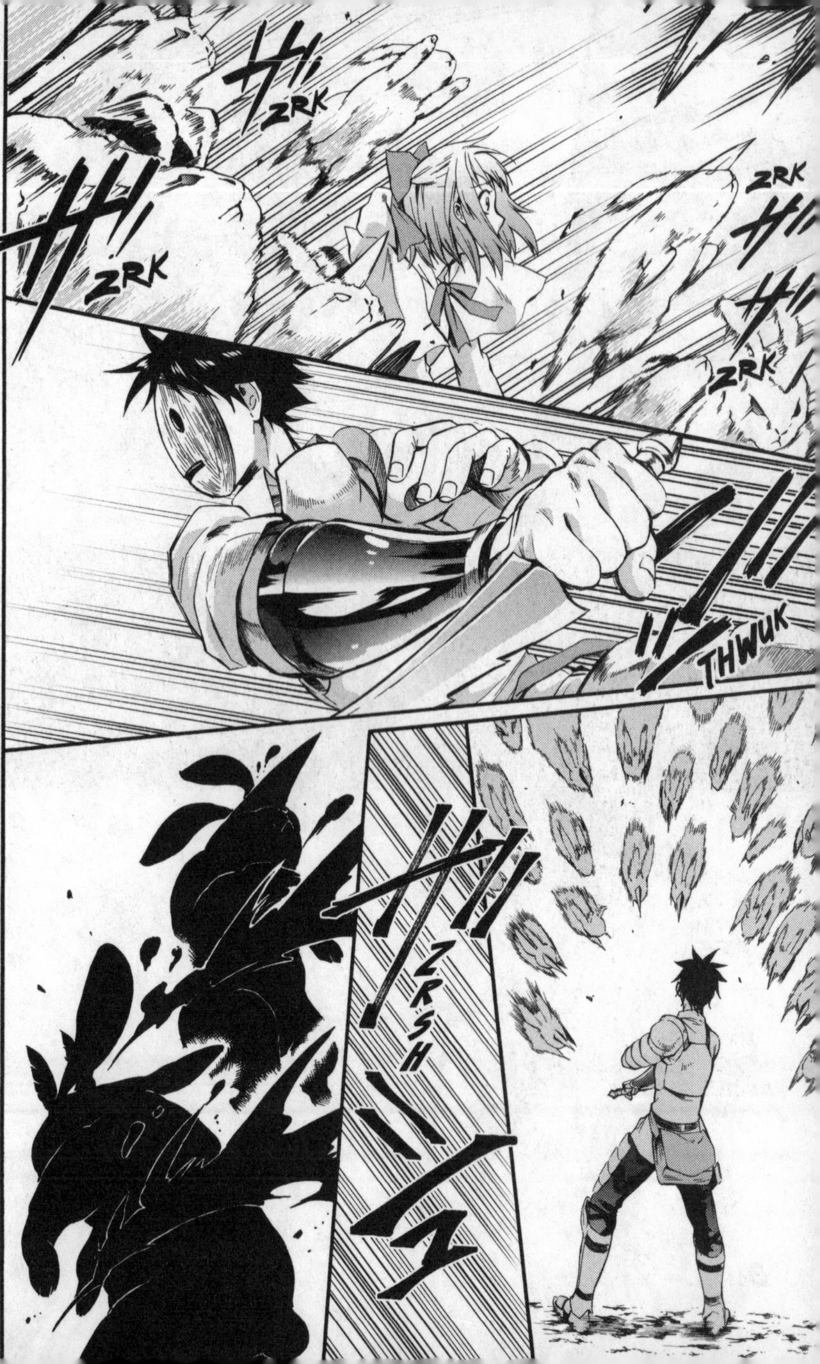
ZRK
ZRK
ZRK
ZRK
THWUK
ZRSH

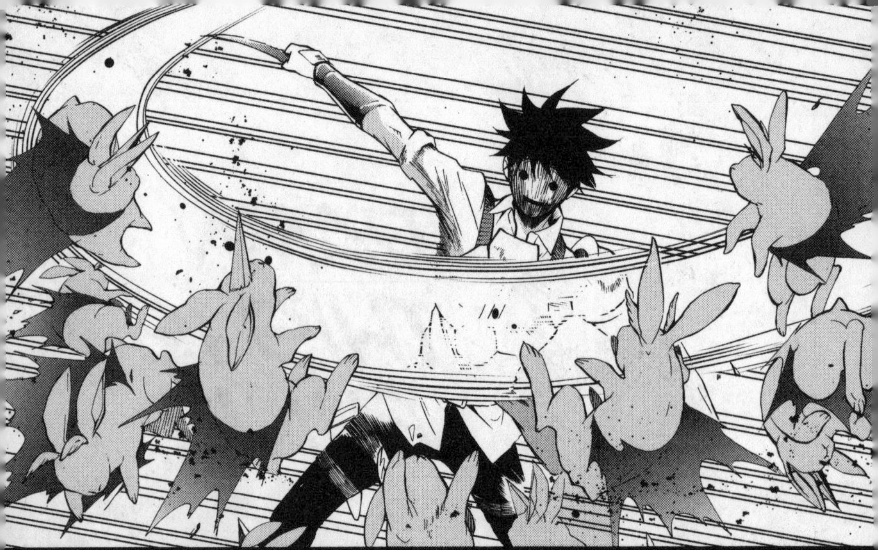

JUST ONE POINT.

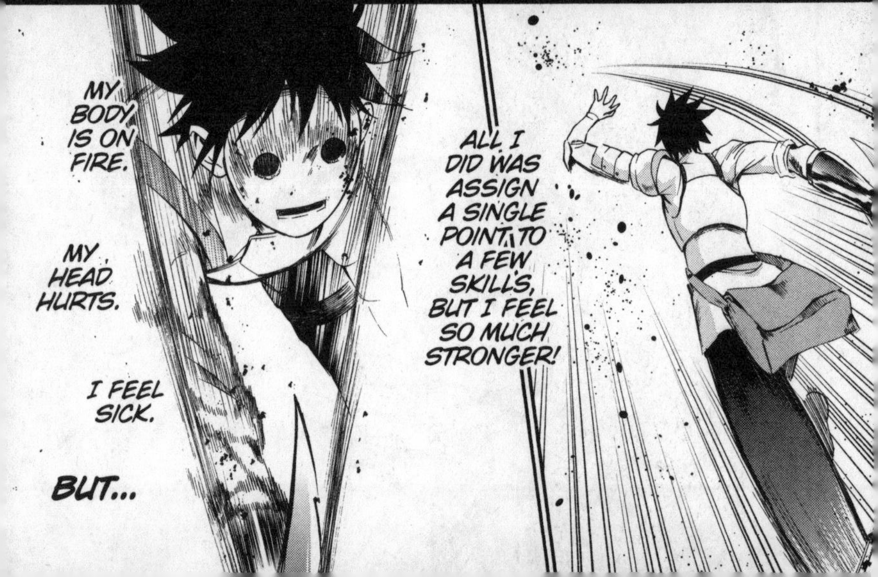
ALL I DID WAS ASSIGN A SINGLE POINT TO A FEW SKILLS, BUT I FEEL SO MUCH STRONGER!
MY BODY IS ON FIRE.
MY HEAD HURTS.
I FEEL SICK.
BUT...

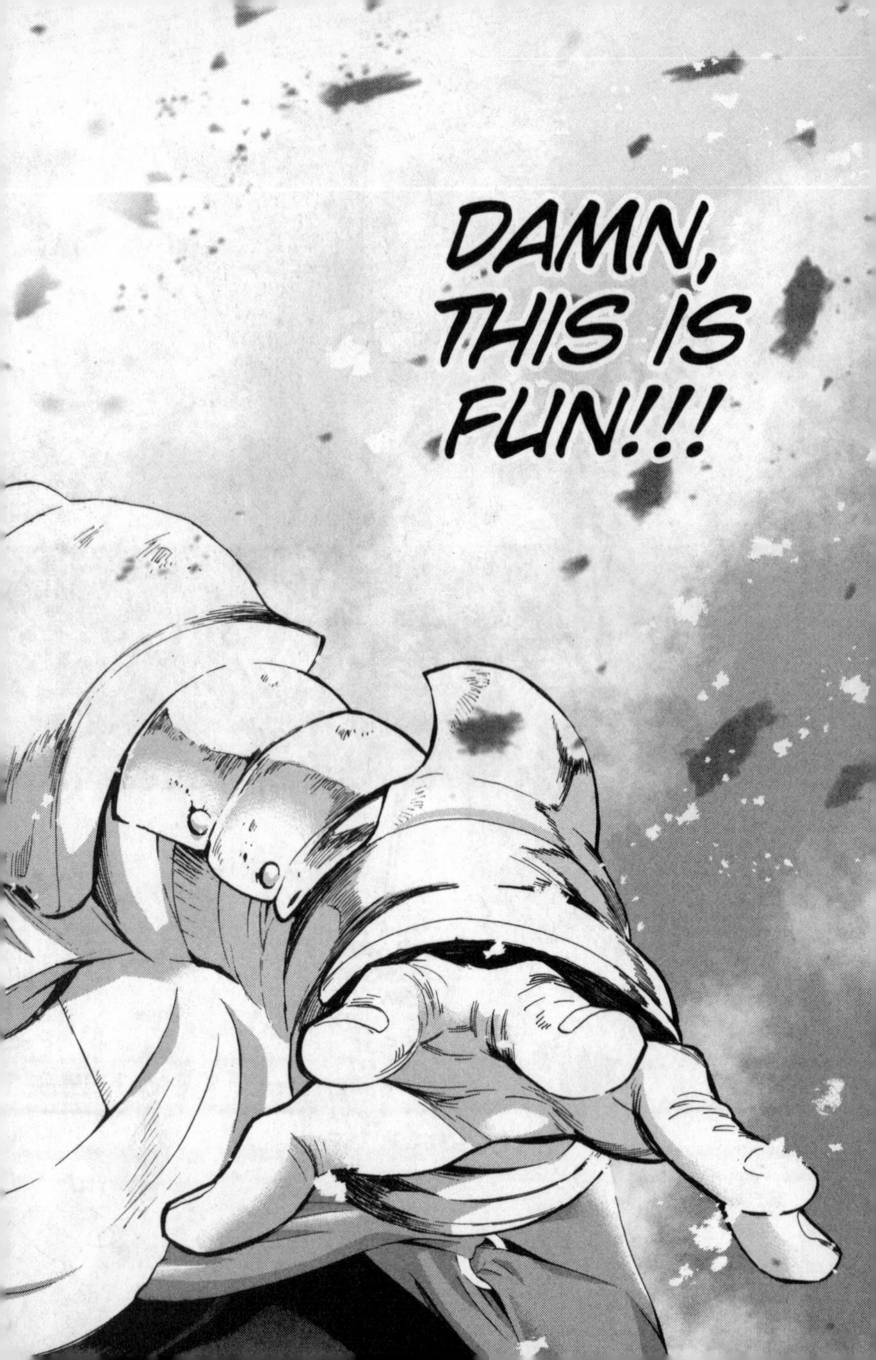
DAMN, THIS IS FUN!!!

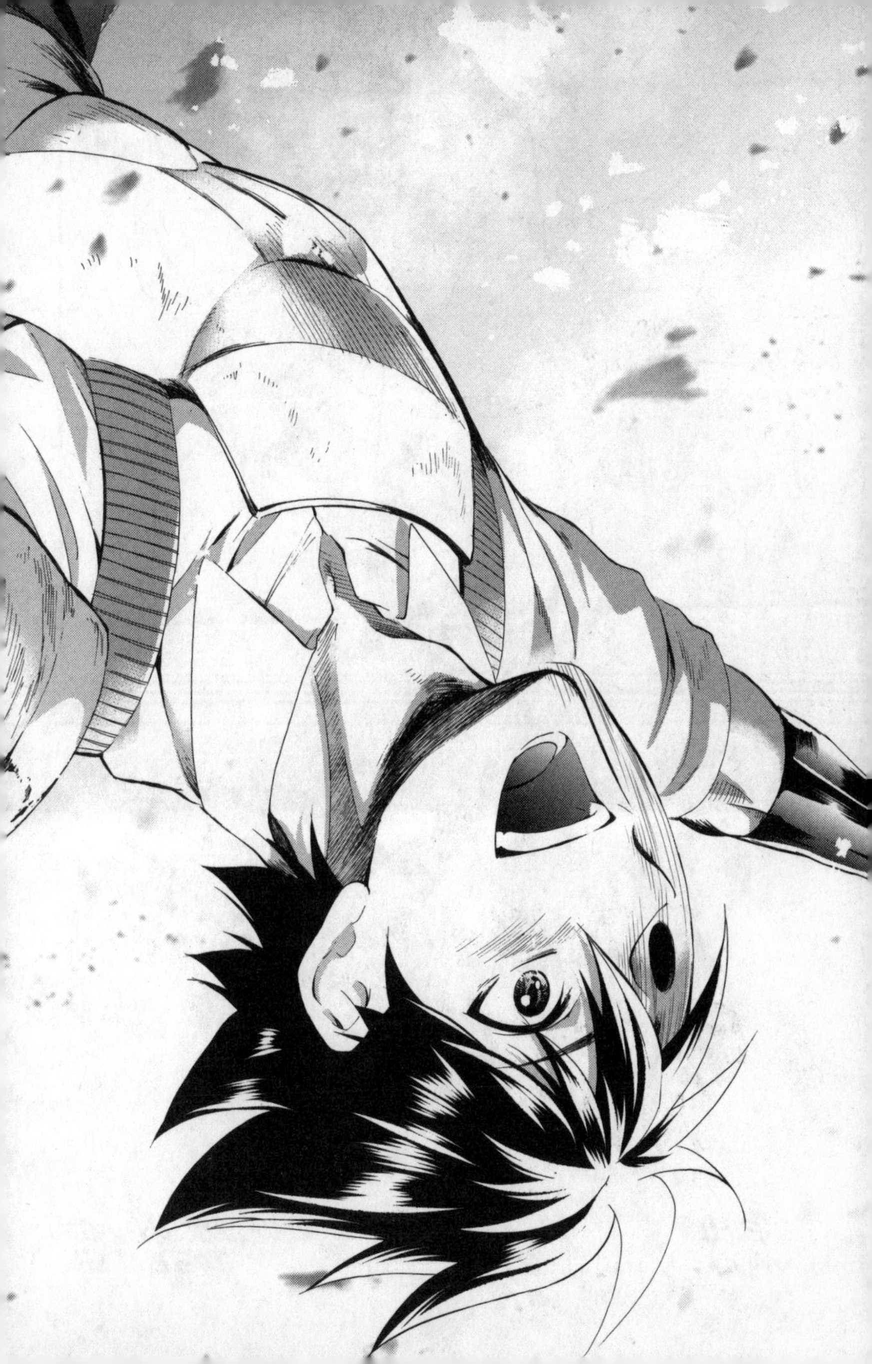

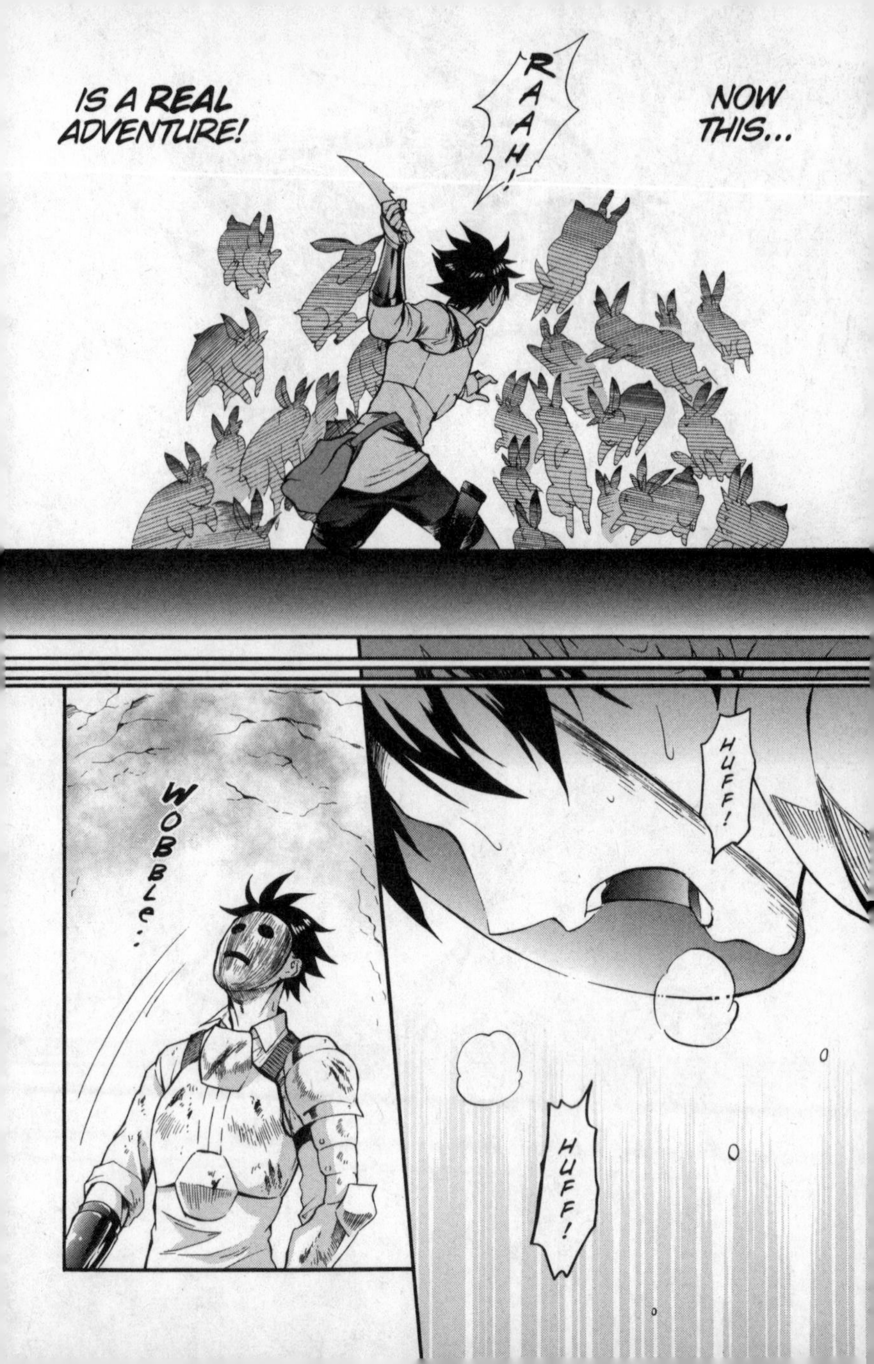
NOW THIS...
RAAH!
IS A REAL ADVENTURE!
HUFF!
HUFF!
WOBBLE...

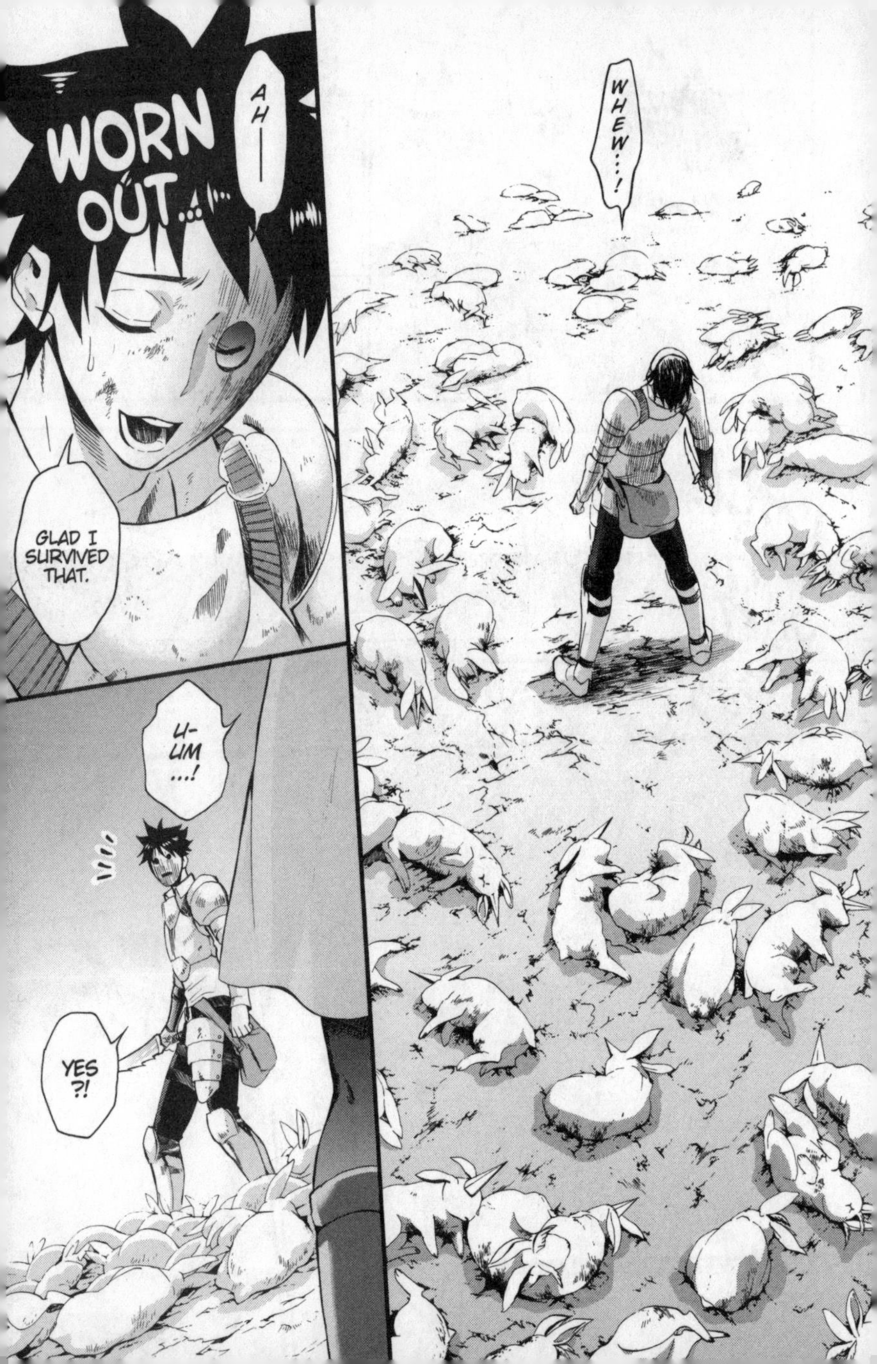
WHEW...!
AH—
WORN OUT...
GLAD I SURVIVED THAT.
U-UM...!
YES?!

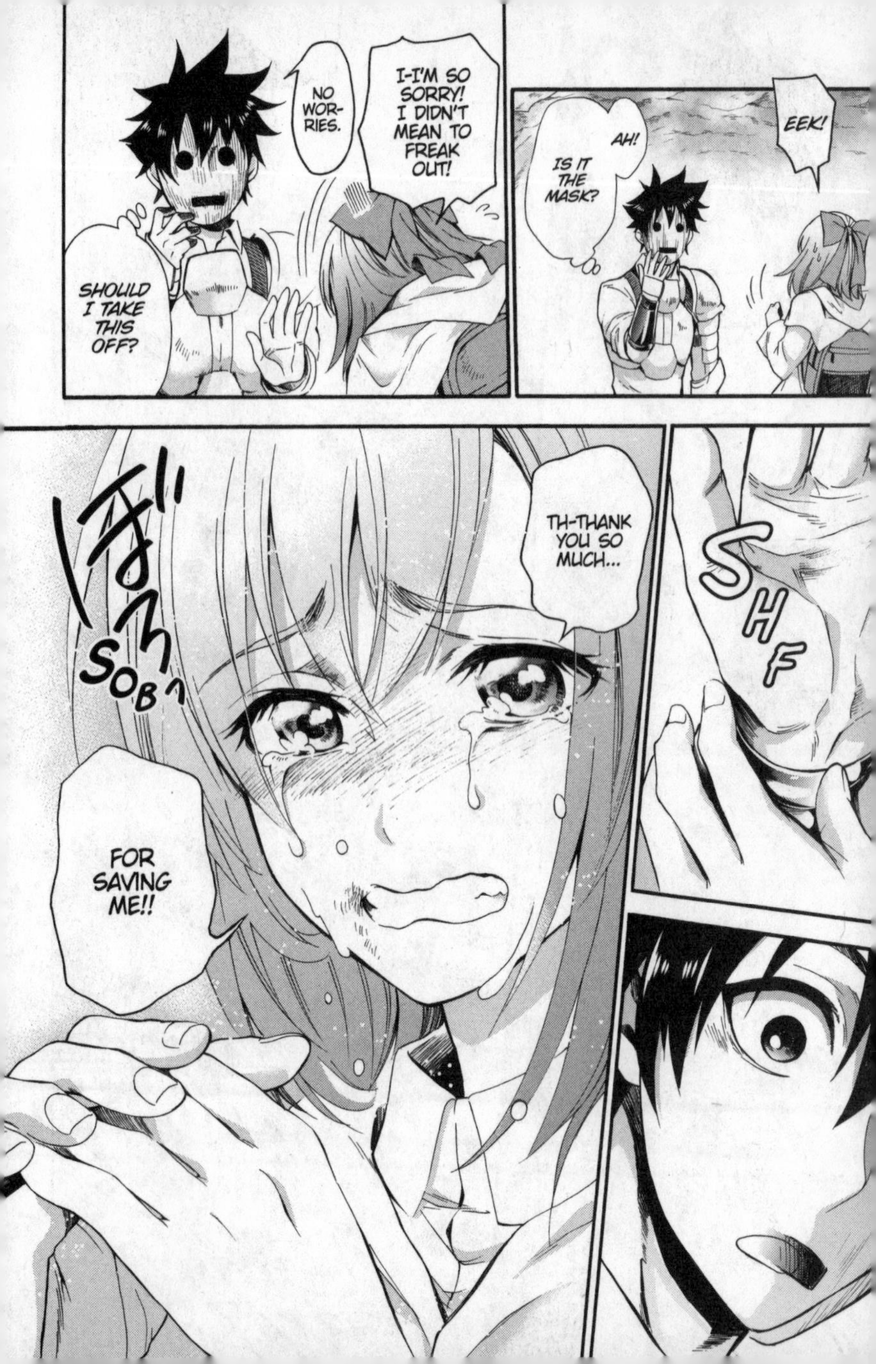
EEK!
AH! IS IT THE MASK?
I-I'M SO SORRY! I DIDN'T MEAN TO FREAK OUT!
NO WOR-RIES.
SHOULD I TAKE THIS OFF?
SHF
TH-THANK YOU SO MUCH...
SOB
FOR SAVING ME!!

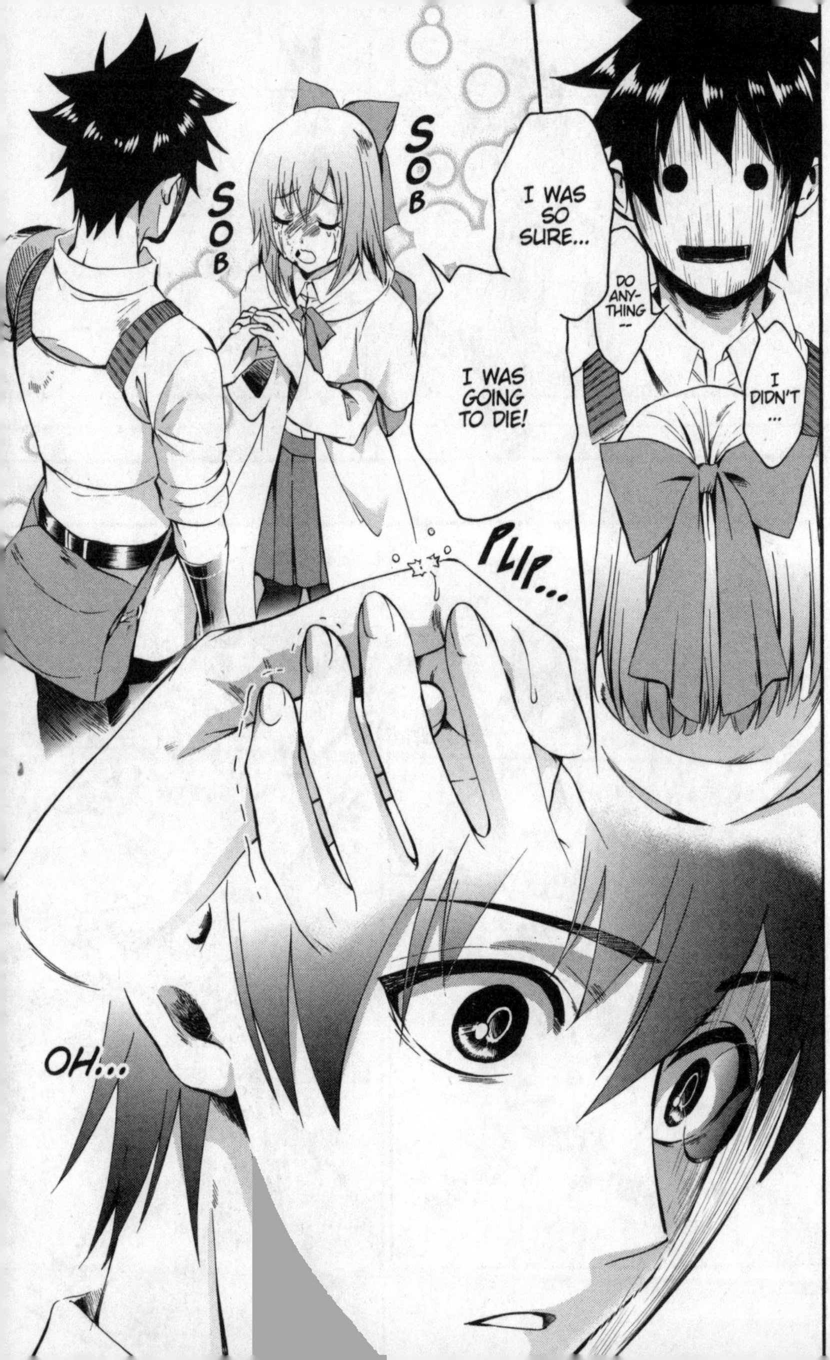
I DIDN'T ...
DO ANYTHING --
SOB SOB
I WAS SO SURE...
I WAS GOING TO DIE!
PLIP...
OH...

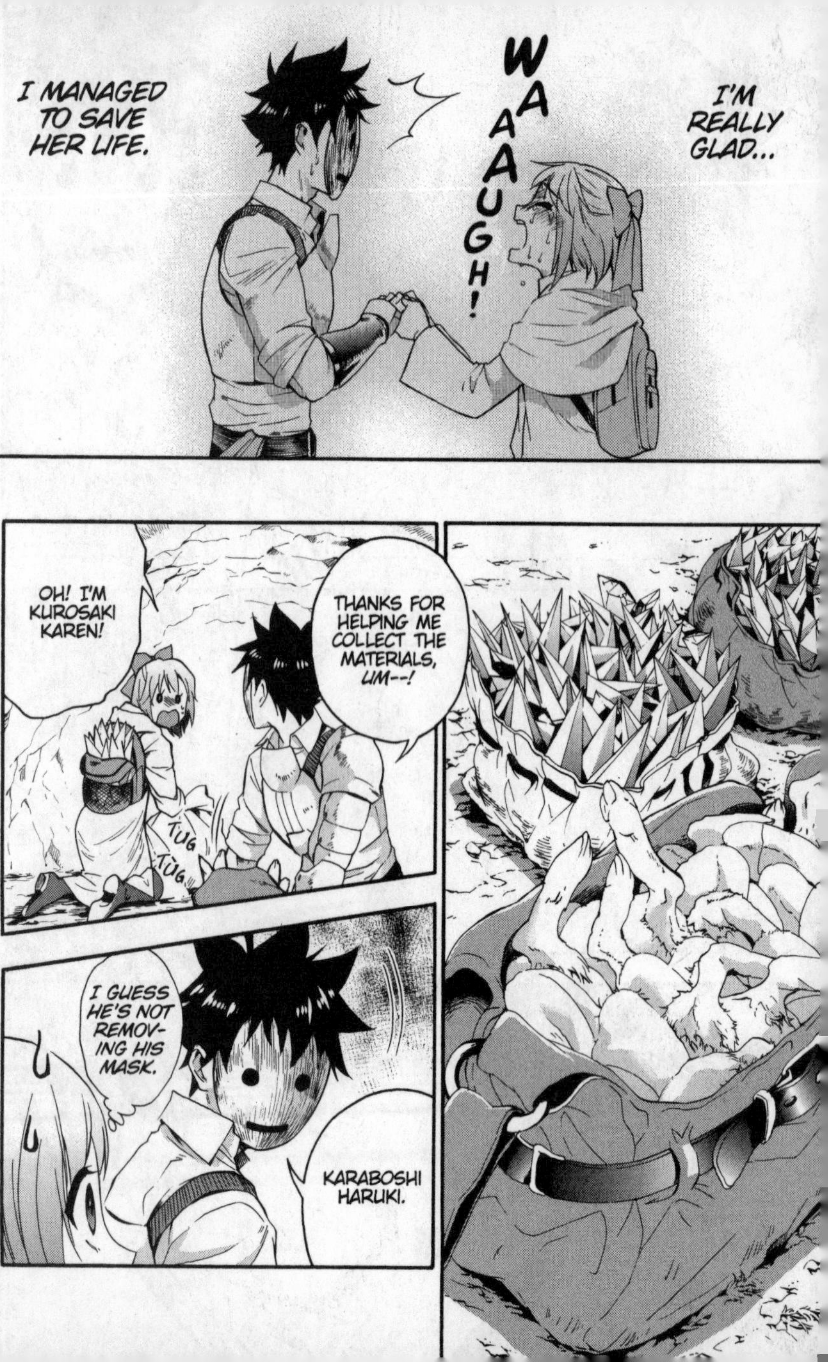
I'M REALLY GLAD...
WAAAUGH!
I MANAGED TO SAVE HER LIFE.
THANKS FOR HELPING ME COLLECT THE MATERIALS, UM--!
OH! I'M KUROSAKI KAREN!
TUG TUG
KARABOSHI HARUKI.
I GUESS HE'S NOT REMOV-ING HIS MASK.

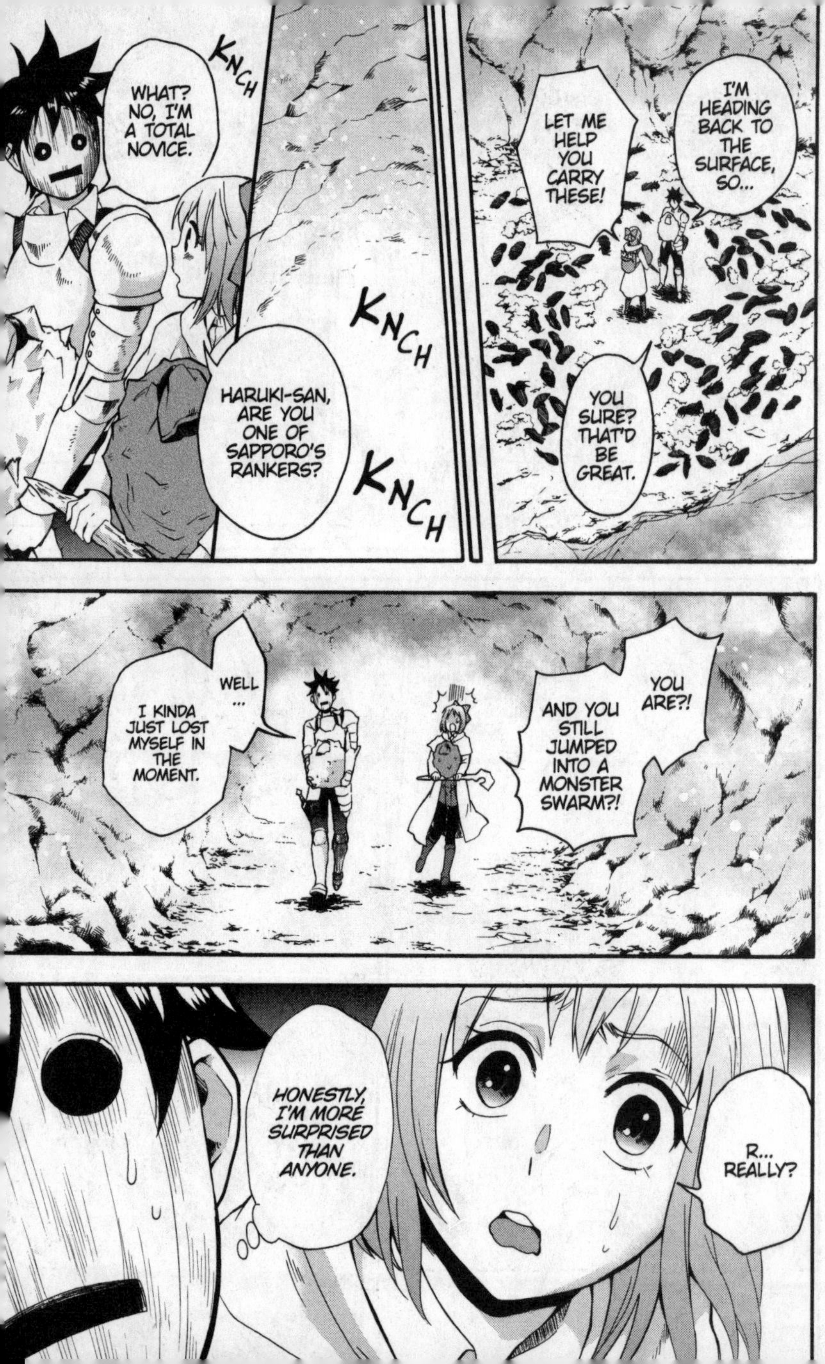
I'M HEADING BACK TO THE SURFACE, SO...
LET ME HELP YOU CARRY THESE!
YOU SURE? THAT'D BE GREAT.
KNCH
KNCH
HARUKI-SAN, ARE YOU ONE OF SAPPORO'S RANKERS?
KNCH
WHAT? NO, I'M A TOTAL NOVICE.
YOU ARE?!
AND YOU STILL JUMPED INTO A MONSTER SWARM?!
WELL ...
I KINDA JUST LOST MYSELF IN THE MOMENT.
R... REALLY?
HONESTLY, I'M MORE SURPRISED THAN ANYONE.

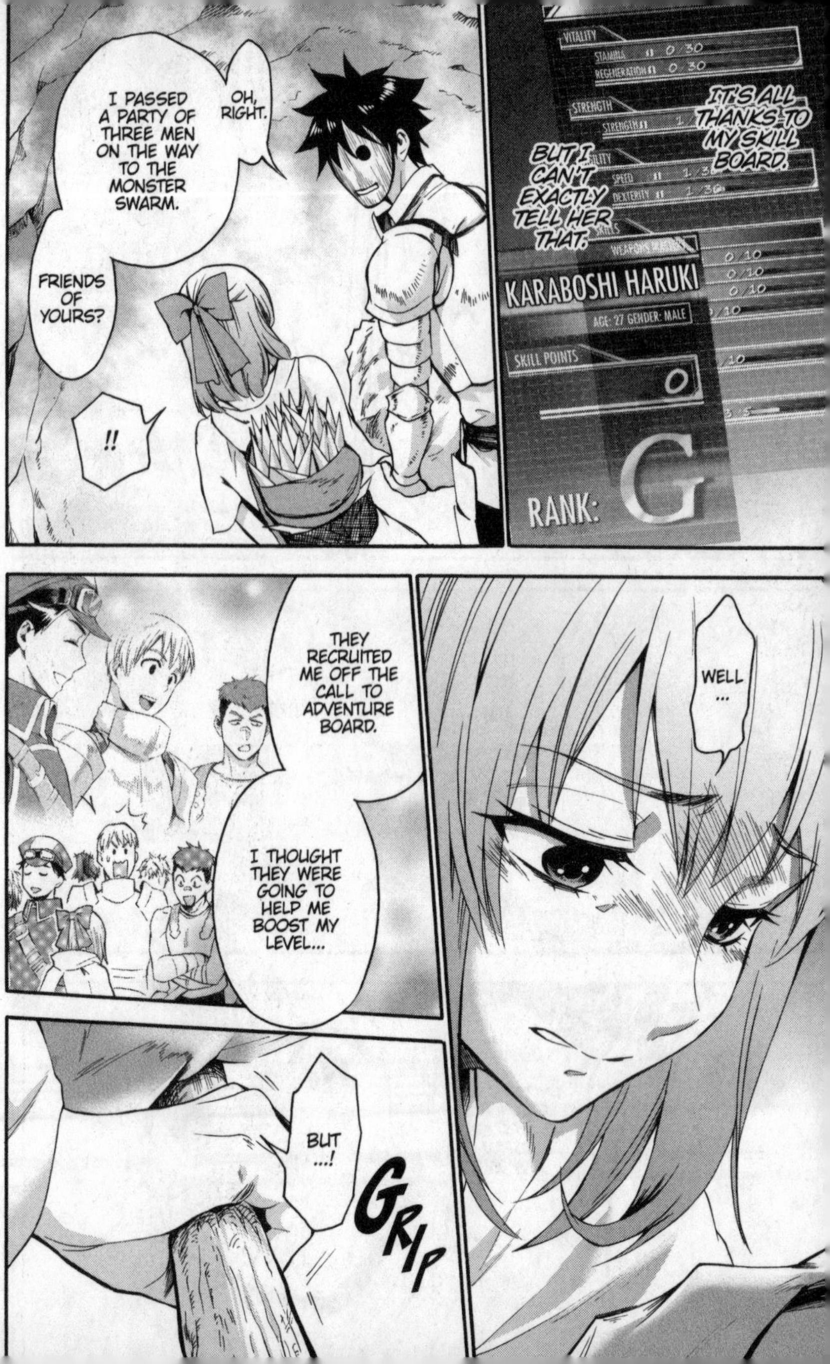
VITALITY
STAMINA 0/30
REGENERATION 0/30
STRENGTH
STRENGTH
SPEED
DEXTERITY
IT'S ALL THANKS TO MY SKILL BOARD.
BUT I CAN'T EXACTLY TELL HER THAT.
KARABOSHI HARUKI
AGE: 27 GENDER: MALE
SKILL POINTS
0
RANK: G
OH, RIGHT.
I PASSED A PARTY OF THREE MEN ON THE WAY TO THE MONSTER SWARM.
FRIENDS OF YOURS?
!!
WELL ...
THEY RECRUITED ME OFF THE CALL TO ADVENTURE BOARD.
I THOUGHT THEY WERE GOING TO HELP ME BOOST MY LEVEL...
BUT ...!
GRIP

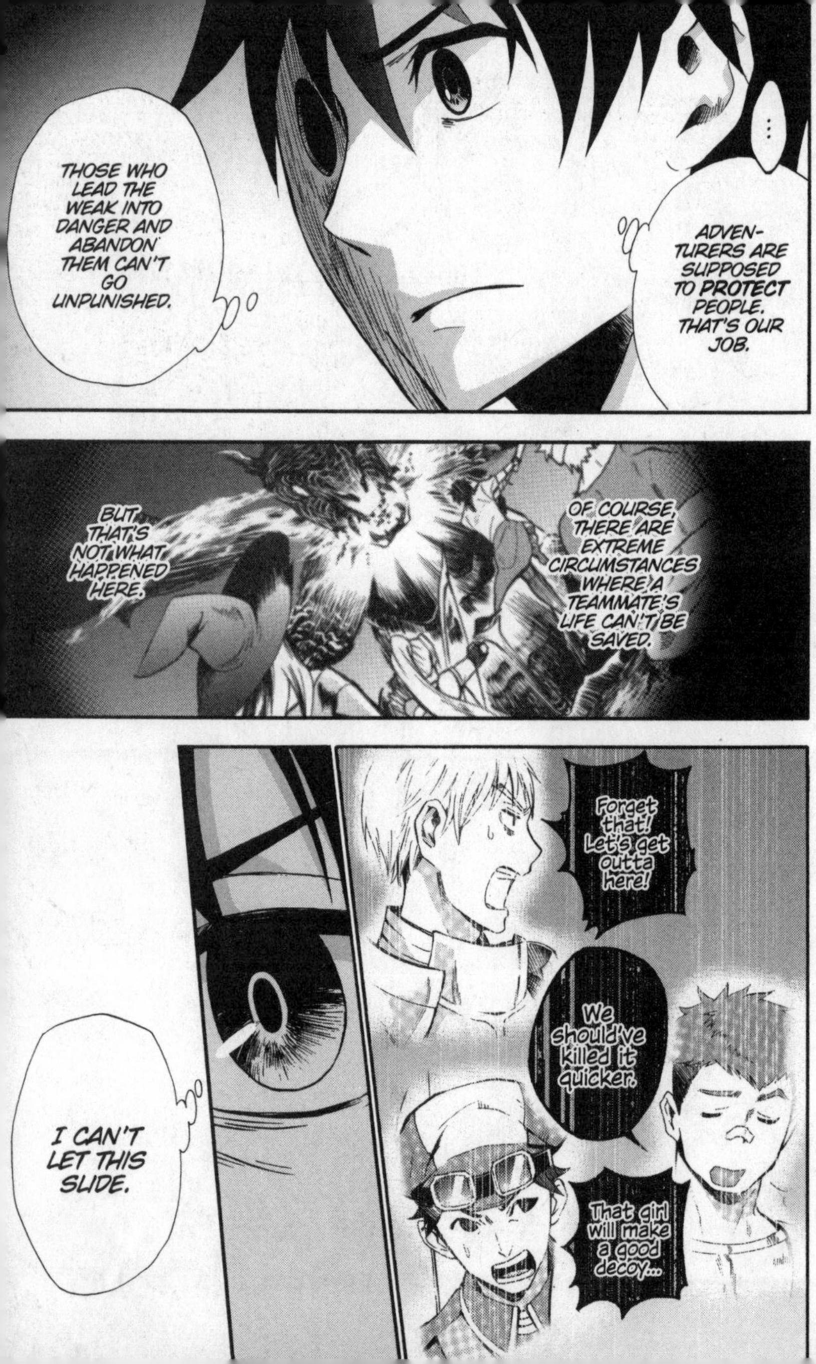
...
ADVEN-TURERS ARE SUPPOSED TO PROTECT PEOPLE. THAT'S OUR JOB.
THOSE WHO LEAD THE WEAK INTO DANGER AND ABANDON THEM CAN'T GO UNPUNISHED.
OF COURSE, THERE ARE EXTREME CIRCUMSTANCES WHERE A TEAMMATE'S LIFE CAN'T BE SAVED.
BUT THAT'S NOT WHAT HAPPENED HERE.
Forget that! Let's get outta here!
We should've killed it quicker.
That girl will make a good decoy...
I CAN'T LET THIS SLIDE.

CALL TO ADVENTURE!

DEFEATING DUNGEONS
WITH A SKILL BOARD

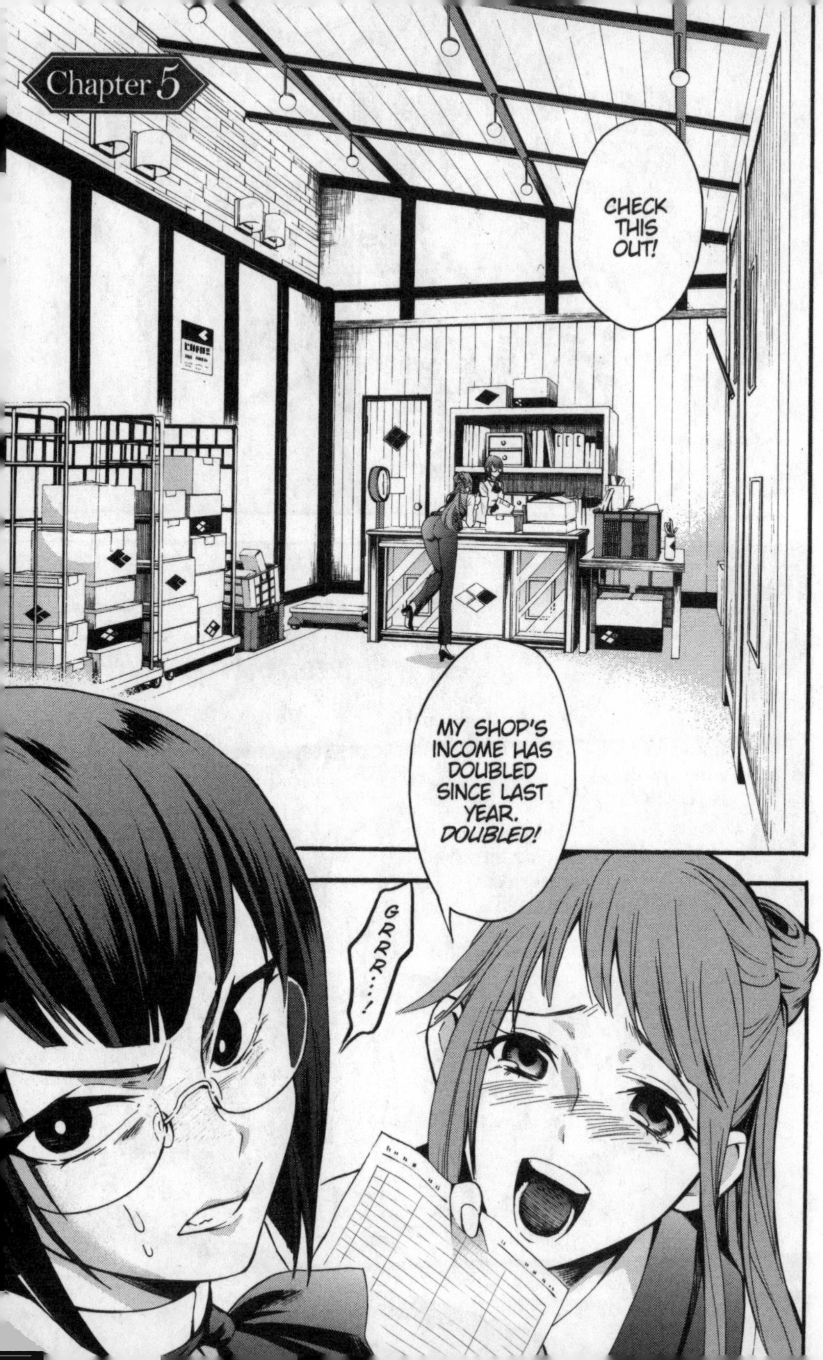
Chapter 5
CHECK THIS OUT!
MY SHOP'S INCOME HAS DOUBLED SINCE LAST YEAR. DOUBLED!
GRRR...!

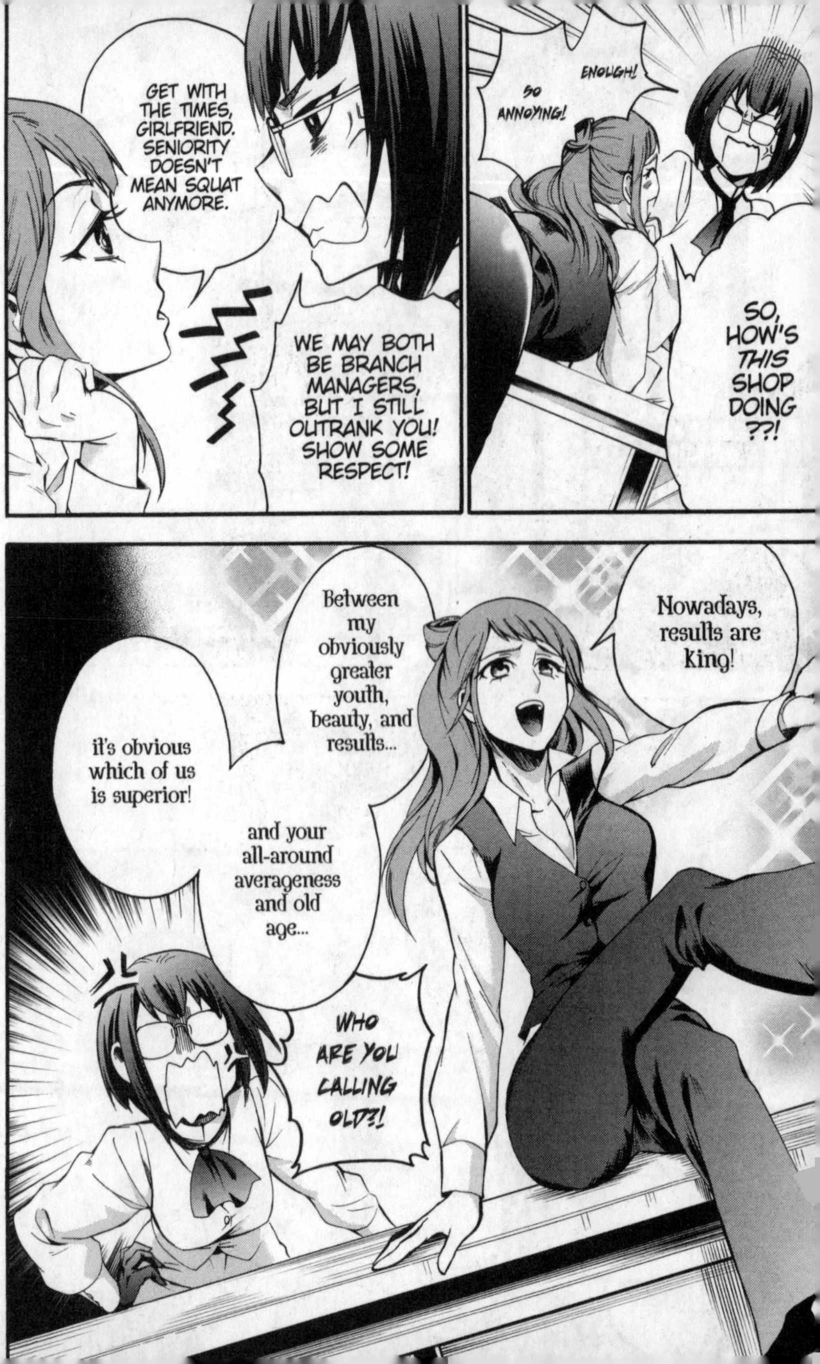
SO, HOW'S THIS SHOP DOING ??!
ENOUGH!
SO ANNOYING!
GET WITH THE TIMES, GIRLFRIEND. SENIORITY DOESN'T MEAN SQUAT ANYMORE.
WE MAY BOTH BE BRANCH MANAGERS, BUT I STILL OUTRANK YOU! SHOW SOME RESPECT!
Nowadays, results are King!
Between my obviously greater youth, beauty, and results...
and your all-around averageness and old age...
it's obvious which of us is superior!
WHO ARE YOU CALLING OLD?!

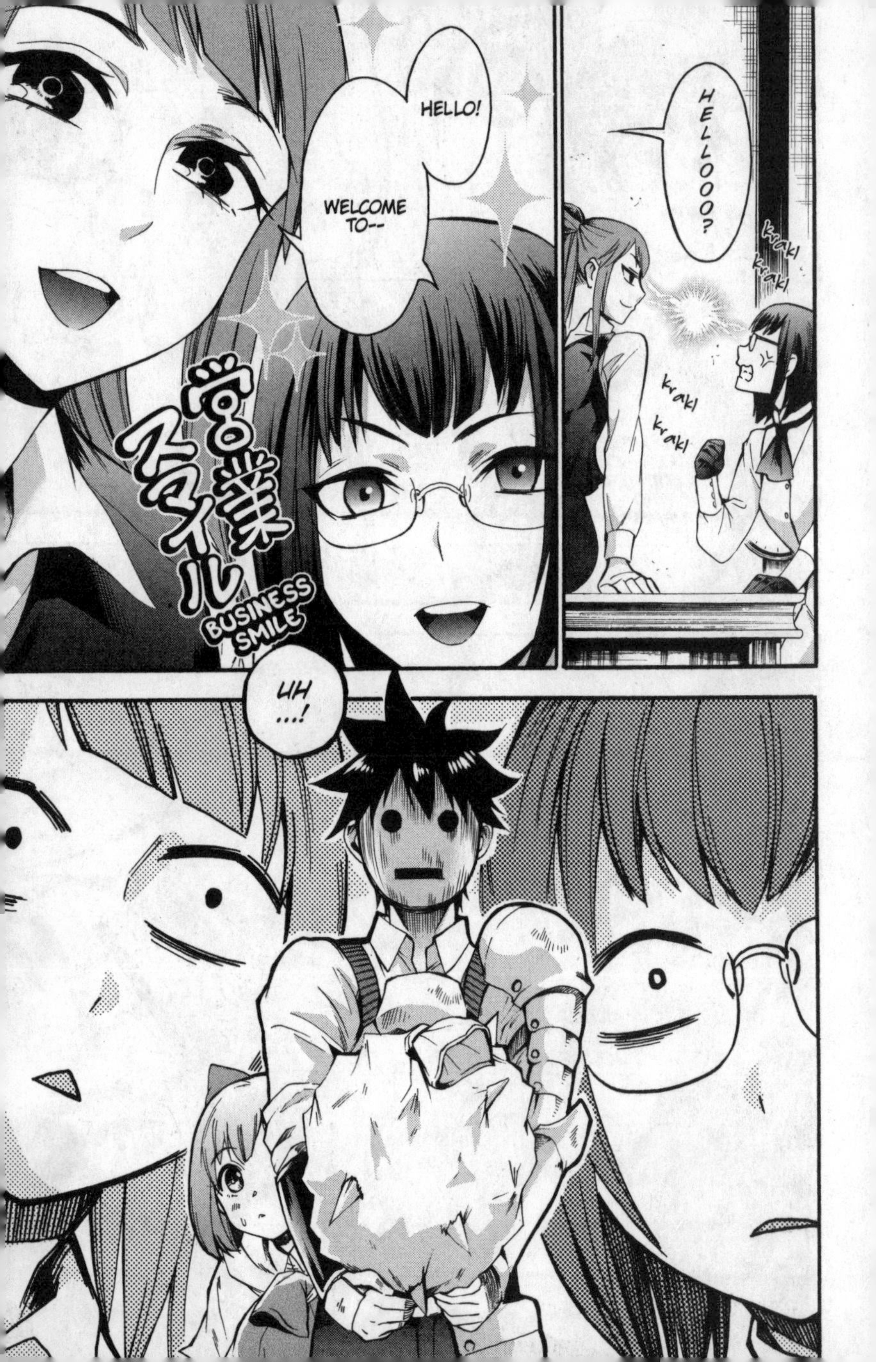
HELLOOO?
kraki kraki
kraki kraki
HELLO!
WELCOME TO--
営業スマイル
BUSINESS SMILE
UH ...!

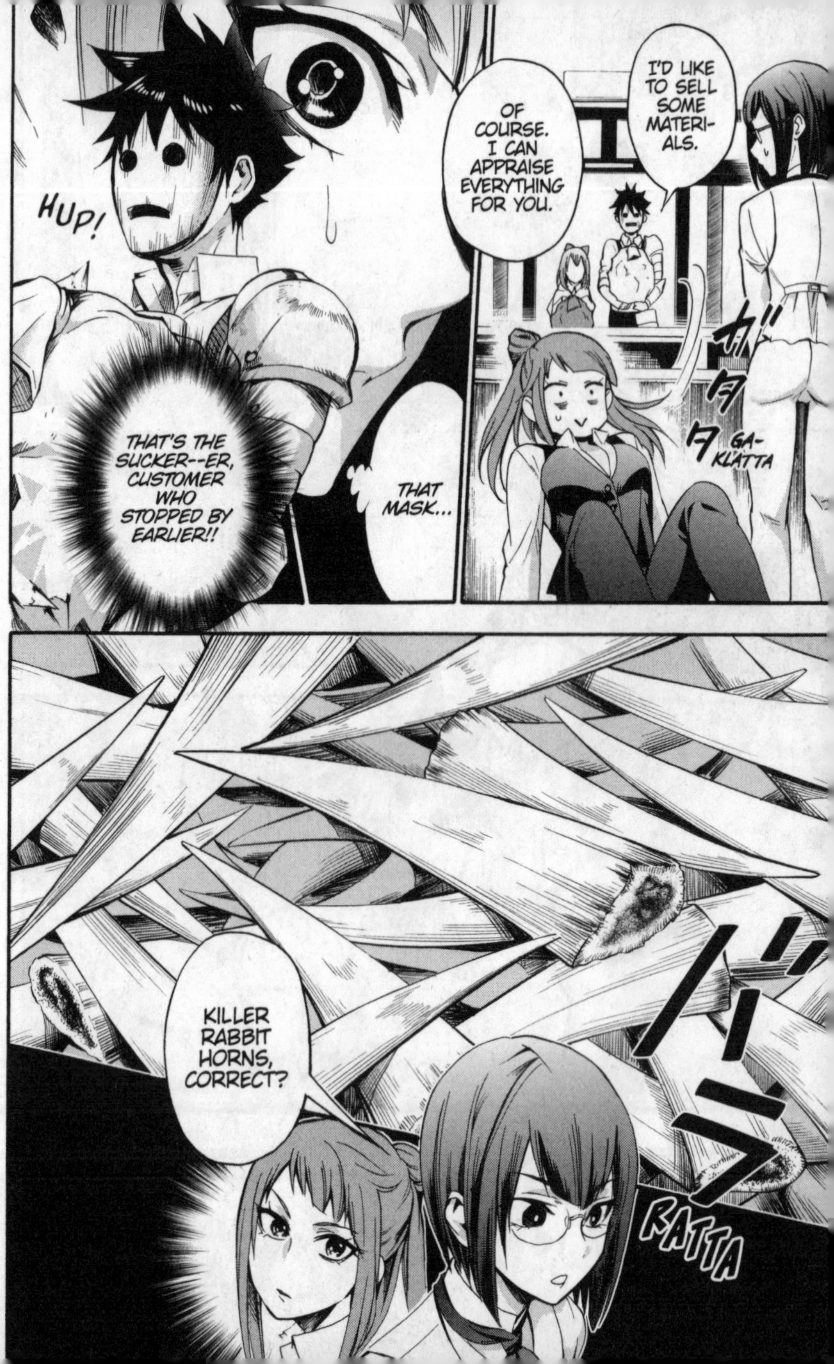
I'D LIKE TO SELL SOME MATERI-ALS.
OF COURSE. I CAN APPRAISE EVERYTHING FOR YOU.
GA-KLÄTTA
THAT MASK...
HUP!
THAT'S THE SUCKER--ER, CUSTOMER WHO STOPPED BY EARLIER!!
RATTA
KILLER RABBIT HORNS, CORRECT?

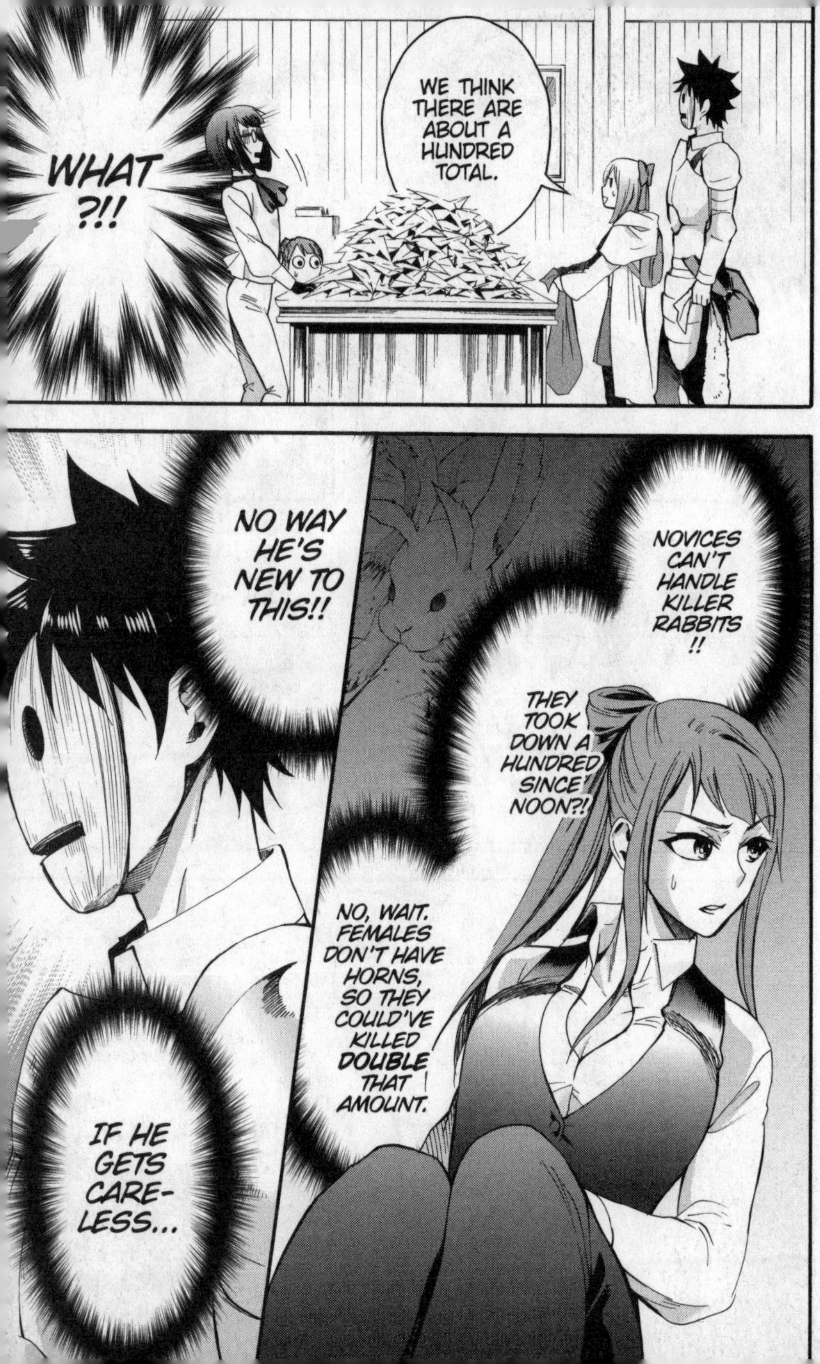
WE THINK THERE ARE ABOUT A HUNDRED TOTAL.
WHAT ?!!
NOVICES CAN'T HANDLE KILLER RABBITS !!
NO WAY HE'S NEW TO THIS!!
THEY TOOK DOWN A HUNDRED SINCE NOON?!
NO, WAIT. FEMALES DON'T HAVE HORNS, SO THEY COULD'VE KILLED DOUBLE THAT AMOUNT.
IF HE GETS CARE-LESS...

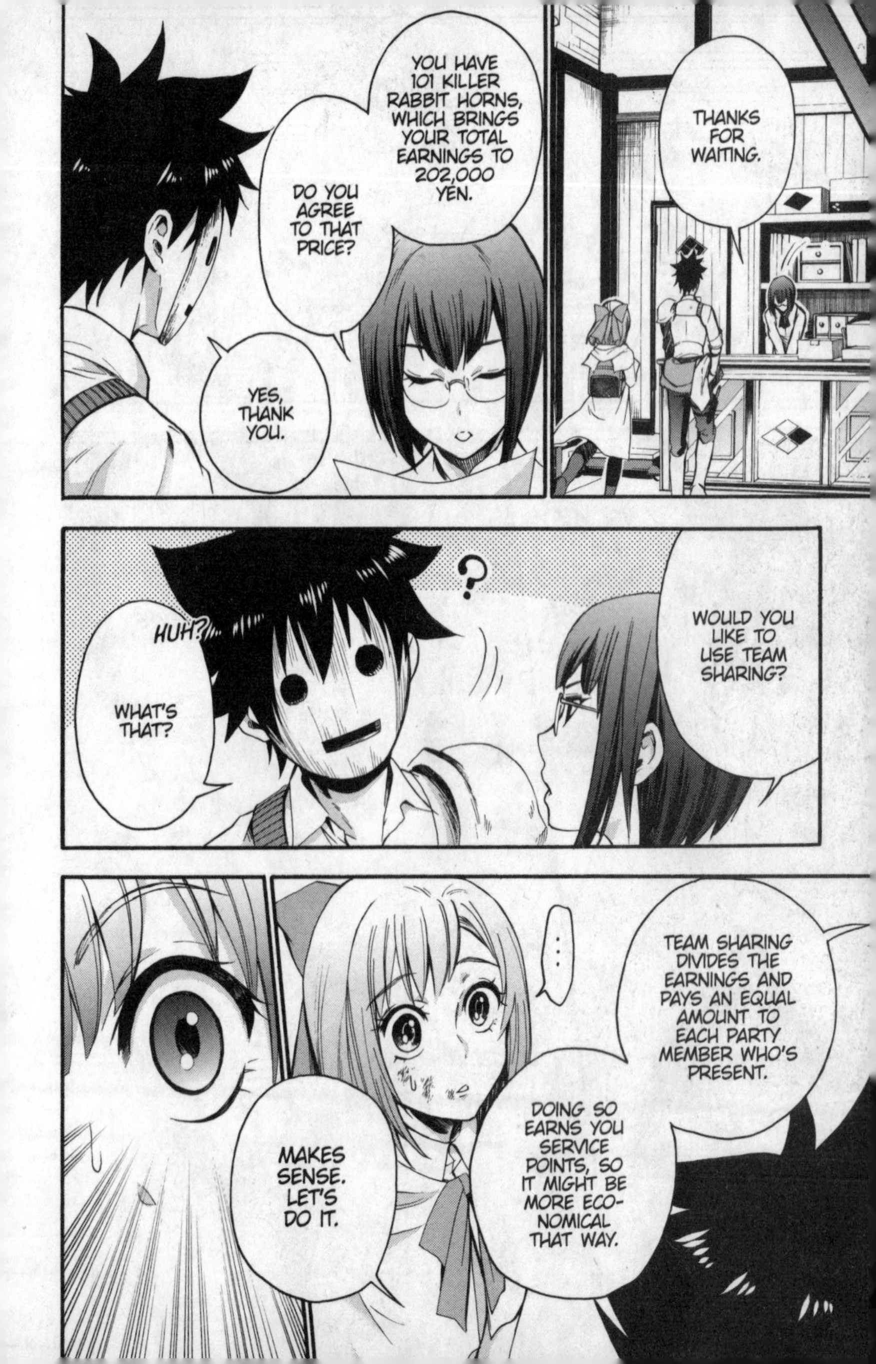
THANKS FOR WAITING.
YOU HAVE 101 KILLER RABBIT HORNS, WHICH BRINGS YOUR TOTAL EARNINGS TO 202,000 YEN.
DO YOU AGREE TO THAT PRICE?
YES, THANK YOU.
WOULD YOU LIKE TO USE TEAM SHARING?
?
HUH?
WHAT'S THAT?
TEAM SHARING DIVIDES THE EARNINGS AND PAYS AN EQUAL AMOUNT TO EACH PARTY MEMBER WHO'S PRESENT.
DOING SO EARNS YOU SERVICE POINTS, SO IT MIGHT BE MORE ECO-NOMICAL THAT WAY.
...
MAKES SENSE. LET'S DO IT.

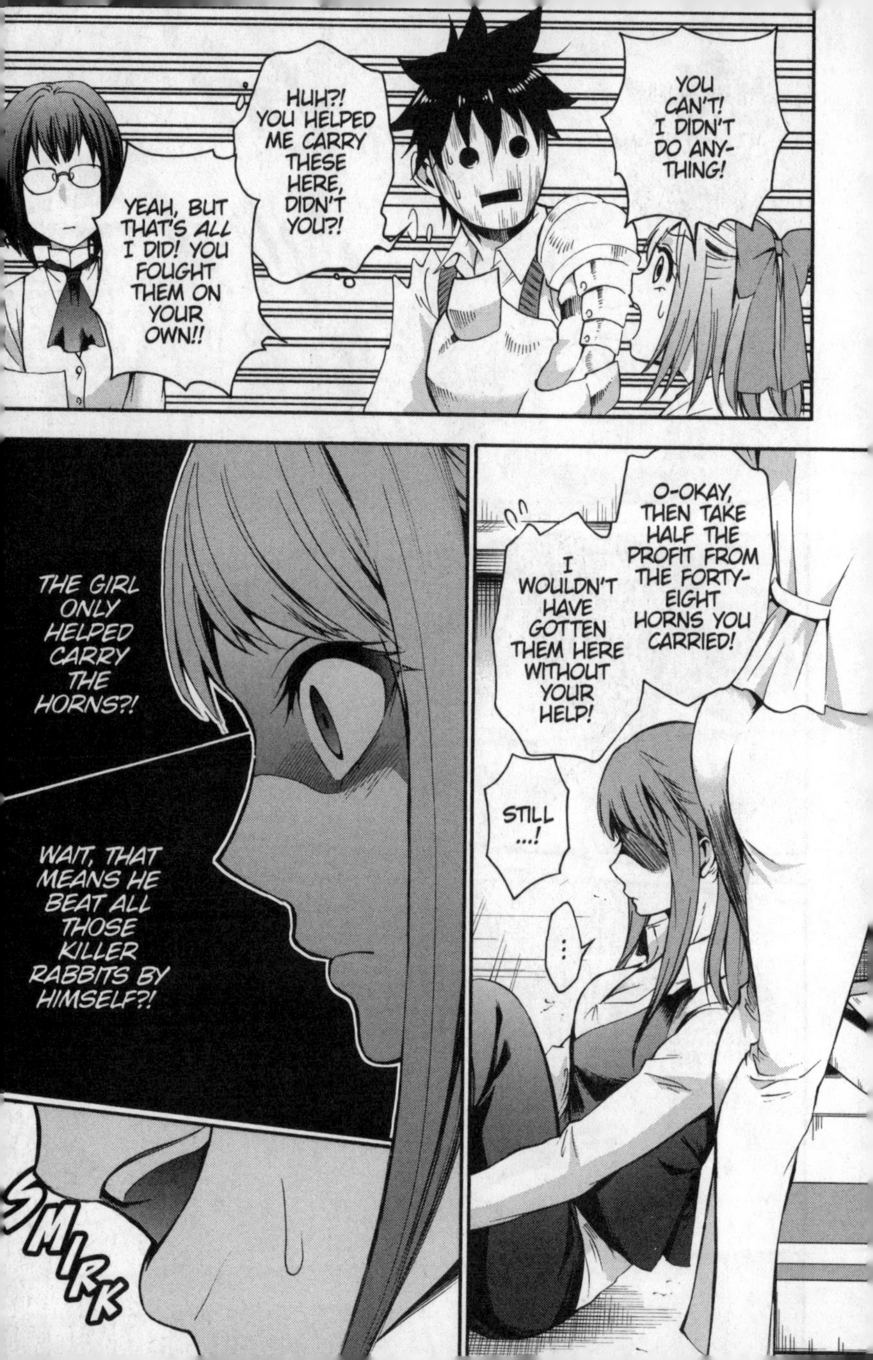
YOU CAN'T! I DIDN'T DO ANY-THING!
HUH?! YOU HELPED ME CARRY THESE HERE, DIDN'T YOU?!
YEAH, BUT THAT'S ALL I DID! YOU FOUGHT THEM ON YOUR OWN!!
O-OKAY, THEN TAKE HALF THE PROFIT FROM THE FORTY-EIGHT HORNS YOU CARRIED!
I WOULDN'T HAVE GOTTEN THEM HERE WITHOUT YOUR HELP!
STILL ...!
...
THE GIRL ONLY HELPED CARRY THE HORNS?!
WAIT, THAT MEANS HE BEAT ALL THOSE KILLER RABBITS BY HIMSELF?!
SMIRK

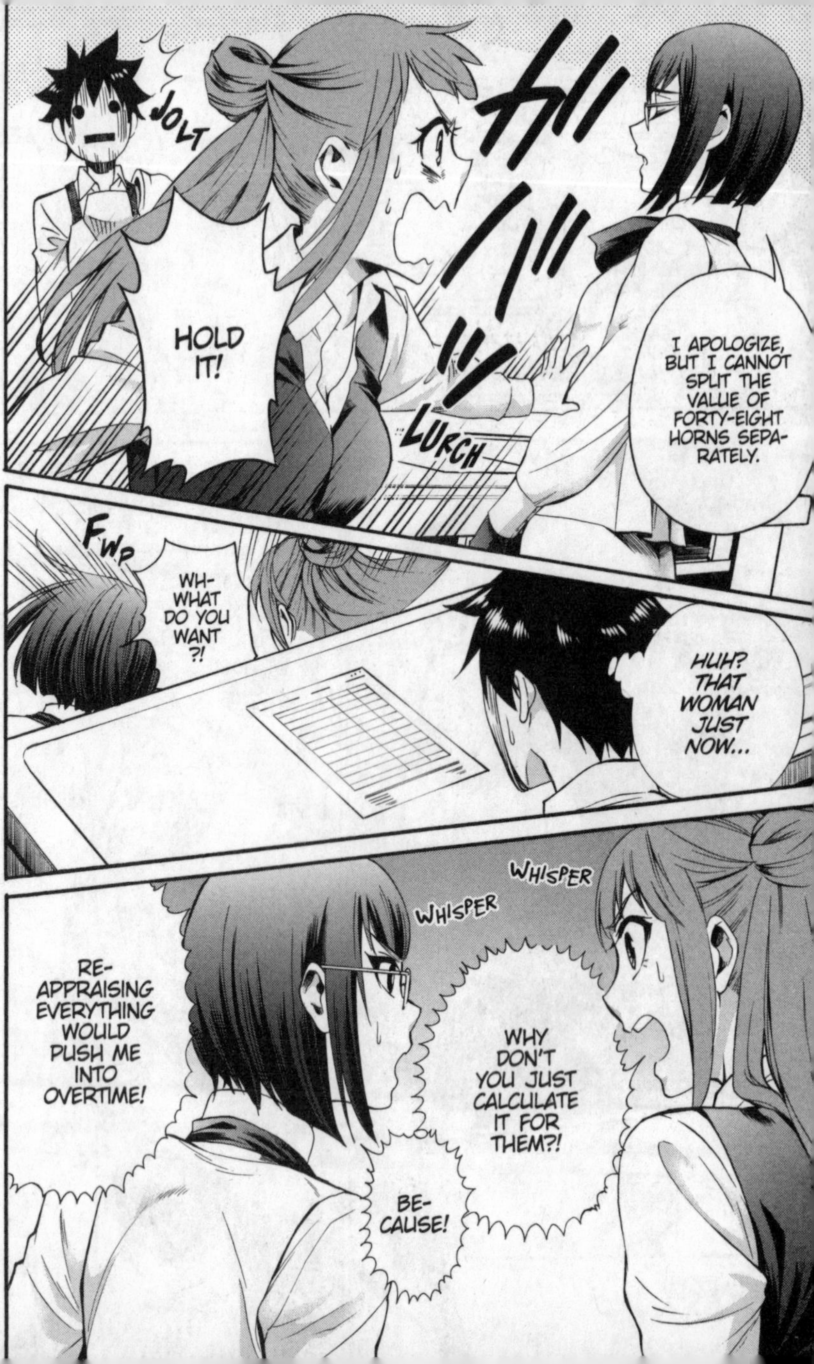
I APOLOGIZE, BUT I CANNOT SPLIT THE VALUE OF FORTY-EIGHT HORNS SEPA-RATELY.
LURCH
HOLD IT!
JOLT
HUH? THAT WOMAN JUST NOW...
WH-WHAT DO YOU WANT ?!
FWP
WHISPER
WHISPER
WHY DON'T YOU JUST CALCULATE IT FOR THEM?!
BE-CAUSE!
RE-APPRAISING EVERYTHING WOULD PUSH ME INTO OVERTIME!

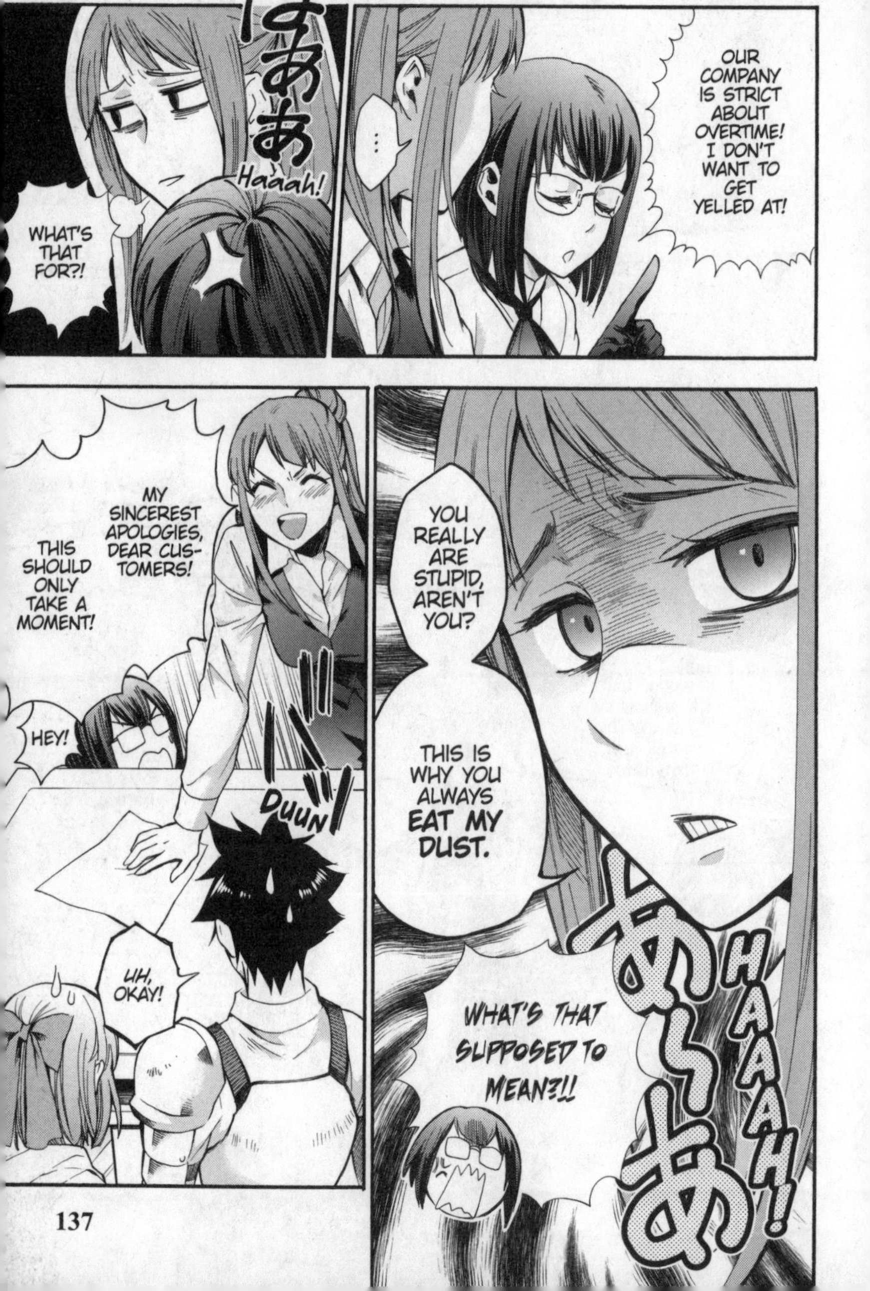

...
OUR COMPANY IS STRICT ABOUT OVERTIME! I DON'T WANT TO GET YELLED AT!
はああ
Haaah!
WHAT'S THAT FOR?!
YOU REALLY ARE STUPID, AREN'T YOU?
THIS IS WHY YOU ALWAYS EAT MY DUST.
HAAAH!
あらあ
WHAT'S THAT SUPPOSED TO MEAN?!!
MY SINCEREST APOLOGIES, DEAR CUS-TOMERS!
THIS SHOULD ONLY TAKE A MOMENT!
HEY!
DUUN
UH, OKAY!

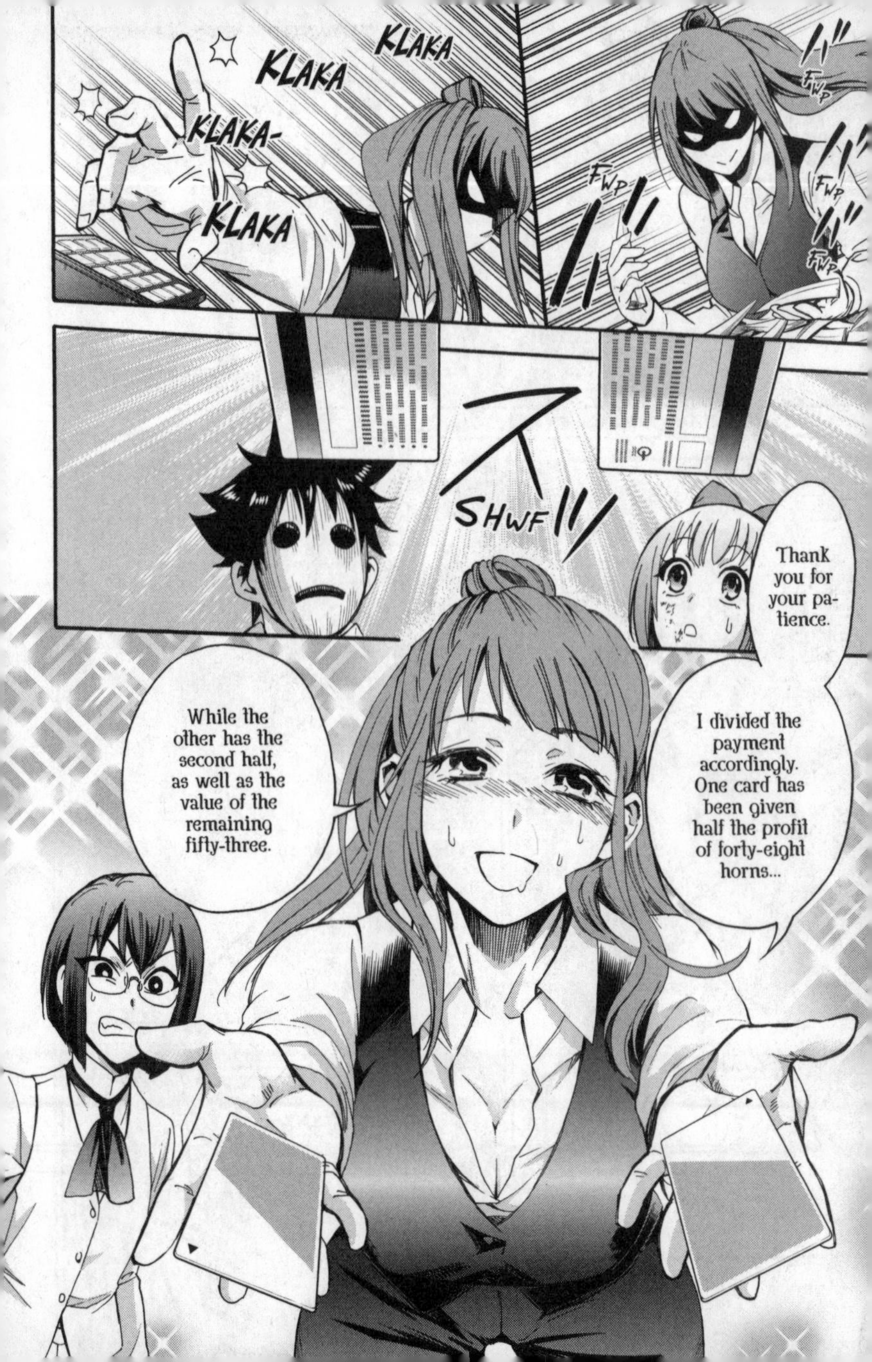
FWP
FWP
FWP
FWP
KLAKA
KLAKA
KLAKA-
KLAKA
SHWF
Thank you for your patience.
I divided the payment accordingly. One card has been given half the profit of forty-eight horns...
While the other has the second half, as well as the value of the remaining fifty-three.

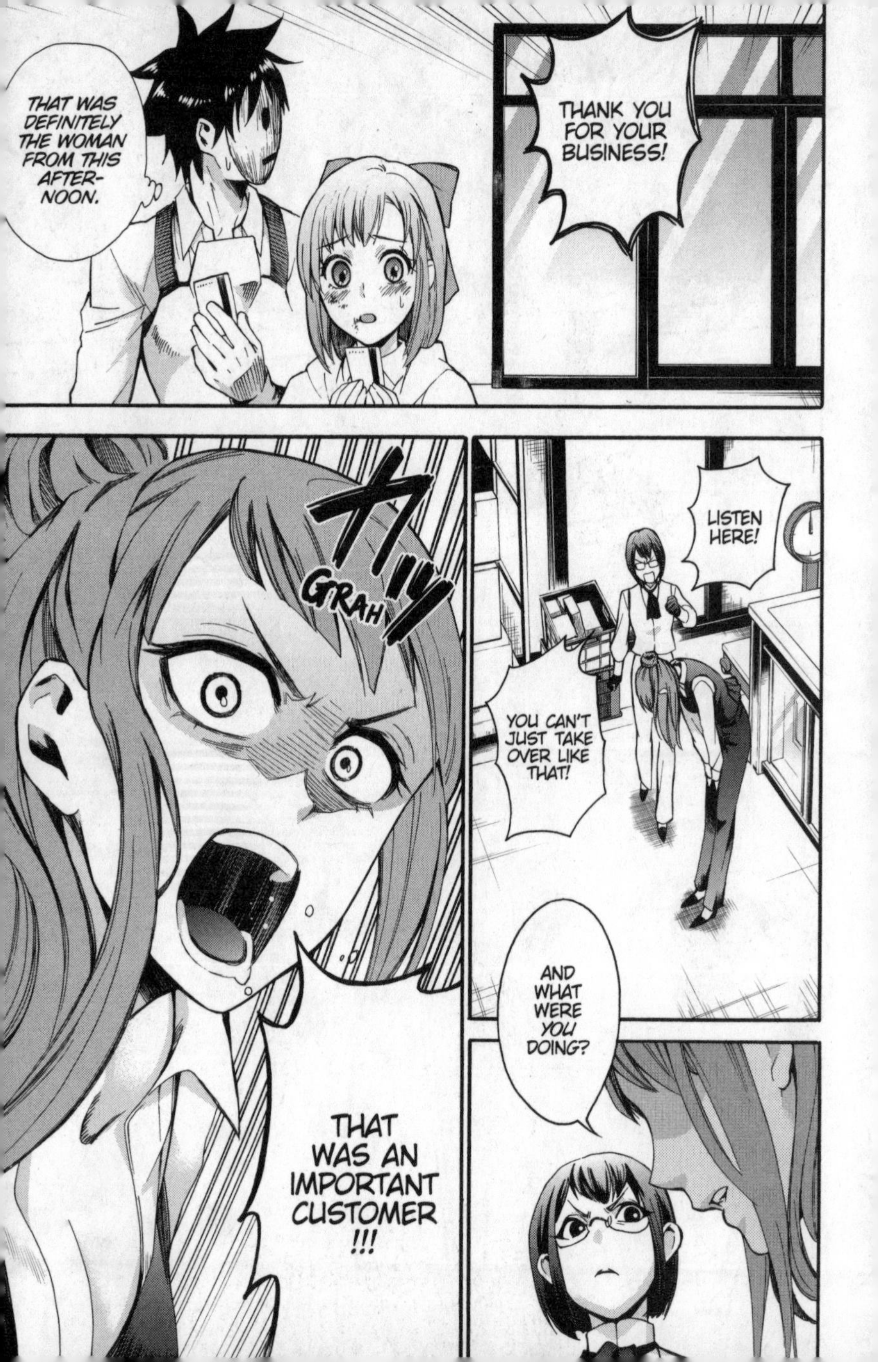
THANK YOU FOR YOUR BUSINESS!
THAT WAS DEFINITELY THE WOMAN FROM THIS AFTER-NOON.
LISTEN HERE!
YOU CAN'T JUST TAKE OVER LIKE THAT!
AND WHAT WERE YOU DOING?
GRAH
THAT WAS AN IMPORTANT CUSTOMER !!!

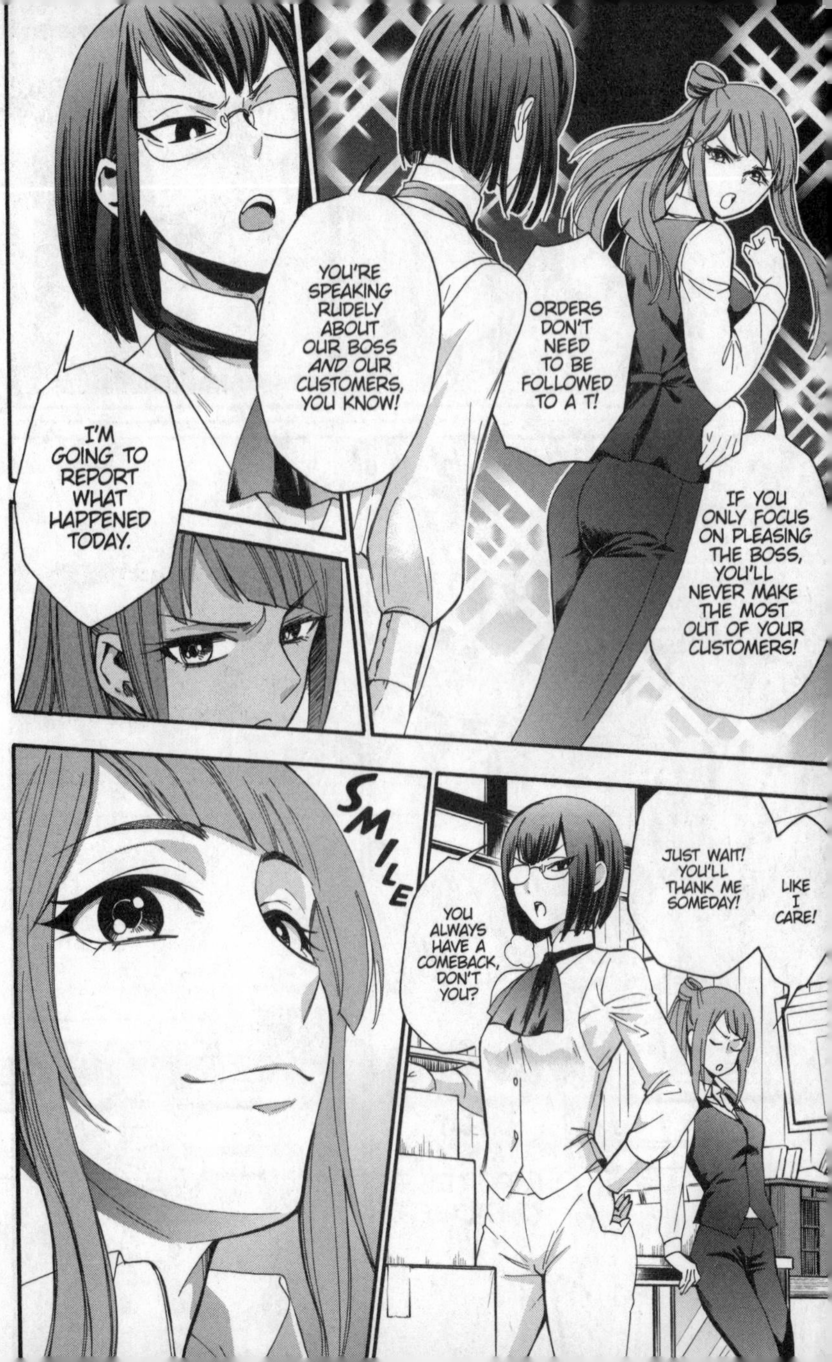
YOU'RE SPEAKING RUDELY ABOUT OUR BOSS AND OUR CUSTOMERS, YOU KNOW!
ORDERS DON'T NEED TO BE FOLLOWED TO A T!
IF YOU ONLY FOCUS ON PLEASING THE BOSS, YOU'LL NEVER MAKE THE MOST OUT OF YOUR CUSTOMERS!
I'M GOING TO REPORT WHAT HAPPENED TODAY.
LIKE I CARE!
JUST WAIT! YOU'LL THANK ME SOMEDAY!
YOU ALWAYS HAVE A COMEBACK, DON'T YOU?
SMILE

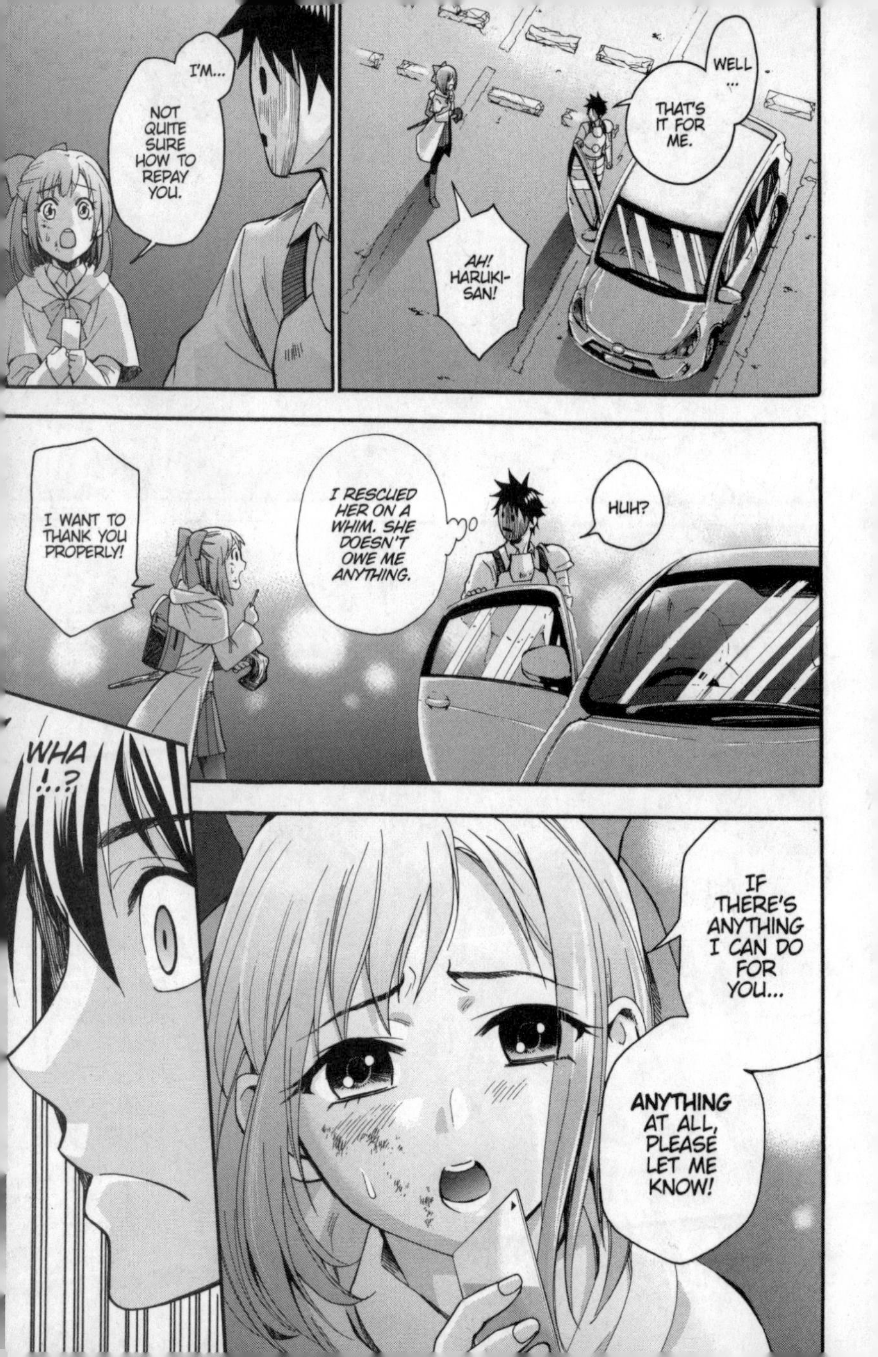
WELL
...
THAT'S IT FOR ME.
AH! HARUKI-SAN!
I'M...
NOT QUITE SURE HOW TO REPAY YOU.
HUH?
I RESCUED HER ON A WHIM. SHE DOESN'T OWE ME ANYTHING.
I WANT TO THANK YOU PROPERLY!
IF THERE'S ANYTHING I CAN DO FOR YOU...
ANYTHING AT ALL, PLEASE LET ME KNOW!
WHA !..?

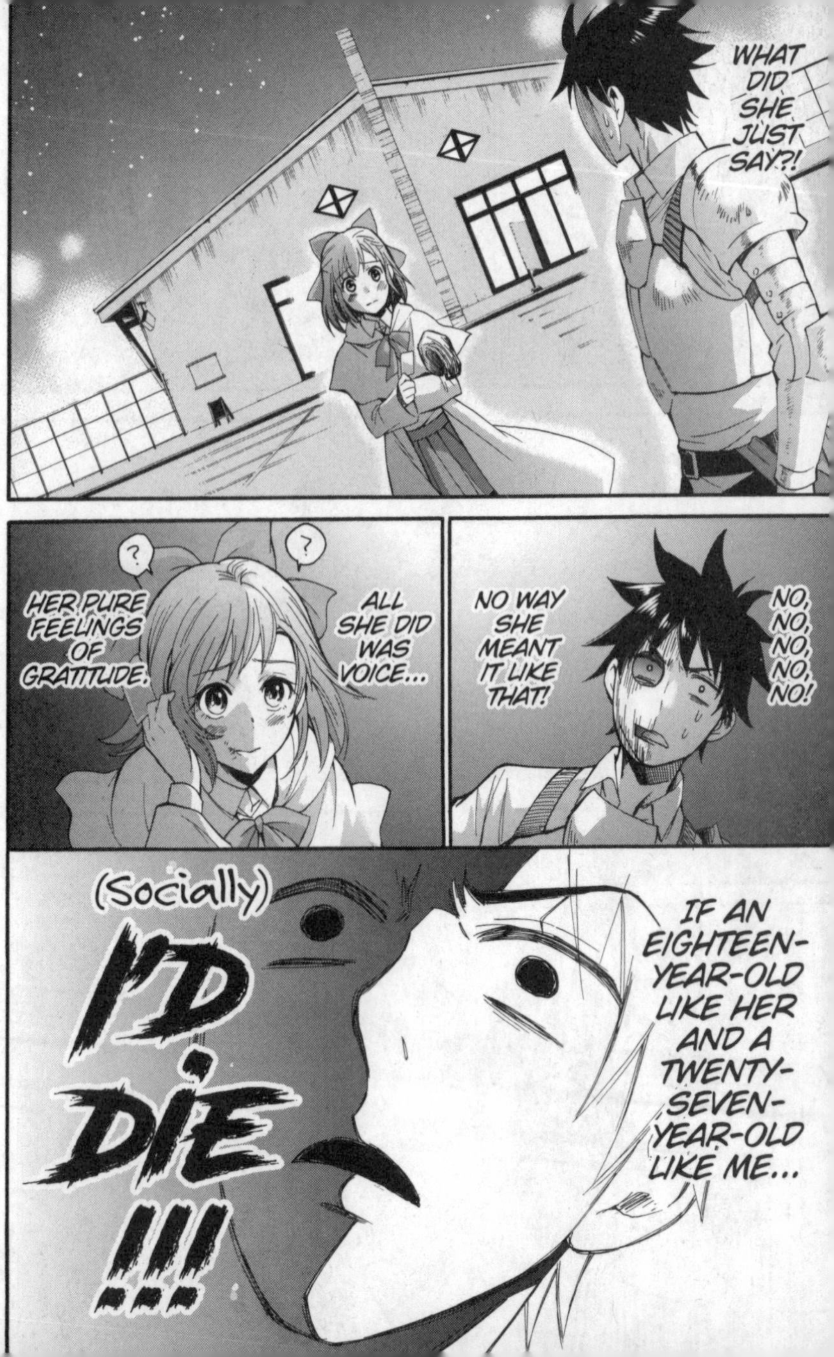
WHAT DID SHE JUST SAY?!
NO, NO, NO, NO, NO!
NO WAY SHE MEANT IT LIKE THAT!
ALL SHE DID WAS VOICE...
HER PURE FEELINGS OF GRATITUDE.
IF AN EIGHTEEN-YEAR-OLD LIKE HER AND A TWENTY-SEVEN-YEAR-OLD LIKE ME...
(Socially)
I'D DIE!!!

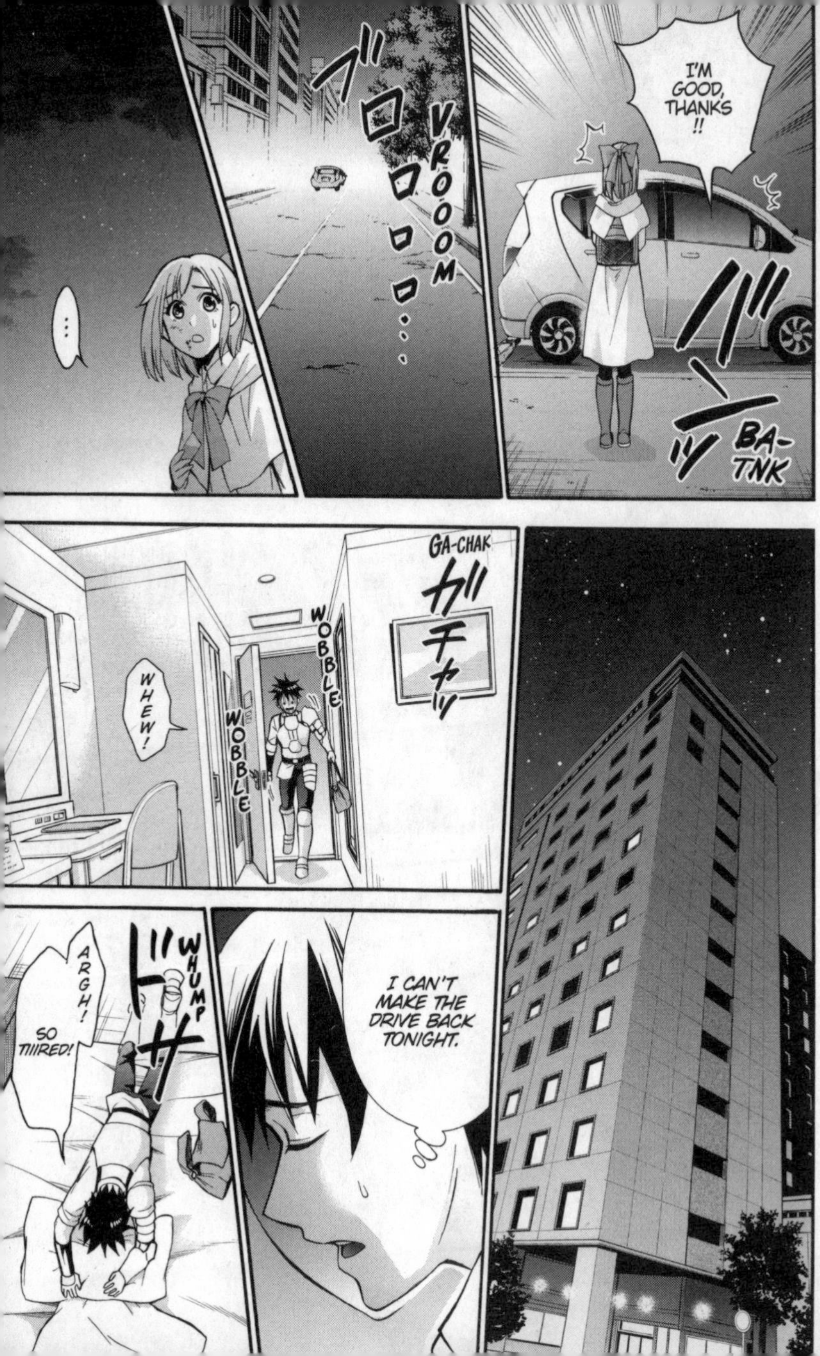
I'M GOOD, THANKS!!
BA-TNK
VROOOM
...
GA-CHAK
WOBBLE
WOBBLE
WHEW!
I CAN'T MAKE THE DRIVE BACK TONIGHT.
WHUMP
ARGH!
SO TIIRED!

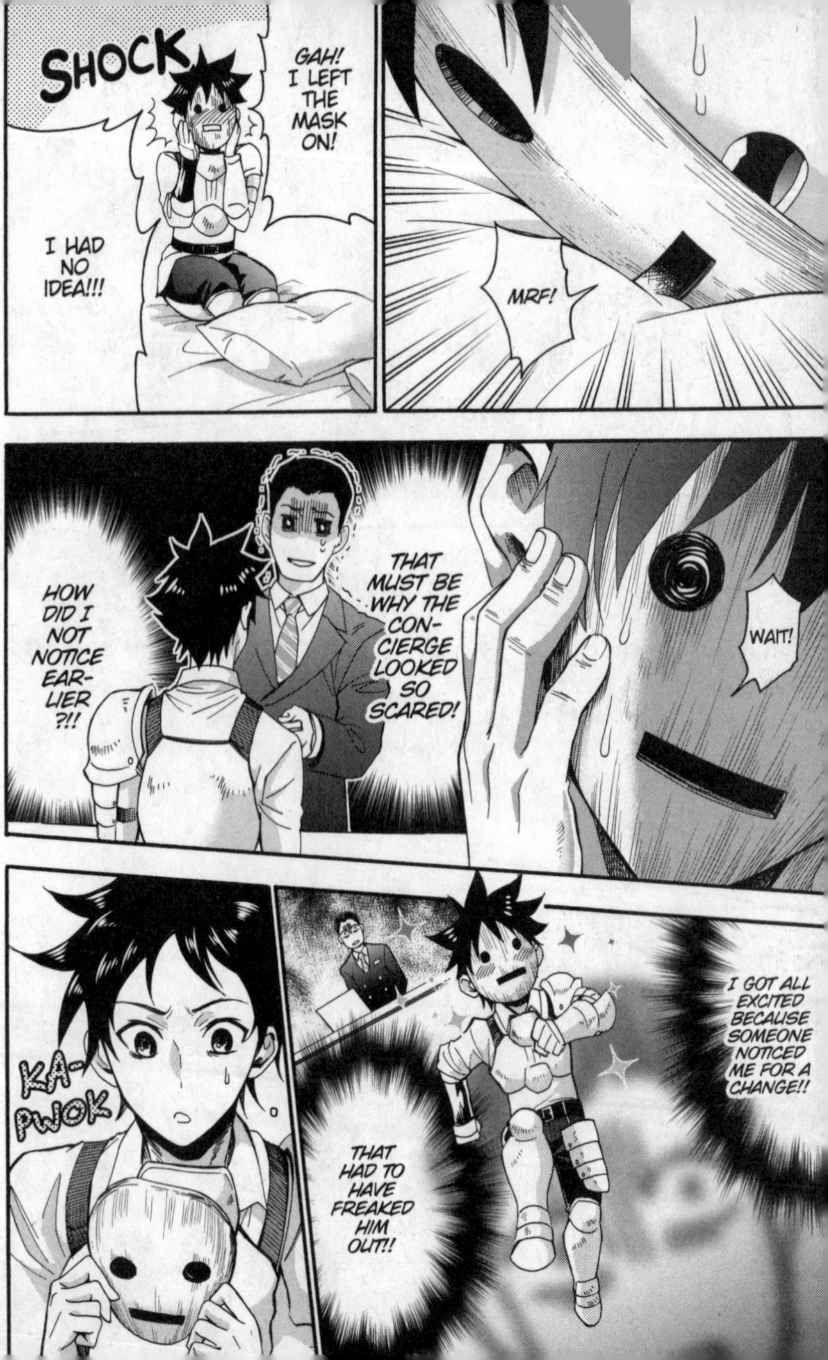
MRF!
SHOCK
GAH! I LEFT THE MASK ON!
I HAD NO IDEA!!!
WAIT!
THAT MUST BE WHY THE CON-CIERGE LOOKED SO SCARED!
HOW DID I NOT NOTICE EAR-LIER ?!!
I GOT ALL EXCITED BECAUSE SOMEONE NOTICED ME FOR A CHANGE!!
THAT HAD TO HAVE FREAKED HIM OUT!!
KA-PWOK

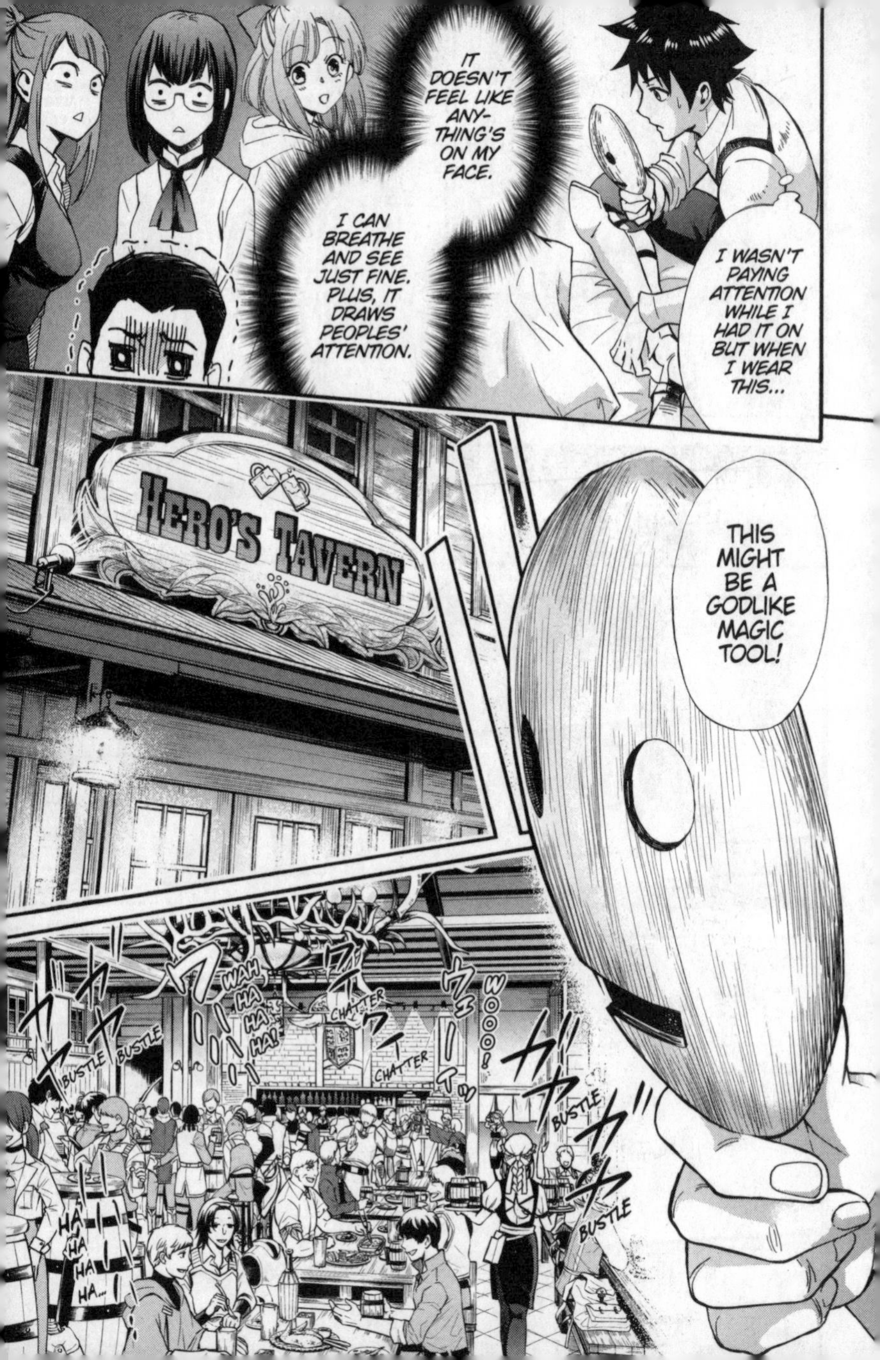
I WASN'T PAYING ATTENTION WHILE I HAD IT ON BUT WHEN I WEAR THIS...
IT DOESN'T FEEL LIKE ANY-THING'S ON MY FACE.
I CAN BREATHE AND SEE JUST FINE. PLUS, IT DRAWS PEOPLES' ATTENTION.
THIS MIGHT BE A GODLIKE MAGIC TOOL!
HERO'S TAVERN
BUSTLE
BUSTLE
WOOOO!
CHATTER
CHATTER
WAH HA HA HA!
BUSTLE
BUSTLE
HA HA HA HA...

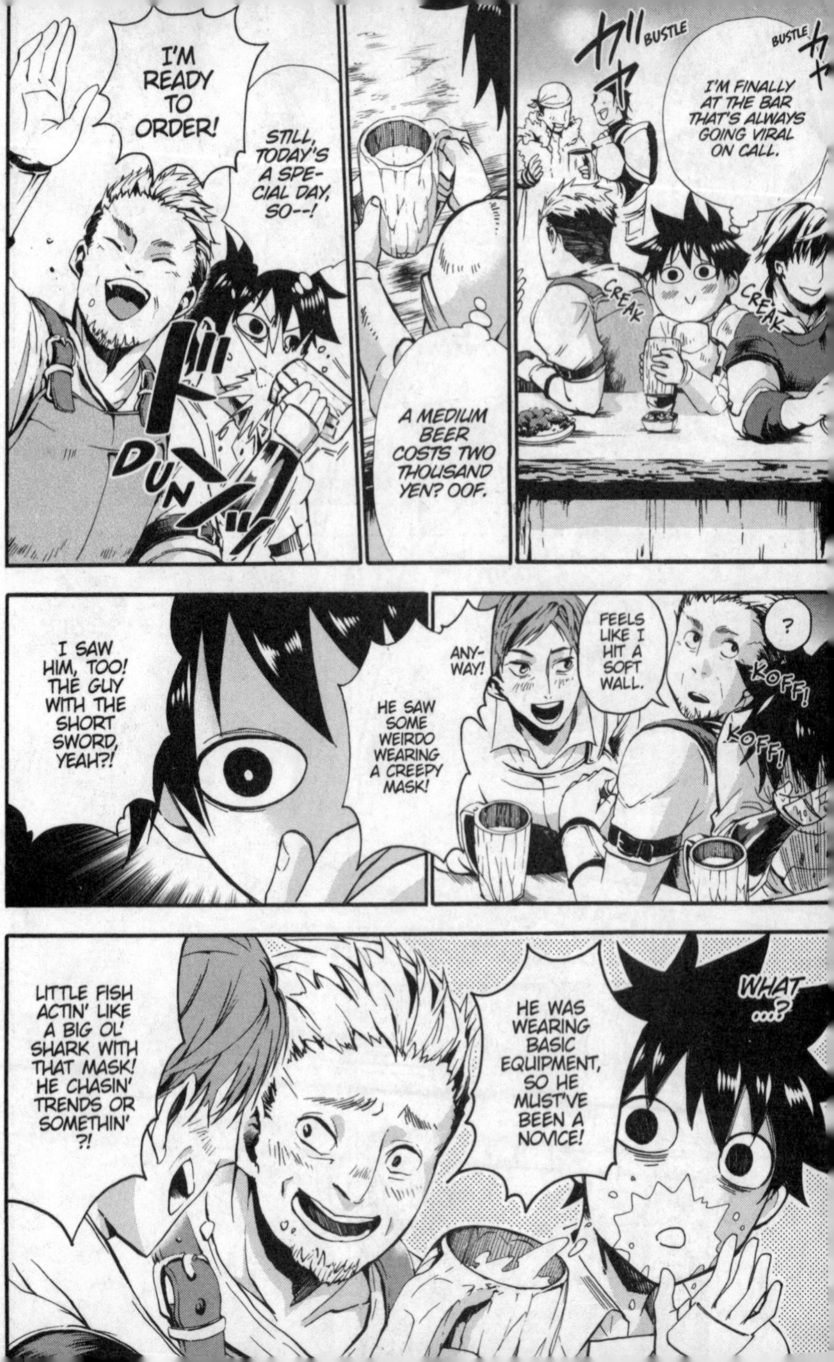
BUSTLE
BUSTLE
I'M FINALLY AT THE BAR THAT'S ALWAYS GOING VIRAL ON CALL.
CREAK
CREAK
A MEDIUM BEER COSTS TWO THOUSAND YEN? OOF.
I'M READY TO ORDER!
STILL, TODAY'S A SPECIAL DAY, SO--!
DUN
?
KOFF!
KOFF!
FEELS LIKE I HIT A SOFT WALL.
ANY-WAY!
HE SAW SOME WEIRDO WEARING A CREEPY MASK!
I SAW HIM, TOO! THE GUY WITH THE SHORT SWORD, YEAH?!
WHAT ...?
HE WAS WEARING BASIC EQUIPMENT, SO HE MUST'VE BEEN A NOVICE!
LITTLE FISH ACTIN' LIKE A BIG OL' SHARK WITH THAT MASK! HE CHASIN' TRENDS OR SOMETHIN' ?!

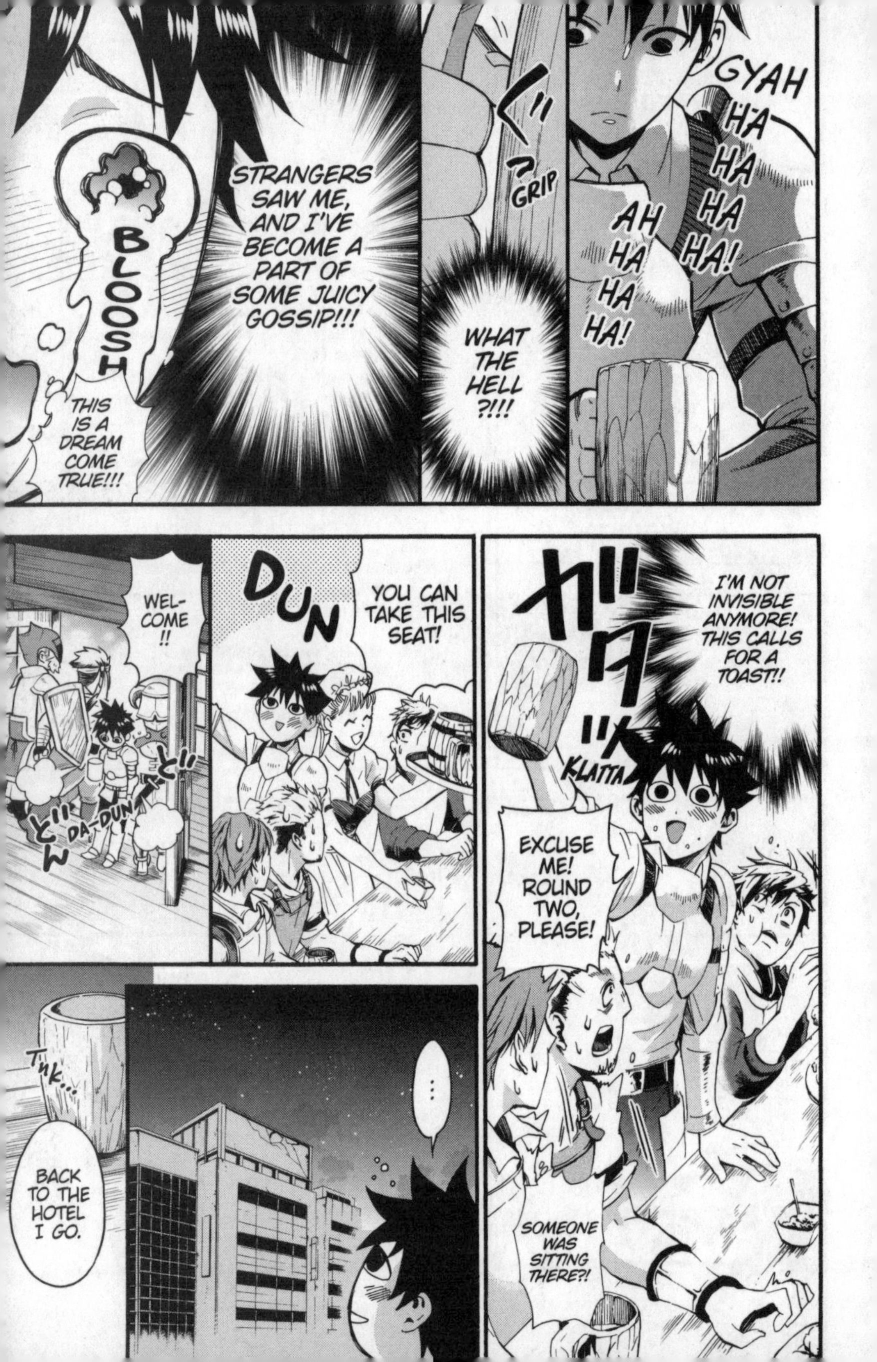
GYAH HA HA HA HA!
AH HA HA HA!
GRIP
WHAT THE HELL ?!!!
STRANGERS SAW ME, AND I'VE BECOME A PART OF SOME JUICY GOSSIP!!!
BLOOSH
THIS IS A DREAM COME TRUE!!!
I'M NOT INVISIBLE ANYMORE! THIS CALLS FOR A TOAST!!
KLATTA
EXCUSE ME! ROUND TWO, PLEASE!
SOMEONE WAS SITTING THERE?!
DUN
YOU CAN TAKE THIS SEAT!
WEL-COME !!
DA-DUN
...
Tnk...
BACK TO THE HOTEL I GO.

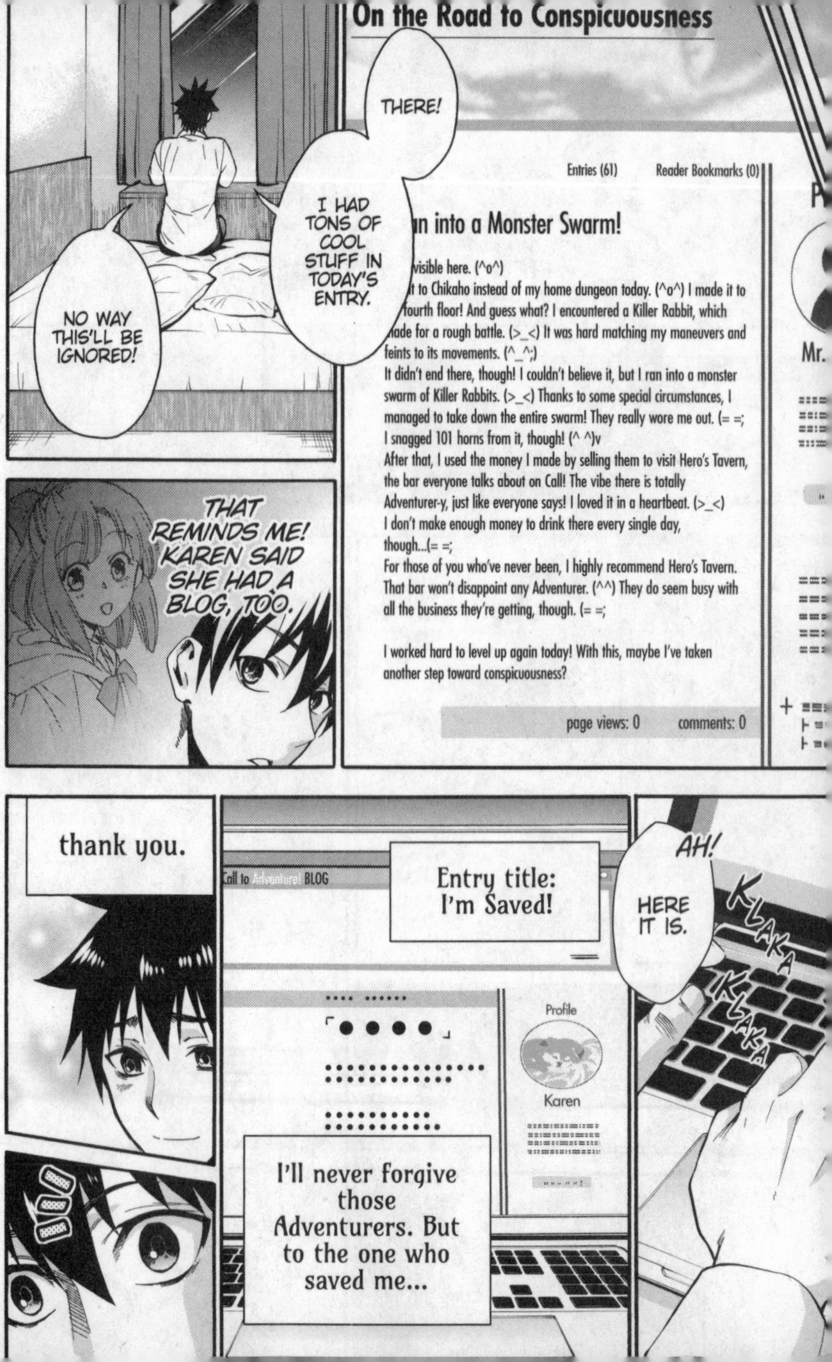
On the Road to Conspicuousness
THERE!
I HAD TONS OF COOL STUFF IN TODAY'S ENTRY.
Entries (61)
Reader Bookmarks (0)
...n into a Monster Swarm!
...visible here. (^o^)
...t to Chikaho instead of my home dungeon today. (^o^) I made it to ...fourth floor! And guess what? I encountered a Killer Rabbit, which ...ade for a rough battle. (>_<) It was hard matching my maneuvers and feints to its movements. (^_^;)
It didn't end there, though! I couldn't believe it, but I ran into a monster swarm of Killer Rabbits. (>_<) Thanks to some special circumstances, I managed to take down the entire swarm! They really wore me out. (= =;
I snagged 101 horns from it, though! (^ ^)v
After that, I used the money I made by selling them to visit Hero's Tavern, the bar everyone talks about on Call! The vibe there is totally Adventurer-y, just like everyone says! I loved it in a heartbeat. (>_<)
I don't make enough money to drink there every single day, though...(= =;
For those of you who've never been, I highly recommend Hero's Tavern. That bar won't disappoint any Adventurer. (^^) They do seem busy with all the business they're getting, though. (= =;
I worked hard to level up again today! With this, maybe I've taken another step toward conspicuousness?
page views: 0
comments: 0
Mr.
NO WAY THIS'LL BE IGNORED!
THAT REMINDS ME! KAREN SAID SHE HAD A BLOG, TOO.
AH!
HERE IT IS.
KLAKA
KLAKA
Call to Adventure! BLOG
Entry title: I'm Saved!
Profile
Karen
I'll never forgive those Adventurers. But to the one who saved me...
thank you.

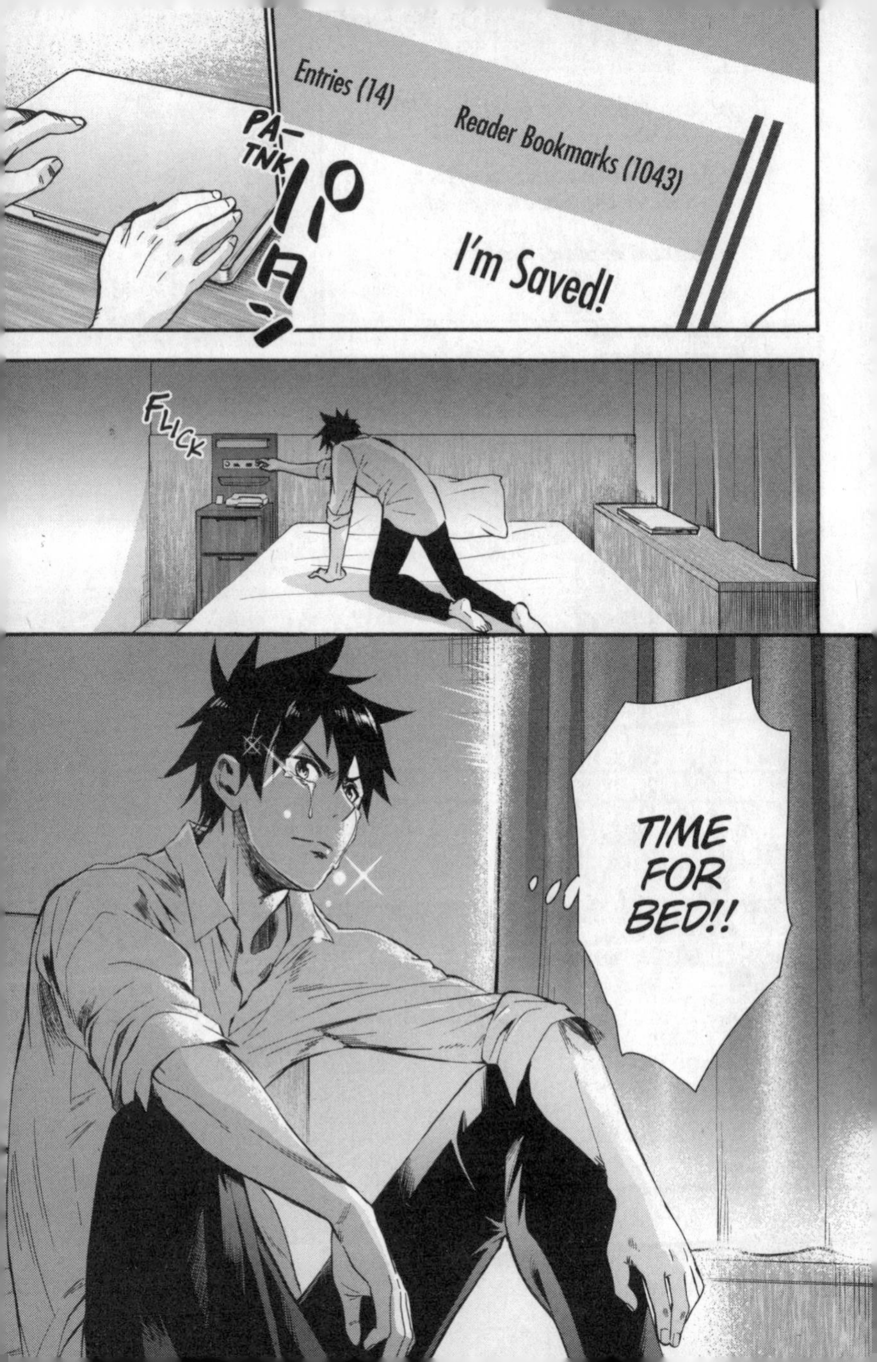
Entries (14)
Reader Bookmarks (1043)
I'm Saved!
PA-TNK
パタン
FLICK
TIME FOR BED!!

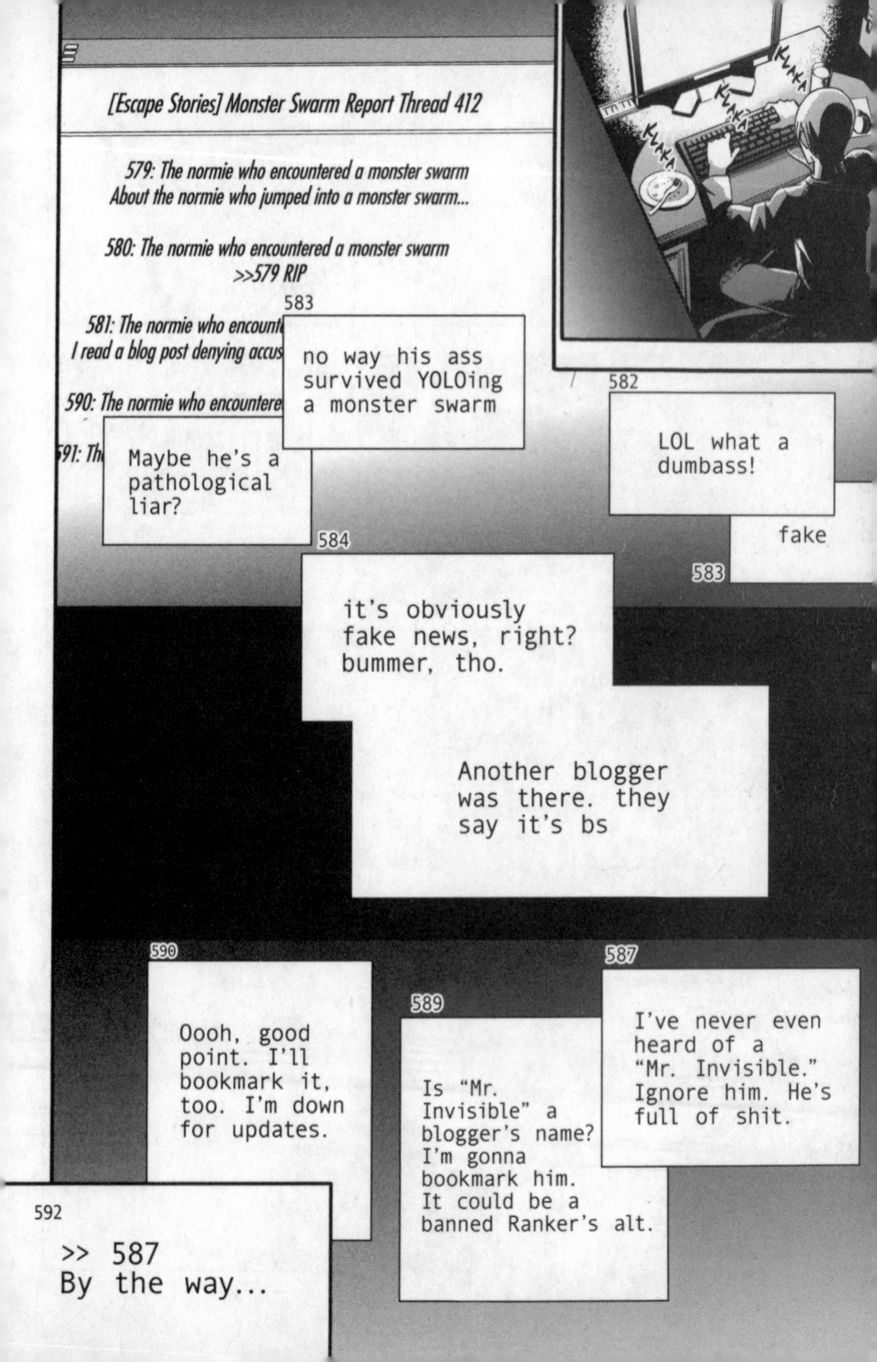
KLAKA
KLAKA
KLAKA
[Escape Stories] Monster Swarm Report Thread 412
579: The normie who encountered a monster swarm
About the normie who jumped into a monster swarm...
580: The normie who encountered a monster swarm
>>579 RIP
581: The normie who encount
I read a blog post denying accus
590: The normie who encountere
591: Th
582
LOL what a dumbass!
583
fake
583
no way his ass survived YOLOing a monster swarm
Maybe he's a pathological liar?
584
it's obviously fake news, right? bummer, tho.
Another blogger was there. they say it's bs
587
I've never even heard of a "Mr. Invisible." Ignore him. He's full of shit.
589
Is "Mr. Invisible" a blogger's name? I'm gonna bookmark him. It could be a banned Ranker's alt.
590
Oooh, good point. I'll bookmark it, too. I'm down for updates.
592
>> 587
By the way...

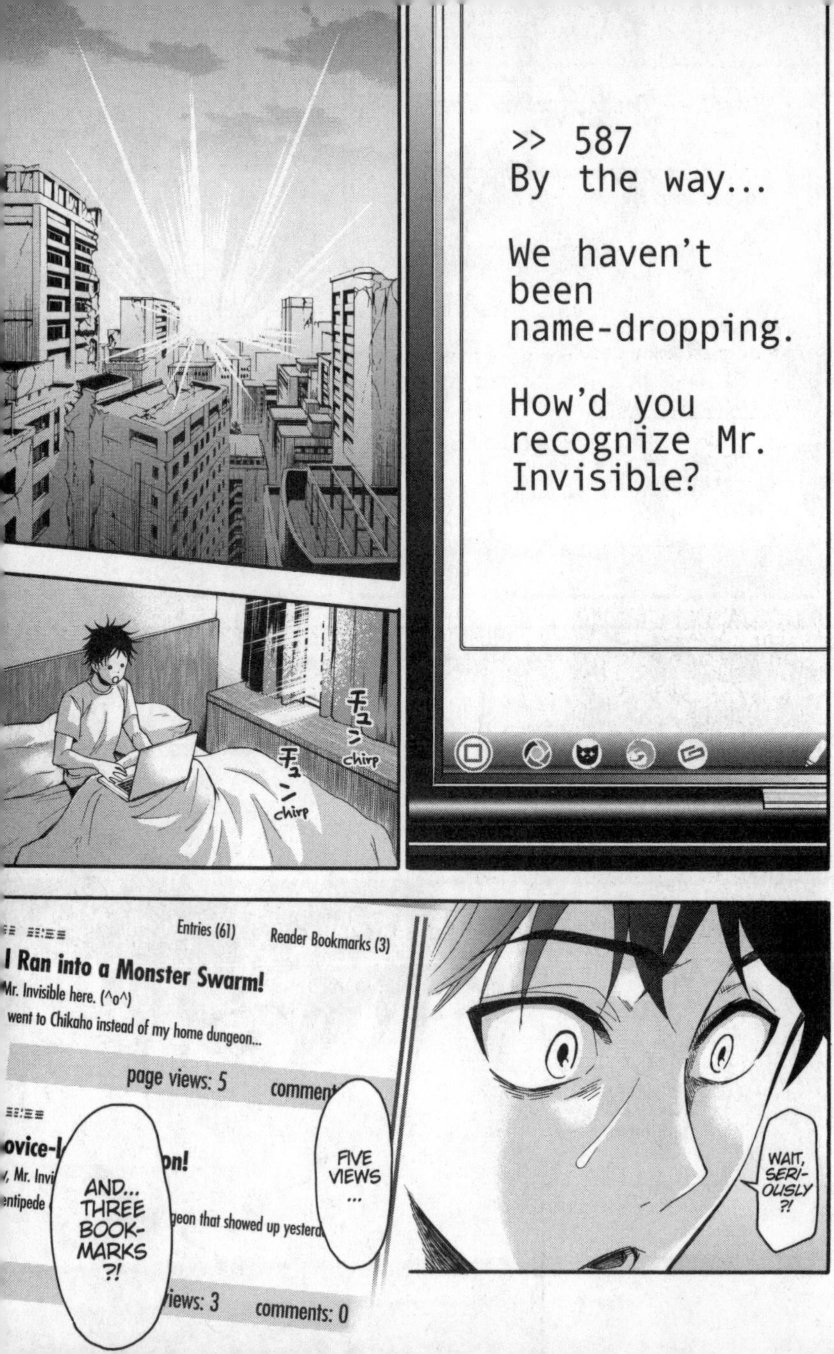
>> 587
By the way...
We haven't been name-dropping.
How'd you recognize Mr. Invisible?
チュン chirp
チュン chirp
WAIT, SERI-OUSLY ?!
FIVE VIEWS ...
Entries (61) Reader Bookmarks (3)
I Ran into a Monster Swarm!
Mr. Invisible here. (^o^)
went to Chikaho instead of my home dungeon...
page views: 5 comment
ovice-l on!
, Mr. Invi
entipede
geon that showed up yesterd
views: 3 comments: 0
AND... THREE BOOK-MARKS ?!

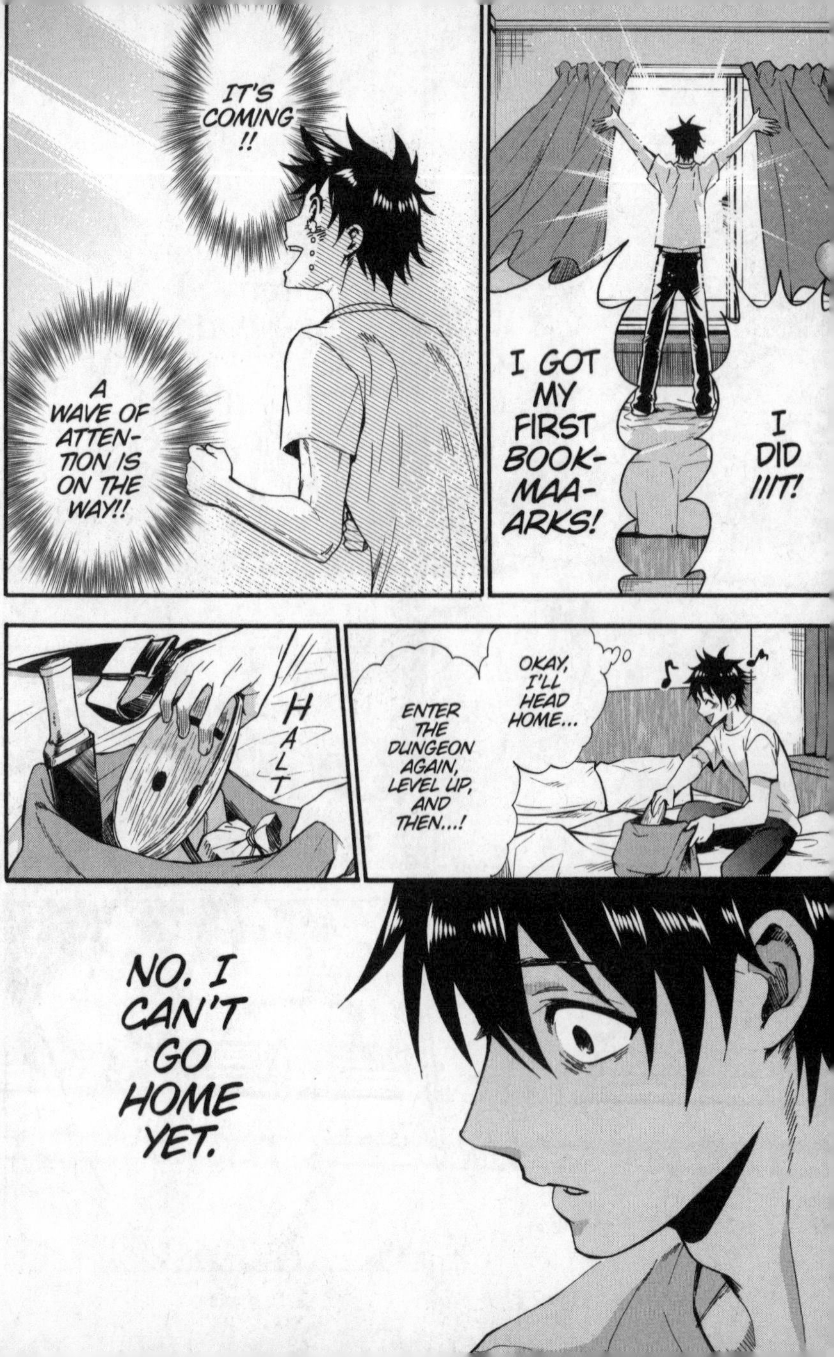
I DID IIIIT!
I GOT MY FIRST BOOK-MAA-ARKS!
IT'S COMING !!
A WAVE OF ATTEN-TION IS ON THE WAY!!
OKAY, I'LL HEAD HOME...
ENTER THE DUNGEON AGAIN, LEVEL UP, AND THEN...!
HALT
NO. I CAN'T GO HOME YET.

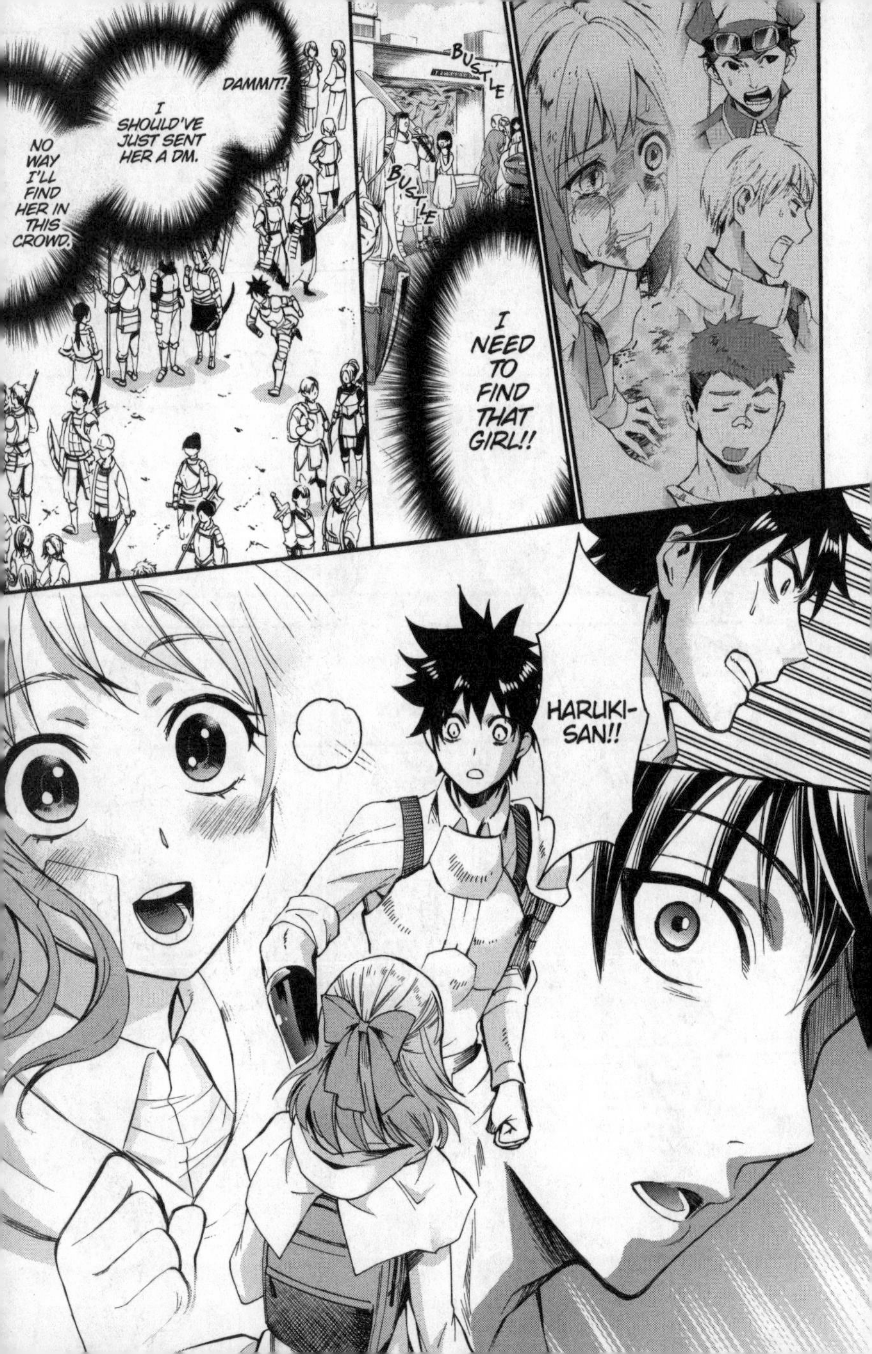
I NEED TO FIND THAT GIRL!!
BUSTLE
BUSTLE
DAMMIT!
I SHOULD'VE JUST SENT HER A DM.
NO WAY I'LL FIND HER IN THIS CROWD.
HARUKI-SAN!!

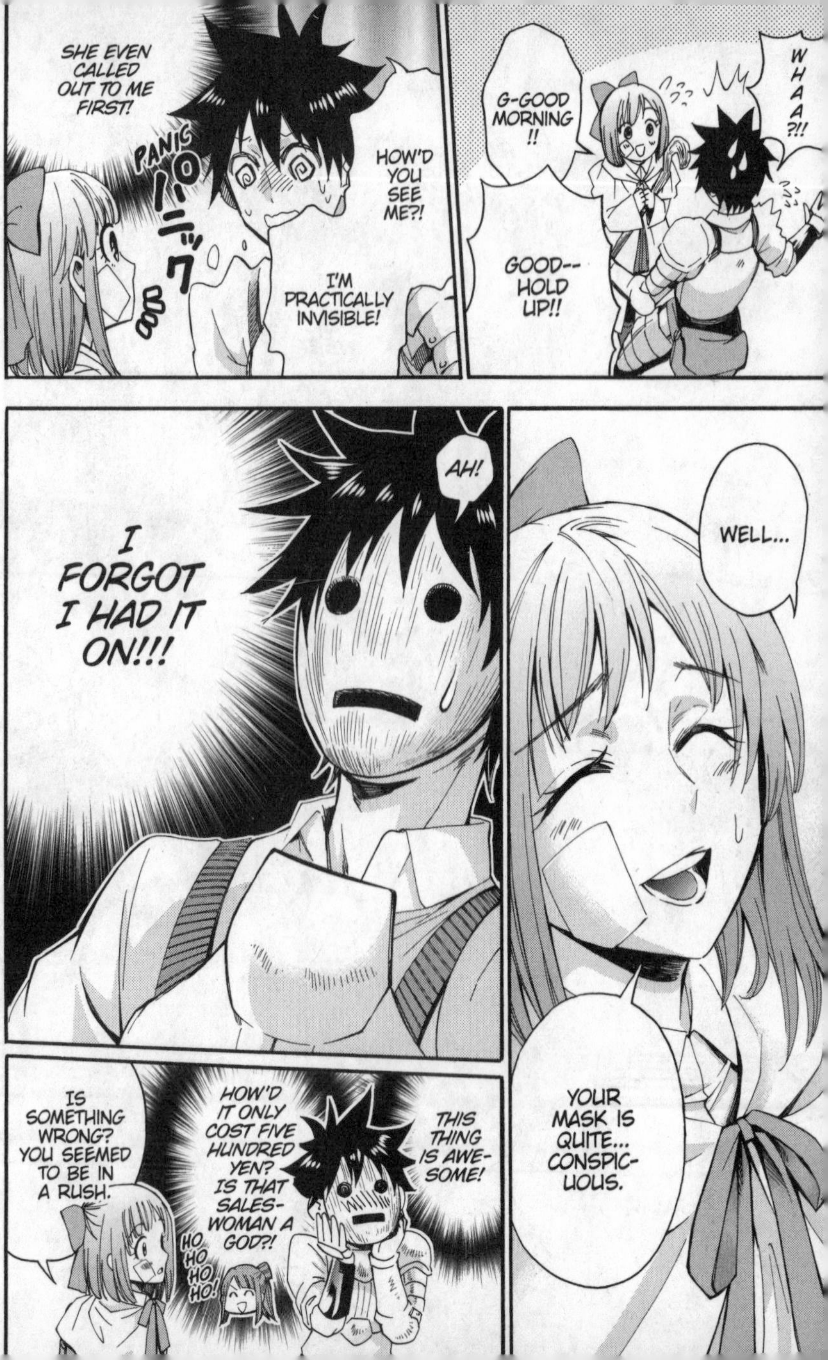
G-GOOD MORNING !!
WHAA?!!
GOOD-- HOLD UP!!
SHE EVEN CALLED OUT TO ME FIRST!
PANIC
HOW'D YOU SEE ME?!
I'M PRACTICALLY INVISIBLE!
WELL...
YOUR MASK IS QUITE... CONSPICUOUS.
AH!
I FORGOT I HAD IT ON!!!
THIS THING IS AWESOME!
HOW'D IT ONLY COST FIVE HUNDRED YEN? IS THAT SALESWOMAN A GOD?!
IS SOMETHING WRONG? YOU SEEMED TO BE IN A RUSH.
HO HO HO HO!

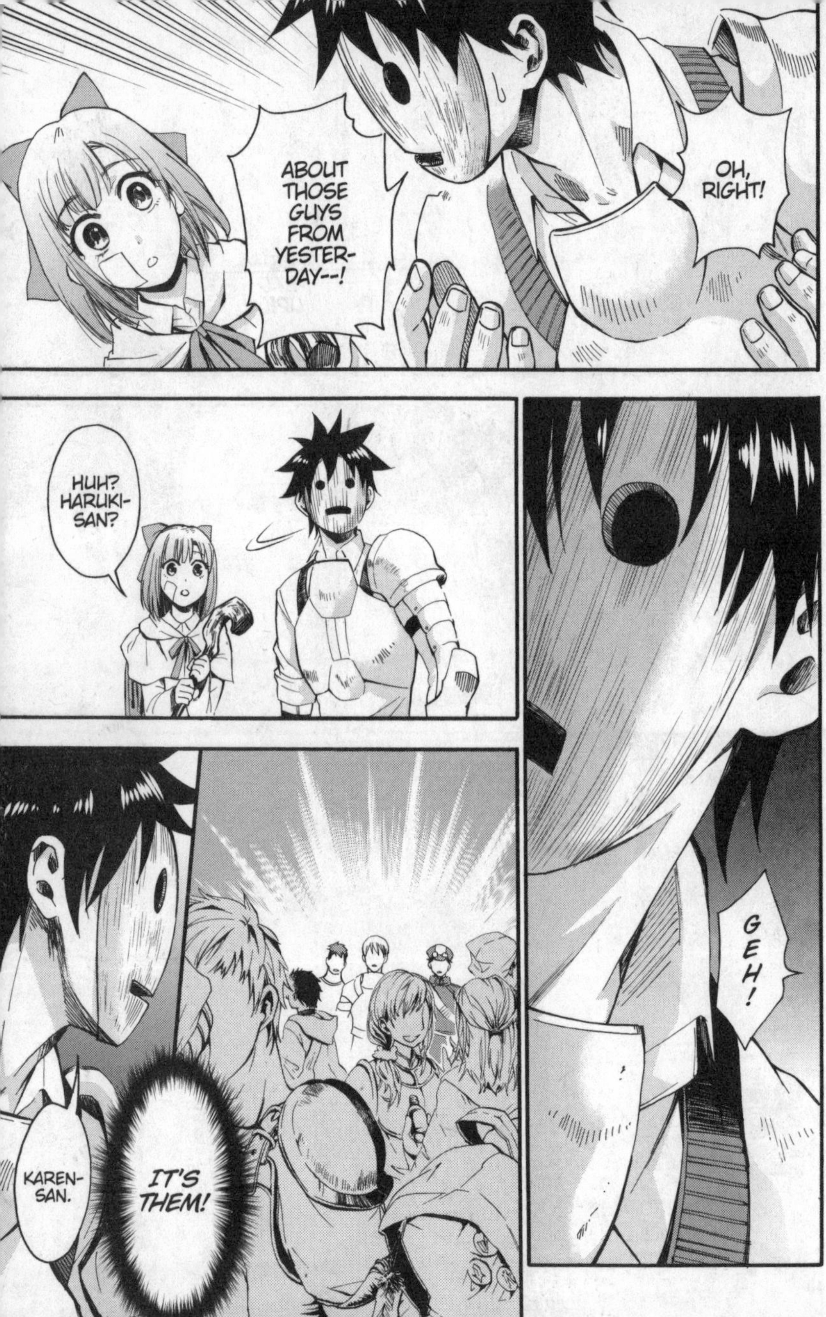
OH, RIGHT!
ABOUT THOSE GUYS FROM YESTER-DAY--!
GEH!
HUH? HARUKI-SAN?
IT'S THEM!
KAREN-SAN.

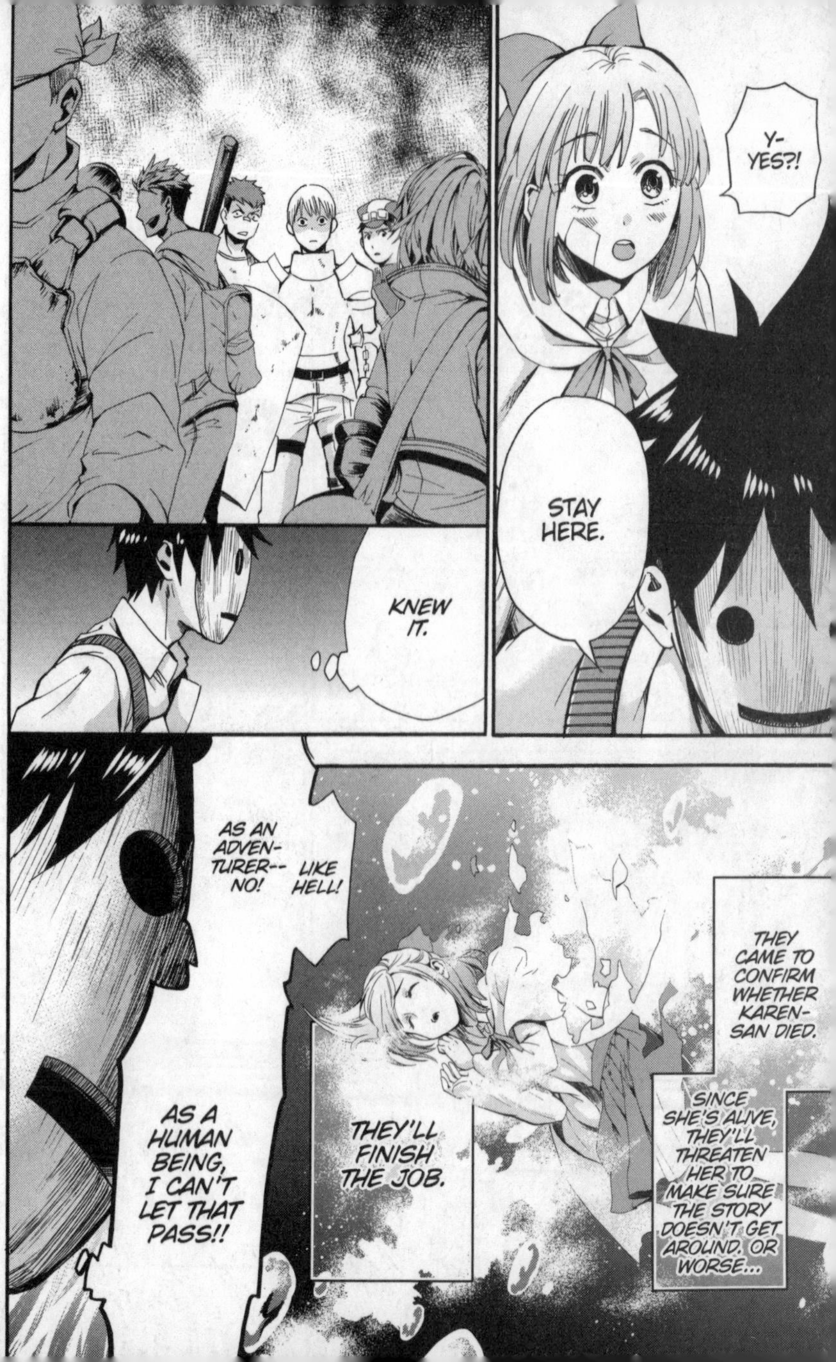
Y- YES?!
STAY HERE.
KNEW IT.
THEY CAME TO CONFIRM WHETHER KAREN-SAN DIED.
SINCE SHE'S ALIVE, THEY'LL THREATEN HER TO MAKE SURE THE STORY DOESN'T GET AROUND. OR WORSE...
THEY'LL FINISH THE JOB.
AS AN ADVEN-TURER-- NO!
LIKE HELL!
AS A HUMAN BEING, I CAN'T LET THAT PASS!!

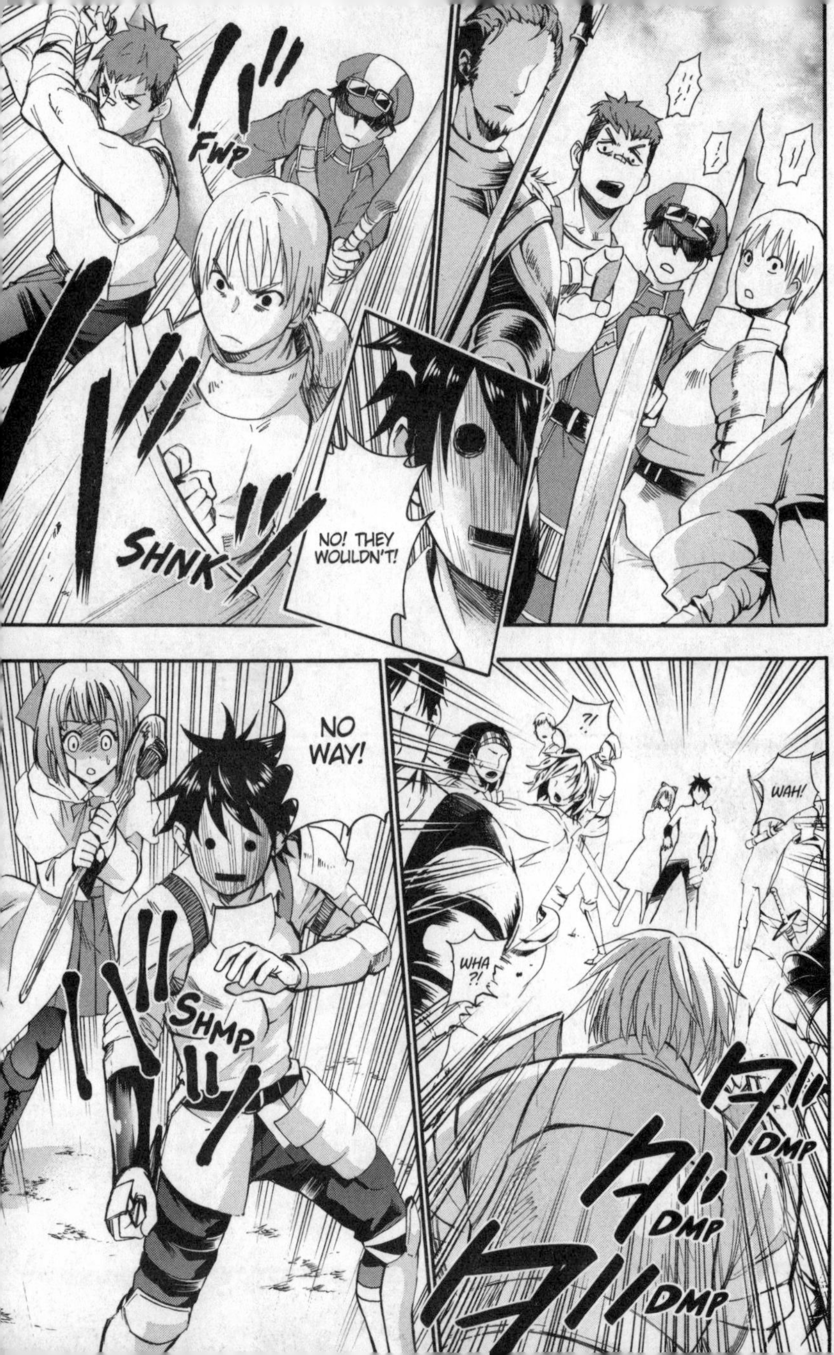
!!
!
!!
NO! THEY WOULDN'T!
FWP
SHNK
?!
WAH!
WHA ?!
DMP
DMP
DMP
NO WAY!
SHMP

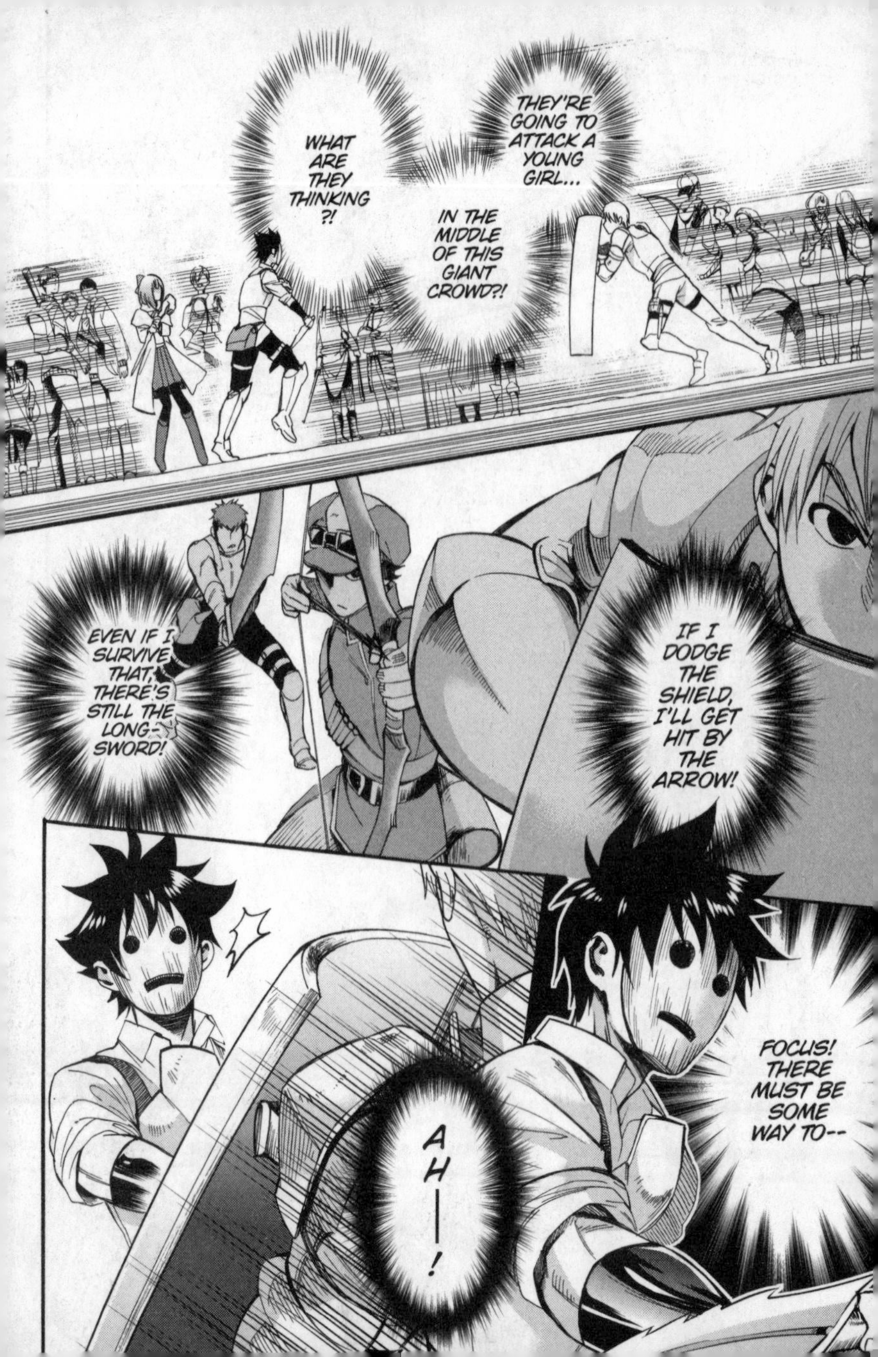
THEY'RE GOING TO ATTACK A YOUNG GIRL...
WHAT ARE THEY THINKING ?!
IN THE MIDDLE OF THIS GIANT CROWD?!
IF I DODGE THE SHIELD, I'LL GET HIT BY THE ARROW!
EVEN IF I SURVIVE THAT, THERE'S STILL THE LONG-SWORD!
FOCUS! THERE MUST BE SOME WAY TO--
AH--!

SEVEN SEAS ENTERTAINMENT PRESENTS

CALL TO ADVENTURE!
DEFEATING DUNGEONS
WITH A SKILL BOARD Vol. 1

story by **AKI HAGIU**   art by **RENJI KURIYAMA**   character design by **TEDDY**

TRANSLATION
Morgan Watchorn

ADAPTATION
Maneesh Maganti

LETTERING
Ochie Caraan

COVER DESIGN
Hanase Qi

LOGO DESIGN
George Panella

PROOFREADER
Kurestin Armada

COPY EDITOR
Dawn Davis

EDITOR
Jenn Grunigen

PREPRESS TECHNICIAN
hiannon Rasmussen-Silverstein

PRODUCTION ASSOCIATE
Christa Miesner

PRODUCTION MANAGER
Lissa Pattillo

MANAGING EDITOR
Julie Davis

ASSOCIATE PUBLISHER
Adam Arnold

PUBLISHER
Jason DeAngelis

Seven Seas press and purchase enquiries can be sent to Marketing Manager Lianne
Sentar at press@gomanga.com. Information regarding the distribution and purchase of
digital editions is available from Digital Manager CK Russell at digital@gomanga.com.

Seven Seas and the Seven Seas logo are trademarks of
Seven Seas Entertainment. All rights reserved.

ISBN: 978-1-64827-587-6
Printed in Canada
First Printing: August 2021
10 9 8 7 6 5 4 3 2 1

READING DIRECTIONS

This book reads from *right to left*,
Japanese style. If this is your first time
reading manga, you start reading from
the top right panel on each page and
take it from there. If you get lost, just
follow the numbered diagram here.
It may seem backwards at first,
but you'll get the hang of it! Have fun!!

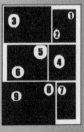

Follow us online: www.SevenSeasEntertainment.com

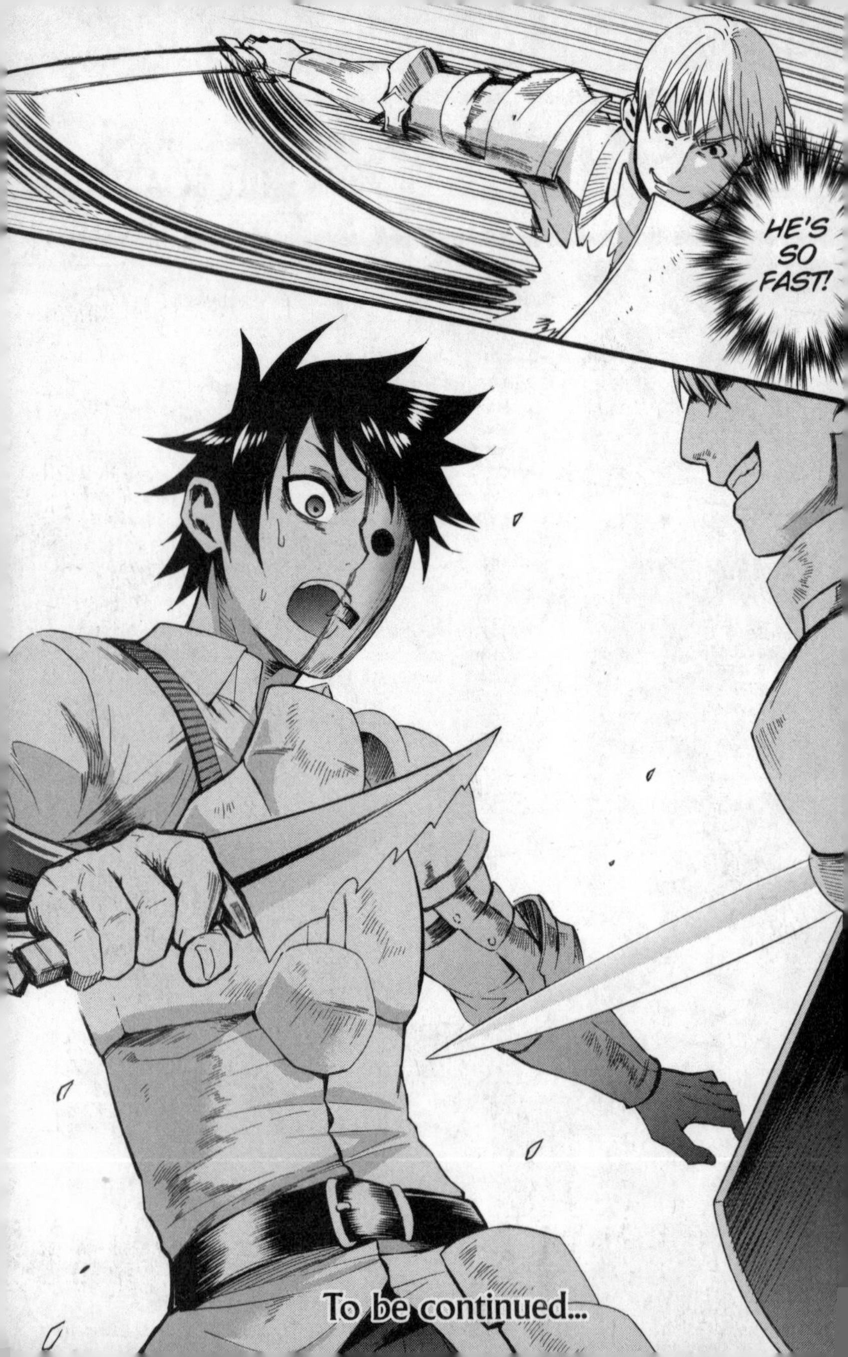
HE'S SO FAST!
To be continued...